Caught Up In Crime

Recent Titles in Libraries Unlimited
Genreflecting Advisory Series

Diana Tixier Herald, Series Editor

Canadian Fiction: A Guide to Reading Interests
Sharron Smith and Maureen O'Connor

Genreflecting: A Guide to Popular Reading Interests, 6th Edition
Diana Tixier Herald, Edited by Wayne A. Wiegand

The Real Story: A Guide to Nonfiction Reading Interests
Sarah Statz Cords, Edited by Robert Burgin

Read the High Country: A Guide to Western Books and Films
John Mort

Graphic Novels: A Genre Guide to Comic Books, Manga, and More
Michael Pawuk

Genrefied Classics: A Guide to Reading Interests in Classic Literature
Tina Frolund

Encountering Enchantment: A Guide to Speculative Fiction for Teens
Susan Fichtelberg

Fluent in Fantasy: The Next Generation
Diana Tixier Herald and Bonnie Kunzel

Gay, Lesbian, Bisexual, and Transgendered Literature: A Genre Guide
Ellen Bosman and John Bradford; Edited by Robert B. Ridinger

Reality Rules!: A Guide to Teen Nonfiction Reading Interests
Elizabeth Fraser

Historical Fiction II: A Guide to the Genre
Sarah L. Johnson

Hooked on Horror III
Anthony J. Fonseca and June Michele Pulliam

Caught Up In Crime

A Reader's Guide to Crime Fiction and Nonfiction

Gary Warren Niebuhr

Genreflecting Advisory Series

Diana Tixier Herald, Series Editor

Libraries Unlimited

An Imprint of ABC-CLIO, LLC

A B C ⬥ C L I O

Santa Barbara, California • Denver, Colorado • Oxford, England

Library of Congress Cataloging-in-Publication Data

Caught up in crime : a reader's guide to crime fiction and nonfiction / [compiled by] Gary Warren Niebuhr.

p. cm. — (Genreflecting advisory series)
Includes bibliographical references and index.
ISBN 978-1-59158-428-5 (alk. paper)
1. Crime writing—Bibliography. 2. Criminal investigation—Bibliography. I. Niebuhr, Gary Warren.
Z5703.4.C728 C39 2009 [PN3377.5.C75]]
016.8083'872—dc22   2009008733

13   12   11   10   9   1   2   3   4   5

This book is also available on the World Wide Web as an eBook.
Visit www.abc-clio.com for details.

ABC-CLIO, LLC
130 Cremona Drive, P.O. Box 1911
Santa Barbara, California 93116-1911

This book is printed on acid-free paper ∞
Manufactured in the United States of America

Because he knows a frightful fiend close behind him tread.
—Samuel Taylor Coleridge, *The Rime of the Ancient Mariner*

Contents

Acknowledgments...xi
Introduction: An Overview of This Book xiii

Part I: Introduction to Crime Literature

Chapter 1—Collection Development and Preservation.....................3
Building the Crime Literature Collection...3
Maintaining the Crime Literature Collection 4
Weeding the Crime Literature Collection 4
Awards 4
    The Agatha Awards..5
    The Anthony Awards 5
    The Arthur Ellis Awards 5
    The Barry Awards 5
    The Dagger Awards...6
    The Dilys Award 6
    The Edgar Allan Poe Awards...6
    The Hammett Awards 6
    The Macavity Awards 6
    The Ned Kelly Awards...7
    The Reading List 7
    The Shamus Awards...7
Critics' Choices..7

Chapter 2—The History of Crime Literature 9
The Earliest Crime Novels 9
The Development of the American Crime Novel....................................10
The Modern Crime Story 11

Part II: The Literature

Chapter 3—Professional Criminals 15
Capers..15
    Caper Novels 15
    True Crime Capers 24
The Mob...27
    Mob Novels..28
    True Crime Mob Stories...36

Chapter 3—Professional Criminals (*Cont.*)

   Robbers 40
      Robber Novels...41
      True Crime Robbers 48
   White Collar Crimes..49
      White Collar Crime Novels..50
      True White Collar Crime 51

Chapter 4—Caught Up in Crime 55

   Amateur Criminals 55
      Amateur Criminal Novels 55
      True Amateur Crime 60
   Crime and Punishment 61
      Crime and Punishment Novels...62
      True Crime and Punishment...68
   Criminals with Good Intentions 73
      Criminals with Good Intentions Novels 74
      True Criminals with Good Intentions 86
   On the Run 90
      On the Run Novels..91
      On the Run True Crime 103
   Serial Killers and Psychos..105
      Serial Killers and Psychos Novels...105
      True Crime Serial Killers and Psychos 116
   Victims 121
      Victims Novels...122
      True Crime Victims...136

Chapter 5—Criminal Detectives 147

   Cops Gone Bad...147
      Cops Gone Bad Novels 148
      True Crime Cops Gone Bad 153
   Lawyers Gone Bad 155
      Lawyers Gone Bad Novels...156
   Private Investigators Gone Bad...157
      Private Investigators Gone Bad Novels.......................................158

Part III: Topics

Chapter 6—Bibliographies 167

Chapter 7—Encyclopedias 171

Chapter 8—Filmography..173

Chapter 9—Guides 175

Chapter 10—History and Criticism..179

Chapter 11—Journals...183

Chapter 12—Book Review Sources..185

Chapter 13—Conventions..187

Chapter 14—Mystery Bookstores..189

Chapter 15—Online Resources..191
General Sites 191
Mystery Listservs 191
Readers' Advisory Sites 191

Chapter 16—Organizations 193

Chapter 17—Publishers...195
Major Publishers 195
Small Presses...195

Author Index and Biographical Notes..197
Title Index 255
Subject Index...269
Locations Index 291

Acknowledgments

Reading fiction is my hobby. Reading about bad people is inexplicable.

In the thirty years that I have been immersed in crime literature fan activities, many individuals have influenced me. In the mystery field, Mary Ann Grochowski got me started, and Marv Lachman has kept me going. Wonderful editors like Jeff Meyerson, Art Scott, George Easter, Bill Ott, Lynn Kaczmarek, and Chris Aldrich have afforded me the opportunities to have my ideas broadcast to the world.

I especially want to thank all the caring and giving crime literature fans who have influenced me since I first entered the community. The readers in The Cloak and Clue Society and the members of the Greendale Park and Recreation Crime Fiction Book Discussion have lent their ideas to this book without their knowledge.

In cyberspace, the daily thoughts of the members of RARA-Avis have proven invaluable to me as I did my research for this work.

This book could not have been written without the awe-inspiring work by Allen J. Hubin, *Crime Fiction*. There may be no greater single contribution to mystery fiction research than this effort, and it is greatly appreciated.

However, this book would not exist except for the pioneering work *Genreflecting*, and the work done by Betty Rosenberg and Diana Tixier Herald. This is a debt that can never be paid. I would like to thank Barbara Ittner for the opportunity to produce this work, and thank all the hard-working folks at Libraries Unlimited. A big thank-you to Emma Bailey and Sharon DeJohn, who edited this book with precision.

Any errors or omissions in this work are unintentional, and in the spirit of maintaining the level of research intended to do a revision, I would appreciate receiving any comments readers may have to improve a later edition. My e-mail address is gniebuhr@wi.rr.com.

I would like to thank my wife, Denice, who can recite this quote with me because it is the same statement from the three books I have written, but it is still true. After twenty-eight years of marriage, she still agrees to live in poverty because of a basement full of books. But she understands, and that is all I need. This book could not have been written without her support.

Introduction:
An Overview of This Book

Caught Up in Crime is designed to help readers' advisors, librarians, and others develop a greater understanding of the crime genre so they can make reading recommendations and successfully answer questions raised by readers who enjoy reading crime literature.

Whereas the mystery genre that I wrote about in *Make Mine a Mystery* has a hero who will restore justice to a world gone wrong, crime literature is about people who revel in the nether regions. Why I enjoy reading about their travails is difficult to explain except for one coda: there but for the grace of God go I.

A crime novel observes the undertaking of a criminal act, but does not necessarily have a detective who pursues either the criminal or a sense of justice. The protagonist may, in fact, be the criminal. The novels in this volume include

> stand-alone crime novels,
>
> crime novels featuring a series character caught up in crimes rather than mysteries,
>
> stand-alone mysteries that function more like crime novels in their intent, and
>
> true crime that reads like a novel.

Because I am attempting to encompass all of crime literature outside of detective novels, I have included titles from the entire history of the genre. Although the development of crime stories could be traced to folktales and religious sources such as the Bible, as a fiction art form, that development began in the 1700s. This book covers publications from then until 2008. I hope this historical approach will deepen the readers' advisor's understanding of the genre and its evolution over time to better comprehend what appeals to readers of this genre. It also serves crime readers, who often take interest in the evolution of the genre and of their favorite characters.

Although crime literature tends to shy away from series characters, some creative artists have managed to sustain one character over time. The titles listed for these authors include all titles in a series.

Titles written by an author in the mystery field and outside the crime genre are not listed.

Many of the books listed in this book are in print. However, some can only be found by searching a quality collection in a large public library or by haunting specialty crime literature stores or used bookstores. Readers who are intrigued should not hesitate to use interlibrary loan at their local library or the World Wide Web to search for out-of-print book dealers that carry crime literature.

Each entry provides publisher and year of publication, listing the first edition first, whether it is the British or the American edition. Alternate titles are provided. Also included are brief plot summaries to help users get a general sense of what the book is about. Individual titles are listed chronologically (by publication date) beneath each author's name; series titles are grouped chronologically under a series designation.

The overall organization groups similar titles, so the subcategories within each chapter can be considered "read-alike" lists. Author, title, subject, and location indexes offer additional access.

Although this book is intended for professionals who advise readers, it will also be useful to fans of the genre, crime literature bookstore owners, educators who teach literature courses in crime literature, crime literature publishers, and writers who want to publish in the genre.

The Subgenres of Crime

What is a *crime story*?

> A crime story observes the undertaking of a criminal act, but does not necessarily have a detective who pursues either the criminal or a sense of justice.

For the purposes of this book, crime literature is divided into three main categories:

Professional Criminals

Caught Up in Crime

Criminal Detectives

Nonfiction crime stories, or "true crime," are listed in separate subcategories under each main category.

"Professional Criminals" are individuals or groups who try to derive their sole income from criminal behavior. This category is divided into the following subgroups:

Capers

The Mob

Robbers

White Collar Crimes

Capers are novels wherein the characters plan a crime with many external dimensions, which can include the commission of the crime and the consequences after the plan is put in place. The central core of a caper story is the development and execution of the plan. It is distinguished from a mystery story in that the emphasis is not on the prevention or apprehension of the criminals. The appeal of the caper is in whether or not the characters will succeed in pulling off the heist. Gangs who become so affiliated that they reach the ranks of "organized crime" have their stories told in the section "The Mob."

Books about *the mob* involve all aspects of organized crime, with the understanding that the perpetrators fall under the standard definition. The main focus of these stories is as much on the organization and its behavior as it is on any criminal activities it undertakes. The main appeal of mob stories is an understanding of the power of an organization's structure and rules over decent moral and ethical behavior. Gangs of criminals who do not reach this status find their tales told in "Capers."

Robbers are defined by their emotional and sporadic behavior rather than their organizational skills. Whereas in a caper novel there is a great deal of planning, robbers act in the moment and often use violent methods in the perpetration of the crime. What a robber steals from the victim can vary from wealth to dignity. The appeal of a robber story is in what motivated the character to commit these acts.

White collar crime stories are about individuals in the business community who decide to take advantage of their knowledge to commit a crime. These crimes can range from the simple act of embezzlement at work to a major computer fraud that will gain the perpetrator millions. Although the main focus of the story's structure is similar to that of a caper, the appeal of this book is the slow descent of a decent character into the netherworld of crime.

Mercenaries and assassins are considered to fall within the category "thriller" and are not covered because their actions are not viewed as crimes per se, because although an assassination is a crime against humanity, for the purposes of this book it is on too grand a scale to be included in a work regarding crime literature. It is more appropriately handled in the thriller category because the focus is on the planning and carrying out of the act, or the hunt for the person after the act, in a style that fits the thriller definition better than it fits the crime fiction definition. That said, a few titles that involve assassination do appear in this volume, some because they involve a series character that I wanted to include:

Max Collins, *Primary Target*

Richard Condon, *The Manchurian Candidate*

Tim Dorsey, *Orange Crush*

Victor Gischler, *Gun Monkeys* and *Shotgun Opera*

Thomas Perry, *The Butcher's Boy*

Mike Weiss, *Double Play*

Novels in "Caught Up in Crime" are defined by the individual problem facing the protagonist. This category is divided into the following subgroups:

"Amateur Criminals"

"Crime and Punishment"

"Criminals with Good Intentions"

"On the Run"

"Serial Killers and Psychos"

"Victims"

Amateur criminals commit one act and suffer the consequences. They are average citizens who never intended to commit a crime or to profit from it. The appeal of these novels is often defined by the character who committed the act and the range of emotions displayed by that person as he or she suffers the consequences.

Crime and punishment novels deal with the actions of individuals after a crime has been committed. These range from the emotional decline of the perpetrator to acts of revenge committed by the victim. What is key in these novels is that the reader sees direct action as a result of a crime. The appeal is that in some fashion, this type of crime literature may be the only one in the genre that delivers a sense of justice or completion.

We make an assumption that some of the tortured characters covered in this book are *criminals with good intentions.* Although their involvement in crime is inevitable, their reasons may be pure. One of the questions to be answered in these stories is whether the main character should get away with criminal activity for a higher moral purpose.

Stories in which the character is *on the run* are the roller-coaster rides of crime. The person in motion can be either a criminal evading the administration of justice or a victim trying to outpace the pursuing criminal. The appeal of this type of literature is both the suspense and the thrill. The suspense asks whether or not the character will be caught. The thrill comes from fast-paced action and the author's ability to raise the reader's heart rate by creating empathy.

Serial killers and psychos fascinate us by their amoral behavior. The appeal is an emotional one based mostly on the thrill of watching a person commit heinous crimes and the challenge of trying to understand what motivates that behavior.

Novels that feature *victims* concentrate on the results of a crime. Whether healing or not, these novels display the range of emotions exhibited by an individual who has been affected by a criminal act. The appeal may be one of hope, as victims claw their way out from under. Other victims novels do not end pleasantly, and the appeal of those could be the attempt to understand and avoid consequences.

The "Criminal Detectives" stories are the allies of the mystery fiction genre. Herein are displayed the actions of characters who lack the moral qualities to be mystery fiction detectives. Although they are assigned the traditional roles from that genre, they often behave badly while occasionally doing the right thing. This category is divided into the following subgroups:

"Cops Gone Bad"

"Lawyers Gone Bad"

"Private Investigators Gone Bad"

Cops, lawyers, and private investigators gone bad share a common denominator. These individuals could choose the path of righteousness and justice, but instead try to illegally profit from their assigned role in the prevention of a crime or apprehension of the criminals. The appeal of these novels is in the characters, the paths they select, and the consequences therein. Some authors have managed to sustain a series character in this genre.

The Appeal of the Criminal Character

The appeal of the criminal character can be defined by two terms: hard-boiled and noir.

According to the *Merriam-Webster Collegiate Dictionary*, to hard-boil an egg, it needs to be cooked in its shell until the white and yolk have solidified. The same source says the adjective *hard-boiled* can be applied to a person who is tough, devoid of sentimentality, and has a matter-of-fact attitude toward violence.

This definition covers the majority of the characters contained in crime literature. The appeal here is that although we would not necessarily want to meet these characters in real life, crime literature affords us the opportunity to observe, study, and even vicariously participate in adventures with individuals whose behavior, and its consequences, fascinate us.

The exception to this in crime literature is when we observe the victims. Although readers are empathetic, they are also secretly hoping that the victims will develop the one character trait that would have kept them from being victimized: a hard-boiled attitude.

In researching the definition of hard-boiled, author Jack Bludis discovered a sentence in Ernest Hemingway's novel *The Sun Also Rises* (1926) that reads, "It is awfully easy to be hard-boiled about something in the daytime, but at night it's another thing."

The nighttime is the correct atmosphere for film *noir*. It was first identified by French scholars, and the term translates from the French as "black film." This film style was first utilized in France but was brought to its peak by low-budget American directors and producers in the 1940s; it was identified as a genre long after the films were made.

Many of the great films noir are based on crime fiction that appears in this book. Ironically, crime fiction has now become defined as noir. It is to the French we turn again for the credit of establishing this term in the world of literature. At the French publishing house Gallimard in 1945, editor Marcel Duhamel founded an imprint called Série noire. This brought American crime fiction to France and featured many of the novels that had been the source materials for the screenplays of film noir.

What defines a story as noir? Film noir scholar Eddie Muller says a film noir has atmospherics, such as being dark and sinister, that can translate to a novel. However, a film noir also has content, such as a doomed protagonist, a femme fatale, etc., that might translate to the printed page. Muller says, "The darkest crime fiction is where the protagonist falls down a moral slope and can't get back—and does not care."

Because much of the source material for film noir was American crime fiction of the 1930s and 1940s, the use of location, language, and attitude can be defined as colloquial to the American urban experience. The urban location is so central to noir literature that nonurban settings are always qualified in discussing titles set outside the confines of a big city.

Mystery author Jim Doherty likes to pare these definitions down to these:

> Hardboiled = tough and colloquial

> Noir = dark and sinister

Bludis makes the definition even shorter and blunter:

> Hardboiled = tough

> Noir = screwed

Here is my definition of a hard-boiled story:

> In a **hard-boiled story**, the action is violent, with sexual content and the language of the streets. A hard-boiled world is a society in which everything is suspect, including established institutions and the people who work for them, even the legal forces. The inclusion of a crime in a hard-boiled world is inevitable. Most violent action takes place onstage. The emphasis is on the perpetration of the crime, and characters are often driven to do what they do by circumstances that are often out of their control. Hard-boiled literature can feature protagonists who are not clearly defined as being on either the right or wrong side of the law. The administration of justice is not certain in a hard-boiled story, and *morality* may have many definitions in a hard-boiled world.

For the noir genre, I would add these sentences:

> The protagonist will suffer the major consequences of his or her decisions. There is no hope for a noir protagonist. If the protagonist is involved in a criminal activity, that person will be punished for his or her actions. The punishment will not necessarily be from organized society, but rather more from fate. The ultimate punishment in a noir story is death.

The appeal of noir literature is in watching the inevitable descent of the protagonist into a situation from which he or she cannot escape. If the person is a criminal, part of the satisfaction may be seeing the world apply justice to him or her.

We hope a hard-boiled hero will be able to remain in control and restore some balance of order to his or her world. Although this may seem contrary when reading about a criminal, it is part of the appeal of this type of fiction: unintentionally identifying with the protagonist and rooting for the wrong side.

In crime series, the challenge is creating a noir-like world with a hard-boiled protagonist wherein the most final application of justice, death, is never applied. The punishment meted out to a series character in this world is often brutal.

Part I

Introduction to Crime Literature

Chapter 1

Collection Development and Preservation

Building the Crime Literature Collection

In a perfect world, a library would be able to select the best crime literature each year and never have to discard or lose a copy. All the titles would be available, in bright, fresh, and attractive copies. Money could be spent on works by new authors, as well as on buying the new titles of the tried and true stalwarts. Paperback originals would be considered the equal of the hardcover, and both would be fully cataloged by author, title, setting, series, character, series title, and type of detective.

Unfortunately, we do not live in a perfect world with unlimited funds. A library must establish a procedure for selecting books that provides fair representation to all the genres. The process should be done with care, as there are many more titles being published than most libraries can afford to buy, catalog, or warehouse. The same principles of the materials selection policy that govern any other type of material added to the library's collection should be applied to crime literature.

Because of the sheer volume of crime titles published each year, many libraries find it relatively easy to locate books to select for their collections. By making a rough estimate of the monthly allotment for crime literature, a library can determine how much effort it wants to put into crime selection. The good news is that crime is a popular genre and is well covered by most of the library professional journals. Journals such as *Publishers Weekly, Library Journal,* and *Booklist* have special sections labeled "mystery" in each issue, which cover some crime fiction and nonfiction. However, please be aware that many of the professional journals review books with major elements of crime as contemporary fiction rather than in a genre-specific category.

Librarians who are able to understand the terminology used in the genre will better understand the reviews. Those who understand their customers may know whether to place a greater emphasis on soft-boiled, cozy mysteries or to stock up on all the latest hard-boiled crime adventures.

If time and the budget allow, you may wish to consult nonprofessional review sources called fanzines. Fanzines are listed in Part III. Each takes a unique approach to reviewing titles in the crime genre, so when you're done with the selection process, place the fanzines in the circulating magazine collection for patrons to use.

Maintaining the Crime Literature Collection

Back in our perfect world, when normal library use requires that the library seek a replacement for a title, a copy would simply be ordered from a major book jobber, and the book would arrive a few days later.

The sad reality is that many crime titles have a short life span. Hardcovers are published and go out of print within a year. Paperback issues (assuming that the book is published in paperback) may extend the life of a title by keeping it in print. Certainly all the normal resources available to the library should be explored to determine if needed titles are in print.

Buying and selling out-of-print crime literature is a very significant and popular activity of the mystery fan community. Most out-of-print bookstores, out-of-print catalogs, and used and antiquarian bookstores have a crime section, although it may be labeled mystery or detective fiction. Become familiar with the resources available in your area. The World Wide Web has several search engines devoted to making the offerings of booksellers readily available. Remember, you will need to understand concerns such as condition, edition, and collectibility before venturing into these sites.

Weeding the Crime Literature Collection

The simple solution to the question of whether to weed a particular work of crime literature is its popularity. Often libraries use circulation as a measure of whether to maintain an item in the collection, and this criteria can also be applied to crime literature. It would be hard to disagree with the argument that if popular genre material is not of interest to the local population, then it should be discarded.

Weeding stand-alone crime novels or true crime books is easier than dealing with series titles in mystery and detective fiction. It is possible to weed some titles in the oeuvre of particular crime writers while retaining others. However, thought should be given to retaining all the works of benchmark crime writers.

Besides using your own circulation statistics, crime literature resources such as those listed in Part III should be consulted to help determine the value of a particular title. If you have any doubt about the value of a particular title, consider creating a display to test interest in that work at the local level.

Part II of this book ensures a library of a comprehensive and quality overview of this genre. However, each library should look at the authors listed and decide which series would be best maintained for the reading interests of its customers.

Awards

One approach to collection development in the genre is to select award-winning titles. Award lists can be used to do retrospective collection building, even though availability is often problematic. Nevertheless, if you want to develop a contemporary collection that reflects the recognition offered by these various awards, checking these lists annually is a wonderful way to develop a collection that includes all the greatest hits of the genre. Including nominated works as well as the winners enhances a library's collection. Of course, as with any award given in the humanities, the choosing of a winner is a very subjective process. And please be aware that these awards rarely distinguish between works of crime literature and those that are mystery or detective fiction.

There has been a proliferation of awards in the mystery and crime field in recent years, particularly during the 1990s. A complete list of the awards given each year can be found at www.stopyourkillingme.com/Awards/index.html.

The Agatha Awards

These awards, first presented in 1988, are given to mystery fiction material published in the previous year that represents the soft-boiled (cozy) and traditional literature and is featured at the annual convention, called Malice Domestic, where the awards are presented each May. The award is named in honor of Agatha Christie and is shaped like a teapot. Malice Domestic attendees create a list of nominees, and the awards are determined by a vote of the convention attendees. Web site: www.malicedomestic.org/agathaawards.html

The Anthony Awards

These awards, first presented in 1986, are given at the Bouchercon, the annual world mystery conference, generally held in October, to mystery fiction of any type published in the previous year. The award and the convention are named in memory of William Anthony Parker White, who wrote mystery fiction and mystery reviews under the pseudonym Anthony Boucher. Each year the Bouchercon committee designs its own Anthony award. The annual attendees of the Bouchercon create a list of nominees, and the membership of the annual convention votes on which works will win the award. Web site: www.bouchercon.info/history.html

The Arthur Ellis Awards

These awards, first presented in 1984, are given by the Crime Writers of Canada, a professional writing organization, at its annual dinner in May, to works of Canadian mystery fiction published during the previous year. The award is named after the name used to disguise Canada's official hangman. The award is a statuette of a wooden gallows with a puppet suspended from it that dances when you pull the hangman's rope. Web site: www.crimewriterscanada.com/cwc/pages/pastawards.html

The Barry Awards

These awards, first presented in 1997, are given at the Bouchercon, the annual world mystery convention, generally held in October, to any work of mystery published during the previous calendar year. The award is named in memory of Barry Gardner, a reviewer for *Deadly Pleasures* and *Mystery News* magazines. The readers of the magazines nominate titles and then vote for winners from that list. Web site: www.deadlypleasures.com/barry.html or www.blackravenpress.com

The Dagger Awards

These awards, first presented in 1980, are given by the Crime Writers Association (CWA), a British professional writing organization, at its annual dinner in December, to works of mystery fiction published from October of the previous year to September of the current year. The main awards are gold and silver daggers. They have a corporate sponsor and are named after the Duncan Laurie bank. Independent committees, created by the CWA chairperson, select the list of nominees and the winners. Web site: www.thecwa.co.uk/

The Dilys Award

This award, first presented in 1992, is given to a work of mystery fiction that the Independent Mystery Booksellers had the most fun selling during the previous year. The award is presented at the Left Coast Crime Conference each year in the spring. The award is named in honor of Dilys Winn, the founder of America's first mystery bookstore, Murder Ink. Web site: www.mysterybooksellers.com/dilys.html

The Edgar Allan Poe Awards

The Edgar awards, first presented in 1946, are given by the Mystery Writers of America (MWA), a professional organization of writers, at its annual banquet in April, to mystery fiction published in the previous year. The award is named after the American writer credited with inventing many of the genre's characteristics. Members of the MWA are assigned to committees that read materials submitted by publishers. A list of nominees is published, with the committees' choices for the best announced at the annual dinner. Web site: www.mysterywriters.org/?q=Edgars-PastWinners

The Hammett Awards

These awards, first presented in 1992, are given by the North American branch of the International Association of Crime Writers, for a work of literary excellence in the field of crime writing by a U.S. or Canadian author that was published in the previous year. The award is named after Dashiell Hammett and is a bronze trophy designed by sculptor Peter Boiger. The winner is chosen by three distinguished judges. Web site: www.crimewritersna.org/hammett/index.htm

The Macavity Awards

These awards, first presented in 1987, are given at Bouchercon by the members of Mystery Readers International, to mystery fiction material published in the previous year. The award is named for the "mystery cat" of T. S. Eliot (*Old Possum's Book of Practical Cats*). Each year the members of Mystery Readers International nominate and vote for their favorites. Web site: www.mysteryreaders.org/macavity.html

The Ned Kelly Awards

These awards, first presented in 1995, are given by The Crime Writers' Association of Australia (CWAA), to works of Australian crime writing published in the previous year. The awards are named after the famous Australian bandit, Ned Kelly. Web site: www.nedkellyawards.com/index.html

The Reading List

These awards, first presented in 2007, are given by The Reading List Council of the American Library Association to highlight outstanding genre fiction that merits special attention by general adult readers and the librarians who work with them. The Council, which consists of twelve librarians who are experts in readers' advisory and collection development, selects books in eight categories. Each year the Council announces the eight winning titles at the CODES Awards Reception, held on the Sunday when the ALA Midwinter Conference takes placev. Web site: www.ala.org/ala/mgrps/divs/rusa/archive/protools/readinglist/lists/currentreadlist.cfm

The Shamus Awards

These awards, first presented in 1982, are given by The Private Eye Writers of America (PWA) to works of private eye fiction published in the previous year. The award's name is a slang term for private eye. The trophy is a mounted and embossed representation of the work. Members of PWA are assigned to committees that read materials submitted by publishers. A list of nominees is published, with the committee's choice for the best announced. Web site: www.thrillingdetective.com/trivia/triv72.html

Critics' Choices

Critics' lists are also useful for collection development. Part III of this book is an example of the kinds of lists that are available in the genre. Many of the other works listed in Part III contain bibliographies that are helpful resources for collection development. Some lists are created each year by critics as a guide to the field. The following magazines produce excellent lists of mystery and crime literature. *Booklist* has an annual issue devoted to mystery and crime literature. *Publishers Weekly* has an annual issue devoted to current developments in the field. *The New York Times Book Review* section produces various lists throughout the year, some tied to the seasons. *Deadly Pleasures* produces reliable annual lists developed by well-respected fan critics in the genre.

An example of a contemporary list that may prove helpful to collection development librarians is the one created by the Independent Mystery Booksellers Association. The list of their favorite mysteries and crime fiction of the previous century can be found at www.mysterybooksellers.com, or in book form in *100 Favorite Mysteries of the Century* (Crum Creek, 2000).

Chapter 2

The History of Crime Literature

Whereas most mystery and detective fiction employs a protagonist who cares about discovering the perpetrator of the crime, crime literature is more focused on examining the crime itself. Because humans have always been interested in both committing and reporting crimes, it is not surprising that pinpointing the origin of crime literature is challenging.

The Earliest Crime Novels

Is it fair to list early works of literature like *The Adventures of Caleb Williams* (1794), written by English philosopher William Godwin, as the first works of crime literature? Certainly many novels like this, in which dark secrets lead to hidden crimes, could qualify. Even romantic adventures like *The Three Musketeers*, by Alexandre Dumas (1844), have elements of criminal activity buried within their intrigue.

Dorothy L. Sayers's *The Omnibus of Crime* (UK title, *Great Short Stories of Detection, Mystery & Horror*) began the hunt for criminal short stories with the biblical or mythological stories of Bel, Susanna, Hercules with Cacus, and Rhampsinitus. Contemporary readers of the three volumes of stories collected by Sayers will likely recognize such contributors as Conan Doyle, E. C. Bentley, G. K. Chesterton, Charles Dickens, Ambrose Bierce, Joseph Conrad, H. G. Wells, Stephen Crane, and Edgar Allan Poe.

Although most mystery and detective fiction scholars are willing to use the works of Edgar Allan Poe (1841) as the starting point for that genre, crime literature started earlier, in an era in which fictionalized memoirs were popular. In fact, crime fiction finds its roots in the "true crime" branch of literature.

Eugène François Vidocq (b. July 23, 1775) was the most prominent example of the cliché "set a thief to catch a thief." Having established a successful career as a criminal and rogue, he volunteered to spy for his country in order to avoid a jail term. Made the first head of the Sûreté Nationale in 1812, he served until 1832, when using ex-criminals as policemen became unpopular. His exploits were published in 1828 and 1829 in ghostwritten volumes. Although some liberties probably were taken with the truth, there is no denying the stories' popularity. Later in life, after establishing the first private detective agency, Vidocq wrote crime fiction, perhaps with the help of Honoré de Balzac. He died in May 1857.

In a sense, Vidocq and his writings served as models for both crime and detective literature. Vidocq is thought to be the model for Victor Hugo's lead character in *Les Misérables*, Emile Gaboriau's Lecoq, and for Vautrin in the works of Balzac. His exploits certainly popularized reading about crime and encouraged others to take up the cause.

When did works of fiction begin to be labeled as genre crime fiction? Penny dreadfuls and yellowback novels (or dime novels) certainly did their share to popularize criminal activities in works of fiction. One of the earliest and most popular was *Recollections of a Detective-Police Officer*, published in 1852. Most of these works were published anonymously and have little merit today except as historical curiosities.

In England, from the 1820s through the 1840s the Newgate novels were all the rage. Based on the exploits of famous criminals locked up in Newgate Prison whose careers had been chronicled in the *Newgate Calendar*, these novels helped open the world of criminality to the world of literature. Less-talented artists like Edward Bulwer-Lytton did little to advance the cause, but more talented authors also began to explore the format.

Charles Dickens experimented with themes and plots that involved criminal activity in such works as *Oliver Twist* (1838) and *Bleak House* (1852). The last work of his life, the unfinished *The Mystery of Edwin Drood* (1870), tells a tale of murder based on jealousy.

Victorian England's Wilkie Collins, mentored by his friendship with Dickens, certainly did his share to lift the literary merits of the genre. His *The Woman in White*, published in 1860, is the gothic tale of a ghostly woman who haunts the countryside and reveals that all may not be well in Cumberland. His second major contribution to crime literature is *The Moonstone* (1868), wherein a diamond is stolen from the Hindus and brought to England, with bad consequences. It is in this book that Collins created Sergeant Cuff, one of the earliest efforts at a legitimate detective character.

Russian author Fyodor Dostoevsky's *Crime and Punishment*, first published in 1867, detailed the thought processes of a desperate individual, Rodion Romanovich Raskolnikov, as he chose murder as the solution to his problems. In that same year, Australian author Fergus Hume posed the intriguing question of how a man ends up murdered on a busy street in *The Mystery of a Hansom Cab* (1886).

By the turn of the century the mystery story, with its heroic detective characters, was successfully developing. On the criminal side of literature, writers like Theodore Dreiser were examining the seamier side of life for source material. Whereas novels like *Sister Carrie* (1900) dealt with the desperate struggles of people to survive in a harsh world, his *An American Tragedy* (1925) lies solidly in the criminal world. It tells of the downward spiral of Clyde Griffiths into a noir nightmare. Central to one of the features that distinguish criminal literature from mystery and detective fiction, the assignment of responsibility for crimes and the application of justice are both vague.

The Development of the American Crime Novel

The period between World War I and World War II was rich with literature in this field. The American publishing phenomenon known as pulp magazines did much to promote the use of criminality in storytelling. While encompassing a wide range of human activities under their scope, the pulps provided a market for fictional crimes. Magazines such as *Black Mask*, *Dime Detective*, and *Spicy Detective* provided a secure outlet for work and a training ground for a new generation of crime writers.

Dashiell Hammett was one of the early graduates of *Black Mask* magazine. Although most of his famous novels feature heroic private detectives based on his own experiences as a Pinkerton agent, Hammett's novel *The Glass Key* (1931) features a professional criminal as the detective.

Another crime writer who apprenticed in the pulps was David Goodis. His second novel, *Dark Passage* (1946), deals with an escaped prisoner who used plastic surgery and the help of a sympathetic woman to hunt down the real killer of his wife. Other pulp graduates who contributed to the oeuvre were Jim Thompson and Horace McCoy. What all three of these writers eventually brought to the table was exploration of the psychological reasons behind criminal behavior. The master of psychological reasoning in crime writing in the period between the wars was James M. Cain. With *The Postman Always Rings Twice* (1934) and *Double Indemnity* (1943), he became the best writer of the period.

W. R. Burnett's *Little Caesar* (1929) established itself as a benchmark mob title. Made into a successful film by Warner Brothers, the story helped to launch a long-running subgenre of organized crime films.

The paperback revolution that caught fire after World War II brought readers to crime writers like Harry Whittington, Gil Brewer, and Peter Rabe. Through paperback original publishers like Gold Medal Lion and others, the public was alerted to the new writers as much by the titles as by the art used on the covers.

Hollywood's use of this type of novel for the screenplays of its film noirs helped fuel interest as well. Perhaps no one can be more credited with combining elements of mystery, detection, crime, and horror to create the noir atmosphere than Cornell Woolrich. With novels under his own name, and more under the names George Hopley and William Irish, he thrilled readers and attracted movie directors to his macabre stories.

The Modern Crime Story

In the post–World War II period, certain crime writers developed new techniques. Patricia Highsmith continued the pattern of emphasis on the psychological development of the characters. Her chief contribution was to contrast the differences between two individuals who are confronted by the worst. Highsmith's first novel, *Strangers on a Train* (1950), is a classic example of the balance between expediency and morality. But not to be overlooked are her series of novels about Tom Ripley, a man who uses his skills as an aspiring actor to become a man of the netherworld.

The examination of two individuals committing a crime together was also the focus of Truman Capote's "true crime" story, *In Cold Blood* (first serialized in 1965). Although maintaining a semblance of journalistic integrity by reporting the facts about a Kansas crime spree as it occurred, Capote bent all the rules when he used the novelistic approach of re-creating the dialogue and thoughts of the characters. This new technique opened the world to the idea of narrative nonfiction, called *new journalism*, blurring the lines between fact and fiction forever.

In 1969, with the publication of *The Godfather* by Mario Puzo, the mob novel was back on the map. When Elmore Leonard moved from Western fiction to novels of crime in 1969 with *The Big Bounce*, he chose to emphasize the caper. His characters want to be more than they are and often more than they are capable of being, but they never reach the level of nobility of Puzo's characters. Leonard's use of humor and dialogue has made him one of the most popular contemporary crime writers. When George V. Higgins arrived on the scene with *The Friends of Eddie Coyle* (1972), his characters' stories were revealed to the reader almost exclusively in dialogue.

Thomas Harris proved it is possible to feature the worst psychopath as a series character when he created Hannibal Lecter in *Red Dragon* (1981). The publication and popularity of *The Silence of the Lambs* (1988) has spawned a subgenre of serial killer protagonists that continues today with the <u>Dexter Morgan series</u>, written by Jeff Lindsay.

A resurgence in the popularity of film noirs and the novels upon which they were based has resulted in a renaissance in neo-noir writing. Authors such as Ken Bruen and Jason Starr are moving crime literature into a new wave of popularity that ensures its health well into the twenty-first century.

Part II

The Literature

Chapter 3

Professional Criminals

Professional criminals are enterprising individuals who want to live off the fruits of someone else's labor by taking what is not theirs. The "professional" tag means most of their income is achieved by devious or illegal means. Professionals have also developed specific skill sets to aid them in their criminal behavior.

Capers

For the purposes of this work, capers are illegal activities that involve a grand plot or scheme. The characters spend an inordinate amount of time planning the enterprise, but often the results are less than they expected. Capers in fiction are usually an adrenaline read. Stories about gangs who reach the ranks of "organized crime" are covered in the section "The Mob."

Benchmark Caper Novel

Biggers, Earl Derr.

Seven Keys to Baldpate. Bobbs-Merrill, 1913.
> When author William H. Magee arrives in the remote upstate New York community of Upper Asquewan Falls, he believes he has the only key to Baldpate Inn, a hotel he intends to use as a refuge in which to write his novel. Then a host of people arrive with keys, all looking for $200,000 that is supposedly locked in the safe of the hotel.
>
> Authors; Hotels; New York—Upper Asquewan Falls

Caper Novels

Bloch, Robert.

Spiderweb. Ace, 1954.
> Eddie Haines is a Midwesterner with dreams of achieving glory in Hollywood. Just about the time he is ready to bag it and head home, he is discovered by Professor Otto Hermann. Under the tutelage of the professor, Eddie becomes self-help guru Judson Roberts, and the world opens up to him. When Eddie begins to have

doubts about what he's doing, the professor is not shy about applying blackmail to keep his invention in line.

California—Los Angeles; Gurus; Self-help

Block, Lawrence.

Mona. Fawcett, 1961. (Also published as *Grifter's Game* or *Sweet Slow Death*).

Joe Marlin is a scam artist, drifting from one hotel to another, always armed with luggage so as not to attract attention prior to skipping out on his bill. So imagine his surprise when one piece of stolen luggage is found to contain a large amount of heroin. When he meets one of the owners, the very married Mona Brassard, the two decide to dispense with the other owner.

Drugs; New Jersey—Atlantic City

The Girl with the Long Green Heart. Fawcett, 1965.

When Johnny Hayden and Doug Rance decide to scam millionaire real estate tycoon Wallace Gunderman, they come up with a plan to sell him some worthless land in Canada. All they need to make the plan perfect is an inside operative, and they find the perfect partner in the recently scorned Evelyn Stone, Gunderman's secretary.

New York—Olean; Real estate; Scams

Bunker, Edward.

Stark. St. Martin's Minotaur, 2007.

Ernie Stark is a con artist with few skills. He thinks he can outsmart everyone, but the reality is that this drug addict has been set up by cop Patrick Crowley to sell out his supplier, Momo Medoza. His love for the beautiful Dorie Williams may blind him to even more obvious clues that he will never be the lord of any empire.

California—Oceanview; Con artist; Drugs

Cain, Tom.

The Accident Man. Viking, 2007.

Samuel Carver is a hit man for hire whose specialty is to make things unarranged. Sent to Paris on assignment in the summer of 1997, he causes the crash of a particular car in a tunnel, supposedly to stop a terrorist. Instead, he finds he has been set up to kill Princess Diana.

Diana, Princess of Wales (1961–1997); Hit men

Carr, A. H. Z.

Finding Maubee. Putnam, 1971.

David Maubee is the Robin Hood of St. Caro, romancing his way into the hearts of the women and earning the wrath of the men. When a tourist is murdered with a machete, the local chief of police, Xavier Brooks, is pressured to arrest the island's number one playboy. But with race relations an issue, the chief finds he may be better off finding another murderer to arrest.

Caribbean—St. Caro, Gracedieu; Race relations

Chavarría, Daniel.

Adios Muchachos. Akashic, 2001.

Alicia rides the streets of Havana, working as a bicycle hooker. The idea is to have your vintage bike ready to fall apart, so that the man you target feels compelled to buy you a new one. Then invite him home for a well-cooked meal with momma, and he'll feel obligated to continue to provide goodies that can be sold on the black market. Alicia likes to concentrate on foreigners, but the day she picks Victor King, a man who is working a sunken treasure scam in Havana, she may have met her match. When someone dies, these two find their schemes may have to be elevated to avoid the long arm of the law.

Cuba—Havana; Scams

Condon, Richard.

The Manchurian Candidate. McGraw, 1959.

When Sergeant Raymond Shaw returns from being a Korean prisoner of war and wins the Congressional Medal of Honor, he appears to be a true American hero. However, he is a brainwashed agent of the Chinese government, a sleeper waiting for the right signal to assassinate a candidate picked out by his own mother. Only Shaw's former commanding officer, Captain Bennett Marco, can uncover the truth and save the nation.

Assassination; Brainwashing; Mothers and sons

Conrad, Mark T.

Dark as Night. Uglytown, 2004.

All chef Morris White would like to do is marry his girlfriend, Vicki Ward, and use her money to open up his own restaurant. Those plans get pushed aside when his ex-con, half-brother Vince Kammer moves in and dreams of another caper. This introduces Morris to a bookmaker, some Mafioso wannabes, and some corrupt cops.

Pennsylvania—Philadelphia

Dodge, David.

The Last Match. Hard Case Crime, 2006.

Con man Curly thinks he is one step ahead of everyone on the French Riviera, until he meets the lovely Regina Forbes-Jones, a woman who will become his "Nemesis." As he is forced to flee the coast of France and sets off across the world, working his scams, he finds she is always in his mind and on his trail.

Con men

1

2

3

4

5

6

7

8

9

10

Dorsey, Tim.

[Serge Storms series].

Tim Dorsey has created a series character, Florida psychopath Serge Storms, who rides the highways and byways of this Southern state pulling one scam after another. The following series titles are listed in order of publication; however, the novels jump around in time, so the chronology of the series is not the same as the publication dates. To keep this all straight, visit Tim Dorsey's Web site at www.timdorsey.com/chronology.html.

Florida Roadkill. William Morrow, 1999.

Sharon Rhodes murders rich men for their insurance money. When she meets Serge and Coleman, she may have found her soul mates. Dentist George Veale has scammed his insured hands into $5 million, but they all watch the suitcase stuffed with the money ride away in a car whose driver is unaware of the contents. They set off in pursuit. The money may belong to sleazy insurance man Charles Saffron, who is laundering it to keep his business afloat. With Serge inflicting damage while quoting Florida trivia, Coleman fried on cocaine, and Sharon willing to do anything to get the cash, the trio has little resemblance to a team, needing to watch each other as much as their targets.

Cocaine; Florida; Money laundering

Hammerhead Ranch Motel. Morrow, 2000.

With $5 million still available for the first taker, spree killer Serge Storms is in hot pursuit, despite the threat of a big hurricane bearing down on him. This time Serge's partner is Lenny Lippowicz, a fallen journalist. Other characters include an alligator wrestler, a worthless pilot, and a scary woman named Ingrid Praline. When everyone ends up locked in the Hammerhead Ranch Motel reenacting the movie *Key Largo,* things come to a head.

Florida—Tampa Bay; Hotels; Hurricanes

Orange Crush. Morrow, 2001.

When incumbent Republican lieutenant governor Marlon Conrad finds himself challenged for office by Democrat Gomer Tatum, he takes to the road in a Winnebago to stir up voters. While he dodges his security and attempts on his life, the bodies are piling up, and the reason may have something to do with Serge. Will it really all be decided by a wrestling match?

Assassination; Elections; Florida; Governors; Wrestling

Triggerfish Twist. Morrow, 2002.

This novel is a prequel in the series. When Jim Davenport moves from Indiana to Tampa, he does not expect to find Serge, Coleman, and Sharon living next door. Oddly, Serge ends up Jim's protector when the other residents on the block are crazier than Serge is. However, he cannot prevent Jim from committing a justifiable homicide that brings the dead man's relatives, the McGraw Brothers, to Tampa on the Fourth of July, seeking revenge.

Florida—Tampa; Neighborhoods

The Stingray Shuffle. Morrow, 2003.

Serge is still trying to find the $5 million that has eluded him since his first adventure. He teams up with his pal Lenny, and the two move up the Eastern Seaboard on a train in search of some Russian mafioso disguised as Latinos. Onstage characters this time include a drug cartel leader trying to keep his bankrupt operation afloat and a novelist named Ralph Krunkleton.

Authors; Florida; New York—New York; Railroads

Cadillac Beach. Morrow, 2004.

Escaped from the psychiatric hospital, Serge teams up with his pal Lenny to move to Miami, where Serge has ties, to open a tourist agency. His grandfather, Sergio, was a bookie in 1964 and got involved in the famous Murph the Surf jewel robbery. But Sergio may have been as nuts as his grandson, and the stories he told may or may not be true. The central question is whether Serge is more interested in finding the long-lost gems or wants to solve the riddle of his grandfather's death.

Florida—Miami; Grandfathers; Jewels; Tourist agency

Torpedo Juice. Morrow, 2005.

Serge is trying to get married! To a librarian named Molly! In his new home, the Florida Keys! But being the upright citizen that he is, he finds himself in conflict with a businessman trying to develop the land and a drug lord who wants to work the territory. He manages all of this while holding down a job as the social director for the No Name Pub.

Developers; Florida—Key West; Marriage; Taverns

The Big Bamboo. Morrow, 2006.

Motivated by a message from his dead grandfather to seek his fortune in California, Serge takes off for Hollywood with Coleman. His mission is to write a screenplay that represents Florida as he knows it. When he gets there, he kidnaps the young starlet Ally Street. He must also deal with the crazy Glick brothers and the weird film director Werner B. Potemkin.

Actors and actresses; California—Los Angeles; Kidnapping; Motion pictures

Hurricane Punch. Morrow, 2007.

Serge is not happy that a serial killer is stalking his home territory, so he decides to hunt down the killer. Also on the trail of the murderer is Serge's archenemy, Agent Mahoney, freshly released from the psychiatric ward himself. Although their quest may be noble, Serge and sidekick Coleman may be having too much fun riding around in their stolen Hummer.

Florida; Hurricanes; Serial killers

1

2

3

4

5

6

7

8

9

10

Atomic Lobster. Morrow, 2008.

> Serge and Coleman are out for a road trip with a stripper named Rachael. Others are on the road with them, including the vengeance-seeking Tex McGraw, two empty nesters, some combative drug dealers, and some government agents who believe a serial killer may be loose in Florida. Is it possible that all of this may have something to do with terrorism?

> Cruise ships; Drugs; Florida; Terrorism

Edgerton, Clyde.

The Bible Salesman. Little, Brown, 2008.

> In the post–World War II South, Preston Clearwater is on the make. Having honed his thieving ways in the Army during the war, he now is a car thief using a cover story that he is an FBI agent. When he discovers Henry Dampier, a young Bible salesman, he finds a dupe willing to drive stolen cars for the glory of helping out the U.S. government. As Clearwater ratchets up the crimes, Henry falls in love and deals with his very religious family.

> Automobile theft; Historical; North Carolina

Gischler, Victor.

Suicide Squeeze. Delacorte, 2005.

> Conner Samson is a repo man on the hunt for Teddy Folger's boat, the *Electric Jenny*. Folger is on the run from an insurance scam and just wants to sail off into the sunset. But the one thing that Folger did not burn in his store was a signed Joe DiMaggio baseball card that also has Billy Wilder's and Marilyn Monroe's signatures on it. What both men do not know is that a Japanese collector has sent his ninja hit men to recover the card and kill its owner.

> Baseball cards; Florida—Pensacola; Repo men

Guthrie, Allan.

Savage Night. UK: Polygon, 2008. (US: Harcourt, 2008).

> Ex-con Andy Park is trying to keep his family together as they follow in their father's footsteps, seeking revenge for an old crime. Although he faints at the sight of blood, his son Ritchie has no problem being a hit man. When Andy's slightly crazy daughter Effie decides to blackmail the man who killed her boyfriend's father, Tommy Savage, it opens a whole new can of worms. Tommy and his brother Phil are not going to take being shaken down well, and when the two families meet, it will lead to bloodshed whether Andy wants to look at it or not.

> Families; Scotland—Edinburgh

Hendricks, Vicki.

Iguana Love. Serpent's Tail, 1999.

> Ramona is on the prowl. She loves the thrill of diving and the thrill of picking up bad boys. When she finds herself attached to Enzo, a diving instructor, she also finds herself acting as a drug runner.

> Bimini; Drugs; Florida—Miami

Higgins, George V.

The Friends of Eddie Coyle. Knopf, 1972.

Eddie Coyle is a gun runner in Boston, aging, along with his wife and three children, while he dreams of the big score. He is still bothered by the consequences of one bad incident early in his career that disfigured his fingers. His life is a drab little spiral of crime, until his work for bank robber Jimmy Scalisi leads a cop named Foley to his doorstep with a request to rat out his boss. And what should he make of part-time contract killer, Dillion, Eddie's favorite bartender and supposed friend, who may believe that Eddie is a stool pigeon?

Bank robbery; Guns; Massachusetts—Boston

Cogan's Trade. Knopf, 1974.

Jackie Cogan's trade is mob enforcer. This time he is after the men who had the nerve to bust one of the mob's high-stakes card games run by Mark Trattman and make off with the money. With his ability to see through other people's weaknesses and an understanding of how a caper is designed, Cogan is able to hunt down the men and apply mob justice as he defines it.

Massachusetts—Boston; Organized crime

Hodgson, Ken.

The Man Who Killed Shakespeare. Five Star, 2007.

During the Great Depression, con man Sam Ransom roars into Shakespeare, New Mexico, with a plan to open a new mine and employee the troubled residents of the town. To his surprise, the mine actually has gold in it, and all goes well until the hit men who have been chasing him arrive to settle an old score.

Con artist; Historical; Mines; New Mexico—Shakespeare

Perry, Thomas.

Metzger's Dog. Scribner, 1983.

The University of Los Angeles is sitting on a million dollars' worth of cocaine, and that proves too much for Vietnam veteran Chinese Gordon. Putting together a gang to steal the drugs seems logical. Unfortunately for the gang, they also make off with some documents that would embarrass the U.S. government unless the CIA can get them back.

California—Los Angeles; Central Intelligence Agency; Drugs

Island. Putnam, 1987.

Here is a good idea: if you just ripped somebody off and need to hide half a million dollars, maybe your own country would be a good place to hide. When Harry and Emma Erskine find themselves in that position, they decide to open up a Caribbean island paradise for folks just like themselves. Sometimes it does hurt to be too popular, especially when other countries decide to invade and take you over.

Caribbean

Westlake, Donald.

[Dortmunder series].

John Dortmunder is a mastermind criminal whose adventures in crime always seem to go awry. The following series titles are listed in the order of publication.

The Hot Rock. Simon & Schuster, 1970.

> John Dortmunder is the leader of a gang of criminals. In this novel, he is hired by Major Patrick Iko, an African ambassador from Talabwo, to steal the Balabomo Emerald worth $500,000 and give it back to its rightful country. When the theft does not go as well as Dortmunder planned, he must set off in pursuit to claim what is not his.
>
> Gangs; Jewels; New York—New York

Bank Shot. Simon & Schuster, 1972.

> When the Capitalists' & Immigrants' Trust Corp. bank moves temporarily into a mobile home during a remodeling, Dortmunder and his gang can't resist the temptation to steal the bank's money, which is left in the bank on Thursday nights. It seems reasonable to back a truck up to the trailer and steal the entire bank. That is, until the safe will not open and Dortmunder needs to hide a bank.
>
> Bank robbery; New York—New York

Jimmy the Kid. Evans, 1974.

> Richard Stark is a great mystery novelist (and is also Donald E. Westlake), but when Dortmunder decides that a Stark novel called *Child Heist* will make the perfect map for his next caper, he sets out to kidnap Jimmy Harrington. Unfortunately, Jimmy is precocious enough to try to organize his own kidnapping. This novel alternates chapters between the Stark novel and the Westlake effort.
>
> Kidnapping; New York—New York

Nobody's Perfect. Evans, 1977.

> Defense attorney J. Radcliffe Stonewiler frees Dortmunder from charges only to set him up to work for Arnold Chauncey. This big-time art collector finances his holdings by getting insurance payments for stolen pieces. Now he wants an oil painting stolen from his Manhattan apartment. Dortmunder goes with the flow, but his instincts make him pick up a few other pieces along the way, and that can only lead to trouble.
>
> Art; England—London; Insurance fraud; New York—New York

Why Me? Viking, 1983.

> The United States has the Byzantine Fire, a 90=carat ruby, which it would like to give to the Turks, but unfortunately it is stolen by the Greeks. Surprisingly, Dortmunder manages to be the next owner of the jewel. Then he finds himself hunted by criminals, including the very scary Tiny Bulcher, the NYPD, and the FBI, as well as some really angry Turks.
>
> Jewels; New York—New York; Terrorists

Good Behavior. Mysterious Press, 1985.

When Dortmunder falls through the roof of the Silent Sisterhood of St. Filumena's cloistered nunnery, the nuns choose to ignore his current attempt at larceny and employ him to locate the long-missing Sister Mary Grace. When he discovers that the sister is not only a prisoner of her millionaire father but also the key to his money, Dortmunder finds this case both a humanitarian and a capitalistic one. So he decides to try to break into a seventy-six-story building to be a hero and a robber.

Kidnapping; New York—New York; Nuns

Drowned Hopes. Mysterious, 1990.

A reunion with a former cellmate, Tom Jimson, means Dortmunder is now a part of his cash recovery team. The $700,000 that he claims is stashed in a hole in upstate New York is now buried under the reservoir system used by New York City. Opposed to blowing up the dam and drowning the cities down river, Dortmunder conceives a new plan.

Dams; New York—Putkin's Corners

Don't Ask. Mysterious, 1993.

Dortmunder has been hired to steal the femur bone of St. Ferghana, a twelfth-century relic that has great religious significance for two Eastern European countries. Possession of the bone will also get one of the two newly formed countries a seat at the United Nations. A plan to steal the bone from a diplomatic boat in the East River leaves Dortmunder a prisoner, needing to devise another plan to get the relic into the right hands.

New York—New York; Relics; Religion; Vermont

What's the Worst That Could Happen? Mysterious, 1996.

When Max Fairbanks points a gun at Dortmunder while he is in the middle of robbing the man's Long Island estate, Fairbanks steals Dortmunder's lucky ring. Seeking revenge, Dortmunder gathers his crew and sets out to get his ring back. Although he gets some swag, he never gets his ring back. A final showdown in Las Vegas will prove who has the stronger will.

Jewels; Nevada—Las Vegas; New York—New York; Revenge

Bad News. Mysterious, 2001.

Fitzroy Guilderpost wants Dortmunder to join him in a takedown of a Native American gambling casino. This calls for a little grave robbing and switching one body for another. Doing this will allow Little Feather Redcorn, a Las Vegas showgirl, to claim a part of the casino through inheritance based on DNA. What Dortmunder and his gang did not anticipate is finding the current casino owners to be as unscrupulous as they are.

Casinos; DNA; Grave robbery; Native Americans; Nevada—Las Vegas; New York—New York

The Road to Ruin. Mysterious, 2004.

> Dortmunder's new caper is to join the staff of rich criminal Monroe Hall and then rip him off from the inside. The ultimate goal is to steal a set of collectible cars. Dortmunder's luck turns when a number of other nefarious folks want to take Hall down for his dirty business dealings. When one of the schemes is to kidnap the boss, who would have guessed that Dortmunder the butler would have to deal with the police.

> Automobiles; Estates; Kidnapping; Pennsylvania

Watch Your Back! Mysterious, 2005.

> Clued in by fence Arnie Albright, Dortmunder knows that the Manhattan penthouse of millionaire Preston Fareweather is empty and ready to be picked of its art collection. While he plans how he is going to do the job, he learns that his beloved O.J. Bar & Grill has been taken over by the mob, and they want to burn it down for the insurance.

> Art; Bars; New York—New York; Organized crime

What's So Funny? Warner, 2007.

> While the world tries to decide who is the rightful owner of an 800 pound gold chess set intended for the last czar of Russia but stolen by U.S. soldiers in 1919, Dortmunder plans to steal it. It is locked in a vault in Manhattan, so Dortmunder's only choice is to create a reason to move it. While it is on the move, so is the Dortmunder gang.

> New York—New York; Relics

True Crime Capers

These works of narrative nonfiction tell the true tales of criminals and the capers that made them infamous.

Bunker, Edward.

Education of a Felon: A Memoir. St. Martin's Press, 2000.

> Being sent to reform school at age ten, on the FBI's Ten Most Wanted List, and the youngest person incarcerated in San Quentin are just some of the exploits divulged here by criminal-turned-pop-hero Bunker.

> Prisons

Coleman, Jonathan.

At Mother's Request: A True Story of Money, Murder and Betrayal. Atheneum, 1985.

> Franklin Bradshaw was one of the richest men in Utah, with vast federal oil and gas leases as well as an auto parts business. But his daughter, Frances Schreuder, board member of the New York City Ballet, could not wait for her inheritance. So she asked her son to murder his grandfather.

> Inheritance; Utah—Salt Lake City

Dolnick, Edward.

The Rescue Artist: A True Story of Art, Thieves, and the Hunt for a Missing Masterpiece. HarperCollins, 2005.

As the Winter Olympics opened in Norway in 1994, two thieves entered the National Gallery in Oslo and stole a painting worth $72 million. *The Scream*, Edvard Munch's iconic antiwar statement, went missing on the world scene, so the embarrassed Norwegian government hired a rescue artist, Charley Hill. The former Scotland Yard detective plunged into the underworld looking for the most and least likely suspects, waiting for the painting to surface.

Art; Munch, Edvard; Norway—Oslo

Farrell, Harry.

Swift Justice: Murder and Vengeance in a California Town. St. Martin's Press, 1992.

In 1933, the son of a department store owner, Brooke Hart, was kidnapped and a ransom demand was made. When the police and FBI got involved, the plot imploded, and Harold Thurmond and Jack Holmes were captured, but not before they murdered the popular young man. Then members of the town took justice into their own hands and lynched the two criminals.

California—San Jose; Kidnapping; Lynching

Fay, Stephen, Lewis Chester, and Magnus Linklater.

Hoax: The Inside Story of the Howard Hughes–Clifford Irving Affair. Viking, 1972.

In the early 1970s, with recluse Howard Hughes a silent enigma, Clifford Irving and his friend Richard Suskind got an idea: publish Hughes's autobiography. The two figured that Hughes was more interested in avoiding publicity than in denouncing their work. They were wrong.

Hughes, Howard

Howard, Clark.

Six Against the Rock. Dial, 1977.

In 1946, an Alcatraz prisoner named Bernie Coy challenged the system by taking control of the main cell house on the island prison. For forty-one hours he battled guards and the military to try to escape his ultimate fate.

Alcatraz Prison; California—Alcatraz Island; Prison breaks

Lindsey, Robert.

A Gathering of Saints: A True Story of Money, Murder and Deceit. Simon & Schuster, 1988.

Over a two-day period in Salt Lake City in 1985, three bombs exploded. One killed Kathy Sheets, the wife of a prominent businessman. The second killed Stephen Christenson, Sheet's business partner. The third injured Mark Hoffman, a man who made his living on the fringes of the rare documents community. Hoffman had recently unearthed early documents from Mormon history, documents long thought to be lost.

Mormons; Rare documents; Utah—Salt Lake City

Olsen, Jack.

Hastened to the Grave: The Gypsy Murder Investigation. St. Martin's, 1998.
When a lawyer decided that Danny Tene was responsible for his elderly client being bilked, he hired the Rat Dog Dick agency and its single employee, Fay Faron, to investigate. Then Hope Victoria Beesley was found dead. Refusing to stop, Faron exposed the activities of the Tene Bimbo clan, a family of gypsies who may have been leaving a trail of victims across the country.

California—San Francisco; Gypsies; Private detectives

Pietrusza, David.

Rothstein: The Life, Times and Murder of the Criminal Genius Who Fixed the 1919 World Series. Carroll & Graf, 2003.
Starting life as a petty criminal and building his personal skills with acumen, Arnold Rothstein grew to legendary status. His most famous scam involved baseball's greatest days and resulted in his being the model for such historic fictional characters as Meyer Wolfsteim (*The Great Gatsby*) and Nathan Detroit (*Guys and Dolls*). It also led to his murder.

Baseball; Bookies; New York—New York; World Series

Rayner, Richard.

Drake's Fortune: The Fabulous True Story of the World's Greatest Confidence Artist. Doubleday, 2002.
During the Great Depression, Oscar Hartzell was able to convince many of his fellow Iowans to give him millions of dollars for shares in a fortune that he never intended to deliver. After living the high life in London, he was deported by Scotland Yard to face a trial in Iowa, all while people continued to send him more money in the hopes of hitting the big time themselves.

Con artist; Iowa

Reit, Seymour.

The Day They Stole the **Mona Lisa.** Summit, 1981.
This book explains how the *Mona Lisa* disappeared for two years from the Louvre. It was taken by Marques de Valfierno and his gang, whose plan was to make copies and sell them to unwitting collectors desperate to own one of the most famous paintings in the world.

Art; France—Paris; Louvre; *Mona Lisa*

Stowers, Carlton.

Careless Whispers. Taylor, 1986.
> In 1982, three teenagers were found murdered in Speegleville Park in Waco, Texas. Two of the victims were women who had been raped, and all three victims had been repeatedly stabbed to death. When the police department gave up, a patrolman named Truman Simons kept at the case until the killer began to drop hints about why he did what he did.
>
> Hit men; Texas—Waco

Walker, Kent, and Mark Schone.

Son of a Grifter: The Twisted Tale of Sante and Kenny Kimes, the Most Notorious Con Artists in America. Morrow, 2001.
> There have been mothers who have led their sons astray before, but perhaps none with the same level of ferocity as Sante Kimes. She and her son, Kenny, roamed the country committing crimes, including murder. This account of their capture is told by Kent Walter, Sante's oldest son and Kenny's half-brother.
>
> Mothers and sons; Sociopath

The Mob

Novels about the mob involve all aspects of organized crime, with the understanding that the perpetrators fall under the standard definition. The main focus of these novels is as much on the organization and its behavior as it is on any criminal activities it undertakes. The main appeal of mob novels is an understanding of the power of an organization's structure and rules over decent moral and ethical behavior. Stories about gangs of criminals who do not reach this status are listed in the "Capers" section.

Benchmark Mob Novels

Burnett, W. R.

Little Caesar. Dial, 1929.
> Cesare "Rico" Bandello is an ambitious, ruthless, power-hungry man who will stop at nothing, including murder, in his rise to fame in the world of crime. Born in Youngstown, Ohio, he moves to the big city of Chicago, obsessed with making it big. From his start as a small-time stick-up man to gang leader, he creates his own image as he gains power. Ironically, it is his vanity and arrogance that decide his ultimate fate.
>
> Illinois—Chicago; Organized crime

Cain, Paul.

Fast One. Doubleday, 1933.

Based on a series of short stories written for *Black Mask* magazine, this novel tells the tale of East Coast hit man and gambler Gerard A. Kells. He is in Los Angeles to cool off from the heat in the East, but when warring gangs square off, he is caught in the middle. He prefers to not take sides, but one gang leader, Jack Rose, goes too far by killing Kells's friend, Shep Berry. So, with his lover Granquist by his side, he decides to take over the L.A. territory and make it home.

California—Los Angeles; Organized crime

Hammett, Dashiell.

The Glass Key. Knopf, 1931.

Ned Beaumont is a gambler and a problem solver for Paul Madvig. Madvig is the heavyweight power behind the throne in an unnamed city where an election is about to occur. Madvig has fallen in love with Senator Ralph Henry's daughter, Janet, to the displeasure of the senator's son, Taylor. Late one night, Ned discovers the body of Taylor lying in the street, bludgeoned to death. From this point on, Ned tries his best to manipulate all the players so everything comes out right for his side. The question is, which side is he on?

Organized crime; Romance

Mob Novels

Abbott, Megan.

Queenpin. Simon & Schuster, 2007.

The female narrator of this novel is hired to cook the books of a small-time. mob-owned club in Vegas in the 1960s when she is taken under the wing of Gloria Denton, the former queen of the underworld. Heading down this dark path, the accountant learns how to make all the right moves, until she falls for a gambler named Vic Riordan.

Nevada—Las Vegas; Organized crime; Triangles (Interpersonal relationships)

Bean, Fred.

Black Gold. Forge, 1997.

Bill Dodd thinks he has struck it rich when his wildcat ways lead to an oil find of major proportions, but he is murdered before he can stake his claim. His widow asks Texas Ranger Lee Garrett to investigate. What Garrett discovers is the first evidence that organized crime elements from the East are infiltrating the Wild West in 1932, and the West will never be the same.

Historical; Oil; Organized crime; Texas—Longview; Texas Rangers

Benioff, David.

The 25th Hour. Carroll & Graf, 2000.

Monty Brogan has twenty-four hours of freedom left before he has to report to the Otisville Federal Prison to serve a seven-year sentence for drug running. Monty wants one final day of partying with friends Frank Slattery and Jacob Elinsky and one last time with his girlfriend, Naturelle. His boss, Uncle Blue, wants to make sure he did not squeal.

Drugs; New York—New York; Prisons

Bowker, David.

Rawhead. UK: Pan Macmillan, 2002. (U.S.: *The Death You Deserve.* St. Martin's Minotaur, 2003).

When journalist Billy Dye's article on Manchester mobster Malcolm Priest ends up being favorable, the crime lord decides he wants Dye to write his biography. However, when things do not go well, Priest puts out a hit on his biographer, and Dye finds himself on the run. The good news is that the hit man is Dye's old pal, Rawhead.

Authors; England—Manchester; Hit men

Breslin, Jimmy.

The Gang That Couldn't Shoot Straight. Viking, 1969.

How innocent does this sound? Let's hold a six day bicycle race. Not so innocent when the idea comes from the mouth of Anthony "Papa Baccala" Pastrumo Sr., one of the five big bosses of the New York mafia. He picks real estate magnate Joseph DeLauria to front the affair for the mob, but things do not go very well. This is not surprising since the others involved include Big Mama Ferrara, her grandson Kid Sally Palumbo, and two guys called Big Jelly and Water Buffalo.

Bicycles; New York—New York; Organized crime

Corbett, David.

The Devil's Redhead. Ballantine, 2002.

After spending ten years in the pen, Dan Abatangelo only wants one thing: to reunite with his love, Shel Beaudry. He finds her connected to Frank Maas, a drug runner for the local mob. When Shel is caught between two warring gangs, Dan uses his old skills to get his girl back.

California—San Francisco; Drugs; Triangles (Interpersonal relationships)

Fisher, Steve.

No House Limit. Dutton, 1958.

When the mob decides that Las Vegas is going to be their domain, they need to take out the small-time operators who are working the strip. Their next target is Joe Martin at the Rainbow's End. Rather than bury him in the desert, they send Bello, the best craps player in the world, to ruin the club. But Martin knows Bello is coming.

Gambling; Nevada—Las Vegas

Gischler, Victor.

Gun Monkeys. Uglytown, 2001.
Charlie "The Hook" Swift is a hit man for Stan's mob. When rivals make things risky for his boss, Charlie does a hit at a strip club that takes out four cops and puts him on the run from everyone. His prize possession, the ledgers that everyone wants, will either save him or put him away permanently.

Assassination; Florida—Orlando; Hit men; Organized crime

Green, Norman.

The Angel of Montague Street. HarperCollins, 2003.
A Vietnam veteran and now a Buddhist, Silvano Iurata does not want to walk the mean streets, but he is compelled to find his missing brother, Noonie. Silvano's family is steeped in mob activities in Brooklyn. Those things that his family hold sacred mean nothing to him as he hunts, except that his relatives could get him killed.

Historical; New York—New York; Organized crime; Vietnamese conflict

[Stoney series].
This series follows the criminal exploits of small-time hood Stoney.

Shooting Dr. Jack. HarperCollins, 2001.
Fat Tommy Rosselli is a junk dealer who uses his business as a front for small-time cons and scams that get him by. He befriends Stoney, an alcoholic but loyal aide, and Tuco, a street kid who needs all the help he can get. When things start to fall apart at the yard, people get shot, South American hit men show up ready for action, and the trio knows they need to step up their game.

Junkyards; New York—New York; Organized crime

Dead Cat Bounce. Harper, 2006.
Stoney has been kicked out of the hose by his wife, Donna, and is attending AA meetings. His daughter Marisa tells him about a man hanging around his wife. As Stoney investigates, with help from Fat Tommy and Tuco, he discovers that the man, named Charles David Prior, is actually stalking his daughter, who is secretly working as a stripper. When Stoney decides enough is enough, it is going to cost someone his or her life.

New York—New York; Organized crime

Huston, Charlie.
Huston writes about small timers who are caught up in the whirlwind of mob-related activities as he chronicles the life of Hank Thompson. The following series titles are listed in the order of publication.

[Hank Thompson series].

Caught Stealing. Ballantine, 2004.

Bartender Hank Thompson is down on his luck and petsitting his neighbor Russ's cat when he is beaten up by some Russian mobsters and left for dead. After he recovers, he returns to Russ's place and finds a key that leads him to millions of dollars. This is the good news; the bad news is that the Russian mobsters are still after him.

New York—New York; Organized crime

Six Bad Things. Ballantine, 2005.

Now living in the Yucatán Peninsula (with $4 million in mob money), Thompson is chilling in Mexico until a Russian with a long memory shows up and he needs to go on the run again. Back in the States, he finds himself depending on the undependable to dodge the bullet that could end it all. His goal: to save his parents from a fate he created.

California; Mexico—Yucatán Peninsula

A Dangerous Man. Ballantine, 2006.

Thompson is back to doing hit man work for Russian mobster David Dolokhov while suffering the mental consequences of taking another person's life. When he is asked to protect a baseball prospect named Miguel Arenas, the job brings back his memories of having been a promising player in his youth. Arenas's gambling problem is going to be a problem for both men before this one is over.

Baseball; Bodyguards; Hit men; Nevada—Las Vegas; New York—New York

Kersh, Gerald.

Night and the City. Joseph, 1938.

Harry Fabian dreams of being a gangster like his heroes in the American films he loves and is trying to raise the money to become a successful wrestling promoter. By selling his girlfriend, he is able to keep going, but his more ambitious scams never seem to pan out. While his honest and hard-working brother, a fruit peddler, tries to pull him into the light, he is fated to seek his fortune in the dark.

Brothers; England—London

McCoy, Horace.

Kiss Tomorrow Good-bye. Random House, 1948.

The reader knows the protagonist of this novel as Ralph Cotter, an alias that hides a Phi Beta Kappa key holder who has descended into a life of crime. When we first meet Ralph, he is breaking out of a prison work farm to return to a life of crime. He needs to commit murder, and then joins the dead man's sister, Holiday, on a dangerous spree. He adds Jinx to his criminal gang and stops at nothing to make money, including bribing the corrupt police officers who will keep him out of trouble and chasing Margaret Dobson, the daughter of the former governor.

Corruption; Gangs

Perry, Thomas.

[The Butcher Boy series].

Perry brings us the life and crimes of a mob hit man in these two books featuring The Butcher's Boy.

The Butcher's Boy. Scribner, 1982.

Told from the perspectives of both the U.S. Justice Department analyst Elizabeth Waring and The Butcher's Boy, this novel looks at what happens when a person has nowhere to run. When The Butcher's Boy assassinates U.S. Senator Claremont from Colorado for the mob, he goes on the run from the legal system and from his own people, who now want him dead.

Assassination; Hit men; Organized crime

Sleeping Dogs. Random House, 1992.

The Butcher's Boy is retired and living the good life in Bath, England. Or at least he is until the day a young mafioso recognizes him and he is forced to return to his killing ways. Now his only choice seems to be returning to the United States and killing the man who wants him dead. Then Elizabeth Waring hears he is back in town.

England—Bath; Hit men; Organized crime

Puzo, Mario.

The Fortunate Pilgrim was Puzo's first attempt to chronicle the history of the mob. He followed that with three series books that continue the sad history of the Corleone family. The Corleone books are listed in order of publication.

The Fortunate Pilgrim. Atheneum, 1964.

Lucia Santa is the matriarch of the Iuzzi-Corbo family. This is the story of how she was born into a Hell's Kitchen tenement and eventually settled on Long Island. In her struggle to protect her family and raise them up in within the American dream, she interacts with various forms of organized crime, from corrupt unions to everyday jobs that depend on the power behind the throne.

New York—New York; Organized crime

[The Corleone series].

The Godfather. Putnam, 1969.

This novel is the story of the Corleone family. They are mobsters ruled by the patriarch, Don Vito Corleone. His sons, Sonny, Freddie, and Michael, are destined to rule the family once he is gone, and this is the story of how the power is beginning to be divided. Most of the power is based on fear and intimidation, with those who are perceived to be in the way being swiftly removed.

Nevada—Las Vegas; New York—New York; Organized crime

The Sicilian. Linden Press/Simon & Schuster, 1984.

The story of Michael Corleone begins again when he returns from exile in Sicily in 1950. By command of the Don, Michael has brought with him a legend from Sicily: the modern-day Robin Hood named Salvatore Guiliano. The problem is that Guiliano battles against the influence of the mafia.

New York—New York; Organized crime

The Last Don. Random House, 1996.

Don Domenico Clericuzio is the head of the new mafia, trying to legitimize their "family" business. He sends two young men into battle to accomplish that: Dante and Cross. When Dante proves to be the better hit man, Cross is left representing the family in Hollywood. There he is set up to meet his own femme fatale, Athena Aquitane.

California—Los Angeles; Nevada—Las Vegas; Motion pictures; Organized crime

Rabe, Peter.

Benny Muscles In. Gold Medal, 1955.

Benny Tapkow is a man on the make in the field of organized crime. When he is not satisfied with how fast he is rising, he decides to kidnap the daughter of his former boss to make himself look good to his new gang. What he does not expect is to have to deal with her once he has her.

Kidnapping; Organized crime

Anatomy of a Killer. Abelard-Schuman, 1960.

Hit man Sam Jordan is a stone cold killer. When he finishes one job, he would like some space, but his contact, Sandy, is ready to send him on another "errand" for the head man. Feeling a little weak, he opens a crack in his life and lets a waitress named Betty sneak in. That is when things start to go bad.

Hit men; Romance

Murder Me for Nickels. Fawcett, 1960.

Jack Stain Louis is the go-to guy for jukebox kingpin Walter Lippit, who rules this racket in a small town near Chicago. Jack walks a fine line, romancing Walter's girl while trying to keep his day job. When Walter feels the pressure from another mob, he turns to his own tough guy to defend his turf.

Gambling; Organized crime

Rozan, S. J.

Absent Friends. Delacorte, 2004.

New York City Fire Captain Jimmy McCaffery died a hero at the World Trade Center on 9/11. But an enterprising newspaper reporter named Harry Randall writes an article that accuses the dead man of being a mob bag man for a payoff to the Keegan family. Markie Keegan was Jimmy best friend when they were kids, and the time he spent in jail was hard on his wife and children. Markie's son, Kevin, was being mentored in the department by Jimmy. When the reporter commits suicide, Laura Stone, also a reporter and Harry's girlfriend, takes on a crusade to reveal the truth.

Firefighters; New York—New York; Newspapers; September 11, 2001, terrorist attack

Sanders, Lawrence.

The Anderson Tapes. Putnam, 1970.

There is a luxury apartment building on East 73rd Street in New York City. In it lives a woman who is having an affair, which is being recorded by a private investigator. The man involved in the affair, John Anderson, is fronting the affair to gain access to the building so he can rob it for the mob. Unfortunately for Anderson, the PI is not the only person or agency listening to what is going on in the building or in Anderson's life.

New York—New York; Surveillance

Schulberg, Budd.

The Harder They Fall. Random House, 1947.

Basing the story on the life of an Italian heavyweight fighter named Primo Carnera, Schulberg tells about corruption in the boxing industry. In the novel, Argentine boxer "El Toro" Molina is working his way to the top. His story is told by a cynical press agent named Lewis. Falling into the hands of an American manager, Nick Latka, El Toro finds himself fighting only to make his handlers rich and to make himself a victim to the sport.

Boxing; New York—New York; Organized crime

Waterfront. Random House, 1955.

Author Schulberg adapted his screenplay, *On the Waterfront*, into a novel and expands the story line used in the famous film. The novel reveals how the mob had its fingers in the harbors of New York and controlled not only the goods brought in but also the workers in the unions who unloaded and moved the materials. Father Peter Barry is the fictional character who takes a stand against this corruption, having been raised in poverty himself. Father Barry uses a damaged former fighter, Terry Malloy, as his ally. Terry's brother is a corrupt union official for Johnny Friendly, and ultimately the issue of right and wrong will irrevocably divide their family.

Brothers; Corruption; Harbors; New York—New York; Organized crime; Priests

Stella, Charlie.

Eddie's World. Carroll & Graf, 2001.

Eddie Senta has problems that making book are not solving. Going legit as a word processor does not hold much appeal, either, with his wife urging him to start a new family, while his teenaged son from a previous marriage wants to get made. So Eddie dips into crime one more time to make the big score. Unfortunately, he picks the wrong gem dealer to rip off.

Jewels; New York—New York; Organized crime; Witness Protection Program

Jimmy Bench-Press. Carroll & Graf, 2002.

NYPD officer Alex Pavlik, who tailed Eddie Senta in the first novel by Stella, reappears in the organized crime unit with a partner, John DeNafria. The two find their paths crossing that of ex-con Jimmy Mangino, who is trying to get back on his feet and back on his game after spending time in prison. The hunt is, on and the question is whether or not Pavlik will be able to put Jimmy back inside.

Ex-convicts; New York—New York; Organized crime

Charlie Opera. Carroll & Graf, 2003.

Charlie Pellecchia is in Vegas for a retirement celebration when the fact that he punched a guy in the jaw in New York for flirting with his wife Lisa returns to haunt him. Too bad that guy happened to be New York mobster Nicholas Cuccia. Charlie is on Nicholas's hit list, and two men, Francone and Lano, are on his trail.

Nevada—Las Vegas; Organized crime; Revenge

Shakedown. Pegasus, 2006.

When Bobby Gennaro retires from the mob, he lives comfortably with his fiancée, Lin Yao. Unfortunately for the couple, their comfort comes from money skimmed from the bookmaking operation Bobby ran for the mob. When the mob comes calling to get its money back, things do not go well.

New York—New York; Organized crime

Mafiya. Pegasus, 2008.

Agnes Lynn has Las Vegas, as well as her life as a call girl, in her rearview mirror. But when she moves to New York and her best friend Rachel Wilson is murdered, she is drawn back into the world of sex for money. She finds an ally in ex-cop Jack Russo and an adversary in the Russian mafia.

New York—New York; Organized crime; Pornography; Prostitutes; Revenge

Thompson, Jim.

Savage Night. Lion Books, 1953.

When the crime syndicate that runs a Long Island city is about to be brought down by the testimony of former mobster Jake Winroy, retired hit man Carl Bigelow is paid $30,000 to take him out. Carl is amazed to discover that his in to Winroy's life is Jake's wayward wife, willing to give up her husband. When he finds himself sympathizing with his intended victim, he suspects a person he believes was sent by The Man to watch over him.

Hit men; New York—Long Island, Peardale; Organized crime

Winslow, Don.

California Fire and Life. Knopf, 1999.

Arson insurance investigator Jack Wade is assigned to find out why a young mother named Pamela Vale died in a fire. Although the local arson police officer dismisses it as an accident, Jack is less likely to do that when he finds out Pamela's husband Nicky is a Russian mobster with issues. Why is there no smoke in the victim's lungs? Also, someone made sure the dog was outside, and a good arson investigator knows no one ever burns their pooch.

Arson; California—Orange County; Organized crime

The Winter of Frankie Machine. Knopf, 2006.

Frank "Machine" Machianno is a retired hit man for the mob, living the quiet life, when he finds himself set up. The problem for those who thought they could take him out is that no matter how old he gets, the Machine has not lost any of his former talents.

California—San Diego; Hit men; Organized crime

Woolrich, Cornell.

The Black Path of Fear. Doubleday, Doran, 1944.

After fleeing Miami and a crime syndicate, Scotty tries to settle down in Havana with his gangster boss's wife, Eve Roman. But when Eve is stabbed with Scotty's knife, he goes on the run, trying to prove he is innocent of all charges.

Cuba—Havana; False accusations; Organized crime

True Crime Mob Stories

Anastasia, George.

The Last Gangster: From Cop to Wiseguy to FBI Informant: Big Ron Previte and the Fall of the American Mob. Regan, 2004.

With remorse but armed with a sociopath's skills, Ron Previte moved from being a cop to joining the mob. He claimed he had committed a felony a day. Then when things went bad, he turned and wore a wire for the FBI, bringing down the Philadelphia mob.

Informants; Organized crime; Pennsylvania—Philadelphia

Blum, Howard.

Gangland: How the FBI Broke the Mob. Simon & Schuster, 1993.

At the pinnacle of the mob sat John Gotti, head of the Gambino family in New York. Arrayed against him was the FBI's C-16 Squad. Through wiretaps and informants, they slowly chipped away at the mob until it cracked, and Sammy Gravano testified against his boss.

Federal Bureau of Investigation; New York—New York; Organized crime

Breslin, Jimmy.

The Good Rat: A True Story. Ecco, 2008.

In 2006, mafioso Burton Kaplan testified at the trial of two New York City police officers who had gone over to the dark side. Taking his testimony, Breslin writes vignettes about daily life in the mob, which despite years of surveillance by local, state, and federal officials, still includes kidnapping, money laundering, drugs, and murder.

New York—New York; Organized crime

Carr, Howie.

The Brothers Bulger: How They Terrorized and Corrupted Boston for a Quarter Century. Warner, 2006.

> While Billy Bulger ran the Massachusetts state government from his Senate presidential chair, his brother, Whitey, ran the city of Boston's Irish mobs and the University of Massachusetts. Each brother looked after the other, and each took everything he could get his hands on for more than twenty-five years.

> Massachusetts—Boston; Organized crime

Cohen, Rich.

Tough Jews. Simon & Schuster, 1998.

> Murder, Inc., was an organization famous for murder that elevated the hit to an art form. When they reigned, their was no one they feared. And when they fell, they all fell hard.

> Jews; Organized crime

Cooley, Robert, with Hillel Levin.

When Corruption Was King: How I Helped the Mob Rule Chicago, Then Brought the Outfit Down. Carroll & Graf, 2004.

> As a lawyer for the Chicago mob, Robert Cooley saw all the corruption that the five families were able to generate. When the U.S. Organized Crime Strike Force decided to turn him into an informant, he wore a wire and brought down the entire operation.

> Illinois—Chicago; Informants; Organized crime

Cowan, Rick, and Douglas Century.

Takedown: The Fall of the Last Mafia Empire. Putnam, 2002.

> In 1992, in a case of mistaken identity, New York City detective Rick Cowan was introduced to the mob. Taking advantage of the open door, he went undercover and wormed his way into the organization. By living a double life for years, he was able to provide the evidence the cops needed to bring down a family deep into the city waste removal business.

> New York—New York; Organized crime; Waste removal

Cummings, John, and Ernest Volkman.

Goombata: The Improbable Rise and Fall of John Gotti and His Gang. Little, Brown, 1990.

> Here is the story of how a street punk named John Gotti became ambitious, rose through the mob, and took over the Gambino family empire in New York.

> New York—New York; Organized crime

Detroit, Michael.

Chain of Evidence: A True Story of Law Enforcement and One Woman's Bravery.
Dutton, 1994.

When the Orange County Sheriff's drug officers turned Cliff Mowery, they gained access to the Hell's Angels bikers. Along for the ride was Victoria Steele, a beautiful woman who also happened to be an officer of the law. Eventually their combined efforts led to seventy arrests, for everything from drugs to death.

Bikers; California—Orange County; Drugs; Hell's Angels

English, T. J.

The Westies: Inside the Hell's Kitchen Irish Mob. Putnam, 1990.

The members of the Irish gang that took over Hell's Kitchen in the 1960s were dubbed the Westies by the media. When Mickey Featherstone, their most vicious enforcer, was charged with murder through the machinations of his colleague, he turned on the old gang and helped bring them down.

New York—New York; Organized crime

Born to Kill: America's Most Notorious Vietnamese Gang, and the Changing Face of Organized Crime. Morrow, 1995.

Forced out of their home country by the Vietnamese conflict, young men were sent from refugee camps to the streets of America. Raised in foster homes, they hit the streets as gang members set on preying on their own people. Known as Chinatown's Born to Kill gang, their downfall came when one member decided to turn informant.

Informants; New York—New York; Organized crime; Vietnamese conflict

Giancana, Antoinette.

Mafia Princess: Growing Up in Sam Giancana's Family. William Morrow, 1984.

After the fall of Al Capone, the man who rose to the top of Chicago's crime syndicate was Sam Giancana. After a lifetime under his control, which included incarcerations in mental institutions, his daughter tells the story of how this corrupt mob giant ruled his family until he was assassinated.

Illinois—Chicago; Organized crime

Hammer, Richard.

The Vatican Connection. Holt, Rinehart & Winston, 1982.

In the early 1970s, the mob managed to put into circulation nearly a billion dollars' worth of stolen and forged securities. That story would have been fascinating enough, but $14 million of these ended up in the possession of the Vatican. This story is told from the perspective of NYPD's Commanding Officer of the Organized Crime Homicide Task Force, Joseph J. Coffey Jr.

Organized crime; Vatican

Humes, Edward.

Mississippi Mud: A True Story from a Corner of the Deep South. Simon & Schuster, 1994.

1

> When Vincent Sherry, a circuit court judge, and his wife Margaret, a city councilperson and candidate for mayor, made the Dixie Mafia nervous with their campaign, they were murdered in their home. Their eldest daughter, Lynne Sposito, unsatisfied with the lack of progress in the police investigation, began a relentless pursuit of the truth, which eventually sent some corrupt individuals to jail, but no one was actually charged with her parents' murder.

2

> Corruption; Mississippi—Biloxi

3

Lehr, Dick, and Gerard O'Neill.

Black Mass: The Irish Mob, the FBI and a Devil's Deal. Public Affairs, 2000.

> James "Whitey" Bulger was the Irish godfather of Boston. His brother, Billy, was president of the Massachusetts State Senate. When their Southie neighborhood childhood friend, FBI John Connolly, was assigned to the Boston area, he thought he had turned Whitey and would be able to bring down the Italian mob. Instead, after a lengthy period of time, in which the Bulgers continued to do whatever they wanted, Connolly found himself providing their side with what they wanted rather than the other way around.

4

5

> Massachusetts—Boston; Organized crime

Maas, Peter.

6

The Valachi Papers. G. P. Putnam's Sons, 1968.

> Joseph Valachi turned from a life in the mob to become a government informant in 1964. At the time he was credited with being the most important source of information about the Cosa Nostra, as he called it. These memoirs were written with the help of freelance writer Peter Maas.

7

> New York—New York; Organized crime

O'Brien, Joseph F., and Andrus Kurins.

Boss of Bosses: The Fall of the Godfather: The FBI and Paul Catellano. Simon & Schuster, 1991.

8

> In the early 1980s, the head of the Gambino family gang in New York City was Paul Castellano. When two FBI agents set out to bring him down, they used listening devices to get the information they needed. As each wing of the family crumbled, Castellano found himself retreating, until he was taken out on a Manhattan street in a gang killing.

9

> Federal Bureau of Investigation; New York—New York; Organized crime

10

Pearson, John.

The Profession of Violence. UK: Weidenfeld & Nicolson, 1973. (U.S.: Saturday Review Press, 1972).

> The Kray twins were an odd and evil genius that ruled England's organized crime activities for years. Ronnie, the paranoid schizophrenic enforcer, and Reggie, the brilliant businessman, ruled by violent means until brought to trial in 1969.

> England—London; Organized crime

Pileggi, Nicholas.

Wiseguy: Life in a Mafia Family. Simon & Schuster, 1985.

> Henry Hill started his crime career at age eleven. Eventually working his way up the food chain of organized crime, he survived for over thirty years before a hit was put out on his life. Turning against his former colleagues, he set the federal investigators on a path to ending their crime empire.

> Organized crime

Pistone, Joseph D., with Richard Woodley.

Donnie Brasco: My Undercover Life in the Mafia; a True Story by FBI Agent Joseph D. Pistone. New American Library, 1987.

> This is the story of how FBI agent Joseph D. Pistone spent six years of his life undercover in the mob, working as the mobster Donnie Brasco.

> New York—New York; Organized crime

Singular, Stephen.

Talked to Death: The Life and Murder of Alan Berg. Beech Tree, 1987.

> Controversial Denver talk radio host Alan Berg was shot in the face as he exited his Volkswagen one night on the way home from work. Police work led to the discovery of a band of neo-Nazis called The Order, who had decided this loud Jewish man had to go.

> Anti-Semitism; Colorado—Denver; Fascism; Radio

Robbers

Robbers are defined by their emotional and sporadic behavior rather than their organizational skills. Whereas in a caper novel there is a great deal of planning, robbers act within the moment and often use violent methods in the perpetration of a crime. What a robber steals from the victim can vary from wealth to dignity. The appeal of a robber novel lies in what motivated the character to commit these acts.

Benchmark Robber Novel

Anderson, Edward.

Thieves Like Us. Frederick A. Stokes, 1937.

Three bank robbers break out of Alcatona Penitentiary and return to their thieving ways. As they ride the back roads, Bowie Bowers falls in love with Elmo Mobley's cousin, Keechie Mobley. When one of the desperados, known as Chicamaw, is taken, things get desperate. Despite the purity of their love, the police have another fate in store for him.

Bank robbery; Oklahoma; Romance; Texas

1

2

3

Robber Novels

Blake, Nicholas.

A Tangled Web. UK: Collins, 1956. (U.S.: Harper, 1956).

When good girl Daisy Bland meets ne'er-do-well cat burglar Hugo Chesterman, fate has a twist for them. Hugo involves Daisy in a housebreaking in Brighton; things go wrong. A police officer is murdered, and their actions will be scrutinized. In the end, with Daisy having given birth to a baby, it will be up to Hugo to decide whether to accept his fate or not.

England—Brighton

4

5

Bourdain, Anthony.

The Bobby Gold Stories. UK: Canongate Crime, 2002. (U.S.: Bloomsbury, 2003).

Bobby Gold was sent to prison when a drug deal went bad, which derailed his medical school education. Ten years later he returns to the fold as a bouncer at mobster Eddie Fish's nightclub. With his love, chef Nikki, he decides to try robbery, with mixed results. On the run, he and Nikki have to decide how best to live their lives.

Ex-convicts; New York—New York; Restaurants

6

7

Bunker, Edward.

No Beast So Fierce. Norton, 1973.

Max Dembo is a professional criminal. He is lucky enough to be paroled and wants desperately to go straight. But when he realizes he has been born to loose, he decides to commit one more jewel robbery to earn enough money to flee the country.

Jewels

8

9

10

Carnahan, Matthew.

Serpent Girl. Villard, 2005.

When a robbery of the Circus Maximus does not go as planned, Bailey Quinn finds himself lying alongside the Columbia River Basin, with his throat slashed and without his pants. He decides to get his revenge by hunting down his fellow robbers, but he fails to calculate the anger of the freak show performers who run the circus and their anger over his betrayal. This is especially true of Serpent Girl, the woman he slept with to get the inside scoop for the robbery.

California—Venice; Coming-of-age; Idaho—Boise

Connelly, Michael.

Void Moon. Little, Brown, 2000.

When Cassie's lover dies during an attempted robbery of a casino penthouse, she is sent to prison as an accomplice on a manslaughter charge. Released, she returns to Las Vegas for one more try to make her retirement money. When her scheme goes haywire, she finds ruthless PI Jack Karch is on her trail, and he is not happy.

Casinos; Nevada—Las Vegas

Guthrie, Allan.

Two Way Split. Dominion, 2004. (U.S.: Pointblank, 2004).

Robin Greaves, his wife Carol, and their ally, Eddie Soutar, are a gang of thieves who are turning on each other. When their post office robbery goes wrong and a woman is killed, they go underground. But Robin knows that his wife is sleeping with Eddie, and he finds it difficult to concentrate on anything except revenge. When a killer comes seeking revenge on him for the hostage death and an unscrupulous PI closes in on the gang, things really get tough.

Armed robbery; Revenge; Scotland—Edinburgh; Triangles (Interpersonal relations)

Miller, Wade.

Branded Woman. Gold Medal, 1952.

Cay Morgan was warned to stay out of the way of The Trader as she plied her international jewel smuggling trade. After having been kidnapped, and with scars to show for her experience, she now vows revenge on the mysterious international thief. Tracing The Trader to Mexico, she sets out in the city to hunt down the person who branded her for life.

Jewels; Kidnapping; Mexico—Mazatlán; Revenge

Price, Richard.

Lush Life. Farrar, Straus & Giroux, 2008.

Eric Cash is accused of murder when he is bar hopping in Manhattan, and Ike Marcus, the new bartender at Eric's job, is murdered. Eric's version is that they were attacked by muggers, but eyewitness statements vary. The teenagers from the projects who were on the grounds that night are still on the loose, pursued by two police detectives,and no one understands the real truth of what happened that night.

False arrest; Mugging; New York—New York

Skármeta, Antonio.

El Baiale de la Victoria. Spain: Editorial Planeta, 2003. (U.S.: *The Dancer and the Thief*, Norton, 2008).

A presidential amnesty has freed Ángel Santiago and his criminal mentor, master thief Nicolás Vergara Grey, from prison. Having once committed a crime by chance, Ángel has now become a grand planner, but he needs Grey's help. Grey is reluctant to once again do something that will put him inside, and things become complicated when an assassin is put on Ángel's trail. He may be redeemed, however, when his motive for robbery is helping a ballerina stage a dance to commemorate her dead father.

Ballet; Chile—Santiago; Hit men

Stark, Richard (pseudonym of Donald Westlake).

[Parker series].

Under this pseudonym, Westlake (the author of the <u>Dortmunder series</u>) wrote a series about a sociopath named Parker, who moves from one place to another, always looking for the score, planning the crime, doing the deed, and moving on. The following series titles are listed in order of publication.

The Hunter. Pocket Books, 1963. (Also *Point Blank*, Gregg, 1973, and *Playback*).

While trying to pull a score on the West Coast with his partner Mal, Parker is double-crossed by his wife, Lynn, and his other partner. When he survives being left for dead, in order to exact his revenge, he will need to take on the mob to get his money back.

New York—New York; Organized crime; Revenge

The Man with the Getaway Face. Pocket Books, 1963. (UK: *The Steel Hit*, Coronet, 1971).

On the run from the mob, Parker heads to Nebraska for a little reconstructive surgery to help hide his identity. Heading back East, he and his crew plan to take down an armored car and mess up the plans of the syndicate again, if the vengeful Alma does not stop him and if he can figure out who killed his surgeon.

New Jersey; Reconstructive surgery

The Outfit. Pocket Books, 1963.

For the third time, Parker finds himself under siege despite a new face and staying on the move. Never willing to back down, he and his crew pull twelve crimes in five days and hit the mob where it hurts: in the pocket book. When Bronson the Godfather does not get the message, Parker decides it is time to go after the kingpin.

Organized crime; Revenge

The Mourner. Pocket Books, 1963.

When Bett Harrow makes off with a gun bearing Parker's fingerprints, Parker knew that slip would come back to bite him, and he is blackmailed into taking on this adventure. He is after The Mourner, an alabaster statute that he can steal from a Russian diplomat. Left for dead with his partner, Handy McKay, during the caper, it is up to Parker to rise from the grave and exact his revenge.

Diplomats; Statutes

The Score. Pocket Books, 1964. (UK: *Killtown*).

If you are in the mood, why not try to take down an entire town? That is the plan presented to Parker. Worried about the amateur planner Edgars, Parker makes some modifications. Then he and ten men try to take everything from the North Dakota mining town of Copper Canyon. What they did not realize is that one woman could spoil their plans.

North Dakota—Copper Canyon

The Jugger. Pocket Books, 1965.

Not averse to covering his tracks using the most brutal of methods, Parker is on his way to Nebraska to silence a man who knows too much and has become senile. Joe Sheer is a retired jugger, or safecracker, and Parker needs to put him away to protect his own secrets. To his great surprise, Parker finds that Sheer is already dead, and his problems just got bigger, because he is now more exposed than ever.

Nebraska—Sagamore; Revenge

The Seventh. Pocket Books, 1966. (UK: *The Split*, Allison & Busby, 1984).

What a brilliant concept: steal the day's proceeds from a college football game at Monequois Stadium and make off with the profits. It only takes Parker and six others to pull it off. Parker's job is to hold the money for five days before the payoff. When someone else decides to make off with the profits, things turn deadly—his girlfriend Ellie Canaday is killed.

Football; Stadiums

The Handle. Pocket Books, 1966. (Also *Run Lethal.* Berkley, 1966).

It seems contrary for Parker to take a job from the mob, but he does when the pot is made sweet enough. Charged with ending the freelancing being done by The Baron, Parker is planning on taking down the latter's offshore gambling operation. Things seem well planned until a fatal error is made and the bullets start flying.

Gambling; Islands; Texas

The Rare Coin Score. Fawcett, 1967.

Why did it take Parker so long to realize that a coin convention is where the money is? When he decides to rip off the rare coins, he does not count on a double cross that will not only threaten him but also his new girlfriend, Claire. He knew he shouldn't work with amateurs like Billy Lebatard.

Coins

The Green Eagle Score. Fawcett, 1967.

> Marty Fusco thinks he has a plan for Parker: Why not take the entire payroll from an Air Force base that employs 5,000 people? With the help of someone on the inside, the planning goes forward, but the crew does not become cohesive. Inevitably, when push comes to shove, Parker has to do some shoving.

> New York—Monequois; United States Air Force

The Black Ice Score. Fawcett, 1968.

> The new African country of Dhaba wants its diamonds back for the current leader, Major Indindu. So they hire Parker to find where the previous leader, Colonel Joseph Lubudi, hid the jewels in New York City. Things seem simple enough to Parker, until he is warned off the case and Claire is kidnapped. The bad guys will find out that making Parker mad is not the best plan of attack.

> Dhaba; Diamonds; New York—New York

The Sour Lemon Score. Fawcett, 1969.

> Although the job goes well, the gang is not happy with the take from the latest bank robbery planned by Parker. George Uhl shoots the two other members of the gang, but he only wounds Parker. It would have been wise of George to take another shot at Parker, for now he is determined to find George and get his revenge.

> Revenge

Deadly Edge. Random House, 1971.

> A four-man crew led by Parker rips off a rock concert and heads to its hideout, only to discover the dead body of a man who was supposed to be on the crew but did not show. The gang scatters with its loot, but soon Parker realizes each man is being hunted down and killed. Can he protect Claire, keep the loot, and save himself?

> Revenge

Slayground. Random House, 1971.

> It seems like just another armored car robbery for Parker and his crew, when things go horribly wrong. While his men are dying around him, Parker manages to escape into Fun Island amusement park. But soon he realizes, as the mob and some crooked cops corner him, that he has just managed to run into a trap that may be his last place of refuge.

> Amusement parks; Ohio—Tyler

Plunder Squad. Random House, 1972.

> It appears that Parker sometimes leaves some things unfinished, and here it is the death of a former associate who now wants to kill the master thief. While distracted by an art heist that should be his focus, Parker has to balance what the world brings him when the mob shows an interest.

> Art; Organized crime; Revenge

Butcher's Moon. Random House, 1974.

Still yearning for the riches he left behind at Fun Island in *Slayride,* Parker decides to return to Ohio and reclaim his reward, with the help of his gang, including Alan Grofield. Instead he steps into a warring town in which the gangs are battling, and he soon finds himself drawn into the conflict. All he wanted was his money; instead he finds himself hunted once again, this time by a hood named Lozini.

Ohio—Tyler; Organized crime

Comeback. Mysterious Press, 1997.

Retired for many years with his love Claire at a retreat in New Jersey, Parker is coaxed back into the game when some thieves want to take down an evangelist named William Archibald and his Christian Crusade. When the preacher's security man proves to be as cold as Parker, he makes a formidable opponent for the hard-boiled crook. But when his own crew turns on itself, Parker finds himself in a dangerous tailspin.

Evangelists

Backflash. Mysterious Press, 1999.

Parker decides to take down the floating casino called the *Spirit of the Hudson.* When he has the money in his hands, his challenge is to get it off the boat and away from the psychopaths who want to take it from him.

Casinos; Cruise ships; New York—Hudson River Valley

Flashfire. Mysterious Press, 2000.

Parker might be best served not to take partners, but he has three with him when he tries to rob a bank in Nebraska. Double-crossed, he decides his best plan is to beat the three to their next job and steal the swag before they get there.

Bank robbery; Florida—Palm Beach; Jewels; Nebraska

Firebreak. Mysterious Press, 2001.

When Parker gets involved in a plan to take down the remote Montana hunting lodge of a billionaire to gain access to all the art in the man's vault, part of his mind is still wrestling with who has set him up for a contract kill. What he does not plan on is the whack job Larry Lloyd, who is a part of the team because of his skills at taking down the sophisticated security at the lodge. In this case, Parker may be able to pick which poison will kill him.

Hit men; Montana

Breakout. Mysterious Press, 2002.

When a job heisting a pharmaceutical company goes wrong, Parker finds himself in the Stoneveldt jail. Forced to break out, he does a payback job, in which he tries to take down a jewelry wholesaler, only to find himself trapped in the ex-armory, which holds the business. When he busts out of that, Parker finds the entire Midwestern town he has angered is after him.

Jewels; Prison breaks

Nobody Runs Forever. Mysterious Press, 2004.

The plan is to steal some dental gold in Cincinnati. What was not in the plan was that one of the gang would be wearing a wire, so he is dispatched. When they decide to rob some armored cars instead, how could they know that a hard-working sheriff and a mean bounty hunter on the trail of the dead guy would mess up the insider information that the gang gets from the bank president's woman?

Bank robbery; Bounty hunters; Informants; Massachusetts; Ohio—Cincinnati

Ask the Parrot. Mysterious Press, 2006.

Still on the run from *Nobody Runs Forever*, Parker hooks up with Tom Lindahl, who has a plan to rip off the racetrack that used to be his employer. Tom knows where the money comes in and how it goes out, so Parker decides this will an easy hit. What he is not prepared for is the local interest and the role a parrot will play in the proceedings.

Gambling; Massachusetts

Dirty Money. Grand Central, 2008.

Parker is on his way back to Massachusetts to settle scores left over from *Nobody Runs Forever*. He needs to reclaim the money he left in a church choir loft and get out of town. When a federal marshal is killed by one of Parker's gang, things begin to fall apart. Pursued and then aided by a relentless bounty hunter named Sandra Loscalzo, Parker still intends to clean up old scores and walk away with the money.

Massachusetts; Revenge

Starr, Jason.

Fake I.D. No Exit Press, 2000.

Tommy Russo dreams of being an actor, but the reality is that he is a bouncer at a Manhattan nightclub with little opportunity for change. So he decides to become a racehorse owner. The only obstacle is the $10,000 he needs to buy into the scheme. The decisions he makes to raise the cash are not going to get him any closer to the winner's circle than he has been to the bright lights of Hollywood.

New York—New York; Robbery

Swierczynski, Duane.

The Wheelman. St. Martin's Minotaur, 2005.

When mute Irish wheelman Lennon is the getaway during a bank heist in Philadelphia, he finds that things do not go according to plan. He is beaten and left for dead, without the loot from the bank. Being the kind of individual he is, he decides to get his share of the loot and get out of town even if it means going through the mob and any cops in his way.

Bank robbery; Pennsylvania—Philadelphia

Thompson, Jim.

The Getaway. New American Library, 1959.

Carter "Doc" McCoy and his wife Carol rob a bank in a small Texas town and leave their partner, Rudy Torrento, for dead. They plan to flee across the country and make it to Mexico, but did not anticipate the tenacity of the police pursuit. Nor did they anticipate that Rudy would not die and also join the chase. As the two are on the run, they find confronting themselves might be as challenging as facing their pursuers.

Bank robbery; Husbands and wives; Police pursuit

The Grifters. Regency, 1963.

Roy Dillion has grown up under the shadow of his mother, Lily, who is only thirteen years older than he. While his mother works for the mob as a gambler, Roy works by day and practices small cons that net him just enough to get by. Then one day he meets Moira Langtry, a woman who pushes him to take bigger risks for the big score. Should he go with her or choose Carol Roberg, the nurse he meets after a bad beating?

California—Los Angeles; Mothers and sons; Nurses

True Crime Robbers

Duncombe, Stephen, and Andrew Mattson.

The Bobbed Haired Bandit: A True Story of Crime and Celebrity in 1920s New York. New York University Press, 2006.

Fame was easy to come by in the jazz age, as proved by the story of a pregnant laundress from Brooklyn, who stuck up stores with her husband and gained national fame as the Bobbed Haired Bandit. Celia Cooney was desperate at first but eventually rode the crest of the publicity to become a symbol of the flapper girl in action.

New York—New York; Robbery

Macintyre, Ben.

The Napoleon of Crime: The Life and Times of Adam Worth, Master Thief. Farrar, Straus & Giroux, 1997.

Adam Worth was a notorious criminal who eluded punishment until he was almost fifty. His daring exploits were so admired that he became Arthur Conan Doyle's model for Professor Moriarty. Because he often stole from the wealthy, Worth took on a Robin Hood-like aura and became a folk hero admired by detectives, including some at Scotland Yard and Alan Pinkerton.

Thieves; Victorian England

Tidyman, Ernest.

Big Bucks: The True, Outrageous Story of the Plymouth Mail Robbery and How They Got Away With It. Norton, 1982.

> In 1962 a gang of six men ripped off the U.S. Post Office for $1.5 million. Despite a trial, all of the men walked away. Twenty years later, one of the insiders confessed how to the author so their tale could be told.

> Mail robbery; Massachusetts—Plymouth

1

2

White Collar Crimes

White collar crimes are thus called because they are linked to a middle- to upper-class business lifestyle. Although the average person would like to think that the daily activities of commerce are free of corruption, the reality is that white collar crimes can include such crimes as embezzlement, fraud, forgery, bribery, and even murder.

3

4

Benchmark White Collar Crime Novels

Cain, James M.

5

Double Indemnity. Avon, 1943.

> Insurance salesman Walter Huff stops by the Nirdlinger household to update the policy of Mr. Nirdlinger. When Mrs. Phyllis Nirdlinger asks about the double indemnity clause in the policy, Huff knows he should run. Instead he falls in lust with her. The two head down a dark path together, beginning to plot a way to get rid of Mr. Nirdlinger.

> California—Glendale; Insurance fraud; Triangles (Interpersonal relations)

6

Fitzgerald, F. Scott.

7

The Great Gatsby. Scribner, 1925.

> Nick Carraway moves to West Egg Village on Long Island to become a bond salesman, searching for a quick way to the wealth that is sweeping America in the 1920s. His next door neighbor is Jay Gatsby, a mysterious man whose vast wealth appears to be as endless as the rumors about how he acquired it. When Nick discovers that Gatsby has an attraction for his second cousin Daisy, who is married to Nick's old college chum, he must decide how involved he wishes to get in their affair.

> New York—Long Island; New York—New York; Organized crime; Revenge; Romance

8

9

10

White Collar Crime Novels

Greene, Graham.

The Third Man. Viking, 1950.

Harry Lime of the International Refugee Office has invited his friend Rollo Martins to Vienna. Normally a writer of pulp Westerns, Rollo's supposed assignment will be to write about the plight of international refugees. But when Rollo arrives in Vienna, he learns that Harry has been killed in a car accident. Anna Schmidt, Harry's lover, believes that the accident may have been murder. She could be right, considering that the police inform Rollo that Lime was a despicable criminal. A witness tells Holly that a third man was at the accident scene, but then Holly sees Harry on the streets of Vienna. When Rollo goes on a quest to discover the truth in the shattered city, he learns a horrible fact that forces him to administer justice for an unspeakable crime.

Austria—Vienna; Refugees; World War II

Perry, Thomas.

Death Benefits. Random House, 2001.

When Max Stillman shows up at the offices of McClaren Life and Casualty in San Francisco, he scares John Walker, a small-time data analyst who sees him from his cubicle. By the time Max is done with the firm and John, he will have been on a roller coaster of a ride, all because he slept with the wrong woman.

California—San Francisco; New Hampshire; Insurance fraud

Stansberry, Domenic.

Manifesto for the Dead. Permanent, 2000.

In the last days of noir writer Jim Thompson's life, as fictionalized here, he is asked to write a novel based on an unproduced screenplay by producer Billy Miracle, who hopes to get the attention of Jack Lombard. The screenplay involves the death of a film executive's girlfriend, and when real life gets too close to the screenplay's plot, Thompson finds himself on the hot seat for murder.

California—Hollywood; Motion pictures; Thompson, Jim

Starr, Jason.

Cold Caller. Norton, 1998.

When advertising executive Bill Moss is fired from his vice president's job, he ends up a telemarketer. Despite having a boss that hates him, Bill manages to weasel his way into management. When his boss decides to dig into his past a little too far, Bill decides that he needs to take action.

New York—New York; Telemarketing

Swan, Mary.

The Boys in the Trees. Henry Holt, 2008.

When William Heath relocates his family to Canada from their native England at the turn of the century, the hope is that they have found a place of comfort. But when William is accused of embezzlement, it leads him to murder his family. The real causes of the crime are explored by all of the Heaths' new neighbors, who search for the truth.

Canada—Emden; Embezzlement; Historical

Thompson, Jim.

A Hell of a Woman. Lion Books, 1954.

Frank "Dolly" Dillon is a door-to-door salesman for the Pay-E-Zee stores, depressed by his marriage to his wife, Joyce. Then one day Dolly makes a call at a home looking for a deadbeat named Pete Hendrickson and instead meets the beautiful Mona Farrell. She is an abused prisoner of her own family, and his act of kindness to her costs him. He is arrested for embezzlement, until the endangered Mona surprisingly comes to his aid, using some of her aunt's money. But Frank's lust for more money will lead him into dangerous areas and spoil any happiness he might have achieved.

Embezzlement; Marriage; Triangles (Interpersonal relations)

True White Collar Crime

Berkow, Ira.

The Man Who Robbed the Pierre: The Story of Bobby Comfort. Atheneum, 1997.

In 1972, $11 million worth of jewelry and cash went out the front door of the Hotel Pierre in New York City in one of the most daring robberies of all time. This book tells the story of Bobby Comfort and how he got to the point of masterminding this crime.

Hotels; New York—New York

Bledsoe, Jerry.

Before He Wakes: A True Story of Money, Marriage, Sex and Murder. Dutton, 1994.

In 1988, Barbara Stager's husband Russ was accidentally shot to death with a gun they kept under their pillow for protection. It was a real tragedy for this churchgoing pair, until police investigations started to reveal that Barbara was active outside the marriage and a compulsive over-spender. Then the police discovered this story had been told before.

Husbands and wives; North Carolina—Durham

Eichenwald, Kurt.

The Informant: A True Story. Broadway, 2000.

Mark Whiteacre was informing on his employer, Archer Daniels Midland, to the FBI. The plan was for him to wear a wire and take down a company planning on stealing millions from its own clients. Then the veracity of the informer came into question, and the search for the truth became clouded.

Commercial crimes; Federal Bureau of Investigation; Illinois; Informants

Greene, Robert W.

The Sting Man: Inside ABSCAM. Dutton, 1981.

The FBI set up a major bribery sting, which eventually involved a U.S. senator, some congressmen, and other government officials who proved eager and willing to behave badly with the public's money.

ABSCAM bribery scandal; Washington, D.C.

Humes, Edward.

Mean Justice: A Town's Terror, a Prosecutor's Power, a Betrayal of Innocence. Simon & Schuster, 1999.

When District Attorney Ed Jagels took over the prosecution of crime in Bakersfield, California, he had the power to clean up the wild town. His conviction rates were high, and crime plummeted. One of his successful prosecutions was of Pat Dunn, a retired high school principal sent away for the murder of his wife, Sandy. But Dunn may be innocent, and as the author probed the techniques of the DA, he uncovered other prosecutions that may have been of a dubious nature.

Attorneys; California—Bakersfield; Trials

McClintick, David.

Indecent Exposure: A True Story of Hollywood and Wall Street. Morrow, 1982.

It all started when actor Cliff Robertson discovered an old movie industry enemy had cashed a $10,000 check in his name. As the case widened, it captured some of the top management in a scandal that would greatly affect the industry.

California—Hollywood; Embezzlement; Motion pictures

Rule, Ann.

Heart Full of Lies: A True Story of Death and Desire. Free, 2003.

Liysa Northon was a sociopath, driven to have everything without compromise. With her third husband, Chris, an airplane pilot who struggled to save his marriage, she found herself unsatisfied. So on a camping trip in remote Oregon, she shot her husband, claimed self-defense, and took every penny of his insurance money. Able to keep up the deception for many years, it was only the smallest of clues that led to the unraveling of this story and the eventual revelation of the truth.

Husbands and wives; Insurance fraud; Oregon—Wallowa County

St. James, James.

Disco Bloodbath: A Fabulous But True Tale of Murder in Clubland. Simon & Schuster, 1999.

> James St. James relates to the reader his path from South Bend, Indiana, to the club scene in New York City. Along the way he met all the individuals who would put everything on the line to be in the line. When big-time party celebrity Michael Alig confessed to St. James one night that he had dismembered Angel Melendez, the author knew the partying was over.

Club scene; New York—New York

Schwartz-Nobel, Loretta.

Engaged to Murder: The Inside Story of the Main Line Murders. Viking, 1987.

> William Bradfield was a sociopath with just a little too much confidence. When he made a broad hint to his alibi for a triple homicide, it led his friend to tell that to the police. What the police discovered was a dead woman, two missing children, and two men who had made a pact with the devil in order to profit from an insurance scam.

Pennsylvania—Harrisburg; Teachers

Stewart, James B.

Den of Thieves. Simon & Schuster, 1991.

> Four men worked to make themselves wealthy in the 1980s, and in the process nearly destroyed Wall Street: Michael Milken, Ivan Boesky, Martin Siegel, and Dennis Levine. By manipulating the system, and each other, they managed to stay one step ahead of the regulatory agencies set up to monitor and stop them.

Insider trading; Wall Street

Zierold, Norman.

Three Sisters in Black. Little, Brown, 1968.

> By 1909, when the arrests were made, this family had left a trail of bizarre behavior across the Eastern seaboard. It was all an attempt to kill Ocey Snead so that the family could collect on her insurance money.

Insurance fraud; New Jersey—East Orange; Sisters

Chapter 4

Caught Up in Crime

Amateur Criminals

Amateur criminals commit one wrong act and suffer the consequences. They are average citizens who never intended to commit a crime or to profit from it. The appeal of these novels lies in the character who committed the act and the range of emotions displayed by that person as he or she suffers the consequences.

Benchmark Amateur Criminal Novel

Cain, James M.

The Postman Always Rings Twice. Knopf, 1934.
> When Frank Chambers is "thrown off the hay truck about noon," he is fortunate to find himself at the Twin Oaks Tavern, owned by Nick Papadakis, a man willing to put him to work. What is not so fortunate is that Nick's wife Cora is willing to move on and willing to remove Nick as an obstacle. As these two desperate characters begin to plot against Nick, all does not go well.
>
> Adultery; California; Romance; Triangles (Interpersonal relations)

Amateur Criminal Novels

Brewer, Gil.

The Vengeful Virgin. Fawcett Publications, 1958.
> Shirley Angela is an eighteen-year-old who wants to get at the riches of her dying stepfather, Victor Spondell. When she meets Jack Ruxton, the owner of a television repair shop, she finds the perfect foil. Together they plan the death of Victor, but things do not go according to plan.
>
> Florida—Florida Keys; Murder for profit

Bruen, Ken, and Jason Starr.

Bust. Hard Case Crime, 2006.

When Max Fisher decides he wants to get rid of his wife, all he has to do is ask the woman with whom he is having an affair. His secretary, Angela Petrakos, knows a man named Dillon, a former IRA hit man, who can get the job done. What Max does not know is that he is now the target.

Affairs; Hit men; New York—New York

Slide. Hard Case Crime, 2007.

Things have not gone well for Max Fisher since he tried to kill his wife, and he now finds himself in Alabama. When Kyle Jordan, a hotel clerk and crack dealer, comes into Max's life, Max decides to become a dealer himself. To his surprise, he is good at it and finds himself back in New York living the high life. Unfortunately, this brings him to the attention of his former secretary and lover, Angela Petrakos, whose new boyfriend Slide, a wannabe serial killer, is perfectly willing to make Max's new life a living hell.

Affairs; Drugs; New York—New York

The Max. Hard Case Crime, 2008.

Max Fisher is wasting away in Attica prison, where he is practicing his best bluster to keep the bad guys at bay. Ironically, his girlfriend, Angela Petrakos, is in prison as well, on the Isle of Lesbos, after an adventure with the dashing Englishman Sebastian that leads to a murder charge. The third person in the mix is true crime writer Paula Segal, who dreams of making it big with Max's story.

Prisons

Bunker, Edward.

Little Boy Blue. Viking, 1981.

Because the author spent most of his life in prison, he may be the perfect person to write the semiautobiographical story of Alex Hammond. Early in his life, Alex spends time in various detention facilities, military academies, reform schools, and mental institutions. From petty crime to doing the time, Alex lives most of his life incarcerated.

California; Children in jeopardy; Prisons

Carpenter, Don.

Hard Rain Falling. Harcourt, Brace & World, 1966.

This novel is the story of Jack Levitt, an orphan from Portland who lives a desperate life outside prison. A large portion of the book is told during the period of Jack's incarceration in San Quentin, yet most of that period of the novel is taken up by the story of Jack's African American cellmate, Billy Lancing. The novel ends with the desperation of Jack trying to create a family once he has been released from prison.

California—San Francisco; Homosexuality; Oregon—Portland; Pool; Prisons; Race relations

Gresham, William Lindsay.

Nightmare Alley. Rinehart & Company, 1946.

Stan Carlisle is a carnival worker with little going for him. When he can't succeed even as a small-time magician, he turns to the art of fortune telling and finds he has a gift for the scam. When he moves up in the world through the use of his newfound skills, he realizes he can manipulate anyone. Along the way he harms many people but manages to ignore the personal consequences. He feels like he is on top of the world, unaware that the one person who can control him is the one person he turns to, to assuage his guilt. Ultimately he is turned into the "geek" he has always been seeking.

Carnivals; Fortune telling; Psychiatrists

Higgins, George V.

The Digger's Game. Knopf, 1973.

Despite his best efforts at petty crime, Jerry "Digger" Doherty has managed to stay out of jail mostly thanks to the interference run by his priest brother. But when he takes advantage of a free businessman's trip to Las Vegas run by the mob, he gets $18,000 in debt to an enforcer known as The Greek. The powers that be are scared that The Greek may not be able to take down the Digger, and things heat up.

Enforcers; Massachusetts—Boston; Organized crime

Hill, Russell.

Robbie's Wife. Hard Case Crime, 2007.

At age 60, Jack Stone escapes L.A. for the English countryside, seeking a jump start to his screenwriting career. His path crosses Sheepheaven Farm, and he meets the seductive temptress Maggie Barlow, twenty years younger and willing to make a change from her husband Robbie. When a crisis hits the bed and breakfast head on, Jack and Maggie must make their decisions and face the consequences.

England—Dorset; Farms; Triangles (Interpersonal relations)

Kirino, Natuso.

Out. Kodansha, 1997. (U.S.: Kodansha International, 2003).

When Yayoi strangles her worthless husband, she turns to her friend Masako for help. Masako enlists the aid of two of their coworkers on the night shift in a Tokyo factory. The quartet decide to quarter the body and dispose of it, but their bond begins to unravel under the pressure of a police investigation. Each woman's personal life is laid bare when the crime comes home to roost. This book won the Grand Prix award in Japan and was a 2004 Edgar award nominee for Best Novel of the Year.

Dismemberment; Factory workers; Female bonding; Japan—Tokyo

Lippman, Laura.

Every Secret Thing. William Morrow, 2003.

The history behind the main story involves a day when two young girls are walking home from a birthday party and decide to rescue an abandoned baby. Seven years later, the girls are released from prison and return to their neighborhood to try to reassemble a life for themselves. When children start disappearing in the neighborhood, the police turn to the two women, while they try to understand both their young lives and the one they are trying to construct after prison. This novel won both the Anthony and Barry awards as the best novel of the year.

Child murderers; Children in jeopardy; Ex-convicts; Maryland—Baltimore

McCarthy, Cormac.

No Country for Old Men. Knopf, 2005.

In all great noir stories, the lead character makes one fatal mistake. In this case, Llewelyn Moss decides to keep the $2 million in drug money that he stumbles on while hunting. Moss leaves behind the carnage of a drug deal gone bad, including the dead bodies of men on both sides of the deal. When the clues at the crime site lead Sheriff Ed Tom Bell to realize that Moss is in very deep trouble, he attempts to rescue him. Bell knows that both sides of the drug deal are after the money. One side sends an ex-Special Forces man. The other side sends a ghost, the extremely talented and dangerous psychotic Anton Chigruh. When everyone is done shooting each other, the key to the novel is who will survive this terrible killing field.

Drugs; Mexico; Texas

McCoy, Horace.

They Shoot Horses, Don't They? Simon & Schuster, 1935.

Robert Syverten is being sentenced for murdering Gloria Beatty as the novel opens, and the rest of the story tells how he got to that point. Both are trying to survive in Depression-era Hollywood, and Gloria has persuaded Robert to enter a dance marathon contest. As the contest begins, the two get to know each other's strengths and weaknesses, and Robert tries to protect Gloria from her own self-destructive tendencies. When an audience member is killed, the marathon grinds to a halt with no winner, and the hopelessness of their situation descends on the characters.

California—Santa Monica; Dance marathons; Marathons; Suicide

No Pockets in a Shroud. UK: Barker, 1937. (U.S.: New American Library, 1948).

Mike Dolan is a crusading newspaper man fighting against the corruption in Coltron, a southwestern city. Choosing to leave his job after his editor refuses to run his story about a baseball team that throws a game for gamblers, he decides to publish his own magazine, *Cosmopolite*, to expose wrongs. As he tries to climb in society, he discovers that those he most wants to be like are some of his bitterest enemies.

Corruption; Newspapers; Unknown state—Coltron

Muller, Eddie.

[Billy Nichols series].

Eddie Muller uses his knowledge of film noir and a little of his own father's history to create the character of Billy Nichols, a newspaperman who becomes involved in crime. The following series novels are listed in order of publication.

The Distance. Scribner, 2002.

Billy Nichols is the boxing columnist on the San Francisco paper *The Inquirer*. When he gets a phone call from boxer Hack Escalante, who claims to have accidentally killed his manager, Billy helps out by burying the body. Then he thinks about it and realizes he is now in deep trouble and needs to find the real killer to stay out of jail.

Boxing; California—San Francisco; Historical

Shadow Boxer. Scribner, 2003.

When Billy Nichols allows himself to get talked into clearing Florence Sander's husband of a murder rap, he should know better. He spent the entire last book pinning the blame for the murder of his lover Claire on Sanders, who is in jail where he belongs. But then some new evidence appears, and Billy begins to doubt his own ability to find the truth.

California—San Francisco; Historical; Prisons; Revenge

Puzo, Mario.

The Dark Arena. Random House, 1955.

Walter Mosca served in Europe in World War II and has now returned to Germany after turning his back on everything the United States had to offer. Working as a civilian on an air base, he falls for Hella, and they have a child. When Hella becomes ill and Walter must turn to the black market for the supplies Hella needs, he proceeds to deal with the real dark side of postwar world Europe.

Germany—Bremen; Germany—History—1945–1955; Penicillin; Revenge; World War II

Sakey, Marcus.

Good People. Dutton, 2008.

Tom and Anna Reed are stressed by the cost of their attempts to have a child by artificial means, despite each having a job and owning rental property in Chicago. When they stumble on almost a half-million dollars in a dead tenant's apartment, they borrow it. What they never expected is the attention brought to their lives by drug dealers, who really want their money back.

Drugs; Illinois—Chicago

Starr, Jason.

Tough Luck. Vintage, 2003.

Mickey Prada agrees to front some sports bets for Angelo Santoro, and when they go bad he is on the hook for the dough. With few choices, Mickey agrees to use his bowling team to commit a robbery. That is when things start to go bad for this down-on-his-luck protagonist.

Gambling; New York—New York

Thompson, Jim.

A Swell-Looking Babe. Lion Books, 1954.

Bill "Dusty" Rhodes is working as a bellhop at the Manton Hotel when he meets the woman in room 1004. Marcia Hillis resembles his dead stepmother, for whom Dusty carries a torch while he is forced to care for his ailing stepfather, a man he hates. Embroiled in Tug Trowbridge's plan to steal from some bookies who use the hotel's safe deposit boxes, he is falsely accused of murder.

Bookies; Gambling; Hotels; Oedipal complex; Texas—Fort Worth

After Dark, My Sweet. Popular Library, 1955.

William "Kid" Collins has been in and out of a series of mental institutions, because despite his friendly nature, he can be vicious when aroused. When he crosses paths with Uncle Bud, Kid finds himself unwittingly involved in a kidnapping plot along with the very seductive widow, Fay Anderson. When their plot to kidnap Charles Vandermeer, the son of a wealthy family, goes awry, Bud and Fay turn on each other, leaving Kid to make the final decision about right and wrong.

Kidnapping; Mental health

Texas by the Tail. Fawcett, 1965.

With girlfriend "Red," whose real name is Harriet, Mitch Corley runs scams against the tables, hoping to skip before the losers realize they have been taken. When the pair lands in Texas, trying to get out from under Mitch's past, which includes a son named Sam and a psycho ex-wife named Teddy, they plan the ultimate scam. What they do not realize is that sometimes those who are burned, like the very wealthy Zearsdale from Houston, know how to start fires of their own.

Fathers and sons; Gambling; Hotels; Scams; Texas—Fort Worth

True Amateur Crime

Englade, Ken.

Beyond Reason: The True Story of a Shocking Double Murder, a Brilliant and Beautiful Virginia Socialite, and a Deadly Psychotic Obsession. St. Martin's, 1990.

Who would murder Derek and Nancy Haysom in their home in Virginia? The viciousness of the crime made it appear like a Manson-like cult ritual. When suspicion turned to the couple's college-aged daughter, Elizabeth fled to Europe with her German boyfriend, Jens Soering. Once across the sea, the couple's behavior brought them to the attention of the police again, and soon Elizabeth found herself extradited to the United States to face a trial for murder.

Parents and children; Virginia—Boonsboro

McGinniss, Joe.

Cruel Doubt. Simon & Schuster, 1991.
> Lieth Von Stein was murdered in his bed and his wife Bonnie was beaten and stabbed while sleeping next to him. Evidence quickly began to point to Bonnie's son from a previous marriage, Chris Pritchard, a drugged-up Dungeons and Dragons player who may have wanted his stepfather's money long before it was due. Bonnie's unwavering belief in her son's innocence may have hindered the author from getting to the truth.

North Carolina—Washington; Patricide

Crime and Punishment

Crime and punishment novels deal with the actions of individuals after a crime has been committed. These range from the emotional decline of the perpetrator to acts of revenge committed by the victim. What is key in these novels is that the reader sees direct action as a result of a crime. The appeal is that in some fashion, this type of crime literature may be the only one that delivers a sense of justice or completion.

Benchmark Crime and Punishment Novels

Bunker, Edward.

Animal Factory. Viking, 1977.
> When Ron Decker, a convicted drug dealer, is sent to San Quentin for two years, all he wants to do is get by. But when he runs into prison lord Earl Copen, he discovers that life on the inside can be as complicated as life on the outside.

California—San Quentin Prison; Prisons

Cain, James M.

Serenade. Knopf, 1937.
> Down-on-his-luck opera singer John Howard Sharp is singing in Mexico when he encounters Juana Montes, a woman of the streets. She rekindles his life, and soon he is singing around the world and making films in Hollywood. However, when they encounter a conductor named Winston Hawes, things turn ugly, and Juana rises to defend her man. The ultimate price is paid.

Homosexuality; Mexico; Opera

Collins, Wilkie.

The Moonstone. UK: Tinsley, 1868. (U.S.: Harper, 1868).

When a Hindu diamond is stolen from a temple in India by Colonel Herncastle, its legacy is a curse upon his descendants. Rachel Verinder, Herncastle's niece, is bequeathed the diamond on her eighteenth birthday, when it is delivered to the Verinders estate by Franklin Blake. Franklin falls in love with Rachel. Some Hindus arrive in the English countryside, intent on returning the diamond to its land of origin, and the diamond goes missing the day after the birthday celebration. The police are represented by the one of fiction's first police detective heroes, Sergeant Cuff.

Diamonds; England—Yorkshire; India; Police

Dostoevsky, Fyodor.

Crime and Punishment. A. F. Bazunov, E. Prats, and Ia. Veidenshtraukh, 1867. (U.S.: Crowell, 1886).

Rodion Romanovich Raskolnikov is a former student living in poverty in St. Petersburg. He tries to save himself by murdering both a pawn broker named Alyona Ivanovna, for her money, and a witness who wanders into the crime scene. Raskolnikov draws the attention of the police investigating the case by acting unnatural while trying to deal with his a visit from his mother and sister. Even the magistrate on the case believes he is guilty, until another man confesses. Still tortured, Raskolnikov makes his own confession, but not before others suffer consequences of his actions.

Russia—St. Petersburg

Crime and Punishment Novels

Cook, Thomas H.

The Cloud of Unknowing. Harcourt, 2007.

When a judge rules that the death of Diana Regan's son, Jason, was an accident, Diana purges herself of her husband, home, and belongings. Her brother, David Sears, worries about his sister's obsessive behaviors, which include fantasies about Jason's death, repeating the bizarre behaviors of their dead father, and seducing David's young daughter into her conspiracies. This novel is told in alternating chapters, with set being David's narrative of the event and the other set being his confession to detective Samuel Petrie. The question is, what is David confessing?

Brothers and sisters; Drowning; Families; Schizophrenia

Dreiser, Theodore.

An American Tragedy. Boni & Liveright, 1925.

Torn from his religious upbringing by alcohol and prostitution, Clyde Griffiths leaves the poverty of his youth for the wild streets of Kansas City. When involvement with a bad woman and an accidental death force him to flee, he heads to New York State, where he becomes a factory foreman in his Uncle Lycurgus's firm. His inability to stay away from bad women haunts him again, and an unwanted pregnancy leads to fatal plans and a trial that seeks the truth.

Kansas—Kansas City; New York—Lycurgus; Pregnancy; Triangles (Interpersonal relationships)

Goodis, David.

Fire in the Flesh. Gold Medal, 1957.

Blazer is a small-time arsonist who hits the big time when he is suspected of setting a fire that killed five people, one of whom is the brother of a gang leader. He cannot remember doing the deed because he was stone drunk, but he feels compelled to try to clear his name and his conscience. Aided by his girl, Cora, he struggles against those who believe in his guilt and want him dead.

Arson; Guilt

Goodman, Carol.

The Seduction of Water. Ballantine, 2003.

Iris Greenfeder lost her mom, Kate Morrissey, when she was ten, and now Iris lives an unfulfilling life as an untenured part-time adjunct professor and struggling writer. When a short story she writes is published by Phoebe Nix at *Caffeine* magazine, it draws the attention of Kate's old agent, Hedda Wolfe. Hedda believes there is a publishable story in the tale of how Kate wrote two novels and then died in a mysterious hotel fire under an assumed name. So Iris takes a job managing the Equinox Hotel where she grew up in the Catskills, where, rumor has it, a third and unpublished manuscript by Kate may still be found.

Authors; Catskill Mountains; Hotels; Mothers and daughters; New York—Arcadia; New York—New York

Highsmith, Patricia.

Strangers on a Train. Harper & Brothers, 1950.

Guy Haines and Charles Anthony Bruno meet as strangers on a train. As each man explores the nature of the other, it becomes evident that they could equally benefit from exchanging a murder. While one man clearly rejects the idea, the other carries out his part in the plan. Then the murderer decides to integrate himself into the life of the man who has failed to do his duty.

Railroads; New York—Great Neck; Texas—Metcalf

Deep Water. Harper & Brothers, 1957.

Victor Van Allen is so weak he is willing to let his wife Melinda sleep around rather than go through the embarrassment of a divorce. But when he begins to claim that he is the murderer of Malcolm McRae in a vain attempt to redeem himself in Melinda's eyes, he finds himself in a world of hurt. So, whether he committed the first murder or not, he is now willing to do the deed in order to eliminate the competition.

Adultery; Divorce; Massachusetts—Little Wesley

A Game for the Living. Harper & Brothers, 1958.

When Lelia is murdered, the finger is pointed at the two men who have been sleeping with her and who do not like each other. Ramón Otero is a furniture repairman in his home country of Mexico. Theodore Schiebelhut is a German expatriate painter who is trying to adopt the local color. When the two men realize they need each other to save themselves, they begin to reach a mutual understanding.

Mexico; Triangles (Interpersonal relationships)

This Sweet Sickness. Harper & Brothers, 1960.

David Kelsey is an engineer at a fabrics manufacturing plant who has become obsessed with a married woman named Annabelle. His plan is to have her join him in a cabin he just bought, hoping they can hide from her husband Gerald under an assumed name. What he ignores is Annabelle's steadfast refusal to join him or to deny her love for her husband. When her husband decides to take action, it results in death. Fleeing, David thinks he has left his problems behind, but he is wrong.

False identity; Triangles (Interpersonal relationships)

The Cry of the Owl. Harper & Row, 1962.

Robert Forester has moved to Pennsylvania to escape New York and his ex-wife Nickie by taking a job with Langley Aeronautics. But when spying on his new neighbor Jenny Thierolf turns him into an obsessive peeping tom, he is invited over to meet his fantasy and her former fiancé, Grey Wyncoop. What Robert discovers is that the reality of the situation next door is not what he dreamed it would be.

Peeping Toms; Pennsylvania—Langley; Triangles (Interpersonal relationships)

Kersh, Gerald.

Prelude to a Certain Midnight. Doubleday, 1947.

A child named Sonia Sabbatani is raped and strangled in London, and her entire neighborhood is devastated. The regular tenants of the local watering hole, The Bar Bacchus, include one Asta Thundersley, who becomes determined to carry out a better investigation than the police. Whether this Bohemian and her friends will bring the murderer to justice may be based on their unique talents.

Children in jeopardy; England—London

Lansdale, Joe R.

Leather Maiden. Knopf, 2008.

Cason Statler is a wreck with post-traumatic syndrome from Iraq and a drinking problem that results in his being exiled from his Pulitzer Prize–nominated career as a journalist. To decompress, he heads home to Camp Rapture to take a job with the small town's newspaper. When he focuses on a cold case involving a missing college coed, he unveils a series of crimes that will rock all of Texas before he uncovers the truth.

Journalism; Texas—Camp Rapture

Marlowe, Dan J.

The Vengeance Man. Gold Medal, 1966.

Construction company owner Jim Wilson thinks he has his bases covered when he has his unfaithful wife followed by a private detective. All he needs is a head's up to cover up her murder, and then he will be free. He desperately wants to advance, and he does not care who he destroys in the process, including the father-in-law he hates. But he does not count on the influence of his new love, Ludmilla Pierson, his wife's best friend.

South Carolina—Moline

Martin, J(ulia) Wallis.

The Bird Yard. UK: Hodder & Stoughton, 1998. (U.S.: St. Martin's Minotaur, 1999).

Based on a childhood memory from her days of living on a counsel estate, Wallis Martin presents a home turned into an aviary, surrounded by wire yet full of the color and song of finches. In the neighborhood where The Bird Yard lies, a young boy named Gary Maudsley has disappeared, echoing a pattern from five years earlier when a young boy named Joseph Coyne also went missing. Detective Superintendent Parker sees the pattern, sees the aviary, and works hard to draw a straight line from one to the other. With the help of profiler Murray Hanson, the detective tries to keep his own paternal feelings intact as he struggles to be objective about this aggravating and intense case of murder.

Children in jeopardy; England—Manchester; Pedophilia

Nunn, Kem.

Tapping the Source. Delacorte, 1984.

Ike Tucker's sister, a runaway, has been missing for years, but now he is committed to discovering the truth. Has she been murdered by the three men who took her to Mexico but did not bring her back? Set in a scary world where drugs affect the thinking of some damaged Vietnam veterans, Tucker explores the world of sun, surf, and sadism.

California—Huntington Beach; Missing persons; Surfing

Pomona Queen. Pocket, 1992.

Earl Dean is a door-to-door vacuum cleaner salesman when he happens to call upon his old schoolmate, Dan Brown. Dan is a cop killer out of prison and one mean biker dude. Brown's brother Buddy has been murdered, and Dan thinks Earl is just the ally he needs to hunt down the killer. That would be the lead singer of a band called Pomona Queen, a beautiful blond.

California—Pomona; Ex-convicts; Musicians; Revenge

Pearl, Matthew.

The Dante Club. Random House, 2003.

In Boston in 1865, a distinguished group of Americans including Henry Wadsworth Longfellow, James Russell Lowell, J. T. Fields, and Oliver Wendell Holmes Sr. form the Dante Club to arrange for the publication of the first American translation of Dante's *Divine Comedy* from its original Italian. When people start dying based on the methods described in the *Inferno*, it is only these men who see the clues for what they are: someone desperately wants to prevent the publication of this book.

Alighieri, Dante; Holmes, Oliver Wendell, Sr.; Longfellow, Henry Wadsworth; Lowell, James Russell; Massachusetts—Boston

Reovoyr, Nina.

Southland. Akashic, 2003.

Jackie Ishida is a lesbian Japanese American who is attending law school in 1994 when her grandfather, Frank Sakai, dies. His estate includes a shoebox containing $38,000, and his will names a benefactor, Curtis Martindale, who was an employee at the store. Curtis was found dead in the store's freezer during the Watts Riots, along with three other black men. Jackie and James Lanier, Curtis's cousin, try to search the past for clues about to the proper course of action to take in the present.

California—Los Angeles; Japanese Americans; Lesbians; Race relations; Watts Riots (1965); Wills

Starr, Jason.

Nothing Personal. No Exit Press, 1998.

Ad executive David Sussman is being blackmailed by his mistress, Amy Lee. His wife Leslie is best friends with Maureen DePino. Then Joey DePino, her husband, who owes two bookmakers and a loan shark, decides he can make some money quick by kidnapping David and Leslie's daughter, Jessica. One crime exposes the other, and things do not go well in David's world.

Blackmail; Kidnapping; New York—New York

Hard Feelings. Vintage, 2002.

Richie Segal is a computer consultant with issues. One is an incident in which he was molested as a child. As an adult, by chance, he sees his molester, Michael Rudnick, now a successful New York lawyer, on the street one day. Richie begins to think of getting a permanent form of revenge.

Molestation; New York—New York; Revenge

Lights Out. St. Martin's Press, 2006.

> When high school baseball star Jake Thomas is facing a statutory rape charge, he decides a wedding with his sweetheart, Christina Mercado, will save his public face. But Christina is more interested in former high school star Ryan Rossetti, now a house painter, who is jealous enough of Jake's success to keep Christina at all costs.

Baseball; New York—Canarsie

Thompson, Jim.

Nothing More Than Murder. Harper & Brothers, 1949.

> Joe Wilmot married up when he joined with Elizabeth Barclay Wilmot in wedded bliss and ownership of the Barclay movie theater. When their relationship becomes irreconcilable, and Joe falls for their maid, Carol Farmer, Elizabeth and Joe concoct a plan to have an accident and defraud their insurance company. Although criminal plans are hard to carry out successfully, sometimes living with the consequences can be even harder.

Insurance fraud; Movie theaters; Stoneville; Triangles (Interpersonal relations)

The Golden Gizmo. Lion, 1954.

> Todd Kent is not happily married, but he is also not happy to discover the corpse of his wife, Elaine. When he revealed to his buyer Milt that he stole an item from one of their marks, he might have set her murder in motion. Todd thought he had found the goose that lays an unlimited source of pure gold eggs, but when he is pursued by a deadly criminal with intent to kill him as well, he needs to run to stay alive.

California—Los Angeles; Gold

The Kill-Off. Lion Library, 1957.

> Twelve narrators tell us the story of the small New England town of Manduwoc, where a woman named Luane Devore lives, waiting to be murdered. Some of those who feared her include her own husband, a doctor with a secret in his past, a youth obsessed with the secret of his birth, a handyman trapped in a marriage to a psychotic woman, and a blind female singer.

Manduwoc; Small town life

Thomson, David.

Suspects. Knopf, 1985.

> By following the lives of characters from Hollywood films, the narrator of this novel is spinning a tale of mystery and intrigue that walks through movie history, film noir, and biography. Amazingly, these disparate characters suddenly begin to have connections. The questions are, What is being confessed, and who is the most likely suspect?

Motion pictures

Walters, Minette.

Acid Row. UK: Macmillan, 2001. (U.S.: Putnam, 2002).

Bassingdale Estate is known as Acid Row to the impoverished residents of this housing project. Things get worse when an agency places a pedophile in this closed community, especially when ten-year-old Amy Rogerson goes missing. When a doctor named Sophie Morrison finds herself held hostage by the pedophile Nicholas Hollis and his vicious father Franek during a riot in the estate, a black man, recently released from prison, decides to save the community with a rag tag band of co-conspirators.

England—Bassingdale Estate; Housing projects; Pedophilia; Riots

Fox Evil. UK: Macmillan, 2002. (U.S.: Putnam, 2003).

Alisa Lockyer-Fox has died in her nightgown and boots outside Shenstead Manor. When her husband James is found not guilty of the murder, a campaign by the local gossips accuses him of murder, which sends him into isolation and depression. His London solicitor, Mark Ankerton, does all he can to defend his client, including facing down the leader of the Travelers, a mysterious man who appears too knowledgeable about the neighborhood.

Depression; England—Dorset, Shenstead; Fox hunting; Grief; Travelers

Westlake, Donald E.

361. Random House, 1962.

When Ray Kelly arrives home from the Air Force, it is only to be next to his father when someone shoots him dead. On the rebound from that death, he discovers his brother Bill's wife has been murdered as well. Taking on his brother as a partner, the two men take to the streets of New York to find out who is murdering their family and to seek their revenge.

New York—New York; Revenge

Wilson, Robert.

A Small Death in Lisbon. UK: HarperCollins, 1999. (U.S.: Harcourt, 2000).

In 1941, German industrialist Klaus Felsen is forced to go to Lisbon and return with wolfram (tungsten) for the Nazi war effort. In 1999, when Catarina Oliviera, the daughter of a prominent lawyer, is found murdered on the beach in Lisbon, police inspector Ze Coehlo is given the case. Eventually these two disparate incidents draw together the story of Portugal and how it suffered in the 1940s, the 1970s, and today.

Nazi Germany; Portugal—Lisbon

True Crime and Punishment

Alexander, Shana.

Nutcracker: Money, Madness, Murder: A Family Album. Doubleday, 1985.

Franklin Bradshaw was a nonpracticing Mormon whose fortune came from auto parts and oil land leases. His family only appreciated his money, no one more than his daughter Frances, who managed to talk her son into murdering their grandfather so she could support her ballet causes.

Mormons; Patricide; Utah—Salt Lake City

Barnes, Margaret Anne.

Murder in Coweta County. Reader's Digest, 1976.

John Wallace ruled over The Kingdom in rural Georgia, a law unto himself. With the law of Meriwether County in his pocket, he felt he could commit any act without repercussions. However, when he murdered a black man in front of eight witnesses, he forgot that he was standing in Coweta County, where Sheriff Lamar Potts worked.

Georgia—Coweta County; Race relations

Black, David.

Murder at the Met: Based on the Exclusive Account of Detectives Mike Struk and Jerry Giorgio of How They Solved the Phantom of the Opera Case. Dial, 1984.

When Helen Hagnes Mintiks, a violinist with the Met, disappeared during the intermission of a performance, New York was mystified until her body was found in an air conditioning shaft in the building. Then it became the task of two NYC homicide detectives to find a murderer and get him convicted by a jury.

Metropolitan Opera House; New York—New York; Trials

Bloom, John, and Jim Atkinson.

Evidence of Love. Texas Monthly Press, 1983.

When Candy Montgomery got bored, she decided to sleep with her fellow church member and next door neighbor, Allan Gore. After their affair was over, Allan's wife Betty discovered the deed and decided to confront her neighbor. What happened in the garage with the axe left one woman brutally murdered and the other on trail claiming self-defense.

Affairs; Revenge; Texas—Wylie; Trials

Bugliosi, Vincent, and Ken Hurwitz.

Till Death Us Do Part: A True Murder Mystery. Norton, 1978.

Already famous for having brought down Charles Manson, Bugliosi stepped into another courtroom with the challenge of bringing down another murderer. This time it was two seemingly random killings that arewere linked by a lack of evidence.

California—Los Angeles; Trials

Cartwright, Gary.

Blood Will Tell: The Murder Trials of T. Cullen Davis. Harcourt Brace Jovanovich, 1979.

> T. Cullen Davis found himself on trial twice despite using his vast resources to keep himself out of court and out of jail. The first trial was for the murder of a young girl and assault on two others. The second trial was for hiring a hit man to take care of the judge in his divorce case.

> Texas—Fort Worth; Trials

Chessman, Caryl.

Cell 2455 Death Row. Prentice-Hall, 1954.

> As a plea to escape the death penalty, lifelong criminal Caryl Chessman wrote and published this book while awaiting his death in San Quentin. It explains how he got on death row.

> California—San Quentin Prison; Death Row; Prisons

Trial by Ordeal. Prentice-Hall, 1955.

> In his sequel, Chessman explained the legal ramifications of his sentence and how he felt about being sentenced to death.

> California—San Quentin Prison; Death row; Prisons

Chester, Giraud.

The Ninth Juror. Random House, 1970.

> Giraud Chester was called to jury duty, and he decided to keep a journal of the proceedings. When two black men were accused of murdering an elderly dentist, he served for three months with eight others, debating the fate of these two men and the course of justice.

> Juries; New York—New York; Trials

Dershowitz, Alan M.

Reversal of Fortune: Inside the von Bülow Case. Random House, 1986.

> Harvard Law Professor Dershowitz was brought in after Claus von Bülow was convicted of killing his wife, Sunny. In a much publicized effort, Dershowitz managed to free von Bülow. While taking readers through the process, Dershowitz also speculates about the guilt of his client and who else could possibly have committed the crime.

> Rhode Island—Newport; Trials

Flynn, Kevin.

Relentless Pursuit: A True Story of Family, Murder and the Prosecutor Who Wouldn't Quit. Putnam, 2007.

> In 1993 the author, then a U.S. District Attorney, was assigned the murder case involving Diane Hawkins and her teenaged daughter, Katrina Harris. Their murders

occurred days before a court hearing regarding child support from Norman Harrell, the father of one of Diane's sons. While Flynn struggled with his trial preparations, he found himself in a family crisis, and comfort came from the extended community that loved Diane.

Families; Fathers and sons; Trials; Washington, D.C.

Godfrey, Ellen.

By Reason of Doubt: The Belshaw Case. Clarke, Irwin, 1981.
On January 15, 1979, Betty Belshaw left a Paris subway and disappeared. Her husband, a Canadian anthropologist named Cyril Belshaw, reported her missing. Two years later her body was found on the slopes of the Swiss Alps, wrapped in garbage bags. Belshaw stood trial for her murder but was acquitted. This book attempts to show how the justice system failed to find a murderer.

Switzerland—Aigle; Trials

Jones, Elwyn.

The Last Two to Hang. Macmillan, 1996. (U.S.: Stein and Day, 1966).
Peter Anthony Allen and Gwynne Owen Evans stole a car and drove to Workington to murder Jack West while their woman accomplice waited in the car with her babies. For that, they were the last two people hanged in England for crimes against their fellow man.

Capital punishment; England—Workington

Lehr, Dick, and Mitchell Zuckoff.

Judgment Ridge: The True Story Behind the Dartmouth Murders. HarperCollins, 2003.
In 2001 two Dartmouth College professors, Half and Susanne Zantop, were murdered in their home. Meanwhile, in nearby Chelsea, Vermont, two high school boys, who had been among the elite at one point, were under suspicion. So James Parker and Robert Tulloch took off on a wild goose chase, only to be caught by the law and brought back to face the charges. The murder had netted them $340.

Dartmouth College; New Hampshire—Hanover; Vermont—Chelsea

Mailer, Norman.

The Executioner's Song. Little Brown, 1979.
Gary Gilmore was the first convict executed in the United States in more than a decade when he died in 1977. Gilmore fought for the right to be executed. Mailer then wrote one of the first works of "faction," or as he called it, a "true-life novel." In this work, he tries to explain how a hopelessly violent man, incarcerated for most of his life, could come to the decision that he wanted to be executed.

Executions; Utah

Maas, Peter.

In a Child's Name: The Legacy of a Mother's Murder. Simon & Schuster, 1990.
Kenneth Taylor, a successful dentist in Marion, Indiana, was accused of beating his third wife, Teresa, to death. After concocting a bizarre story, which matched his excuse for a beating she received in Mexico on their honeymoon, he was convicted of killing his wife. Meanwhile, the families battled over custody of the last victim, their son, Philip.

Indiana—Marion; Uxoricide

Naifeh, Steven, and Gregory White Smith.

Final Justice: The True Story of the Richest Man Ever Tried for Murder. Dutton, 1993.
T. Cullen Davis was found guilty when sent to trial for the murder of one and the assault on two other women he had been involved with in a bitter divorce suit. But one of the richest men in America could spend a lot of money, and his sociopathic personality stopped at no trick to get him judged innocent.

Texas—Fort Worth; Trials

Prendergast, Alan.

The Poison Tree: A True Story of Family Violence and Revenge. Putnam, 1986.
Richie and Deborah Jahnke suffered their father's abuse for years. Finally taking measures into their own hands, they murdered Richard Jahnke. When put on trial, the issue became whether children should take revenge on their parents or rely on a flawed governmental system to protect them.

Child abuse; Children in jeopardy; Trials; Wyoming, Cheyenne

Rule, Ann.

Dead by Sunset: Perfect Husband, Perfect Killer? Simon & Schuster, 1995.
Brad Cunningham was tired of his fourth wife Cheryl, so they divorced and engaged in a bitter custody battle for their children. When Cheryl was found dead in a minivan parked in traffic on the highway, investigators were unable to prove that she had been murdered and that the accident had been staged. But the Keeton family, unable to rest until Cheryl's killer was brought to justice, filed a civil suit that led investigators to crack the case.

Oregon—Portland; Uxoricide

Savage, Mildred.

A Great Fall. Simon & Schuster, 1970.
When a young housewife named Dorothy Thompsen was murdered at midday in a quiet rural area of Connecticut, it terrified and mystified the entire community. The crime led to Agnes Thompsen, a woman who had religious hallucinations and was the mother-in-law of the victim. But the man who went on trial twice for the crime was Harry Solberg, a twenty-year-old man whose suspicious actions led to his arrest.

Connecticut—Litchfield County; Trials

Schutze, Jim.

"My Husband's Trying to Kill Me!": A True Story of Money, Marriage, and Murderous Intent. HarperCollins, 1992.

Former showgirl Linda Edelman was living the high life with her real estate speculator husband Robert in the boomtown of Dallas during the 1970s. When things started to go sour economically, she decided to file for divorce. Then the FBI told her that her husband was trying to put out a contract on her life.

Divorce; Hit men; Texas—Dallas

Stannard, David E.

Honor Killing: How the Infamous "Massie Affair" Transformed Hawai'i. Viking, 2005.

Hawai'i in 1931 was not a workers' paradise, and things got worse when a white naval officer accused five native men of rape. The trial ended in a hung jury, but that did not keep Thalia Massie's mother and husband from arranging for the murder of one of the accused. This led to front page headlines, as world famous defender Charles Darwin arrived in the islands to defend the killer.

Hawai'i—Honolulu; Rape; Trials

Tucker, John C.

May God Have Mercy: A True Story of Crime and Punishment. Norton, 1997.

When Wanda Fay McCoy was raped and murdered in 1981, the police arrested the most likely suspect, her brother-in-law, Roger Coleman. Coleman had served time for sexual assault and he was tried, convicted, and sentenced to death based on the evidence. However, as time went by, the evidence became more and more tainted, and with the help of lawyer Kitty Behan, he fought against the order of execution.

Capital punishment; Virginia—Grundy; Trials

Weiss, Mike.

Double Play: The San Francisco City Hall Killings. Addison-Wesley, 1984.

In 1978 the nation was shocked when the mayor of San Francisco, George Moscone, and gay supervisor Harvey Milk were assassinated by a former supervisor named Dan White. What shocked the nation even more was that a jury could only convict the murderer of manslaughter.

Assassination; California—San Francisco; Trials

Criminals with Good Intentions

We make an assumption that some of the tortured characters in the novels included in this bibliography have good motives, or are "criminals with good intentions." Although their involvement in crime is inevitable, their reasons may be pure. One of the questions to be answered in these novels is whether the main character should get away with the criminal activity for a higher moral purpose. For other criminals, the question is the exact opposite: Why would a person, who seems to have everything, throw it all away by committing a criminal act? Why would someone whom the community assumes is pure of heart turn on another human with acts of unkindness?

Benchmark Criminals with Good Intentions Novels

Irish, William.

Phantom Lady. Lippincott, 1942.
> Roaming the streets in a bad mood, Scott Henderson picks up a woman because he likes her hat and takes her for a night on the town. When he arrives at home, he finds the police in his apartment because his wife Marcella has been murdered. Now, as his execution nears, he is relying on friends like Carol Richman to hunt for the mysterious stranger who can provide him with an alibi before he goes to the chair.

> Affairs; False accusations; Husbands and wives

I Married a Dead Man. Lippincott, 1948.
> Helen Georgesson is a troubled woman, eight months pregnant and abandoned by her lover, when she meets the lovely newlyweds Hugh and Patrice Hazzard on a train from New York. When a train wreck takes both of the young people's lives, it is relatively easy for Helen to be mistaken for and assume the life of Patrice. Easy, that is, until her past comes calling and she has to decide whether she wishes to live as Patrice or Helen.

> False identity; Railroads

Woolrich, Cornell.

Rendezvous in Black. Rinehart, 1948.
> When Johnny Marr's fiancée Dorothy is killed by a bottle that has been thrown from a passing plane, he decides to hunt down the men on the plane and exact his revenge. Rather than kill them, his plan is to kill their women.

> Revenge

Criminals with Good Intentions Novels

Atwood, Margaret.

The Blind Assassin. N.A. Talese, 2000.
> "Ten days after the war ended, my sister drove a car off the bridge." After that compelling opening sentence, Iris, an elderly woman suffering from a heart condition, begins to tell the story of her sister Laura. Laura's death in 1945, ruled an accident, is only the beginning of a family history that includes death, false love, and greed. Mysterious elements are introduced into Iris's life, including the strange

disappearance of her husband in a sailing accident and the death of Iris's daughter. The novel also introduces a science fiction work called *The Blind Assassin*—a book within the book. A companion story to Iris's reminiscences, this story eventually proves to be as much about Iris's life as it is a lavish tale of science fiction pulp writing. Atwood's complex novel intrigues readers, and finally reveals the horrific truths behind the incidents in Iris's life.

Canada—Port Ticonderoga; Great Depression (1929–1939); Sisters; Widows

Bardin, John Franklin.

The Deadly Percheron. Dodd Mead, 1946.
Dr. George Matthews is seeing his last patient of the day when he hears a story of leprechauns who pay to have the patient wear flowers in his hair and a request to deliver a horse to a Broadway actress. The patient, Jacob Blunt, thinks he might be crazy. The next day, when Blunt is arrested for the murder of Frances Raye, the most famous actress on Broadway, Matthews agrees to be his custodian before his trial. The problem is that the man in jail is not the man who came to his office, and this leads to the good doctor himself being incarcerated in a mental ward.

Actors and actresses; New York—New York; Psychiatrists

Baron, Alexander.

The Lowlife. UK: A. S. Barnes, 1963. (U.S.: Yoseloff, 1964).
Harryboy Boas is a man who has little connection to his fellow human beings except through the highs and lows of gambling at the dog or horse tracks. He finds no escape in the swinging sixties Soho scene or the books he loves to read. An obsession with the Deaner family leads to a mood swing that finds Harryboy deep in debt and deep in despair.

England—London; Gambling

Block, Lawrence.

[Bernie Rhodenbarr series].
Lawrence Block's series about bookstore owner and burglar Bernie Rhodenbarr features a criminal with a heart of gold. The following series titles are listed in order of publication.

Burglars Can't Be Choosers. Random House, 1977.
Bernie Rhodenbarr is a normal guy with an unusual occupation: burglar. When he is forced to do a job from a customer who wants a blue leather box stolen from a rich man's apartment, Bernie does not expect to meet two cops willing to go on the take, Ray Kirschmann and Loren Kramer. He also does not expect to have to hide from the police while they examine a corpse in the next room. Now instead of making a living, Bernie has to find a killer to keep himself out of jail.

Burglars; Frames; New York—New York

The Burglar in the Closet. Random House, 1978.

> While he has Craig Sheldrake's hands in his mouth, Bernie allows his dentist to talk him into stealing some diamonds from Crystal Sheldrake, his ex-wife. When Bernie finds the diamonds are gone and Crystal is dead via a dental instrument, he feels like he has been set up. It also means he has to spend time dodging his unwanted partner and nemesis, Detective Kirschmann.

> Dentists; Jewels; New York—New York

The Burglar Who Liked to Quote Kipling. Random House, 1979.

> Is Bernie going legitimate by opening a bookstore called Barnegat Books? What does it mean that his best friend is a lesbian dog groomer named Carolyn Kaiser? Evidently not all that much, as Bernie is interested in stealing a legendary anti-Semitic book by the famous Rudyard Kipling. When Bernie finds another corpse while trying to deliver the goods, he has to protect himself once again.

> Bookstores; Kipling, Rudyard; New York—New York

The Burglar Who Studied Spinoza. Random House, 1980.

> With Carolyn now firmly established as a sidekick in his burglary world, Bernie is set to take on more jobs. What he does not expect to find on the job is that another burglar has preceded them without taking the collection, a single rare coin. When he learns that bodies are discovered in the Colcannon's carriage house, he knows someone followed Carolyn and him onto the job. Meanwhile, Bernie works to fence the coin, which he did manage to steal the night of the burglary.

> Coins; New York—New York

The Burglar Who Painted Like Mondrian. Arbor House, 1983.

> When bookseller Bernie is asked to evaluate a book collection, he takes the opportunity to steal Gordon Onderdonk's stamp collection. Arriving home, he finds that his partner in crime Carolyn's cat has been catnapped and is being held for ransom. The prize is a Mondrian painting, which is held secure in the Hewlitt Museum, so Bernie decides to substitute the Mondiran hanging in Onderdonk's home.

> Mondrian, Piet; New York—New York; Stamps

The Burglar Who Traded Ted Williams. Dutton, 1994.

> After a decade running his bookstore and staying away from crime, Bernie suddenly finds that his new landlord, Borden Stoppelgard, wants to jack his rent ten grand a month. While Bernie is pulling a small-time operation to pay the rent, he stumbles on another corpse, this time in the bathtub. Worse, another burglar is stealing a rare baseball card collection, and the police want to pin that crime on Bernie. Not being able to use the corpse as an alibi, Bernie finds himself in the hot seat once again. Why not steal the cards from the thief and return them to their rightful owner?

> Baseball cards; New York—New York

The Burglar Who Thought He Was Bogart. Dutton, 1995.

While Bernie is romancing the beautiful foreigner, Ilona, by attending a Bogart film festival, he is also stealing a portfolio for a client named Hugo Candlemas. When Hugo goes missing, someone ends up dead, and the CIA ends up interested in what Bernie is doing, he discovers that there may be more to Ilona than he thought.

Bogart, Humphrey; New York—New York; Romance

The Burglar in the Library. Dutton, 1997.

Bernie drags Carolyn along with him to a New England bed and breakfast called Cuttleford House, when his girlfriend goes there to marry another man. However, he is also interested in stealing a signed copy of *The Big Sleep* from the inn's library. But when the whole crew is snowbound in the inn, and people start to die, Bernie finds himself scrambling to hide his secret identity in this new locale.

Bed and breakfasts; Libraries; New York—Pattaskinnick; Weddings

The Burglar in the Rye. Dutton, 1999.

Bernie is asked to break into the Paddington Hotel suite of literary agent Anthea Landau, who represented the reclusive writer, Gulliver Fairborn. The object is to steal the letters of the writer and give them to his former lover, Alice Cottrell. But instead Bernie discovers a corpse and falls under suspicion of murder by his nemesis, Kirschmann. His only choice is to try to sort it out by gathering all the suspects for a climactic finale.

Authors; New York—New York

The Burglar on the Prowl. Morrow, 2004.

While planning on breaking into a mobbed up plastic surgeon house in the Bronx, Bernie gets sidetracked when he breaks into a Manhattan apartment. He witnesses a rape, a tragedy that leads to a series of unfortunate incidents that involve his store, and his own apartment is also burglarized.

New York—New York; Rape

Bunker, Edward.

Dog Eat Dog. St. Martin's, 1996.

Troy Cameron is a Beverly Hills kid gone bad but now, having suffered the consequences of his actions, he wants to go clean. As a mastermind, his plan is to only rip off the bad guys. He partners with one guy named Mad Dog and another named Diesel, perhaps an indication of why things do not go the way he planned.

California—Los Angeles; Ex-convicts; Gangs

Clark, Robert.

Mr. White's Confession. Picador, 1998.

Herbert White, an odd fellow, records the minutiae of his life in notebooks and romances Hollywood starlets from a distance. A loner who loves photography, he amuses himself by taking pictures of the "taxi dancers" from the Aragon Ballroom. Then Charlene Mortensen, one of the girls, is found strangled. One month later, when Herbert's special friend Ruby Fahey is found murdered, Lieutenant Wesley Horner arrests Herbert. It seems like an easy case for the police, until Horner realizes Herbert's confession is not right. Herbert can only remember the distant past.

Amnesia; Memory; Minnesota—St. Paul

Collins, Max (Allan).

[Quarry series].

Quarry is a Vietnam veteran who works as a hired killer. The following series titles are listed in order of publication.

The Broker. Berkley, 1976. (Also *Quarry*).

Quarry is a hit man who takes his assignments from The Broker. When he takes out a victim and some heroin is involved, the hit man is not happy. So he travels to Port City and finds himself up against a conspiracy that leads right back to him and a confrontation that could cost him his life.

Drugs; Hit men; Port City

The Broker's Wife. Berkley, 1976. (Also *Quarry's List*).

Quarry knows that someone is going to exact revenge for his decision making in the previous book, so he is prepared when two hit men come to take him out. Although he manages to kill the first, the second man offers the one thing he needs: the name of who is seeking revenge on Quarry.

Hit men; Revenge

The Dealer. Berkley, 1976. (Also *Quarry's Deal*).

Quarry is on an assignment that allows him to romance one woman while lining up another for the kill. He is in possession of a list of hit man assignments, and his plan is to out the assassin to the victim and pick up some protection money. But things do not go according to plan.

Hit men

The Slasher. Berkley, 1977. (Also *Quarry's Cut*).

Quarry finds himself involved in the pornography business when someone puts out a hit on a skin flick film director. But when people start to die and Quarry is not the one doing the killing, he has to act like a detective to figure out who is the amateur in the killing business.

Hit men; Pornography

Primary Target. Foul Play Press, 1987. (Reprinted as *Quarry's Greatest Hits* [Five Star, 2003] with three additional short stories).

Quarry is living quietly, out of the game, in Paradise Lake, Wisconsin, with his pregnant wife Linda when he is offered a job to assassinate a presidential candidate. He turns the job down but loses his wife and brother-in-law during the bloodbath that follows. What the killers forgot was key: take out Quarry or be taken out.

Assassination

The Last Quarry. Hard Case Crime, 2006.

From his retirement home in the Minnesota woods, hit man Quarry returns to action from retirement when a rich Chicago media mogul puts more money in front of him than he can refuse. The question becomes, why would this man pay to have a young librarian named Janet Wright killed? When his old skills are difficult to rekindle and he realizes he has feelings for his victim, it is time for the hit man to ask himself hard questions.

Hit men; Homewood

The First Quarry. Hard Case Crime, 2008.

Quarry's roots are showing in this flashback novel that explains how he became a hit man. With his Vietnam experience and a few bad choices, Quarry became an agent for hire. The first case he was ever given involved taking out a college professor who had dallied with the wrong woman: the daughter of a Chicago mob boss.

Hit men; Iowa, Iowa City

Goines, Donald.

Daddy Cool. Holloway House, 1974.

As a hit man, Larry "Daddy Cool" Jackson is the man to call when you want a hit to go down. But he has to take a different route when his beloved daughter Janet falls under the spell of a pimp named Ronald. The problem is, his daughter may not want to be rescued.

Hit men; Michigan—Detroit; Prostitutes

Goodis, David.

The Burglar. Lion, 1953.

When Nat Harbin falls in love with the seductive Della, he decides to abandon his burglary gang. However, life on the outside of crime is also fraught with stress. His partners will not leave him alone, especially the suspicious men named Baylock and Rizzio. His love for Della will test his attempt to walk on the right side of the law.

Gangs; Jewels; Pennsylvania—Philadelphia

Black Friday. Lion, 1954.

Wandering the streets, trying to survive the cold while dodging the police, Hart comes across a man in the snow, dying. When the dying man offers

Hart his wallet, Hart is surprised to discover $11,000 in it. Shortly, some bad men try to take the wallet away from Hart and find him more than they bargained for. Held prisoner by the gang's leader, Charley, Hart is soon involved with the gang, two women, and the consequences of walking on the dark side.

Gangs; Pennsylvania—Philadelphia

Down There. Fawcett, 1956.

Eddie has tried to escape the family business with a career as a concert pianist, but when his wife commits suicide, he ends up playing piano in a dive called Harriet's Hut. When his brother Turley arrives and needs his protection from the two men who are after him, it draws Eddie out of his simple life and into the world of danger. His actions to save his brother lead him to a tragic loss and make him question his choices.

Brothers; Musicians; Pennsylvania—Philadelphia

Gores, Joe.

A Time of Predators. Random House, 1969.

Paula Halstead witnesses a gang beating. When the gang manages to track her down and rape her to keep her quiet, she commits suicide. This turns her husband, Professor Curtis Halstead, from an average man back into the commando he was in the military. Those skills will allow him to track down each of the four boys responsible for his wife's death.

California—Los Feliz; Revenge

Hamilton, Donald.

Night Walker. Dell, 1954. (UK: *Rough Company.* Wingate, 1954).

While hitchhiking, U.S. Navy Lieutenant David Young is picked up by a man named Larry Wilson. When David comes to in the hospital, his face is bandaged and everyone thinks he is Wilson, including his "wife." Worse, Wilson is wanted for treason.

False identity

Hassler, Jon.

The Love Hunter. Morrow, 1981.

Larry Quinn is dying of multiple sclerosis. His best friend is Chris MacKensie, with whom he teaches at the local college. Chris wants to take Larry on a hunting trip to make him forget his illness. Chris is also in love with Larry's wife Rachel and plans to kill his friend on the hunting trip.

Hunting; Mercy killings; Minnesota—Rookery

Hendricks, Vicki.

Miami Purity. Pantheon, 1995.

Having finished her career as a stripper and just got out of jail for killing her abusive husband Hank, Sherry is working at the local Miami Purity Dry Cleaners. She finds herself in lust with her boss, Payne Mahoney, but has little time for Payne's mother, who actually owns the business. That is, until Momma is all over Sherry's business and her baser instincts go to work again.

Dry cleaners; Florida—Miami

Highsmith, Patricia.

Those Who Walk Away. Doubleday, 1967.

Ray Garrett is on his honeymoon when his bride commits suicide. Because the Rome police believe that was the case, Ray is free to go. However, his father-in-law, painter Ed Coleman, is now determined to hunt down his son-in-law and seek revenge for the murder of his daughter. A shot is fired, someone survives, and two men circle each with murder in mind.

Fathers and daughters; Honeymoons; Italy—Rome; Italy—Venice; Suicide

Japrisot, Sébastien.

Un Long Dimanche de Fiançailles. France: Denoël, 1991 (U.S.: *A Very Long Engagement*, Plume, 1994).

When Mathilde Donnay loses her fiancé, Jean "Manech" Etchevery, to the trenches of World War I in 1917, she suffers like all war widows. When she is summoned to a French hospital in 1919 to meet with a dying sergeant named Daniel Esperanza, he informs her of the details of Manech's death. He was one of five soldiers who had mutilated their own hands to try to escape the horrors of war. The five soldiers were ordered over the wire at a location called Bingo Crépuscule, left to wander between the French and German lines with their hands tied, waiting to be executed by enemy fire. When Esperanza gives Mathilde a slight hope that Manech might have survived, she begins a search that will reveal the truth of what happened at Bingo Crépuscule.

Battlefield executions; France—Landes, Capbreton; France—Somme, Bingo Crépuscule; Handicapped; Historical; Trench warfare; War; World War I

Khadra, Yasmina.

L'attentat. France: Julliard, 2005. (U.S.: *The Attack.* Doubleday, 2006).

Dr. Amin Jaafari works in a Tel Aviv hospital, an example of how a Bedouin can represent his race well in Israeli society. Then one night the police inform him that his wife has died in a terrorist attack. They also inform him that her injuries are consistent with those of the attackers.

Israel, Tel Aviv; Marriage; Palestinian–Israeli relations; Terrorism

Lee, Harper.

To Kill a Mockingbird. Lippincott, 1960.

Jean "Scout" Finch tells us the story of her home town of Maycomb, Alabama. Over a three-year period, she details the consequences of her lawyer father Atticus Finch's decision to defend a black man, Tom Robinson. Robinson has been accused of raping a white woman named Mavella

Ewell. Scout, her brother Jem, and their friend Dill Harris have many coming-of-age experiences over the course of the novel, including witnessing the racial prejudice of their small town and the mystery of their neighborhood boogeyman, "Boo" Radley.

African Americans; Alabama—Maycomb; Coming-of-age; Race relations; Rape; South, The; Trials

Lehane, Dennis.

Mystic River. Morrow, 2001.

Twenty-five years prior to the main action of this novel, three childhood friends in a blue-collar Boston neighborhood are playing on the street when one makes the mistake of getting into the car of a pedophile. Missing for four days, the young boy returns to grow up in his neighborhood. In the main action of the book, the lives of the three men now intersect when one man's daughter is murdered, one friend is the investigator, and one is the chief suspect in the case.

Children in jeopardy; Coming-of-age; Friendship; Massachusetts—Boston, East Buckingham

Manchette, Jean-Patrick.

La Position du Tireur Couché. France: Editions Gallimard, 1981. (U.S.: *The Prone Gunman.* City Lights, 2002).

Martin Terrier is a hit man, but he wants to give it all up to marry his girlfriend, Anne. However, the organization that he works for is not willing to lose him to retirement and takes his life savings. His employer would like him to take out one more man, an Arab sheik named Hakim, before calling it quits. Nothing goes as planned.

France; Hit men

Meyer, Deon.

Infanta. South Africa: Afrikaans, 2004 (U.S.: *Devil's Peak.* Little, Brown, 2008).

When former mercenary Thobela Mpayipheli's son is murdered in a gas station robbery and the perpetrators go free, he goes on a crusade to take out the people who prey on children in South Africa. Eventually anointed as the media hero Artemis, he is hunted by Detective Inspector Benny Griessel. Griessel is an alcoholic who needs to redeem his career and his personal life. He finds an unusual ally in Christine Van Rooyen, a Cape Town sex worker, when her daughter goes missing.

Pedophilia; Revenge; South Africa—Cape Town

Mills, Mark.

Amagansett. Putnam, 2004. (UK: *The Whaleboat House.* Fourth Estate, 2004).

Amagansett is a fishing community on the tip of Long Island. In 1947, a Basque fisherman named Conrad Labarde and his only friend, Rollo Kemp, pull the body of a beautiful woman from the ocean in their fishing net. Dismissed as a suicide by the police, the case disturbs Deputy Police Chief Tom Hollis so much that he keeps investigating on his own. Unknown to Hollis, the death has also upset Labarde, and the fisherman has decided to investigate the death as well.

Basque Americans; Fishermen; Historical; New York—Long Island, Amagansett; World War II

Nunn, Kem.

Tijuana Straits. Scribner, 2004.
Sam Fahey is an ex-con farming worms who dreams of his former surfing days and catching the "Mystic Peak." His chance meeting with a Mexican worker named Magdalena Rivera, who is investigating the environment on the Tijuana border, finds him embroiled in the lives of the workers in the foreign-owned factory there. When a killer named Armando Santoya decides that his mission is to remove the reformer, it places Sam in a situation in which he has to decide to rejoin the world.

California—Tijuana River Valley; Environment; Mexican–American border; Pollution

O'Connell, Jack.

The Skin Palace. Mysterious, 1996.
Sylvia Krafft has found some old negatives locked in an antique camera, and now she wants to discover things about the photographer. The person to ask is Hugo Schick, owner of the town's pornographic theater, Herzog's Erotic Palace. There she finds Jakob Kinsky, the son of the town's mob boss, who is trying to avoid the family business and start a film career. Can these two keep Dad from taking over Hugo's business?

Massachusetts—Quinsigamond; Movie theaters; Photography

Picoult, Jodi.

Plain Truth. Washington Square Press, 2000.
Katie Fisher is a teenaged Amish farm girl in Lancaster, Pennsylvania. When she is accused by the outside world of having smothered her newborn child, she denies both the birth and the murder. Through a family connection, Philadelphia attorney Ellie Hathaway takes her case, only to find the judge assigning her to live on the Amish farm as a condition of Katie's bail. While living on the farm, Ellie must confront the truths in her own life while trying to force Katie to do the same.

Amish; Infanticide; Pennsylvania—Lancaster; Teenaged mothers

Setterfield, Diane.

The Thirteenth Tale. Atria, 2006.
Vida Winter is one of England's most celebrated authors, and she has selected Margaret Lea to be her biographer. This proves to be a daunting task, as Vida has been telling tall tales about her life for over sixty years. However, now that she is dying, Vida has decided to tell Margaret all

about the English estate where there was a fire with devastating consequences for the twin girls who lived there with their governess. Not to mention the mad woman in the attic. All of this dissembling opens Margaret up to examining her own past, which appears to have an eerie parallel to Vida's story.

Authors; Biographers; England—Cambridge; England—Yorkshire; Ghosts; Haunted houses

Smith, Mitchell.

Stone City. Simon & Schuster, 1990.

Bauman, a history professor jailed for a drunk driving–related death, is forced to act as a detective when two inmates are murdered in the prison where he is being held. The question becomes, how will an ordinary man deal with the very scary and divided prison residents who make up the prison population.

Prisons

Thompson, Jim.

Recoil. Lion Books, 1953.

Pat Cosgrove has been in jail for fifteen years for bank robbery when he suddenly finds himself paroled into the good graces of Dr. Roland Luther. Set up with everything he wants, he realizes his life will not settle down until he finds out what the good doctor wants from him. Dr. Luther is a psychologist, working with local politicians, and appears to be willing to give up everything, including his ex-wife Madeline, to influence the ex-con. Then Pat finds out he may need to worry more about Madeline than about Roland.

Ex-convicts; Psychologists; Unknown state—capital city

Waiwaiole, Lono.

[Wiley series].

The hard-knocks life of Wiley is displayed with grim consequences by Lono Waiwaiole. The following series titles are listed in order of publication.

Wiley's Lament. St. Martin's Minotaur, 2003.

Wiley is eking out a living playing poker and robbing drug dealers. When his estranged daughter, Lizzie, is found murdered in a motel, Wiley believes her death ties in to Oregon's sex trade and its leader, Leon. This is difficult for Wiley because Leon is a friend, and when the truth turns the two in different directions with similar missions, they unite in a fight to reap revenge.

Drug Enforcement Agency; Drugs; Fathers and daughters; Oregon—Portland; Sex industry

Wiley's Shuffle. St. Martin's Minotaur, 2004.

Dookie, a Portland pimp, is threatening a hooker named Miriam who is close to Wiley, so he saddles up with Leon to settle the score. Their quest takes them to two other cities before they return home for the inevitable showdown.

Nevada—Las Vegas; California—Los Angeles; Oregon—Portland; Pimps; Prostitutes

Wiley's Refrain. St. Martin's Minotaur, 2005.

A jazz musician named Ronnie has been murdered. Wiley and Leon decide to hunt down his killer; they focus their efforts on a music promoter who uses thugs to enforce his will. While hunting for a killer from outside his family, Wiley still wrestles with his own inner demons and his regrets about his personal life. When the trail takes him to his ancestral home and the land of his deceased father, Wiley finds himself on the Big Island.

Hawai'i—Big Island; Musicians; Oregon—Portland; Poker

Walter, Jess.

Citizen Vince. ReganBooks, 2005.

In Spokane, Washington, Vince Camden is living a strange life in the Witness Protection Program. He can run the same scams that brought him to the attention of the authorities, gamble with some low-life equals, and dream about moving into the life of a regular, upright citizen. Then the world of his new identity begins to shatter when his partners get greedy, someone tries to muscle into his scam, and the cops get nosy.

Historical; Hit man; Organized crime; Washington—Spokane; Witness Protection Program

Wignall, Kevin.

For the Dogs. Simon & Schuster, 2004.

Ella Hatto is vacationing in Italy when her entire family is wiped out by a mob hit. Turning to the body guard sent to watch over her by her now dead father, Ella talks Stephen Lucas into a plan to avenge the death of her relatives. Lucas had retired from the hit man business, but now he has to decide if he wants in or out of the big plan.

Bodyguards; Hit men; Italy—Tuscany; Revenge

Winslow, Don.

The Death and Life of Bobby Z. Knopf, 1997.

As a three-time loser who has a prison contract on his head, Tim Kearney agrees to a proposal from the DEA: impersonate a drug smuggler named Bobby Z and get traded for an agent who is being held captive. When things do not go according to the DEA's plan, Tim finds himself on the outside but with none of the pleasures he had anticipated. Instead, he becomes Bobby Z.

California; Drug Enforcement Agency; Drugs

Woodrell, Daniel.

Give Us a Kiss. Holt, 1996.

When crime novelist Doyle Redmond needs to leave a messy divorce behind in California, he returns to his family in the Ozarks for a little rest and recreation. By helping his brother Smoke bring in the fall harvest of marijuana, he finds work and a little play with a local woman he falls for. He also finds himself deep in a feud between his family and the infamous Dollys. When he is done, he is finally the famous man he wants to be.

Drugs; Families; Missouri—Ozarks

True Criminals with Good Intentions

Alexandra, Shana.

Very Much a Lady: The Untold Story of Jean Harris and Dr. Herman Tarnower. Little, Brown, 1983.

When best-selling Scarsdale diet author and physician Dr. Herman Tarnower was shot by his lover, educator Jean Harris, the nation's interest was peaked. Did Harris go to Tarnower's house to commit suicide, and did the good doctor die saving her life, or did she shoot him four times in cold blood?

Affairs; Doctors; New York—Purchase; Virginia—McLean

Brand, Christianna.

Heaven Knows Who. Scribner's, 1960.

When servant Jess M'Pherson's body was discovered by her friend Jessie M'Lachlan, Jessie did not expect to be charged with the deed. In 1862, police work was sketchy, and this was the first case handled by the newly formed Glasgow Police Detective Branch. Although Jess's employer, the eighty-seven-year-old James Fleming, stood accused during the trial, it was Jessie who was sentenced to death.

Scotland—Glasgow; Trials

Carcaterra, Lorenzo.

Sleepers. Ballantine, 1995.

When four childhood friends from New York City's Hell's Kitchen grew up as punks, they pulled one too many pranks, and a man was almost killed. Sent to the Wilkinson Home for Boys, they chose different paths. Two of the boys became mob hit men and found themselves about to be prosecuted by one of their old pals from Hell's Kitchen. The fourth boy tells the tale.

New York—New York; Reform schools; Trials

Cornwell, John.

Earth to Earth. Allen Lane, 1982. (U.S.: Ecco, 1982).

When the police were called to an isolated farm near Winkleigh, they discovered the brutally slaughtered bodies of Alan, Robbie, and Frances Luxtons. The Luxtons had been recluses, living on a farm that had been in their family since the fourteenth century. Centuries of family history is displayed here to explain what led to the deaths of these souls trapped in a long forgotten past.

England—Mid-Devon, Winkleigh; Families; Farms; Suicide

Feuerlight, Roberta Strauss.

Justice Crucified: The Story of Sacco and Vanzetti. McGraw-Hill, 1977.

Nicola Sacco and Bartolomeo Vanzetti have stood through time as the romanticized and persecuted radicals who were falsely accused of the deaths of a paymaster and guard at a South Braintree, Massachusetts —shoe factory. Feuerlight's research tries to reveal what we really know about their crimes and punishments and the rush to judgment about their guilt.

Massachusetts—Braintree; Massachusetts—Denham; Radicals; Sacco and Vanzetti; Trials

Finkel, Michael.

True Story: Murder, Memoir, Mea Culpa. HarperCollins, 2005.

Michael Finkel was about to be fired from his *New York Times* magazine job when he was charged with falsifying a character contained in a story he wrote about child labor in Mali. At the same time, a tip led him to a bizarre discovery: a murderer named Christian Longo had just been arrested in Mexico, living under the false identity of Michael Finkel, reporter. Once able to make contact, Finkel and Longo fell into a dance, each trying to gain the upper hand and escape his fate.

False identity; Oregon—Lincoln County

Harrison, Kathryn.

While They Slept: An Inquiry into the Murder of a Family. Random House, 2008.

When Billy Gilley Jr. killed his parents and his eleven-year-old sister, he freed himself and his sixteen-year-old sister Jody from the abuse their parents had heaped on them. Years later, in interviews with the author, the two siblings, one in jail for life and the other a communications strategist, shared their differing views on what happened in their lives, that night, and why their younger sister had to die.

Oregon—Medford; Parricide

Holmes, Paul.

The Sheppard Murder Case. David McKay, 1961.

Marilyn Sheppard, the pregnant wife of Dr. Sam Sheppard, was beaten to death in her home in Bay Village on the Fourth of July in 1954. Her husband was put on trial and convicted of her murder. This book was the first to suggest that he was innocent.

Ohio—Bay Village; Trials

Horne, Jed.

Desire Street: A True Story of Death and Deliverance in New Orleans. Farrar, Straus & Giroux, 2005.

Curtis Kyles was arrested for the murder of Delores Dye based on the evidence found in his house, including the murder weapon. But even a case with concrete evidence like this can have strange twists and turns. Five trials and fourteen years later, Curtis Kyles found himself once again wondering if he would ever be a free man.

Louisiana—New Orleans; Trials

Junger, Sebastian.

A Death in Belmont. Norton, 2006.

In the midst of the reign of terror of the Boston Strangler, a woman named Bessie Goldberg was strangled to death in the suburb of Belmont. Roy Smith, a black man who was working on Goldberg's house, was arrested and convicted for her murder. However, it was revealed later that a man named Albert DeSalvo had also been working in construction in that neighborhood that time, on the house of one of Goldberg's neighbors.

Boston Strangler; Massachusetts—Boston; Race relations

Keyes, Daniel.

Unveiling Claudia: A True Story of Serial Murder. Bantam, 1986.

When the owner of the Eldorado Club, his dancer girlfriend, and his elderly mom were all found murdered with a .22 caliber weapon, the case seemed initially straightforward to the investigating police. This was especially true when Claudia Yasko approached the police with a confession. But while she was waiting for trial, more murders with the same weapon took place. Now investigators not only had to find a murderer but also to explain a false confession that contained details only the perpetrator should know.

False confessions; Ohio—Columbus

Lefkowitz, Bernard.

Our Guys: The Glen Ridge Rape and the Secret Life of the Perfect Suburb. University of California Press, 1997.

Why would successful and respected high school football stars in the upscale town of Glen Ridge, New Jersey, commit a horrific crime? Why would they entice a seventeen-year-old girl with the mental age of an eight-year-old into their clutches? Why would they rape her with a baseball bat and a broomstick? Why would none of the thirteen boys involved in this incident report it as a crime?

High school athletics; New Jersey—Glen Ridge; Rape

McDougal, Dennis.

In the Best of Families: The Anatomy of a True Tragedy. Warner, 1994.

While father Roy Miller was a successful attorney within the Ronald Reagan inner circle, his wife Marguerite had to deal with two troubled sons. She tried to raise them in a religious setting with a steady diet of health foods. Oldest son Jeffrey, after attending Dartmouth, fell into Christian fundamentalism, went through a rough deprogramming, and eventually committed suicide. Michael, in the clutches of mental illness, raped and clubbed his mother to death.

California— Palos Verdes Estates; Mental health; Mothers and sons

McNamara, Eileen.

Breakdown: Sex, Suicide, and the Harvard Psychiatrist. Pocket, 1994.

After entering Harvard Medical School, student Paul Lozano had adjustment difficulties. He turned to psychotherapist Dr. Margaret Bean-Bavog, who regressed Paul back to age three and became his pseudo-mother. When she ended her relationship with Paul he committed suicide, and his parents sued her.

Massachusetts—Cambridge; Psychotherapy; Suicide

O'Brien, Darcy.

Murder in Little Egypt. Morrow, 1989.

Dr. John Dale Cavaness was a small town success, having moved away to gain a medical degree and moved back to Saline County to become a pillar of the community. Known as a kind and considerate man at work, few knew of his violent temper, his wife beating, and the tormenting of his four sons. Eventually, two suffered the ultimate consequences of their father's desperate nature.

Fathers and sons; Illinois—Saline County; Physicians

Protess, David, and Rob Warden.

Gone in the Night: The Dowaliby Family's Encounter with Murder and the Law. Delacorte, 1993.

One night seven-year-old Jaclyn Dowaliby disappeared from her home, only to be found dead four days later. When the police became desperate for a solution, they charged both parents. One went to jail. Protess and Warden's investigation led to a new trial.

Children in jeopardy; Husbands and wives; Illinois—Midlothian; Trials

Rubinstein, Julian.

Ballad of the Whiskey Robber: A True Story of Bank Heists, Ice Hockey, Transylvanian Pelt Smuggling, Moonlighting Detectives and Broken Hearts. Little, Brown, 2004.

In the 1990s, Attila Ambrus moved to Hungary from his native Transylvania. After proving a financial failure as the third-string goalie for one of the best hockey teams, he turned to a life of crime. Working a variety of schemes, he made millions, became a legend in his adopted country, and still occasionally played hockey.

Capers; Hungary; Hockey

Russell, Francis.

Tragedy in Dedham: The Story of the Sacco-Vanzetti Case. McGraw-Hill, 1971.
Russell had the benefit of hindsight and new research to cast a fresh light on the two radicals, Nicola Sacco and Bartolomeo Vanzetti. Were they properly prosecuted for the crimes they committed? Or were they falsely accused, deserving to become cultural icons?

Massachusetts—Braintree; Massachusetts—Denham; Radicals; Sacco and Vanzetti; Trials

Schiller, Lawrence.

Cape May Court House. HarperCollins, 2002.
When Eric Thomas sued the Ford Motor Company for the wrongful death of his wife Tracy, he seemed like an angry widow and single father. When doctors determined that Tracy had died from manual strangulation, not from a faulty air bag, Eric found he had some explaining to do.

Auto accidents; New Jersey—Cape May Court House; Trials

Wolfe, Linda.

Wasted: The Preppie Murder. Simon and Schuster, 1989.
This case drew the attention of the nation when the accused attempted to use a "rough sex" defense. When Robert Chambers and Jennifer Levin had sex in Central Park, Robert claimed that things got out of hand and he strangled Jennifer because she was too wild. The defense suggested that he had been brought up as a revered male who was now a sociopath. It was left for the jury to decide.

New York—New York; Sex; Trials

On the Run

Novels in which the character is on the run are the roller-coaster rides of crime. The person in motion can be either a criminal evading the administration of justice or a victim trying to outpace a pursuing criminal. The appeal of this type of literature is both the suspense and the thrill. The suspense asks whether or not the character will be caught. The thrill comes from the fast pacing and the author's ability to raise the reader's heart rate by creating empathy.

Benchmark On the Run Novel

Collins, Wilkie.

Armadale. UK: Smith, Elder, 1866. (U.S.: Harper, 1866).
> One young man, Ozias Midwinter, struggles against a legacy of murder and denial of his heritage, while another young man, Allan Armadale, lives a life using a name not his. By fate, the two meet, and their lives become even more intertwined when they fall under the spell of the real Alan Armadale's mother's maid, Lydia Gwilt. Lydia is looking for love and revenge, a deadly combination.

> England—Norfolk, Thorpe Ambrose; False identity; Families

On the Run Novels

Bigsby, Christopher.

Beautiful Dreamer. UK: Methuen, 2002. (U.S.: Thomas Dunne, 2006).
> When a black man walks through the front door of a white man's business in Tennessee, the effrontery would be enough to get him lynched without the additional accusation of rape by the store owner's wife. This plot alone might be enough to propel the novel, but the real story begins when a white man who witnessed the confrontation makes a verbal defense of the black man and is branded with an "N." He is forced to go on the run with the lynched man's son, and the novel becomes a tale of redemption and a journey of discovery.

> Hate crimes; Lynching; Race relations; Tennessee

Brown, Fredric.

Night of the Jabberwock. Dutton, 1950.
> Doc Stoeger puts the Carmel City *Clarion* out each Friday morning, so there is not a Thursday night that passes without him wishing for more to write about than the local flea market dates. On this particular Thursday, through the haze of alcohol and local shenanigans, he is going to witness criminal activities the likes of which his town has never seen. With the help of some knowledge of Lewis Carroll, he will make sense of the weird happenings on this one night.

> Carroll, Lewis; Illinois—Carmel City; Journalists; Newspapers

Choi, Susan.

A Person of Interest. Viking, 2008.
> Wen Ho Lee is an undistinguished math professor with an unsuccessful personal life that includes two failed marriages and an estranged daughter, Esther. When a mail bomb injures a colleague, Lee finds himself

slightly satisfied that the popular young Dr. Hendley has been hurt. Lee finds his remorseless behavior has gotten him targeted as "The Brain Bomber," a terrorist who has menaced prominent thinkers. Then Lee receives a missive from the past from a former friend named Gaither that makes him think he is being set up for things in his past that he has always run from.

Asian Americans; Bombs; Terrorists

Chute, Verne.

Flight of an Angel. Morrow, 1946.

The man's first memories are of standing on a Los Angeles street corner. When he discovers that his name is Jamey-Boy Raider and that he is a mechanic at a defense plant, it means nothing. Nor does he recognize the blond stripper named Violet Manners, with whom he lives. As he begins to put together the pieces of the puzzle, he does not like the direction that his "new" life is taking him. Especially when a local hood named Norm Severen decides to put him away.

Amnesia; California—Los Angeles

Colapinto, John.

About the Author. HarperCollins, 2001.

Bookstore stock boy Cal Cunningham has always had big dreams of being a novelist. When Cal discovers his lawyer roommate Stewart has actually written (but not published) a pretty good novel based on Cal's miserable life, he is jealous. So when Stewart dies in a bike accident, Cal decides to pass off the work as his own. It all works well until someone threatens to reveal the fraud.

Authors; Forgery; New York—New York; Vermont—New Halcyon

Cook, Thomas H.

The Chatham School Affair. Bantam, 1996.

This novel represents the memories of attorney Henry Griswald, who carries the guilt for actions taken in 1926. Henry's father was headmaster of Chatham School when he hired Elizabeth Channing to teach art there. The emotional impact she had on the boys and on one teacher, Leland Reed, led to a series of tragic events and deaths. As the story is slowly revealed, incident by incident, the reader discovers who may be responsible for the actions that occurred on Black Pond so many years before.

Academia; Affairs; Massachusetts—Cape Cod, Chatham; Historical; Private schools

Master of the Delta. Harcourt, 2008.

Jack Branch has returned to his hometown to teach high school. He encourages a young man named Eddie to write a paper about his father, who was The Coed Killer. As the two explore the past, they realize they are discovering more than just the facts about Eddie's dad.

Fathers and sons; Historical; Mississippi—Lakeland

Doolittle, Sean.

Dirt. Uglytown, 2001.

Quince Bishop is burying his best friend when some ecoterrorists bust up the funeral, so Quince busts up a few of them. Falling under the spell of the head of the group, Maria Casteneda, he soon finds himself undercover with the group. All of this is at the encouragement of Quince's ex-girl-friend, a journalist named Melanie Roth, who can sense a story.

California—Los Angeles; Funerals; Journalists; Undertakers

Burn. Uglytown, 2003.

When Gregor Tavlin, a famous fitness instructor, is found dead in his Alfa Romeo in a wildfire outside of L.A., the findings indicate homicide. The case falls to Adam Timms, who teams up with a retired arson-for-hire mobster named Andrew Kindler. Kindler, who just wanted to retire from the heat of his East Coast mob connections, finds himself working on the right side of the law to keep out of jail.

California—Los Angeles; Wildfires

The Cleanup. Dell, 2006.

Matthew Worth is a cop who works security at an Omaha supermarket, where he has fallen for a checkout girl named Gwen. When Gwen whacks her boyfriend, she expects Matthew to take pity on her and help. And he does.

Drugs; Nebraska—Omaha; Romance

Rain Dogs. Dell, 2006.

When Chicago journalist Tom Coleman's daughter dies and his marriage fails, he moves to his home state of Nebraska to manage a campground and canoe rental business. He manages to drink himself into oblivion, until one night his old journalist skills are needed when a local corrupt policeman comes calling for him after a drug lab explodes in Tom's backyard.

Drugs; Nebraska—Valentine; Police corruption

Earling, Debra Magpie.

Perma Red. BlueHen, 2002.

Louise White Elk is pursued throughout her life by the magical Baptiste Yellow Knife. She rebels against his constraining love and the abusive poverty of life on the Flathead Indian Reservation in the 1940s. Her life is observed by tribal police office Charlie Kicking Woman, a man who walks in both the white and native worlds and is obsessed with Louise. As time passes and desperate measures are taken, Louise's affair with white businessman Harvey Stoner leads to a series of events that bring even more tragedy into these damaged and dysfunctional lives.

Coming-of-age; Flathead Indians; Historical; Montana—Flathead Indian Reservation; Montana—Perma; Native Americans; Poverty; Reservations; Runaways; Salish

Ellis, David.

Line of Vision. Putnam, 2001.

Investment banker Marty Kalish has been having an affair with a married woman named Rachel Reinhardt. When her husband Derrick disappears, Marty becomes suspect number one. Eventually Marty is arrested and goes on trial. Marty is guilty of something, but exactly what is only explained as the novel unfolds. One thing is certain: Marty's narrative is not to be trusted.

Illinois—Highland Woods; Trials; Triangles (Interpersonal relations)

Faust, Christa.

Money Shot. Hard Case Crime, 2008.

Angel Dare has retired from the pornography business to open Daring Angels, an adult modeling and talent agency. To her surprise, she is asked by old friend Sam Hammer to make one last appearance on the silver screen as a substitute hitter. She agrees and is beaten, raped, shot, and left to die in the trunk of a Honda Civic. Turning to security cop Lalo Malloy for support, Angel decides to seek revenge.

California—Van Nuys; Pornography; Revenge

Fearing, Kenneth.

The Big Clock. Harcourt Brace, 1946 (Also published as *No Way Out.* Perennial, 1987).

Janoth Enterprises is an all-encompassing organization that rules its employees' lives. It publishes *Crimeways*, a true crime magazine, and one of its writers is George Stroud. He is at the organization's mercy when it asks him to investigate the murder of Pauline Delos, because Stroud knows he is the culprit.

New York—New York; Publishing

Fergus, Jim.

The Wild Girl: The Notebooks of Ned Giles, 1932. Hyperion, 2005.

Ned Giles is a teenaged photographer who volunteers to join The Great Apache Expedition. The expedition is going into the Sierra Madre Mountains of Mexico to hunt for a kidnapped seven-year-old boy. Leaving from Douglas, Arizona, the expedition team is made up of an odd combination of adventurers, scientists, newspapermen, and even a gay college student. What begins as high adventure turns wicked under the leadership of Chief of Police Leslie Gatlin, especially after the capture of La Niña Bronca, the wild girl the expedition will try to use as trade bait for the boy. With the added perspective Ned receives from the two Native Americans who are the guides for the expedition, he begins to think that the real crime may not be the first kidnapping.

Apaches; Coming-of-age; Mexico—Sonora, Bauispe; Photography; Westerns

Gischler, Victor.

The Pistol Poets. Delacorte, 2004.

1

Jay Morgan is trying to survive in the academic world as a poet, but the dead coed in his bed is not going to help. When Fred Jones makes the body disappear in exchange for some poetry evaluation, Morgan thinks he is in the clear, until a PI appears on his tail. When one of his graduate students turns out to be a drug runner named Harold Jenks, who is on the run and is using a dead student's identity to get by at college, it means someone is going to show up on campus looking for his drugs and some revenge.

2

Academia; Drugs; Oklahoma—Fumbee

Shotgun Opera. Dell, 2006.

3

Mike Foley is hiding from his past in Oklahoma and surviving by making wine. But his nephew, Andrew Foley, is on the run from some mob guys in New York and needs his help. The mob has sent a professional hit woman named Nikki Enders to take him out, and Uncle Mike is going to have to revive some old skills to save the farm.

Assassination; Hit men; Oklahoma; Organized crime

4

Goodis, David.

Dark Passage. Messner, 1946.

5

San Quentin cannot hold Vince Parry, who is desperate to escape and prove his innocence. Falsely accused of murdering his wife, he meets a woman named Irene Jannery, who is willing to help him find justice. Along the way he makes desperate choices, including plastic surgery to hide his identity from the cops and to let him get close to the real killer.

6

California—San Francisco; False identity; Prison breaks

Nightfall. Messner, 1947.

While on his way to a new job in Chicago, Donald Vanning innocently became involved in a bank robbery. When the gang forced him to cooperate, they had no idea he would take off with the loot, or that he would kill one of their members, even in self-defense. Now Vanning is hiding in New York and hoping that neither the police nor the criminals will be able to find him. Then one night he meets a woman named Martha.

7

Bank robbery; Gangs; New York—New York

8

Street of No Return. Fawcett, 1954.

Eugene "Whitey" Lindell is a former singer whose life with Celia led to alcoholism and his downfall. Celia belonged to gang leader Sharkey, and when Whitey refused to give her up, he lost his career as a result of the physical injuries from a beating and lost his voice to the bottle. Years later, Whitey sees one of the men who beat him and has to make a choice between staying in his personal fog or seeking the revenge most men would crave. Soon a cop is dead, there is a race riot, and the once withdrawn Whitey finds himself in the midst of the danger.

9

10

Alcoholism; Revenge; Riots

The Wounded and the Slain. Fawcett, 1955.

James Bevan has decided to save his marriage to his wife Cora by taking her on a vacation to Jamaica. Once there, James is forced to murder a robber. Before he can leave, James feels obligated to try to clear the man who is falsely accused of the crime he committed. Meanwhile, Cora has begun to stray from her marriage vows, and James must decide if she is worth saving.

Husbands and wives; Jamaica—Kingston

Gottlieb, Eli.

Now You See Him. Morrow, 2008.

When Nick Framingham learns that his childhood friend, Rob Castor, has murdered his girlfriend. Kate Pierce. in Manhattan, he begins to obsess about the memories of their relationship. As Caster remains on the loose, Nick falls further and further into a paranoid state of mind as he examines his childhood, his parents, his wife and kids, and his job. All of these ruminations circle around Rob, and as new details are revealed to the reader, the reason for Nick's state of mind are revealed, right up to the shocking conclusion.

Fathers and sons; Friendship; New York—Monarch; Paranoia

Green, Norman.

Way Past Legal. HarperCollins, 2004.

Ex-con Manny Williams and his son are on the run after Manny rips off his former partner in crime, Rosey. Forced to lay over in Maine, the two adopt their new surroundings. When Rosey comes calling, Manny has to decide whether to stand and defend his new friends or cut and run again.

Ex-convicts; Maine—Machias

Highsmith, Patricia.

The Two Faces of January. Doubleday, 1964.

Rydal Keener is an expatriate American whose money is running out in Athens. His law degree comes in handy when he becomes involved in the death of a policeman at the hands of the rich American businessman Chester MacFarland. With MacFarland and his wife Colette, Rydal helps hide the body and then joins the duo on the lam. The question is how long this trio can remain a trio.

Crete; Greece—Athens; Triangles (Interpersonal relations)

Hoffman, William.

Tidewater Blood. Algonquin Books, 1998.

Vietnam vet and ex-con Charles Le Blanc is the black sheep of his blue-blood Virginia family, living on his own in his shack in the woods. When a bomb kills Charles's older brother, wife, and children while they are celebrating the 250th anniversary of his family at their ancestral home, Bellerive, Charles becomes suspect number one. When the evidence is not strong enough to hold him, his first choice is to flee to Montana. But when he discovers someone has pursued him, Charles decides to find out who killed his family.

Family feuds; Montana; Virginia—Tidewater; West Virginia

Hopley, George.

Fright. Rinehart, 1950.

When Prescott Marshall strays from the path with a woman named Leona just before his intended marriage to his girl, Marjorie, he ends up killing the prostitute when her demands for money get out of hand. Fleeing with Marjorie to a job in a small town far from New York, Prescott finds that his life is no better there, because he cannot forget the corpse he left behind.

Infidelity

Hunter, Stephen.

Dirty White Boys. Random House, 1994.

Lamar Pye, his cousin Odell, and a third prisoner named Richard Peed bust out of the Oklahoma State Penitentiary and race across the country-side on a crime spree. Chased by state troopers, the gang picks up a young girl who murdered her parents and worships convicts. What the quartet does not expect is the dogged pursuit of one Sergeant Bud Pewtie, determined to revenge a weakness that may have set off this entire affair.

Oklahoma; Prison breaks; Texas

Irish, William.

Deadline at Dawn. Lippincott, 1944.

By sheer coincidence, Bricky Coleman, a dance hall girl for hire in New York, is from the same Iowa home town as a customer she meets, Quinn Williams. When circumstances make him look guilty of murder and pit Quinn against the clock, he finds Bricky an unlikely ally in hunting through the streets of New York for a murderer.

New York—New York

Kernick, Simon.

The Murder Exchange. UK: Bantam, 2003. (U.S.: St. Martin's Minotaur, 2003).

Max Iversson, a former mercenary, now works as a bodyguard. When a case he is on goes wrong and the client, club owner Ray Fowler, and two of his staff are murdered, he goes on the run from the killers and the cops. Chasing him is Detective Sergeant John Gallan, a man eager to right his ship and regain his position as inspector. The two narrators share the book, and each has a part of the solution, if they could just learn to trust each other.

Bodyguards; England—London; Nightclubs

Lankford, Terrill Lee.

Earthquake Weather. Ballantine, 2004.

Mark Hayes hates his boss, Dexter Morton, but slugs out a career in Hollywood as a development executive for the movie producer. When Morton ends up dead in his pool, murdered during an earthquake, Hayes finds himself suspect number one.

California—Hollywood; Earthquakes; Motion pictures

Manchette, Jean-Patrick.

Petit Bleu de la Côte ouest. Gallimard, 1976. (U.S.: *Three to Kill*, City Lights, 2002).
When business manager Georges Gerfaut witnesses a murder, he becomes the target of two hit men, named Carol and Bastien. Despite going on the run, Gerfaut decides that this might be a defining moment in his life, and soon the tables are being turned on Mr. Taylor, the man who ordered the hit.

France—Paris; Hit men;

Marlowe, Dan J.

The Name of the Game Is Death. Gold Medal, 1962. (UK: *Operation Overkill*, Coronet, 1973).
A man who calls himself Roy Martin (or Chet Arnold) has been a criminal his entire life. After robbing a bank in Phoenix and killing three men, he is on the lam with a bullet wound. When his partner, Bunny, takes off to Florida with most of the money, Bunny agrees to mail some of it back for Martin. When the envelopes stop coming, Martin decides to go on the warpath to avenge his friend and safeguard the money. Marlowe later turned this character (known later as Earl Drake) into a series hero as a secret agent.

Arizona—Phoenix; Bank robbery; Florida—Hudson; Revenge

Martin, J(ulia) Wallis.

A Likeness in Stone. UK: Hodder & Stoughton, 1997. (U.S.: St. Martin's Minotaur, 1998).
A reservoir has flooded an area where a murder has been committed, and twenty years later, when a diver uncovers a corpse hidden in a submerged house, it confirms the worst fears of retired Thames Valley Chief Inspector Bill Driver. He now knows where the body of Helena Warner has rested all these years. His new mission becomes revisiting her three friends, who years ago, as undergraduates, hid the truth from the investigator.

England—Marshfield; England—Oxford; Oxford University; Reservoirs

Millar, Margaret.

Beast in View. Random House, 1955.
When Helen Clarvoe, a rich and recently widowed woman living in a Hollywood hotel, receives a call from Evelyn Merrick, it reminds her that her brain has made her forget. In order to make sense of what she does not remember, Helen must reach out beyond the hotel for help from an attorney. His investigation will prove whether Helen is mad or is being driven mad.

California—Los Angeles; Hotels; Pornography; Revenge

Norris, Frank.

McTeague: A Story of San Francisco. Doubleday & McClure, 1899.

McTeague is an unlicensed dentist who loses all when he is betrayed to the authorities. Meanwhile his wife, Trina, has won the lottery. Although that should bring the couple great joy, the reality is that sharing the prize will be a problem, because McTeague is a drunken, violent man who thinks more of riches than he does of love, and Trina insists that they live off his money, not hers. As the couple's fortunes diminish but the lottery money is still there, it becomes too great a temptation for a man like McTeague.

California—San Francisco; Greed; Husbands and wives; Lottery

O'Connor, Joseph.

Star of the Sea. Harcourt, 2002.

Sailing from Ireland in 1847, the *Star of the Sea* is attempting to leave behind all the difficulties of a country wracked by famine. On board are Lord David Merridith and his family, the targets of an assassin named Pius Mulvey. The Merridith's nanny, Mary Duane, is Mulvey's former fiancée and the widow of Mulvey's dead brother. American journalist Grantley Dixon is traveling home, hoping to continue his affair with Lady Merridith, while providing the narrative in the form of his diaries about the voyage. On the storm-tossed seas, this mix of characters, all with different goals, is heading more for tragedy than for a safe port.

Immigration; Ocean travel

Perry, Thomas.

Dead Aim. Random House, 2002.

When Robert Mallon is out for a walk on the beach, he manages to save the life of Catherine Broward, who apparently was attempting to commit suicide. A few days later, he reads that she may have been successful in a second attempt. Telling the police what he knows and hiring his own detective puts Mallon on the run from a killer who wants him dead as well.

California—Santa Barbara; Suicide

Reasoner, James.

The Dust Devils. Point Blank, 2007.

When Toby McCoy looks for work on the farm, he does not expect to find a woman as attractive as Grace Halligan, the owner of the farm. But when some people from Grace's past show up and reveal her true identity, they end up in the ground, and the couple goes on the run. The couple wants to reunite Grace with the money she is owed from a bank robbery, and they intend to take it from the man who has it.

Texas

Robotham, Michael.

Suspect. UK: Little, Brown, 2004. (U.S.: Doubleday, 2005).

Joe O'Loughlin, psychologist and Parkinson's disease sufferer, is dragged into a murder investigation when the victim is a former client who once charged him with sexual assault. Once Joe exhibits an interest in the case, he begins to discover that he is the most likely suspect in the girl's murder. As his personal life spins out of control and he becomes the target of the police, he is the only one who believes in his innocence.

England—Liverpool; England—London; Parkinson's disease; Psychologists

Ruis Zafón, Carlos.

La Sombra del Viento. Spain: Planeta, 2001. (U.S.: *The Shadow of the Wind.* Penguin, 2004).

On his tenth birthday, Daniel Sempere's father takes him to the Cemetery of Forgotten Books, where he is allowed to select one title as his own. He selects *The Shadow of the Wind*, by Julián Carax. Soon after, a threatening and mysterious man offers to buy the book. When Daniel refuses, he sets off a voyage of discovery that will explain why all the works of Carax have been systematically destroyed by the man named as the devil in Carax's novel, *Laín Coubert*.

Authors; Bibliomystery; Coming-of-age; Rare books; Spain—Barcelona

Schickler, David.

Sweet and Vicious. Dial, 2004.

Floyd, Roger, and Henry Dante all work for Honey Pobrinks, the mobster. Their job is to recover The Planets, a set of Spanish diamonds that were stolen from Honey by Charles Chalk. When an opportunity arises to go on the lam with The Planets, Henry is game. What he does not expect is to pick up Grace McGlone, a disappointed Christian looking for adventure, at the car wash where she works. The two go on the lam, until Grace discovers why and insists on ditching their ill-gotten gains for the greater glory of God.

Jewels; Religion; Romance; Wisconsin—Janesville

Shubin, Seymour.

Witness to Myself. Hard Case, 2006.

Alan Benning, now a successful lawyer, has always been troubled by an incident in his teen years wherein he may have caused the death of a young girl. When he falls in love with a nurse named Anna Presiac, his ability to have a relationship is inhibited by his past. So he goes to Cape Cod and begins to dig into the past, seeking answers that will either free him or punish him for his deeds.

Massachusetts—Cape Cod; Memory

Sidor, Steven.

Skin River. St. Martin's Minotaur, 2004.

Buddy Bayes is hiding out in northern Wisconsin, running a small bar in a fishing and hunting haven, with designs of romancing his upstairs tenant, Margot. When an evil serial killer called the Goatskinner operates in this remote area, and Buddy just happens to be the search party member who finds a severed hand floating in the Skin River, unwanted attention is focused on him. The consequences of an old crime come calling, and Buddy finds himself caught between his past and the evil of the present.

Alcohol; Revenge; Wisconsin—Gunnar

Stansberry, Domenic.

The Last Days of Il Duce. Permanent Press, 1998.

Niccolo Jones is a lawyer who fell in love with his brother's wife, Marie. As he moves back and forth in time telling his story of obsession, the Italian North Beach area of San Francisco goes through as many changes as the characters. When his brother Joe is murdered, Nick finds himself under suspicion but also on a quest for revenge.

California—San Francisco; Obsession; Revenge

Starr, Jason.

Twisted City. Vintage, 2004.

Journalist David Miller's favorite sister has died recently, he hates his girlfriend, and he was just fired from his job at the *Wall Street Journal*. While cruising the bars one night, he discovers his wallet is missing. Now he is negotiating with a hooker who claims she knows where his wallet is. When her boyfriend dies, David finds himself running from a murder charge.

Drugs; Journalists; New York—New York

Thornburg, Newton.

Cutter and Bone. Little, Brown, 1976.

After Bone witnesses the murder of a young girl, he tells his friend, Cutter. Cutter, damaged by his Vietnam War experiences, is just obsessed enough to agree to pursue the perpetrator based on some rather limited information. The two set off across the country in pursuit of J. J. Wolfe, a successful businessman, accompanied by the dead girl's sister. When their chase leads them to the end of the trail, it becomes evident to Bone that there is more to this than meets Cutter's eye.

Ozarks; Vietnamese conflict

Walters, Minette.

The Ice House. UK: Macmillan, 1992. (U.S.: St. Martin's, 1992).

Phoebe Maybury is living in Streech Grange with her lesbian companions, interior designer Diana Goode and journalist Anna Cattrell. Phoebe's long-missing ex-husband had abused their daughter and disappeared. When a corpse is found in an unused icehouse on the property, Chief Inspector Walsh focuses his investigation on Phoebe. And why not? He suspected her of foul play ten years ago when her husband disappeared.

England—Hampshire; Homosexuality

The Scold's Bridle. UK: Macmillan, 1994. (U.S.: St. Martin's, 1994).

When the body of Mathilda Gillespie is found in her bathtub, her head is encased in a scold's bridle. Oddly, she has bequeathed her fortune to her doctor, Sarah Blakeney, instead of her hated daughter, Joanna, or unreliable granddaughter, Ruth. Even Blakeney's ne'er-do-well husband Jack gets dragged into this investigation by Detective Sergeant Cooper. It becomes the task of the doctor to prove that she is innocent of murder.

Children in jeopardy; England—Dorset, Fontwell; Inheritance; Wills

The Dark Room. UK: Macmillan, 1995. (U.S.: Putnam, 1996).

Jinx Kingsley has been found wandering around an abandoned airfield, apparently after trying to kill herself. And why not? Her husband was murdered ten years ago. Recently her fiancé, Leo, and her best friend, Meg, have cheated on her, and both have been murdered. Jinx is the logical suspect. With her memory of the recent crucial days lost, she turns to Dr. Alan Protheroe for help.

Amnesia; England—London; Photography

The Echo. UK: Macmillan, 1997. (U.S.: Putnam, 1997).

When a homeless man named Billy Blake is found dead in the garage of successful architect Amanda Powell, journalist Michael Deacon begins to probe into the reasons why Blake would choose to starve to death in front of a well-stocked refrigerator. As it is revealed that Blake may have been a banker who disappeared with an enormous fortune, the mystery deepens. What happened to the banker's wife? And how does all of this relate to the stoic Amanda Powell?

England—London; Homeless; Journalists

Woolrich, Cornell.

The Black Curtain. Simon & Schuster, 1941.

When Frank Townsend receives a blow to the head, he forgets who he is and lives a lie for three years. Then, after another blow, his memory of his previous life is restored, but he forgets who he has been during the last three years. When some people he cannot remember come calling for him, he must scramble to restore the missing three years to find out why he is a wanted man.

Memory

On the Run True Crime

Alexander, Shana.

Anyone's Daughter. Viking, 1979.
> When Patty Hearst became the most baffling crime queen of the 1970s, it confused all of America. Here the author tries to take a backward look and explain how this heiress ended up on the front page of the newspaper, toting a gun.

> Hearst, Patty; Symbionese Liberation Army

Bommersbach, Jana.

The Trunk Murderess: Winnie Ruth Judd: The Truth About an American Crime Legend Revealed at Last. Simon & Schuster, 1992.
> In 1931 Winnie Ruth Judd, a medical secretary, shot and killed Annie LeRoi and Hedvig Samuelson. To make matters worse, she dismembered one body and placed both in a trunk. Then, to make herself a national media sensation, she checked the luggage onto a train bound for Los Angeles. After her conviction, she escaped seven times from various mental hospitals and spent numerous years on the outside.

> Arizona—Phoenix; Escapes

Capote, Truman.

In Cold Blood: A True Account of a Multiple Murder and Its Consequences. Random House, 1966.
> In 1959, members of the Clutter family were murdered in the small town of Holcomb, Kansas. This random and seemingly insignificant crime was turned into a compelling work of nonfiction that incorporated fictional techniques by Capote and Harper Lee, who arrived to research the crime before the killers were even apprehended. When Perry Smith and Dick Hickock were caught, Capote completed the story by tracing their escape route and defining the reasons why they appeared that dark night in Kansas to commit this crime.

> Kansas—Holcomb; Robbery; Trials

Cook, Thomas H.

Blood Echoes: The True Story of an Infamous Mass Murder and Its Aftermath. Dutton, 1992.
> In 1973, two Issac brothers escaped from a Maryland jail and headed south with another convict, picking up a third brother on the way. When they hit Georgia, they murdered six members of the rural Alday family. They were captured after an intensive manhunt, only to spend years in and out of courtrooms, avoiding the ultimate punishment for their crimes.

> Gangs; Georgia—Seminole County; Trials

Evans, Wanda Webb.

Trail of Blood: A Father, a Son and a Tell-tale Crime Scene Investigation. New Horizon, 2005.

When twenty-four-year-old Scott Dunn disappeared, his father James worried about his son's whereabouts. It took six years of hard efforts for James to find out what had happened to his son, mostly thanks to the forensics expertise of The Vidocq Society.

Forensics; Texas—Lubbock

France, Johnny, and Malcolm McConnell.

Incident at Big Sky: The True Story of Sheriff Johnny France and the Capture of the Mountain Men. Norton, 1986.

Olympic biathlete Kari Swenson was on a training run when she was kidnapped by mountain man Daniel Nichols as a bride for his son, Dan. When a rescue attempt was launched by law enforcement officials, Alan Goldstein was killed, and the Nicholses escaped into the Montana wilderness. Despite a massive manhunt, they remained at large until Sheriff Johnny France hunted them down and brought them in.

Kidnapping; Montana—Madison County; Mountain men

The Goldman Family.

If I Did It: Confessions of the Killer. Beaufort, 2007.

When Ron Goldman lost his life on the same night that O. J. Simpson's wife Nicole Brown Simpson was murdered, who knew that the circus surrounding this case would include a confession from O. J. published by Goldman's relatives in an attempt to prove that O. J. did it?

California—Brentwood; Confessions; Simpson, O. J.

Gourevitch, Philip.

A Cold Case. Farrar, Straus & Giroux, 2001.

Andy Rosenzweig was a former New York Police Department officer who became an investigator with the Manhattan DA's office. Haunted by a murder that took place in 1970, when hit man Frankie Koehler took out two men in cold blood, he decided to discover why the fugitive had never been brought to justice. The reason Rosenzweig was interested in this cold case is that he knew the victims.

Cold cases; New York—New York

Jackson, Joe.

Leavenworth Train: A Fugitive's Search for Justice in the Vanishing West. Carroll and Graf, 2001.

Petty thief Frank Grigware had the misfortune to fall into the clutches of a gang of train robbers in 1909. When he was falsely accused of their crimes and convicted, he was sent to Leavenworth Federal Penitentiary. His successful escape and life in

Canada as the mayor of his town did not save him from the wrath of the American government when his new identity was revealed.

Prison breaks

Thompson, Thomas.

Blood and Money. Doubleday, 1976.
Joan Robinson was the favored daughter of Texas oilman Ash Robinson. When she married plastic surgeon Dr. John Hill and subsequently mysteriously died, her father sought revenge against the man he thought had murdered his daughter.

Physicians; Revenge; Texas—Houston

Serial Killers and Psychos

Serial killers and psychos fascinate us by their amoral behavior. The appeal is an emotional one, mostly based on the thrill of watching a person commit heinous crimes and trying to understand what motivates that behavior.

Benchmark Serial Killers and Psychos Novel

Dickens, Charles.

The Mystery of Edwin Drood. Fields, Osgood, 1870.
Choirmaster John Jasper is in love with Rosa Bud, his nephew Edwin Drood's fiancée. Rosa and Edwin are friends, but their marriage, arranged by their parents when they were children, may not happen. Jasper, a drug addict and practitioner of the art of mesmerism, is intent on stealing Rosa. He begins by setting Neville Landless, a young man from Ceylon, against Edwin. Edwin disappears. Dickens died before completing the manuscript, and the reader is left to speculate whether Jasper was the perpetrator or if Dickens had someone else in mind.

Drugs; England—Cloisterham; Mesmerism

Serial Killers and Psychos Novels

Blanchard, Alice.

The Breathtaker. Warner, 2003.
Charlie Grover, the sheriff of Promise, Oklahoma, is a single parent with a precocious daughter named Sophie. He is trying to balance his own personal problems against the stresses of his job. When a tornado strikes his town, the damage is severe, but things get really creepy when it becomes obvious that three of the victims in the storm were actually murdered. As Charlie begins to discover evidence that a serial killer may be working

Tornado Alley, he must turn to storm chasers for help. Although a potential relationship with scientist Willa Bellman adds spice to his life, it also forces Charlie to reestablish communication with his storm-chasing father. As Charlie chases across the Plains looking for the right storm to trap his killer, he also races against time to save his family from self-destructing.

Fathers and daughters; Oklahoma—Promise; Serial killers; Tornadoes

Brown, Fredric.

The Screaming Mimi. Dutton, 1949.

When Bill Sweeney is roaring drunk, he lives in the gutter. When he is sober, he is one of Chicago's great journalists. When he sees a naked woman in a doorway guarded by a fierce dog, he is not sure if he is stoned or sober—but he knows he wants the woman. When he discovers she may have been attempt number four, staged by a serial killer named The Ripper, he decides to play detective, drunk or sober.

Alcoholism; Illinois—Chicago; Journalist; Serial killers

The Lenient Beast. Dutton, 1956.

From five different points of view, we hear the story of John Medley. John is only at peace when he can help his fellow man by showing his merciful love. Meanwhile, the police are trying to find the serial killer working the streets of their town.

Arizona—Tucson; Serial killers

Caspary, Vera.

Bedelia. Houghton Mifflin, 1945.

Charlie Horst thought he was the luckiest man in the world when he married Bedelia. But as time passes, he begins to think his wife may have a past. Worse, she may be a serial killer. Even worse, she may make him her next victim.

Connecticut; Historical; Husbands and wives; Serial killers

Connelly, Michael.

The Poet. Little, Brown, 1996.

Denver homicide detective Sean McEvoy kills himself with a shotgun in his squad car, leaving a cryptic suicide note on the dash. His twin brother Jack, a journalist, is eager to try to solve the mystery behind his brother's death. As Jack digs into his brother's background, he discovers that other cops have died by suicide, leaving similar notes, all of which appear to have something to do with Edgar Allan Poe. He teams up with the FBI's Rachel Walling and finds in her an able partner in the search for a serial killer.

Poe, Edgar Allan; Serial killers

Cooke, John Peyton.

Torsos. Mysterious, 1993.

It is the 1930s in Cleveland, and a serial killer is taking out male victims by dismembering them and dumping their bodies in the Kingsbury Run section of town. The town's safety commissioner is Eliot Ness, and he is determined to find the killer. One of the city's homicide detectives, Hank Lambert, is leaning to the gay life but keeping that secret from his family. Hank recognizes the victims as men from the city's homosexual population. When Lambert links up with a gay hooker named Danny Cottone, he finds he has an in to catching a murderer, but not before the raw side of Depression era sexuality is exposed.

Historical; Homosexuality; Ohio—Cleveland; Serial killers

Denton, Bradley.

Blackburn. St. Martin's Press, 1993.

Jimmy Blackburn is a young man who grew up in a small Kansas town, abused and unloved. Knowing the unjust hatred of those who hurt him, he decides to start a campaign to eliminate only those who prey on the undeserving.

Kansas; Serial killers; Texas

Dobyns, Stephen.

The Church of Dead Girls. Metropolitan, 1997.

A small town is always affected by a tragedy, and when a murder occurs it can topple the community's sense of well-being. When the murder of Janice McNeal, a woman of ill-repute, is followed by the disappearance of three girls, it completely fractures this community. The citizens of Aurelia, New York, are quick to take on roles and make decisions, while the rights of individuals are trampled with impunity. Although Janice's son is one suspect, the high school biology teacher who narrates this creepy tale does nothing to eliminate himself from the list.

Children in jeopardy; Missing persons; Serial killers

Floyd, Bill.

The Killer's Wife. St. Martin's Minotaur, 2008.

After testifying against her husband, Randal Mosley, a serial killer who is now serving time, Leigh Wren has moved her son to a new life in Cary, North Carolina. Her former life with Mosley is exposed when the father of one of his victims targets Leigh. Worse, a copycat serial killer is now on the loose, using her ex-husband's methods to create more victims among people who knew Leigh.

North Carolina—Cary; Serial killers; Stalkers

Fowles, John.

The Collector. Little, Brown, 1963.

Frederick Clegg is a clerk in the Rates Office at the Town Hall Annexe when he wins £73,091 in the pools. After packing his guardian aunt and handicapped niece off to Australia on a family trip, he buys a remote country cottage near Lewes in Sussex. He moves his butterfly collection to his new home and makes plans to add one more unique specimen to his collection: art student Miranda Grey.

Captivity; England—London; England—Sussex, Lewes; Kidnapping; Obsession

Girard, James Preston.

The Late Man. Athenuem, 1993.

A serial killer who has been working the Wichita area has been quiet for awhile, but now a new body has been found. For Captain L. J. Loomis, this puts him back on the trail of a killer who has troubled him for years and broke up his marriage. For Stosh Babicki, the new body may mean a hot story for an eager reporter. For San Haun, his coworker who mans the night desk, it reminds him of the death of his family in a car accident. How each man will handle the pressure assures that it will not be easy to find a killer.

Kansas—Wichita; Serial killers

Glynn, Jonny.

The Seven Days of Peter Crumb. Portobello, 2007. (U.S.: HarperPerennial, 2007).

When Peter Crumb decides that he will be dead in a week, he realizes his behavior no longer has any moral boundaries. So he begins a series of killings of savage randomness, all while carrying on a dialogue with himself about life in general.

England—London; Serial killers; Sociopaths

Gores, Joe.

Menaced Assassin. Mysterious, 1994.

San Francisco detective Dante Stagnoro, a member of the Organized Crime Task Force, has the task of babysitting Will Dalton, a paleoanthropologist. While the man lectures his students on violence and sexuality in apes, the detective ponders why the hit man, known as Raptor, started his killing spree with Dalton's unfaithful wife, Molly.

California—San Francisco; Hit men; Organized crime; Serial killers

Gray, John MacLachlan.

The Fiend in Human. UK: Century, 2002. (U.S.: St. Martin's Minotaur, 2003).

Newspaperman Edmund Whitty is writing about the execution of Chokee Bill, the serial killer who has been preying on prostitutes in London in 1852. William Ryan, the man accused, is protesting that he is innocent. Whitty is trying to make hay with the idea that the police may have arrested the wrong man, a theory supported by additional murders.

England—London; Historical; Journalists; Prostitutes; Serial killers

Harris, Thomas.

[Hannibal Lecter series].

1

Thomas Harris ignited contemporary interest in the doings of serial killers when he created Dr. Hannibal Lecter for this series of novels. The following series titles are listed in order of publication.

Red Dragon. Putnam, 1981.

2

Will Graham was almost killed when he brought the serial killer, Dr. Hannibal "The Cannibal" Lecter, to justice. But now he needs the keen insight of the demented doctor when Graham is asked to bring in Francis Dolarhyde, a film lab assistant who has been murdering entire families after previewing their home movies. As Graham closes in on Dolarhyde, Dolarhyde prepares for his pursuer, while The Cannibal plots from within his cell.

3

Federal Bureau of Investigation; Missouri—St. Louis; Serial killers

The Silence of the Lambs. St. Martin's, 1988.

4

Dr. Hannibal Lecter is a brilliant psychiatrist who himself is a serial killer. The FBI sends a behavioral science trainee, Clarice Starling, to interview the doctor in his prison cell, and the games begin. With the serial killer Buffalo Bill, known to skin his female victims, on the loose, it seems logical to follow the doctor's advice on how to hunt him down.

5

Federal Bureau of Investigation; Prisons; Serial killers

Hannibal. Delacorte, 1999.

Clarice Starling is not the darling of the FBI, but she finds a way is open to redeem her career when the Bureau decides it is time to rein in the long-missing Dr. Hannibal Lecter. Their interest has been peaked by Mason Verger, a victim of Lecter's who has survived on a respirator and now wants to use his vast inherited resources to get revenge.

6

Federal Bureau of Investigation; Revenge; Serial killers

7

Hannibal Rising. Delacorte, 2006.

This is the novel that tells all about how a man became a famous serial killer and cannibal. When Hannibal's uncle Robert finds the young man in an orphanage, it is after his family has lived in the woods hiding from the Nazis who invaded their homeland of Russia. But the worst thing that Hannibal saw was the death of his beloved sister, Mischa. As he becomes the youngest person ever admitted to medical school in France, he is already plotting his revenge on the world.

8

9

France; Serial killers; World War II

10

Highsmith, Patricia.

[Tom Ripley series].

Sociopath Tom Ripley may be one of the most fascinating characters to follow in crime fiction. The following series titles are listed in order of publication.

The Talented Mr. Ripley. Coward-McCann, 1955.

> Tom Ripley is a chameleon with a black heart. He uses false pretenses and Herbert Greenleaf's concern for his son Dickie to get a sponsored trip to Italy to bring the wayward son home. Once in Mongibello, Tom begins an insidious campaign to both win Dickie's affections and assume his identity. When murder occurs, Tom balances his criminal skills against the concerns of the Greenleafs and the police in a monstrous attempt to live someone else's life and escape his own.

> Identity theft; Italy—Mongibello; Sociopaths

Ripley under Ground. Doubleday, 1970.

> Ripley has been living in the suburbs of Paris for fifteen years since he left Italy, enjoying his beautiful wife Heloise, his vast house, and his impressive art collection. He is threatened when the façade he has built begins to crumble. The forgeries he has been selling to finance his lifestyle are claimed to be by Derwatt, a reclusive artist who actually committed suicide years before. When an American art connoisseur named Thomas Murchison starts an investigation, Ripley once again takes on another's personality to hide his crimes. One death may release the pressure, but two deaths only brings the police to his doorstep again.

> Art; France—Villeperce-sur-Seine; Identity theft; Sociopaths

Ripley's Game. Knopf, 1974.

> Although he is willing to kill for the sheer purpose of propelling his own life forward, Ripley rejects the proposal of a man named Reeves Minot to find someone to kill two mobsters who are running a gambling empire in Hamburg, Germany. However, he is mad at Jonathan Trevanny—an Englishman living in France and running a picture framing store—for snubbing him at a party. He manages to get Trevanny to do the dirty work, while he plans on collecting the money. For a brief moment, Ripley has a heart, and this leads him to Hamburg to commit the murder he never wanted to.

> Gambling; France—Villeperce-sur-Seine; Germany—Hamburg

The Boy Who Followed Ripley. Crowell, 1980.

> After murdering his father by pushing his wheelchair off a cliff, sixteen-year-old Frank Pierson shows up at the Ripley estate, where he confesses his sins. The two develop a friendship that may be growing into something else. Is Ripley mellowing by developing a heart, or is he stalking this innocent for his own evil purposes? Ripley will be tested when Frank is kidnapped.

> France—Villeperce-sur-Seine; Germany—Berlin; Kidnapping

Ripley under Water. Knopf, 1991.

> After many years of quiet and peaceful life at home with his wife Heloise, Ripley is disturbed by his new neighbors. David and Janice Pritchard appear to Ripley to be too interested in him and know a few too many details about his past adventures. When Pritchard begins to hunt for the bodies of Ripley's past enemies, he rises to the occasion and defends his home against this intrusion.

France—Villeperce-sur-Seine; Morrocco; Revenge

Hyde, Christopher.

Wisdom of the Bones. New American Library, 2003.

> It is 1963 in Dallas, Texas, and Homicide Detective Ray Duval has a serial killer on his hands. This killer has resurfaced to dismember girls and put them back together like a puzzle. Duval is in a race against time as he is dying from a fatal heart condition. Who will protect the young girls if he cannot bring the killer to justice before he is forced to retire or the historical events sweep away any interest in these crimes?

Children in jeopardy; Historical; Serial killers; Terminally ill; Texas—Dallas

Katzenbach, John.

The Madman's Tale. Ballantine, 2004.

> Francis Xavier Petrel is writing the history of his madness, and his stay at the Western State Hospital for the insane, on the walls of his apartment. Over twenty years earlier, he had been nicknamed C-Bird by inmate Peter the Fireman as the two struggled to stay as sane as possible with the doctors and the drugs stacked against them. When the nurse called Short Blond is found raped and murdered in a storage closet and their fellow inmate Lanky is falsely accused of the crime, the two decide to act as detectives. They are joined in that struggle by Suffolk County prosecutor Lucy Kyoto Jones, herself a rape victim, who believes a serial killer may be hiding in the hospital. That story is interspersed with the contemporary struggles of C-Bird to adapt to life on the outside of the asylum while his internal voices torment him about the past.

Massachusetts—Suffolk County; Memory; Prosecutors; Psychiatric hospitals; Serial killers

Landay, William.

The Strangler. Delacorte, 2007.

> In 1963, with the city in turmoil after the president's assassination, a serial killer known as The Boston Strangler is working the streets. Three brothers, sons of a cop killed on the job, have each taken a different path. Joe Jr., who followed in his father's footsteps, has to deal with the confession of The Strangler while dealing with his own gambling debts and connections to the mob. Michael is the assistant district attorney involved in the case.

The last brother, Rickey, is a burglar who gets one job to close to The Strangler and finds the heat turned on him.

Boston Strangler; Brothers; Historical; Massachusetts—Boston; Serial killers

Levin, Ira.

A Kiss Before Dying. Simon & Schuster, 1953.

Dorothy Kingship was born with a silver spoon in her mouth, and her calculating boyfriend wants to get it by marrying into her family. But when she becomes pregnant before the groom-to-be can even meet the father who wants to disown her, he decides to take matters into his own hands. Then things get complicated.

Pregnancy

Levison, Iain.

Since the Layoffs. Soho, 2003.

Things have not been going so well for Jake Skowran. Having lost his job when the factory where he worked closed, he has been hounded by everyone to whom he owes money. Now with his girl gone and his unemployment ended, he accepts a job as a hit man to kill drug dealer Ken Gardocki's wife. The problem is that he discovers killing is something he is good at.

Hit men; Unemployment

Lindsay, Jeff.

[Dexter Morgan series].

Dewter Morgan is a blood splatter expert for the Miami Police Department. He gets his expertise from having been a serial killer since he was a small boy, avenging the good by killing only those people who deserve it, like other serial killers and child molesters. The following series titles are listed in order of publication.

Darkly Dreaming Dexter. Doubleday, 2004.

Who would guess that the blood splatter expert working in the Miami Police Department lab is also a serial killer, with a heart of gold? Following the voice he hears in his head, called the Dark Passenger, Dexter hunts down other serial killers and bad people like pedophiles. When a copycat serial killer begins to kill prostitutes, Dexter needs to make sure his foster sister, Deborah Morgan, assigned to the homicide cases, does not discover her brother's secret before she finds the real killer.

Florida—Miami; Serial killers

Dearly Devoted Dexter. Doubleday, 2005.

Now that he is under the suspicion by Miami Sergeant Doakes, Dexter needs to keep a low profile. When another serial killer named Danco begins to practice in the turf covered by Deborah Morgan, she finds her foster brother's help invaluable, especially because he knows Danco has Doakes on his shortlist of potential victims.

Florida—Miami; Serial killers

Dexter in the Dark. Doubleday, 2007.

When the murder of two coeds on a university campus brings blood splatter expert Dexter to the scene, his inner voice, the Dark Passenger, inexplicably deserts him. What frightens him is that he may have finally met his match, a serial killer so powerful that he can compete with Dexter. Now he is being stalked like one of his victims and needs to look within himself for something other than his guardian angel.

Florida—Miami; Serial killers

MacDonald, John D.

The End of the Night. Simon & Schuster, 1960.

This novel begins with a prison guard's account of the execution of four gang members. Through the backstory, we then learn how Kirby Stassen, a privileged young man, is corrupted in Hollywood to join Robert Hernandez, Sander Golden, and Nanette Koslov on a rampage across the country, raping and killing their way into infamy.

Gangs

Matheson, Richard.

Fury on Sunday. Lion Books, 1953.

Mad as a hatter, Vincent escapes from a mental institution and takes to the streets. He is a mad killer, unsure whom he wants to hurt but knowing his father is to blame. When a woman named Ruth stands in his path, the people around her become the victims he needs to feed his inner demons.

New York—New York; Serial killers

Someone Is Bleeding. Lion Books, 1953.

Dave Newton is a Santa Monica writer who happens to fall in love with a woman named Peggy. Peggy's problem is that she seems to be leaving a trail of male corpses in her wake, and Dave has to decide if he has fallen in love with a serial killer.

California— Santa Monica; Serial killers

Murray, Sabrina.

A Carnivore's Inquiry. Grove, 2004.

Katherine is on a journey of discovery. It starts with her arrival in New York and an affair with a Russian novelist named Boris Nrvshkin. Then she is off to Maine and Mexico, leaving a trail of corpses in her wake. She is not shy about revealing her fascination with the dark culinary arts to the reader, but can this really be blamed on her mother?

Cannibalism; Maine—Portland; Mexico; Mothers and daughters; New York—New York; Serial killers

O'Connell, Jack.

Wireless. Mysterious Press, 1993.

When a local priest with a popular radio show is murdered, Detective Hannah Shaw is given the case. She is up against a former FBI agent named Speer, who is determined to silence the "jammers," or those radio pirates who broadcast below the radar. Their gathering spot is a club called Wireless, and it is there that those who want to get the message out will confront the one who wants to silence them.

Massachusetts—Quinsigamond; Radio; Serial killers

Peace, David.

Tokyo Year Zero. Knopf, 2007.

Detective Minami works the devastated streets of post–World War II Tokyo. When a serial killer starts leaving dead women in a local park, Minami is assigned the case. It should be no surprise that Minami is flawed himself, and his own weakness may keep him from uncovering a serial killer on the war-torn streets of the city.

Historical; Japan—Tokyo; Serial killers; World War II

Perry, Thomas.

Nightlife. Random House, 2006.

Portland homicide cop Catherine Hobbes is given the case when Dennis Poole, the cousin of Los Angeles mafioso Hugo Poole, is killed in Portland. While Catherine searches for a woman seen on a security tape, Poole hires a PI, who begins his own investigation. As the two unwilling cohorts combine their investigation, it begins to look like they are on the trail of a serial killer, who now has a contract on Catherine.

Oregon—Portland; Organized crime; Serial killers

Phillips, Scott.

Cottonwood. Ballantine, 2004.

Photographer and saloon keeper Bill Ogden lives in Cottonwood, Kansas, in 1872. When Chicago businessman Marc Leval comes to town looking for an ally to develop the one-horse town, he finds his patsy in Ogden. Then Ogden falls for Leval's wife, Maggie, and things get ugly when the townsfolk turn against the plan. As if things were not bad enough, who wants to bring the railroad to a town where people are mysteriously disappearing thanks to The Bloody Benders? But after leaving, Odgen finds you can go home again.

Historical; Kansas—Cottonwood; Serial killers; Westerns

Stansberry, Domenic.

The Confession. Hard Case Crime, 2004.

Forensic psychologist Jake Danser works all day trying to break down the testimonies of murderers, psychos, and serial killers. His outlet is to be a sexual predator, a little secret he keeps from his colleagues and his loving wife, Elisabeth. When a woman named Sara Johnson ends up dead, he is on the hot seat and in need of all his own confessional skills to keep out of jail.

California—Sausalito; False confessions; Infidelity

1

Thompson, Jim.

Lou Ford series.

The Killer Inside Me. Lion Books, 1953.

2

Lou Ford is a folksy deputy sheriff working the dusty streets of a small Texas town. When "the sickness" overtakes him, the abuses that molded him into the man he is begin to manifest themselves in contemporary behavior. Someone has died, his brother has suffered, and now he has fallen in love with a prostitute, Joyce Lakeland. As his inner demons force him to behave violently, he finds it harder and harder to hide behind the benign façade that is his public persona. That means those around him are going to suffer.

3

Psychotics; Sheriffs; Texas—Central City

4

The Nothing Man. Dell, 1954.

Newspaper man Clinton Brown is a World War II veteran who lost his manhood on the battlefield. When he returns to civilian life, he discovers that alcohol is not the distraction he needs when women find him attractive. Unable to control his urges, he turns to murder. But is he a reliable narrator?

5

California—Pacific City; Emasculation; Newspapers; Serial killers

Wild Town. New American Library, 1957.

6

Mike Hanlon, wheelchair-bound owner of the Hanlon Hotel, senses that his wife, Joyce, is going to get rid of him. He turns to the town's chief deputy sheriff, a man named Lou Ford. When Ford is less than helpful, Hanlon finds himself relying on his new house detective, David "Bugs" McKenna. What Bugs, an ex-con, does not know is that the job may involve more than he bargained for, especially because Ford asked him to take the job and Bugs is falling for Ford's girl-friend, Amy.

7

Hotels; House detectives; Texas

8

Williams, Charles.

Dead Calm. Viking, 1963.

John and Rae Ingram are honeymooning in the Pacific on their yacht when they come across a man on a sinking ship. He tells them that he had to bury his wife and another couple when they suffered food poisoning. But then the story begins to fall apart.

9

Honeymoons; Pacific Ocean; Shipboard

10

Woolrich, Cornell.

Black Alibi. Simon & Schuster, 1942.

In the South American city of Ciudad Real, a jaguar breaks away from a singer's publicity stunt. Then it is believed to be stalking women at night and killing them. Suspicion begins to grow that this may not be the work of a jaguar but rather the work of a man.

Serial killers; South America—Ciudad Real

True Crime Serial Killers and Psychos

Bledsoe, Jerry.

Death Sentence: The True Story of Velma Barfield's Life, Crimes and Execution. Dutton, 1998.

When Velma Barfield and Stuart Taylor were engaged, no one expected Stuart to be poisoned, least of all by Velma. More shocking, this was not her first murder. Despite all this, there was widespread debate about whether she should be executed for her crimes.

Capital punishment; North Carolina—Robeson County; Serial killers

Bugliosi, Vincent, and Curt Gentry.

Helter Skelter: The True Story of the Manson Murders. Norton, 1974.

The prosecutor in the Tate-Labianca trials reveals all that he knows about the serial killings that riveted a nation and put Charles Manson on the map as an archetypal murderer.

California—Hollywood; Manson, Charles; Serial killers; Tate, Sharon

Burn, Gordon.

Somebody's Husband, Somebody's Son: The Story of the Yorkshire Ripper. Viking, 1984.

After six years and thirteen victims, Peter Sutcliffe was finally arrested as the Yorkshire Ripper. In this book Burn attempts to probe backwards into the life of this serial killer to show how he became one of the most feared men in English criminal history.

England—Yorkshire; Serial killers; Yorkshire Ripper

Cray, Ed.

Burden of Proof: The Case of Juan Corona. Macmillan, 1973.

When bodies were discovered on a farm in Yuba City, it was revealed that someone was killing off migrant workers with an ax. Juan Corona, who was responsible for supplying the workers to the farm, was tried and convicted. Cray was on his defense team and believes there were holes in the prosecution's story.

California—Yuba City; Migrant workers; Serial killers

Elkind, Peter.

The Death Shift: The True Story of Nurse Genene Jones and the Texas Baby Murders. Viking, 1989.

> Bexar County Hospital was where Genene Jones settled into working the second shift in the pediatric ward. When the hospital became concerned about the high number of infant mortalities on the ward during her shift, they kicked her out. Moving into the private sector, she continued her work, and the number of dying children continued to grow.

Children in jeopardy; Infanticide; Serial killers; Texas—San Antonio

Fanning, Diane.

Written in Blood: A True Story of Murder and a Deadly 16-Year Old Secret That Tore a Family Apart. St. Martin's Paperbacks, 2005.

> Michael Peterson was driven to success. A Marine decorated for action in Vietnam, he worked to become a published fiction author. Along the way, he searched for love and supposedly found it with Kathleen Atwater. But when Kathleen was found at the bottom of the stairs of the couple's house, the evidence began to point toward a husband who may have wanted out. Then echoes of an old case surfaced and made Michael look even worse.

Husbands and wives; North Carolina—Durham; Uxoricide

Farber, Myron.

"Somebody Is Lying": The Story of Dr. X. Doubleday, 1982.

> Riverdell Hospital in New Jersey was the scene of a number of extraordinary deaths. An investigation was held; it was discovered that Dr. Mario Jascalevich's patients were dying from curare and that he had access to the material. When put on trial, he was acquitted of all charges. Farber pries open the lid on this case to show what went wrong.

Doctors; Hospitals; New Jersey—Bergen County; Serial killers; Trials

Frank, Gerold.

The Boston Strangler. New American Library, 1966.

> Albert DeSalvo was accused of a reign of terror in Boston that included the strangulation deaths of thirteen women and assault on hundreds more. Here is his story.

Massachusetts—Boston; Serial killers

Fuhrman, Mark.

Murder in Spokane: Catching a Serial Killer. Cliff Street, 2001.

> Spokane's prostitutes suffered the wrath of a serial killer who was active for ten years before two of his victims were found in separate locations on the same day. Finally spurred to action, the local police task force found itself shadowed by the author of this book, a former cop involved in the Simpson case.

Prostitutes; Serial killers; Washington—Spokane

Graysmith, Robert.

Unabomber: A Desire to Kill. Regnery, 1997.

For eighteen years, a crazed Harvard graduate lived in the woods in Montana, mailing bombs and terrorizing the nation. This book tries to answer the questions about the motives of Theodore Kaczynski and why it took the FBI so long to find him.

Bombs; Federal Bureau of Investigation; Montana; Unabomber

Indiana, Gary.

Three Month Fever: The Andrew Cunanan Story. Cliff Street, 1999.

Andrew Cunanan was a manufactured story from the start. A challenging childhood and his struggles with being gay led him to a lifestyle of wildness on the edge of criminality. Eventually he snapped and became a nationally sought-after serial killer.

Homosexuality; Serial killers

Keyes, Edward.

The Michigan Murders. Reader's Digest, 1976.

In the first year one college girl disappeared. In the second year, another. By the third year the serial killer preying on college-aged girls had accelerated to four in one year, and the police faced a public outcry to stop him before he killed again.

Michigan—Washtenaw County; Serial killers

Lancaster, Bob, and B. C. Hall.

Judgment Day. Seaview/Putnam, 1983.

When Kenneth Rex McElroy was murdered in broad daylight on main street in front of witnesses in Skidmore, the whole town banded together to protect his killers. McElroy had spent most of his forty-seven years terrorizing the citizens of the small town, and his murder went unsolved as the town's final revenge.

Missouri—Skidmore; Trials

Larson, Eric.

The Devil in the White City: Murder, Magic, and Madness at the Fair That Changed America. Crown, 2003.

This book tells two stories. The first details the life of Henry H. Holmes, a doctor who preyed on innocent women by ritualistically torturing and murdering them. Holmes set up shop just west of the World's Columbian Exposition of 1893 in Chicago, and the book also details the building of this magnificent fair and how it changed American society forever.

Illinois—Chicago; Serial killers; World's Columbian Exposition of 1893

MacLean, Harry N.

In Broad Daylight. Harper & Row, 1988.

Ken Rex McElroy was a holy terror in northwestern Missouri, having been indicted twenty-one times on various charges from robbery, to shooting, to raping and maiming. Only once was he sent away, and then he came back. Having had enough, the town's men conspired to execute McElroy in broad daylight, on main street, in front of forty-five witnesses, and they got away with murder when no trial was ever held.

Missouri—Skidmore; Trials

Meyer, Gerald.

The Memphis Murders. Continuum, 1974.

During the summer of 1969, the city of Memphis was gripped by the terror of unexplained deaths. As the police searched for a killer, those who were near to the case began to wonder who was guilty. This was especially true for Mary Putt, who lived too close to the almost identical brothers, Clifford and Buster Putt.

Brothers; Serial killers; Tennessee—Memphis

Mitchell, Corey.

Strangler. Pinnacle, 2007.

Anthony Allen Shore could have been a musician. Instead, after floundering in the music community, he turned his rage against four woman, whom he strangled to death, one as young as nine. Evidence began to mount that he might be the "I-45 Serial Killer," responsible for many more deaths than he would admit.

Musicians; Serial killers; Texas—Houston

Olsen, Jack.

"Son": A Psychopath and His Victims. Atheneum, 1983.

When a rapist was working the streets of Spokane for over two years, Gordon Coe, managing editor of the *Spokane Chronicle*, offered an award for the arrest of a suspect. Then the police arrested his son. That was when Fred Coe's mother Ruth began a campaign to free her son.

Mothers and sons; Rape; Washington—Spokane

The Misbegotten Son: A Serial Killer and His Victims: The True Story of Arthur J. Shawcross. Delacorte, 1993.

Odd as a child and affected by his service in Vietnam, Arthur J. Shawcross settled into the small town of Watertown, New York. At some point he decided to murder two small children. After serving his time in prison, he was released and went on the move from town to town. When he settled down in Rochester, the bodies began to turn up again—this time prostitutes.

Children in jeopardy; New York—Rochester; New York—Watertown; Prostitutes; Serial killers

I: The Creation of a Serial Killer. St. Martin's, 2002.

> In February 1990, Oregon police arrested, tried, and convicted two people for the murder of Taunja Bennett. This just made the real killer angry. Soon, through letters to the newspapers and graffiti on the walls of highway rest stops, he challenged the police to find him.

> Oregon; Serial killers

Preston, Douglas, and Mario Spezi.

The Monster of Florence. Grand Central, 2008.

> When world-famous thriller writer Douglas Preston moved to Florence, he was surprised to hear that the famous Italian serial killer The Monster of Florence had once left two victims in the olive grove next to his villa. Joining with a journalist named Mario Spezi, Preston found himself both hunting a killer and being accused of being an accomplice.

> Italy—Florence; Police corruption; Serial killers

Rule, Ann.

The Stranger Beside Me. Norton, 1980.

> When author Ann Rule first met Ted Bundy at a Seattle crisis clinic, she did not know that telling his story would set her on a path to becoming America's premiere true crime writer. Her first book, which details the life and activities of one of America's most active serial killers, is a classic in the true crime field.

> Serial killers

Green River, Running Red: The Real Story of the Green River Killer—America's Deadliest Serial Murderer. Free, 2004.

> America's most active serial killer was Gary Ridgeway, known to the world as the "Green River Killer." For two decades he preyed on prostitutes, dumping the first bodies in the river that gave him his name. Before Ridgeway was done, forty-eight women had lost their lives. This book tells the tale of each victim and how she fell into the clutches of this mass murderer.

> Prostitutes; Serial killers; Washington—Seattle

Too Late to Say Goodbye: A True Story of Murder and Betrayal. Free, 2007.

> Dr. Bart Corbin was a wealthy dentist in the Atlanta area, happily married to his wife, Jean. But his constant violent outbursts strained the family and eventually stressed the marriage. After Jean committed suicide, investigators were troubled by some clues that did not add up. When the trail led back to the suicide of a woman who had dated Corbin while he was in dental school, the situation began to clear up.

> Georgia—Atlanta; Serial killers; Uxoricide

Stewart, James B.

Blind Eye: How the Medical Establishment Let a Doctor Get Away with Murder. Simon & Schuster, 1999.

> Michael Swango led a charmed life. While in medical school at Southern Illinois, an intern at the Ohio State University Medical Center, and a physician in various

parts of the United States, he made no secret about his obsession: serial killings. He is thought to be responsible for more than thirty-five deaths of patients under his care, and has served a prison sentence for poisoning (but not killing) some of his patients and another term for fraud. When things became too complicated in the United States, Swango fled overseas, where he practiced medicine in Zimbabwe.

Physicians; Serial killers

Victims

Novels that feature victims concentrate on the results of a crime. Some are healing and some are not, but all display the range of emotions exhibited by an individual who has been affected by a criminal act. The appeal is often one of hope, as victims claw their way out from under. However, some victims novels do not end pleasantly, and the appeal of these lies in the attempt to understand and avoid the consequences.

Benchmark Victims Novels

Collins, Wilkie.

The Woman in White. UK: Low, 1860. (U.S.: Harper, 1860).
> Laura Fairlie is in danger of losing her inheritance when the evil Count Fosco and her equally evil husband, Sir Percival Glyde, hatch a diabolical plot. Laura is left without resources, except for the help of Walter Hartright, a drawing student who has fallen in love with her while acting as her tutor, and her faithful half-sister, Marian Halcombe. The key to Laura's redemption is a mysterious fugitive from a mental asylum, who dresses in white, resembles Laura, and knows the secret that could set her free.
>
> England—Cumberland; Ghosts

Dickens, Charles.

Oliver Twist; or, the Parish Boy's Progress. UK: Bentley's Miscellany, 1838. (U.S.: Carey, Lea & Blanchard, 1839).
> Oliver is a victim of the workhouse orphanages. He escapes, only to fall into the clutches of Fagin, a fence who trains young boys in the ways of the criminal world. From the Artful Dodger, Fagin's assistant, the boys learn how to become master pickpockets. When Oliver also crosses paths with Bill Sikes, a robber and murderer, he learns the ultimate fate of those who lead a life of crime.
>
> Coming-of-age; England—London; Orphans; Victorian England

Hume, Fergus Wright.

The Mystery of a Hansom Cab. Kemp & Boyce, 1886.
> Outside the Scots Church in Melbourne, two men enter a cab. While one departs at Domain Road, the other man continues to St. Kilda Junction. But upon arrival, the hansom cab driver discovers that his fare is dead. The police try to identify the dead man as the first step on a journey to find the explanation for his death.

> Australia—Melbourne; Hansom cabs

Victims Novels

Abbott, Megan.

The Song Is You. Simon & Schuster, 2007.
> Gil "Hop" Hopkins, a public relations man for the studios, finds himself in a tailspin when actress Jean Spangler disappears. Although Hop knows that Jean was last seen with the song and dance duo of Mary Sutton and Gene Merrel, he also knows that the Hollywood gossip mill says those two can be bad news. Then the woman who opened the case disappears, and Hop realizes he might be on the trail of a murder.

> Actors and actresses; California— Hollywood; Missing persons

Bock, Charles.

Beautiful Children. Random House, 2008.
> Twelve-year-old Newell Ewing lives in Las Vegas. When he disappears, it has a devastating effect on his parents, Lincoln and Lorraine. Trying to find their son leads the parents into the seamy world of runaway children and pornography, where they meet a comic book artist and a stripper. Their story mirrors the urban nightmare that Sin City has become and the waste of human life possible when all hope is abandoned for what is perceived as pleasure.

> Children in jeopardy; Comic books; Nevada—Las Vegas

Bojanowski, Marc.

The Dog Fighter. Morrow, 2004.
> Set in Mexico in the 1940s, this is the story of an unnamed narrator who runs dog fights for a living. Exiled to Mexico after murdering a man in California, the man goes to work under the tutelage of a corrupt businessman named Cantana. Abandoning construction work on Cantana's hotel, he turns to dog fighting in order to find the glory he wishes for in his life. Eventually he discovers that he might have to fight his boss to really gain the respect he wants.

> Construction; Dogs; Historical; Mexico—Canción

Braddon, Mary Elizabeth.

Lady Audley's Secret. Tinsely Brothers, 1862. (U.S.: S.H. Goetzel, 1864).

After the marriage of Lucy Graham to Sir Michael Audley, their relationship is challenged when the fortune hunting George Talboys returns to England looking for Helen, the woman he left behind. George is destroyed by the news that his Helen is dead. Robert Audley, Michael's nephew and a barrister, is a friend of George and sets off on a personal journey to prove that his friend's wife may still be alive. This search for the truth becomes more crucial when George disappears.

Bigamy; England; False identity

Bradley, James.

Wrack. UK: Review, 1998. (U.S.: Henry Holt, 1999).

Dr. David Norfolk, archaeologist, has taken on a mission to find evidence of a sixteenth-century Portuguese sailing vessel buried in the sand hills of New South Wales, Australia. He is convinced that his discovery will rewrite Australian history. But instead of the ship, David finds the fifty-year-old corpse of a murdered man. Does a dying man, Kurt Seligman, who lives near the excavation site, hold clues to what happened in the 1930s? Moving among three different time periods, this novel tells tales of the Portuguese sailors, the university politics that led to a murder, and the obsessive love expressed by the characters in the present. Eventually all seven definitions for the word "wrack" are revealed to the reader through the heartbreaking stories of the characters.

Archaeologists; Australia—New South Wales; Excavations; Historical; Shipwrecks

Brown, Fredric.

The Far Cry. Dutton, 1951.

It is recommended to George Weaver that he recover from his nervous breakdown by vacationing in New Mexico, so he rents a house in Taos. When he discovers that the house was the sight of a murder eight years earlier, he obsessively begins to probe into the life of Jenny Ames, a woman who was killed by her fiancé.

New Mexico—Taos; Obsession

Connelly, Michael.

Chasing the Dime. Little, Brown, 2002.

The L.A. Darling Web site, advertising the services of a woman called Lilly, has just put Henry Pierce's telephone number on the World Wide Web as theirs. When he pays the Web service a visit to complain, Henry discovers that Lilly is now amongst the missing. Pierce identifies with Lilly because his sister, a prostitute, has also been missing for years, so he launches a personal crusade to find Lilly.

California—Santa Monica; Prostitutes; World Wide Web

Cook, Thomas H.

Breakheart Hill. Bantam, 1995.

Kelli Troy bravely writes a school essay about "the race problem" for her high school newspaper, edited by Ben Wade. As upset as this makes the community in 1962, no one anticipates that she will suffer for her honesty, let alone be murdered. Local ruffian Lyle Gates is tried and convicted for the deed, and the community tries to forget. Years later, Dr. Ben Wade is helping Kelli's mother close her estate. This small act opens a floodgate of memories that move the doctor to explain the real reasons for what happened and his own culpability.

African Americans; Alabama—Choctaw; Race relations; South, The

Red Leaves. Harcourt, 2005.

One quiet night, Eric Moore sees his son Keith returning from a babysitting job, the flash of car headlights illuminating the family's house. The next day it is revealed that eight-year-old Amy Giordano is now missing, and suspicion falls on Keith. As Eric and his wife Meredith begin to splinter over their sense of guilt, time passes, and Amy is not found. The corrosive effects of the current crime raise memories in Eric of the death of his sister and mother and lead him to confront his brother Warren and father Edward about his family's past.

Children in jeopardy; Families; Fathers and sons; Kidnapping; Teenagers; Unknown state—Wesley

Corbett, David.

Done for a Dime. Ballantine, 2003.

Raymond "Strong" Carlisle, a jazz musician whose career peaked years before and was then left destitute, is found shot to death in his front yard. Initially the investigating officers, Dennis Murchison and Jerry Stluka, think he might have been murdered by the person he fought with at a bar the night before. As they probe into the local drug scene, they find much more to ponder, including the very character of the town in which they work.

California—Rio Mirada; Drugs; Musicians

DeMarinis, Rick.

A Clod of Wayward Marl. Dennis McMillan, 2001.

While Guido Tarkenen, a slightly boozy English instructor at La Siberia Tech, tries to hold his life together, the institution contends with rumors of its sale to an overseas computer company. His literary career, writing pulp detective fiction, does not hold much academic weight. When faculty members begin to be murdered, Guido tries to stay sober long enough to solve the crimes and save the school.

Academia; Authors

du Maurier, Daphne.

Rebecca. Doubleday, 1938.

"Last night I dreamt I went to Manderley again." This line begins the sad tale of the second Mrs. de Winter. When she falls for her husband, Maxim, little does she know that she will be taken to his estate, Manderley, where the ghost of the first Mrs. de Winter haunts the grounds, while the hostile housekeeper Mrs. Danvers rules the manor. As the true story of the death of her rival is revealed, it tests the courage of the young bride.

England—Cornwall; Estates; Marriage

Enger, Lin.

Undiscovered Country. Little, Brown, 2008.
Seventeen-year-old Jessie Matson is hunting with his father, Harold, when he discovers his father dead from a self-inflicted wound. Jessie is unable to reconcile his feelings for his father and the facts of his death. Most troubling to Jesse is the question of his Uncle Clay's role in the events of the day. By exploring the secrets of his own family, Jesse is able to deal with the truth and grow into a man.

Coming-of-age; Fathers and sons; Minnesota—Battlepoint

Goodis, David.

The Moon in the Gutter. Gold Medal, 1954.
Bill Kerrigan is a dock worker whose daily existence is disrupted by the memory of his sister Catherine's suicide after she was raped. His girl-friend, Bella, obsesses about him to the point of wanting him dead when he wants out. His ticket out is socialite Loretta Channing, but Bill must decide if marriage to this woman will really let him leave the docks behind.

Docks; Pennsylvania—Philadelphia; Rape; Suicide

Green, George Dawes.

The Caveman's Valentine. Warner, 1994.
Romulus Ledbetter graduated from the Julliard School of Music, but his quest to understand the music he loved led him to a life of mental illness. Now living in a cave in Manhattan's Inwood Park, he stumbles over the corpse of a photographer's model named Scotty Gales. He decides to find the killer, who he believes works for the evil Cornelius Gould Stuyvesant, a man who rules the world from high atop the Chrysler Building.

Homeless; New York—New York—Inwood Park; Paranoia

Grubb, Davis.

The Night of the Hunter. Harper, 1953.
When their father, Ben Harper, confesses in jail to Harry Powell, a.k.a. The Preacher, about some money he stole from the bank, it sets Powell, an insane killer, on the trail. Unfortunately, it leads to the small town where Ben's children live. Young John and his sister are not prepared for the terror that the sins of their father will send them.

Children in jeopardy; Historical; West Virginia—Moundsville

Guterson, David.

Snow Falling on Cedars. Harcourt Brace, 1994.

On the Puget Sound Island of San Piedro, a community struggles with the lingering effects of World War II. Despite having sent its sons to fight in Europe, the Japanese community is ostracized, and it is divided physically as well as racially. When conflict develops over ownership of land between a white man and his Japanese neighbors, it leads to a charge of murder. As the trial develops, the author shifts time to slowly reveal the dark history of this community and who carries the guilt for the sad events as they unfold.

Historical; Japanese Americans; Journalists; Romance; Trials; Washington—Puget Sound, San Piedro Island; Winter weather

Haddon, Mark.

The Curious Incident of the Dog in the Night-Time. Doubleday, 2003.

When his neighbor's poodle, Wellington, is killed with a pitchfork, a young boy with Asperger's syndrome named Christopher Boone decides to investigate. The story of Christopher's path to the truth is told in a manuscript he has written as a part of a class assignment. At first an attempt to emulate Sherlock Holmes, the actual journey Christopher keeps will reopen old wounds and make him reevaluate his entire life.

Asperger's syndrome; Autism; Coming-of-age; Dogs; England—London; England—Swindon; Historical; Mathematics

Harrison, Colin.

Bodies Electric. Crown, 1993.

Having lost his wife to street crime, businessman Jack Whitman decides to adopt a Dominican woman named Dolores Salcines and her four-year-old daughter Maria after a chance encounter on the subway. At work his boss is trying to engineer a deal that will merge their company without the knowledge of the board of directors and has made Jack the lead person in the deal. Meanwhile, Dolores's savage husband Hector begins to hunt his family down.

Corporations; New York—New York; Spousal abuse

Highsmith, Patricia.

The Blunderer. Coward-McCann, 1954. (Also *Lament for a Lover*, Popular Library, 1956).

Melchoir Kimmel, a pornographic book dealer, has murdered his wife Helen and planned it so well that he appears to be getting away with it. Meanwhile, Walter Stackhouse is fantasizing about the death of his wife, Clara, and figuring out how Kimmel got away with murder so he can copy the crime. When Clara dies and Walter crumbles, the police find themselves watching both men to determine who killed whom.

New Jersey—Newark; New York—New York; Uxoricide

The Glass Cell. Doubleday, 1964.

Philip Carter, an engineer, has spent six years in prison, falsely convicted of fraud for overcharging for materials on the job at Triumph. When he is released, he is not rehabilitated, he is really angry. Carter sets out to find out who set him up, and woe be to anyone who stands in his way, including his once loyal wife, Hazel, and his lawyer, David Sullivan.

False imprisonment; New York—New York; Prisons; Revenge

A Suspension of Mercy. UK: Heinemann, 1965. (U.S.: *The Story-Teller*, Doubleday, 1965).

Sydney Smith Bartleby is the principal writer on a British television show called *The Whip*, and his notebook full of nefarious measures is his source of inspiration when writing scripts for the crime program. When Sydney's wife Alicia, a woman he wishes were dead, disappears, the police suspect his notebook was a guidebook to murder. However, after Sydney makes a startling discovery, he takes steps to ensure that he is found not guilty.

England—Suffolk; Suicide; Television shows; Uxoricide

Hopley, George.

Night Has a Thousand Eyes. Farrar & Rinehart, 1945.

Does the psychic Jeremiah Tompkins have the ability to see the future? When he predicts that millionaire Harlan Reid will be attacked by a lion and crushed in its jaws, it seems far fetched. Then a circus loses its lion, and Jean Reid begins to think her father may soon be killed, so she turns to police detective Tom Shawn for help.

Fathers and daughters; Lions; Psychics

Inness-Brown, Elizabeth.

Burning Marguerite. Knopf, 2002.

James Jack lives an idyllic life on Grain Island, until one winter he discovers the body of his "aunt" Tante, the woman who raised him after his parents' death when he was age four. As it turns out, this will not be the only crime or death that will have to be explained. This novel's parallel narrative is split between Jack's third-person isolation and the first-person voice of Tante. Jack's path to the truth will lead him to a troubled woman named Faith, who might be his future. Tante's mysteries, including her time in New Orleans, will keep the reader guessing about the realities sheltered on this tiny island.

Coming-of-age; Islands; Louisiana—New Orleans; New England—Grain Island; Romance

Irish, William.

Waltz into Darkness. Lippincott, 1947.

Louis Durand is a wealthy businessman who starts a lonely-hearts correspondence with a woman from St. Louis. When she comes down the river to New Orleans, he finds her more beautiful than he had expected. After they are married, he also finds her more stealthy than he expected, when she cleans him out and leaves him dry.

Historical; Louisiana—New Orleans; Romance

King, Laurie R.

A Darker Place. Bantam, 1999.

Eighteen years before the start of this novel, Anne Waverly left a cult in Texas and survived a mass suicide. Her husband and daughter did not. Now a professor in Oregon and an FBI special investigator, she is asked to penetrate a Northern California commune called Change. Once there, it is difficult for her to know whether she is being demonized by her own past and whether the Change, under the leadership of Jonas Seraph, is really a cult.

Arizona; Cults; Federal Bureau of Investigation; Mothers and daughters

Kirino, Natsuo.

Riaru Warudo. Japan: Shueisha, 2006. (U.S.: *Real World*, Knopf, 2008).

Four female best friends are struggling through the summer as they cram to pass their college entrance exams. Toshi Yamanaka, the dependable one of the group, overhears an incident that may have been the murder of her neighbor. The girls decide that the most likely suspect is Worm, the son of the victim, who has fled with Toshi's bicycle and her cell phone. The girls have to decide whether they are going to help or hinder Worm, because their lives are affected as much as his is by this random act of murder.

Japan—Tokyo; Teenagers

Matheson, Richard.

Ride the Nightmare. Ballantine, 1959.

One night during dinner, Helen answers the telephone and tries to dissuade the caller when he asks for her husband but uses a name unfamiliar to Helen. Her husband, Chris, now running a music store and helping to raise their young daughter, is not happy to hear this voice from his past. It seems he thought he had run far enough, but the past has caught up to him now, and he will need to make a stand to protect his new family.

California; Revenge

Millar, Margaret.

The Listening Walls. Random House, 1959.

Amy Kellogg is accompanying her restless, and drunk, friend Wilma Wyatt when Wilma takes a dive off their Mexican hotel balcony and kills herself. After a week in a Mexican hospital, Amy returns to the states, only to leave her husband. When Amy's brother Gill becomes suspicious about Amy's absence, he hires PI Elmer Dodd to go to Mexico to find out who is killing whom.

Husbands and wives; Mexico—Mexico City

A Stranger in My Grave. Random House, 1961.

Daisy Harker has a dream in which she visits her gravesite and discovers that her tombstone bears a death date four years before the date of this story. Her obsession with discovering why the date December 2, 1955, should be on her tombstone leads her to hire PI Steve Pinata. What Steve discovers is that there is more to Daisy than meets the eye.

California—San Felice; Memory

Moore, Susanna.

In the Cut. Knopf, 1995.

Franny is a divorced NYU creative writing professor who teaches under-privileged youth while writing a book about the vernacular of the streets. Her inability to relate to other humans is contrasted with her desire for risky sexual encounters and her obsession with language. One night she observes two people having sex, and when the woman ends up a murder victim, Franny thinks she might be able to identify the killer from a tattoo he had on his wrist. Soon there is another victim, and she is going to see that tattoo again. Now she needs to decide what to do.

Academia; New York—New York; Sex

Pamuk, Orhan.

Benim Adim Kirmizi. Turkey: Ileti sim, 1998. (U.S.: *My Name Is Red*, Knopf, 2001).

As the Ottoman Empire begins to fade and Western ways move to the forefront, Islamic culture is being challenged on all fronts. The sultan commissions a work in the style of the West, which leads to a dangerous situation for the miniaturists who are conassigned to the work. When a gilder named Elegant is murdered, it calls into question the fundamental beliefs of this closed society of artists.

Art; Historical; Illumination; Islamic culture; Miniaturists; Turkey—Istanbul

Pears, Iain.

An Instance of the Fingerpost. UK: Jonathan Cape, 1997. (U.S.: Riverhead, 1998).

In 1663, Oxford University is still reeling from the end of Cromwell's era and the Restoration of Charles II to the kingdom. This society in turmoil is presented to the reader from four distinct perspectives: the Italian soldier, Marco da Cola; the mad student, Jack Prestcott; the surly mathematician, John Wallis; and the humble historian, Anthony Wood. Each tells his version of the murder of one of their fellow scholars and the charge of murder against a fetching and engaging wench named Sarah Blundy.

England—London; England—Oxford; Great Britain—History—Restoration, 1660–1688; Oxford University; Theology; Truth

Pelecanos, George.

The Turnaround. Little, Brown, 2008.

In 1972, three white boys, Alex Pappas, Billy Cachoris, and Pet Whitten, drove into an all-black neighborhood of Washington, D.C., to cause trouble. When it was all done, Billy was dead and Alex badly beaten. The only person to go to prison was one of the black men. Forty-five years later, Alex is approached by Raymond Monroe, one of the black men involved in the incident, in an attempt to heal the wounds. What neither knows is that the jailed man is about to get out of prison, and he has a different mission in mind.

Race relations; Revenge; Washington, D.C.

Pierre, D. B. C.

Vernon God Little. UK: Faber and Faber, 2003. (U.S.: Canongate, 2003).

Vernon Gregory Little is the fifteen-year-old best friend of Jesus Navarro, who has just shot up their high school using one of Vernon's father's guns. Accused of being an accessory, Vernon takes off, and as he runs he finds there are very few who will not want to make something off him and then betray him.

School massacres; Texas—Martirio

Rabe, Peter.

A Shroud for Jesso. Gold Medal, 1955.

When mobster Jackie Jesso goofs up doing a task for mob boss Gluck, he flees overseas to cool his heels. He is living in the house of Kator, a spy, and his lovely sister Renette and her husband, the Baron Helmut von Lohe. When things start getting complicated on the romance side and a half-million dollars is suddenly at stake, Jackie is tempted to take action.

Germany—Hanover; Triangles (Interpersonal relations)

Rossner, Judith.

Looking for Mr. Goodbar. Simon & Schuster, 1975.

This book opens with the murder confession of Gary Cooper White. Then we meet Theresa Dunn, a schoolteacher living alone in the city, who trolls bars looking for a man to make her happy.

New York—New York; Sex

Saul, Jamie M.

Light of Day. Morrow, 2005.

Professor Jack Owens has fled New York for a small college campus in Indiana. He is shocked one day when he is told that his fifteen-year-old son Danny has committed suicide. Wallowing in his grief, he speculates on his role in the death of his son. Then one day he is visited by a police officer, who begins to open a door that Jack may not want to go through.

Academia; Children in jeopardy; Indiana—Gilbert; Suicide

Schutz, Benjamin M.

The Mongol Reply. Five Star, 2004.

Dr. Morgan Reece is appointed by a judge to resolve the issues of custody in a divorce case. On one side is pro football coach Tom Tully, a hard-boiled man who surprised his wife with the divorce petition. On the other side is Serena Tully, who desperately wants custody of her children. Tom's attorney, Albert Garfield, is vicious in outmaneuvering Serena, so she hires attorney Lou Carlson to represent her cause. As the case probes further and further into the lives of the combatants, it reaches dangerous places that lead to murder.

Custody of children; Divorce; Trials; Virginia

Sherman, Dayne.

Welcome to the Fallen Paradise. MacAdam/Cage, 2004.

Jesse Tadlock has finished a twelve-year stint in the army and now has returned to his parish to claim an inheritance after the death of his mother and to redeem his name in the community. Taking a job as a deputy sheriff, he earns enough to become romantically involved with his old girlfriend and set up a homestead in his new home. Then his neighbor, Balem "Cotton" Moxley, threatens his life, trying to oust him from his new house. This threat unites Jesse with his roguish Uncle Red, a man willing to do whatever it takes to protect his family.

Inheritance; Louisiana—Baxter Parrish, Mount Olive

Shreve, Anita.

The Weight of Water. Little Brown, 1997.

Jean, a photographer, is cruising the Isle of Shoals in her brother-in-law Rich's boat. She is ostensibly photographing the infamous site where, in 1873, Karen and Anethe Christensen died and Maren Hontvedt survived by hiding overnight in a wintry cave. Jean battles her own demons on shipboard with her poet husband, Thomas; her five-year-old daughter, Bille; and Rich's temptress girlfriend, Adaline. When Jean finds a confession that explains all the odd events that occurred in 1873, some eerie parallels develop in her own story.

Historical; Islands; Maine—Isle of Shoals, Smuttynose Island; New Hampshire—Portsmouth; Norway—Laurvig; Norwegian immigrants; Shipboard

Simmons, Kelly.

Standing Still. Atria, 2008.

Clair Cooper, a broadcaster and working mother of three, is home one night when a kidnapper bursts into her home. Despite her panic disorder, she sacrifices herself for her child by talking the man into taking her away. For seven days she lies in a motel room, connecting with her kidnapper and wondering about the connections she does not have with her own husband, Sam.

Kidnapping

Smith, Peter Moore.

Raveling. Little Brown, 2000.

Pilot James Aire is a schizophrenic who lives in a world of hurt for twenty years, wondering if he had anything to do with the disappearance of his seven-year-old sister, Fiona. After returning home to take care of his sick mother, Pilot must deal with his arrogant neurosurgeon brother, Eric. When he is assigned to Katherine as a new therapist, he begins to recount what he remembers of that fateful night so that he can live in peace.

Children in jeopardy; Schizophrenia

Los Angeles. Little, Brown, 2005.

Angel Veronchek is an albino who hangs out in his apartment, avoiding the Hollywood of his father, a successful movie producer, but taking drugs and endlessly working on a screenplay. However, he has fallen in love with his neighbor, the stripper named Angela. When she calls one night and just says his name, Angel knows she is in trouble and ventures out of his safe haven to help the only woman he has ever loved.

Albinos; California—Los Angeles; Missing persons; Motion pictures

Stella, Charlie.

Cheapskates. Carroll & Graf, 2005.

When Reese Walters made a promise to his cell mate at Fishkill Penitentiary, it stuck. So when Peter Rizzo is killed, Reese decides to do something about it. Unfortunately, the something includes a missing $50,000 in cash, a greedy ex-wife, a police investigation, and one angry mobster named Wigs.

Ex-convicts; New York—New York; Revenge

Stout, Rex.

How Like a God. Vanguard, 1929.

Told from the perspective of the inner voice of the main character, Bill Sidney, this is a novel about sexual obsession. It all starts when Bill is in college and is seduced by the ten-year-old daughter of his laundress, Millicent Moran. Eventually he falls under the spell of his sister, Jane; his wife, Erma; and the woman he really loved, named Lucy. Later in life, Millicent returns to plague him. Finally, Bill decides only he can break her power over him.

Obsession; Sex

Swierczynski, Duane.

The Blonde. St. Martin's Minotaur, 2006.

Journalist Jack Eisley is minding his own business in an airport lounge when a blonde named Kelly White poisons his cocktail. With the anecdote for his poison, she is able to keep him within ten feet of her, a solution she needs for her own infection with nanites, which will cause her death if she does not have human companionship. Mike Kowalski, with Homeland Security, is on her trail, but he also wants to hunt down and kill the scientist behind this tracking technology.

Hit men; Nanotechnology; Pennsylvania—Philadelphia

Tartt, Donna.

The Little Friend. Knopf, 2002.

Harriet Cleve Dufresnes lives in Alexandria, Mississippi, under the shadow of the black tupelo tree where her brother Robin hanged himself when she was six months old. The tragedy has fractured her parent's marriage, depressed her mother Charlotte, and sent her older sister Allison into a near catatonic state. Harriet's three aunts and grandmother Edie are trying to preserve a bygone lifestyle in this Southern town, when one summer, at age twelve, Harriet decides to find out what really happened to her brother.

Coming-of-age; Mississippi—Alexandria; Mothers and daughters; Sisters; Suicide

Thiong'o, Ngũgĩ wa.

Petals of Blood. Dutton, 1978.

This novel begins with the information that three owners of the Theng'eta Breweries and Enterprises, Ltd., have been murdered. The police arrest three individuals who may be connected to the crime, while a fourth suspect lies injured in the hospital. The balance of the book is the story of the four suspects—the struggling teacher, the wounded revolutionary, the disillusioned social activist, and the lonely prostitute—who have settled in the rural village of Ilmorog to escape from the world. Told from various points of view over the twelve years leading up to the murders, the novel reveals the harsh realities and disappointments of life in independent Kenya, struggling to join the contemporary world without sacrificing its deep-rooted Kenyan traditions and beliefs.

Colonialism; Kenya; Kenya—Ilmorog

Thompson, Jim.

Cropper's Cabin. Lion Books, 1952.

Tommy Carver lives with his no-good dad and the prostitute his father keeps to nanny his son. While the boy deals with all of his issues, including his love for the mixed-race daughter of the richest man around, he finds himself facing a murder charge when that man is found dead.

Fathers and sons; Oklahoma

The Criminal. Lion Books, 1953.

A fifteen-year-old boy named Bob Talbert is accused of raping and strangling a girl in his neighborhood. Forced to confess and abandoned by his father, Al, Bobby is also condemned by the local newspaper, *The Star*, which needs his story to increase its circulation numbers. Bob's only defender, a lawyer named Kossmeyer, is one of the nine points of view from which this story is told.

Fathers and sons; Newspapers; Rape

South of Heaven. Fawcett Gold Medal, 1967.

South of heaven is the area in west Texas where a gas pipeline is being laid by a mixture of people, including some hoboes, during the 1920s. Tommy Burwell tells us the story of these times from a forty-year perspective. He relates his childhood difficulties, including the death of his grandparents in a dynamite explosion. This leads to a meeting with Four Trey Whiteside, who wants Tommy to use explosives on the pipeline. He also meets Carol, a townie who is willing to give herself to the young man. But then while he goes about his job, he begins to see suspicious things on the line, especially regarding the Long Gang. Then he is arrested for murder.

Historical; Hoboes; Pipelines; Texas—Odessa

Child of Rage. Lancer Militaria, 1972.

Allen Smith is a mixed-race child raised by his white mother, a prostitute, who sexually abuses him. At school, he identifies with a black family, but in an evil way: he wants everything they have. When school staff members get in the way, Allen finds a method of revenge on them and his mom.

Children in jeopardy; New York—New York; Prostitutes; Sexual abuse

Walters, Minette.

The Sculptress. UK: Macmillan, 1993. (U.S.: St. Martin's, 1993).

Convicted of chopping up her mother and sister with an ax, Olive Martin is passing her life in prison carving human figures out of wax. When her publisher suggests there may be a book in Olive's story, writer Rosalind Leigh grudgingly decides to interview Olive. Once she meets Olive, Roz is drawn back into her cell repeatedly as she begins to redefine what the truth surrounding this case is.

Convicts; England; Journalists; Prisons

The Breaker. UK: McClelland & Stewart,1998. (U.S.: Macmillan, 1998).

When Kate Sumner's body washes ashore at Dorset, it becomes apparent she has been drugged, raped, and thrown in the sea to drown. Equally chilling, her three-year-old daughter Hannah is founded wandering the streets of the town of Poole. As the police investigate, credible suspects surface, ranging from the victim's husband William, to a randy actor named Steven Harding, to a teacher named Tony Bridges. The case is investigated from two different angles, that of the outsider, Detective Inspector John Galbraith, and that of local constable Nick Ingram, with whom Galbraith matches wits. Ingram is attracted to Maggie Jenner, a local stable owner who has fallen on hard times. As each lie in the case is exposed, the detectives get one step closer to understanding the horror of this crime.

Children in jeopardy; England—Dorset; Sailing

The Shape of Snakes. UK: Macmillan, 2000. (U.S.: Putnam, 2001).

M. Ranelagh, who has been on a twenty-year mission to explain the death of her neighbor on Graham Road, "Mad Annie" Butts, narrates this story. It was M. who found Butts dying in a gutter one night following months of abuse at the hands of her neighbors due to Butts's Tourette's syndrome and alcoholism. Driven by a sense of justice and a need for revenge, M. pursues a line of investigation that puts her own family at risk and sets neighbor against neighbor as each truth is revealed.

England—Dorset, Dorchester; England—London; Race relations; Revenge; Tourette's syndrome

Watson, Larry.

Montana 1948. Milkweed, 1993.

Wesley Hayden is the sheriff of the small Montana town of Bentrock in 1948. His brother Frank is a returned war hero and the town's doctor. When the sheriff's maid, Marie Little Feather, a Sioux, is reluctant to be seen by Frank, Wesley begins to suspect that all is not well in this community. Later Marie is found dead, and Wesley is forced to make a difficult choice. All of the complex maneuverings in this small town are witnessed by twelve-year-old David Hayden, Wesley's son, including a crucial clue that may determine if murder occurred.

Coming-of-age; Montana—Bentrock; Native Americans

Welch, Louise.

The Cutting Room. UK: Canongate, 2002.

Rilke is an auctioneer for a Glasgow firm. When assigned to retrieve the belongings of Roddy McKindless, he is stunned to find a snuff film among a vast collection of pornography. Rilke feels compelled to find out who murdered the girl in the film and moves into the dark side of Glasgow to get the answers.

Auctions; Homosexuality; Pornography; Scotland—Glasgow

Willeford, Charles.

Pick-up. Beacon, 1955.

Helen Meredith is a loose woman who will take on any man when she was drunk. She is on a quest to loose herself in the depths of society, trying to forget her mother and her abusive husband. Harry Jordan is a former artist, now a coffee-shop counterman, who decides that Helen could be more than a drinking partner. As the two try to develop a relationship, they are unable to find solace in any of their actions and begin a spiral down into tragedy.

Alcoholism; California—San Francisco

Williams, Charles.

Man on a Leash. Putnam, 1973.

Eric Romstead has returned to his hometown, where he finds his father, Gunnar, dead in what is described as a drug deal gone bad. Then Eric finds a corpse in his father's house that further links him to the underworld. As Eric works to prove his father was innocent, he realizes that he himself may be the next victim.

Drugs; Fathers and sons; Nevada—Coleville

Williams, Darren.

Angel Rock. UK: HarperCollins, 2002. (U.S.: Knopf, 2002).

When twelve-year-old Tom Ferry and his four-year-old stepbrother Flynn are neglected by their ne'er-do-well father, they wander away from a construction site and are lost for a week in the Australian bush outside of the community of Angel Rock. When after a week only Tom returns, the boy is too traumatized to explain what has happened. Local Sheriff Pop Mathers fails to find out, and a big-city investigator named Gibson, originally sent to solve the suicide of Darcy Steele, takes up the challenge of trying to pry open the secrets of this rural Australian community.

Australia—New South Wales—Angel Rock; Children in jeopardy; Families

Woolrich, Cornell.

The Bride Wore Black. Simon & Schuster, 1940.

Julie Killeen is a serial killer. She methodically hunts down men and kills them. At the end of her tale, it is revealed why she is doing this, and a lesson is learned about responsibility and revenge.

Revenge; Serial killer

The Black Angel. Doubleday, Doran, 1943.

When her husband Kirk is falsely accused of murdering his lover, Mia Mercer, his very faithful wife Alberta takes on a crusade to free him. In order to find the truth, she must integrate herself with the many suspects, which requires her to assume various roles and jobs as a detective.

False imprisonment

True Crime Victims

Behn, Noel.

Lindbergh: The Crime. Atlantic Monthly, 1994.

All of the possible scenarios are laid out in this book, which tries to examine who could have done what when the Lindberghs' child was kidnapped in 1932. The basic premise here is that Bruno Hauptmann was innocent.

Kidnapping; New Jersey—Hopewell

Bryan, Patricia L. and Thomas Wolf.

Midnight Assassin: A Murder in America's Heartland. Algonquin, 2005.

In 1900, an Iowa farmer named John Hossack was murdered in his bed with an ax. Although logic dictated that his wife was the culprit, she was tried twice and acquitted of the murder, perhaps due to a hint of abuse.

Husbands and wives; Iowa—Indianola; Trials

de Ford, Miriam Allen.

The Overbury Affair: The Murder Trial That Rocked the Court of King James I. Chilton, 1960.

During the reign of King James I, Thomas Overbury and Robert Carr formed an association that would lead them to the halls of power. Along the way, Overbury opposed a romantic liaison of his friend and was locked in The Tower for his troubles. Then someone decided he had to die.

England—London; James I, King of England—1566–1625

Dumas, Timothy.

Greentown: Murder and Mystery in Greenwich, America's Wealthiest Community. Arcade, 1998.

In 1975, a fifteen-year-old girl named Martha Moxley was beaten to death with a golf club during an annual town revelry known as Mischief Night. The club came from the home of Thomas Skakel, the last person to see Martha alive and a relative of the Kennedy family through marriage. The wealth and power of this town's families allowed the whole community to avoid punishment for this crime, but it did not allow the truth to be hidden.

Connecticut—Greenwich; Corruption

Fisher, Jim.

The Ghosts of Hopewell: Setting the Record Straight in the Lindbergh Case. Southern Illinois University Press, 1999.

The sad tragedy of the kidnapping of Charles Lindbergh's baby is compounded by the historical dissatisfaction with the arrest and execution of Bruno Hauptmann. Contemporary researchers like Fisher want to take another look at the evidence to evaluate whether there could have been another solution to this case.

Kidnapping; New Jersey—Hopewell

Fosburgh, Lacey.

Closing Time: The True Story of the "Goodbar" Murder. Delacorte, 1977.

When reporter Lacey Fosburgh was assigned to cover the murder of Katherine Cleary, she became obsessed with discovering why this pretty young schoolteacher would hang out all night in bars and go home with a stranger. Did this behavior mean she would inevitably meet the end she did?

Bars; New York—New York

Frasca, John.

The Mulberry Tree. Prentice-Hall, 1968.

When Mulberry experienced a crime wave, the local police arrested Robert Watson. After he went to jail, the crime wave continued. It was not until the author, an investigative reporter, showed interest in the case that justice was served and the true guilty parties were punished.

Florida—Mulberry; Trials

Gentry, Curt.

Frame-up: The Incredible Case of Tom Mooney and Warren Billings. Norton, 1967.

When a bomb went off during a parade on Market Street in San Francisco in 1916, the powers that be found two radical labor leaders, Tom Mooney and Warren Billings, the perfect scapegoats for the crime. For twenty-three years the men languished in prison for a crime they did not commit. The author shows that the district attorney of San Francisco suppressed key evidence that would have freed them.

California— San Francisco; Trials

Golden, Harry.

A Little Girl Is Dead. World, 1965.

When the body of fourteen-year-old Mary Phagan was found in the basement of the National Pencil Company in Atlanta, the factory's superintendent, Leo Frank, was arrested. With a black man testifying against a capitalist Jew, the trial became a national sensation. Found guilty, Frank had his sentence commuted by the governor, only to be lynched by a gang of prominent men from the community. The question still remains: Who murdered May Phagan.

Anti-Semitism; Children in jeopardy; Georgia—Atlanta

Grisham, John.

The Innocent Man: Murder and Injustice in a Small Town. Doubleday, 2006.

When the body of Debra Sue Carter, a waitress, was found in 1982, the police were initially baffled. Then they focused on Ron Williamson, a former glory days boy who was down on his luck and seemed like the type to be capable of murder. The problem was that he was innocent.

Oklahoma—Ada; Trials

Harwell, Fred.

A True Deliverance: The Joan Little Case. Knopf, 1980.

When Joan Little murdered a prison guard who was trying to rape her in her cell, the case might have disappeared from public view. What brought it to the front page of American newspapers was the fact that Joan was black and the rapist was white.

North Carolina—Washington; Prisons; Racism; Rape

Hodel, Steve.

Black Dahlia Avenger: The True Story. Arcade, 2003.

In 1947, a woman's body was found in Los Angeles, brutally murdered. Her death went down in history as The Black Dahlia mystery. One of the great unsolved crimes of American crime lore, it fascinated Hodel, a former L.A. homicide detective, and during his retirement he stumbled on a clue to this crime that involved him personally.

Black Dahlia murder; California—Los Angeles; Fathers and sons

Howard, Clark.

Zebra: The True Account of the 179 Days of Terror in San Francisco. Richard Marek, 1979.

In 1973 and 1974, five black men, following the call of their Black Muslim beliefs, tried to become Death Angels. In order to qualify, they had to sacrifice nine white victims to Allah. How this mission left the state of California in the grip of terror is portrayed by following the police investigation.

Black Muslims; California—San Francisco; Racism

Jentz, Terri.

Strange Piece of Paradise. Farrar, Straus & Giroux, 2006.

While in college at Yale, Terri Jentz and her friend, Shayna Weiss, decided to bike across the country. While camping in Oregon's Cline Falls State Park, the two were deliberately run over by a cowboy, who then attacked them with an ax. Both women survived, and as a catharsis, Jentz decided to return to the area fifteen years later to find out who attacked them.

Oregon—Cline Falls State Park; Revenge

Jonas, George, and Barbara Amiel.

By Persons Unknown: The Strange Death of Christine Demeter. Grove, 1977.

Real estate developer Peter Demeter was married to former model Christine Demeter, and they lived apparently happily together with their daughter. That is, until the night Christine was brutally murdered in the family garage. At Peter's trial, a bizarre story of long distance love affairs and shadowy hit men fascinated the nation as the rich man's world crumbled and the police struggled to name the hit man.

Canada—Ontario; Models

Kates, Brian.

The Murder of a Shopping Bag Lady. Harcourt Brace Jovanovich, 1985.

When reporter Brian Kates stumbled onto the sad murder of homeless bag lady Phyllis Iannotta, he launched a four-year investigation into her life, trying to explain how she ended up dead on the streets of New York City.

Homeless; New York—New York

Kennedy, Ludovic.

The Airman and the Carpenter: The Lindbergh Kidnapping and the Framing of Richard Hauptmann. Viking, 1985. (Also *Crime of the Century: The Lindbergh Kidnapping and the Framing of Richard Hauptmann*, Penguin, 1996).

Kennedy's perspective on the nation's most famous kidnapping is made clear from the subtitle of this book. How did such a famous case end up with the wrong man being convicted for the crime?

Kidnapping; New Jersey—Hopewell

Keyes, Daniel.

The Minds of Billy Milligan. Random House, 1981.

Students on the campus of The Ohio State University could breath a sign of relief when the serial rapist who had terrorized them was arrested. When the police psychologist examined the suspect, Billy Milligan, he found a man with twenty-four separate personalities.

Multiple personalities; Ohio—Columbus; Rape

Kleiman, Dena.

A Deadly Silence: The Ordeal of Cheryl Pierson; a Case of Incest and Murder. Atlantic Monthly, 1988.

When popular electrician James Pierson was murdered in his own driveway, the community was shocked. But they were even more shocked when it was revealed that his eldest daughter and her boyfriend had arranged for his murder. Then the community found out why, and they were shocked all over again.

Incest; New York—Selden

Levitt, Leonard.

Conviction: Solving the Moxley Murder. Regan, 2004.

See Dumas, above, for a summary of this case. Here, investigative reporter Levitt is able to include the updated information from when Michael Skakel was put on trial for the murder of Martha Moxley.

Connecticut—Greenwich; Corruption

Lincoln, Victoria.

A Private Disgrace: Lizzie Borden by Daylight. Putnam, 1967,

As a native from Fall River, the author believes she can bring special insight into the Lizzie Borden case. Her claims include a previously unknown motive, a new murder method, and insight into the clothes Lizzie wore on the day she did the deed.

Massachusetts—Fall River

Mayer, Robert.

The Dreams of Ada. Viking, 1987.

In Ada, Oklahoma, a convenience store clerk named Denice Haraway disappeared late one night. Six months later, based on the ramblings of one man and a recounting of his dreams, the police arrested Tommy Ward and Karl Fontenot. Eventually the two were on death row, convicted of murder by a jury who never heard evidence about a body, a murder weapon, or a motive.

Oklahoma—Ada; Trials

Miller, Gene.

Invitation to a Lynching. Doubleday, 1975.

When a gas station was robbed and two attendants were murdered, two black men were arrested, tried, and convicted of the crime. Years later, when a white man wished to confess to the crime and free the men, his testimony was ignored.

False confessions; Florida—Highland View; Race relations

Neff, James.

Unfinished Murder: The Capture of a Serial Rapist. Pocket, 1995.

For five years, Ronnie Shelton terrorized Cleveland, raping more than a hundred women even though he was brought to the attention of the police for other, petty crimes. When he was finally captured on a rape charge, thirty of his victims came together to testify and keep him off the streets forever.

Ohio—Cleveland; Rape

The Wrong Man: The Final Verdict on the Dr. Sam Sheppard Murder Case. Random House, 2001.

In 1954, Dr. Sam Sheppard was accused, tried, and convicted for killing his pregnant wife Marilyn, despite his defense of having wrestled with a mysterious intruder. In the 1990s, lawyer F. Lee Bailey got Sheppard a new trial, at which he was acquitted; he died four short years later. Although popular opinion still believes that he was the killer, this book attempts to point the finger in a different direction, identifying the mysterious man for the first time.

Acquittals; Ohio—Bay Village; Trials

Olsen, Jack.

"Doc": The Rape of the Town of Lovell. Atheneum, 1989.

For over twenty-five years, Dr. John Story raped his female patients. He was able to get away with this because most of his patients were Mormon small-town women, too naïve to doubt their physician, and with no power to challenge a pillar of the community.

Doctors; Mormons; Rape; Wyoming—Lovell

O'Malley, Suzanne.

"Are You There Alone?": The Unspeakable Crimes of Andrea Yates. Simon & Schuster, 2004.

> Who speaks for a mother when she deliberately drowns five of her children in a bathtub? At the time of her trial, Andrea Yates received a sentence that ignored her attempt to use a postpartum depression defense, partially based on false testimony. As other evidence of past suicide attempts and mental illness surfaced after the trial, they led to the question, Is there another fate for this woman?
>
> Children in jeopardy; Postpartum depression; Texas—Houston; Trials

Oney, Steve.

And the Dead Shall Rise: The Murder of Mary Phagan and the Lynching of Leo Frank. Pantheon, 2003.

> The murder of thirteen-year-old pencil factory worker Mary Phagan was a sensation. Leo Frank was accused, tried, and convicted for the crime. When the governor of Georgia commuted Frank's sentence to life in prison, he was removed from prison by a mob and lynched. Over time, questions have arisen about Frank's Jewish faith, the continuing influence of the North in the postwar South, the testimony of the African American witness, and the zealousness of a police force eager to get a conviction.
>
> Children in jeopardy; Georgia—Atlanta; Georgia—Marietta; Lynching; Trials

Pomeroy, Sarah B.

The Murder of Regilla: A Case of Domestic Violence in Antiquity. Harvard University, 2007.

> Regilla married Herodes at the age of fifteen and bore him five children over the next twenty years. But when she died while pregnant with the sixth, from a blow to the stomach, Herodes was put on trial for her murder. After being acquitted, he erected statues to his dead wife all over Rome, but this author still thinks he was guilty.
>
> Husbands and wives; Italy—Rome

Robins, Natalie, and Steven M. Aronson.

Savage Grace: The True Story of Fatal Relations in a Rich and Famous American Family. Morrow, 1985.

> All the Baekeland heirs lived the high life on the profits from Bakelite, invented by Leo Hendrik Baekeland, but that did not make them happy. When son Brooks married Barbara Daly, it should have been an ideal marriage. Instead it led to madness, incest, and matricide.
>
> Incest; Matricide

Ruddick, James.

Death at the Priory: Sex, Love, and Murder in Victorian England. Atlantic Monthly, 2001.

Charles Bravo married Florence Ricardo in 1875. The successful attorney moved his bride into The Priory, a mansion outside of London, and then began to make her life unbearable. When Charles was poisoned, the courts were unable todetermine who was the murderer. With the passing of time, Ruddick can study the evidence and point a finger at the most likely suspect.

England—London; Husbands and wives; Poisons; Victorian England

Rule, Ann.

Small Sacrifices: A True Story of Passion and Murder. New American Library, 1987.

When Diana Downs arrived at an Oregon hospital, she said she and her three children had been shot by a stranger on a remote road. After one child died, investigators began to explore her story. Eventually the details did not add up.

Children in jeopardy; Oregon—Springfield

If You Really Loved Me: A True Story of Desire and Murder. Simon & Schuster, 1991.

When technology wizard David Brown decided to get rid of his wife Linda, he convinced his fourteen-year-old daughter Cinnamon to murder her and take the fall. While his daughter wasted away in prison, David went on to marry Linda's sister. Five years after this tragedy, a suspicious prosecutor decided to reinvestigate the case, and things began to fall apart.

California—Orange County; Matricide

Everything She Ever Wanted: A True Story of Obsessive Love, Murder & Betrayal. Simon & Schuster, 1992.

Patricia Taylor Allanson was a master manipulator. Raised to think of herself as the reincarnation of Scarlett O'Hara, she was an obsessive narcissist who wreaked havoc among her family, friends, and acquaintances. In her wake she left arson, suicides, poisonings, and even murder.

Georgia—Atlanta; Obsession

Bitter Harvest: A Woman's Fury, A Mother's Sacrifice. Simon & Schuster, 1997.

Dr. Debora Green was a trusted physician with a loving physician husband and three children. Behind the surface lived a monster, a woman who slowly poisoned her husband after he began an affair. Then one night her demons led her to light a fire, with tragic consequences.

Arson; Kansas—Prairie Village; Missouri—Kansas City; Physicians

And Never Let Her Go: Thomas Capano: The Deadly Seducer. Simon & Schuster, 1999.

"Tommy" Capano was the power behind the throne in Delaware politics. Anne Marie Fahey was the secretary for Delaware's governor, Thomas Carper. They had an affair. Then Anne disappeared. When Capano's secret world began to disintegrate, more of his emotional victims were revealed.

Adultery; Delaware—Wilmington; Politics

Every Breath You Take: A True Story of Obsession, Revenge and Murder. Free, 2001.

When Shelia Blackthorne Bellush divorced multimillionaire Allen Blackthorne, she told how he said he would track her down and know "every breath you take." Although he was in San Antonio on the day Shelia was murdered in Sarasota, an evidence trail eventually led back to an obsessive ex-husband who just could not let go.

Divorce; Florida—Sarasota; Obsession; Texas—San Antonio

Schutze, Jim.

By Two and Two: The Scandalous Story of Twin Sisters Accused of a Shocking Crime of Passion. Morrow, 1995.

Betty and Peggy Woods were twins, born in a Southern way of life that looked down on women and still had racist aspects in every day life. When Betty married a prominent ophthalmologist named Jack Wilson, all should have gone well. But personal problems on both sides of the marriage drove her to alcoholism and affairs with black men. Then Wilson was murdered, and a schizophrenic alcoholic named James White claimed Betty and Peggy had hired him to murder Jack.

Alabama—Huntsville; Trials; Twins

Serrano, Richard A.

One of Ours: Timothy McVeigh and the Oklahoma City Bombing. Norton, 1998.

When the Alfred P. Murrah Federal Building in Oklahoma City was blown up in 1995, 128 people were killed and over 500 injured. When the shock of the explosion wore off, the nation was shocked again: the terrorist was one of us.

Bombs; Oklahoma—Oklahoma City; Terrorism

Siegel, Barry.

A Death in White Bear Lake: The True Chronicle of an All-American Town. Bantam, 1990.

Over twenty years after the death of Dennis Jurgens, a jury finally found someone guilty for his death. Given up by his birth mother, Jerry Sherwood, in 1962, Dennis had spent his childhood in a small Minnesota town. Despite the mysterious circumstances that surrounded his death, no one was convicted of the crime until Jerry began a quest in 1980 to find the truth.

Adoption; Children in jeopardy; Minnesota—White Bear Lake

Stashower, Daniel.

The Beautiful Cigar Girl: Mary Rogers, Edgar Allan Poe, and the Invention of Murder. Dutton, 2006.

> Mary Rogers was a tobacco store clerk, whose body was found floating in the river in 1841. Her death was turned into a media circus but remained unsolved. Then writer Edgar Allan Poe decided to step in and solve the case by writing *The Mystery of Marie Rogêt.*

> New York—New York; Poe, Edgar Allan

Stowers, Carlton.

To the Last Breath: Three Women Fight for the Truth Behind a Child's Tragic Murder. St. Martin's Press, 1998.

> In 1994, two-year-old Renee Goode died in her crib at her father Shane Goode's house. Shane and his wife Annette were separated, and she was suspicious about how her daughter had died. Enlisting the aid of her mother, Sharon Crouch, and a female detective who believed in her cause, she began a dogged investigation that eventually led to a revelation that shocked their small town.

> Children in jeopardy; Divorce; Texas—Alvin

Sullivan, Robert.

The Disappearance of Dr. Parkman. Little, Brown, 1971.

> Dr. George Parkman was one of the richest men in Boston in 1850, and when his headless corpse was found it created a sensation. Professor John Webster of the Harvard Medical College was accused of the murder, and his trial is still considered a travesty. The charge to the jury by Chief Justice Shaw is still studied in law schools today, but the question of who murdered Dr. Parkman may still be unanswered.

> Massachusetts—Boston; Trials

Swindle, Howard.

Trespasses: Portrait of a Serial Rapist. Viking, 1996.

> Dallas was terrorized by the Ski Mask Rapist, suspected of having raped nearly a hundred women from 1985 to 1990. Very careful, he was able to stay free despite being the police department's number one suspect. When finally apprehended, Gilbert Escobedo proved to be the archetype serial rapist.

> Rape; Texas—Dallas

Taylor, John.

The Count and the Confession: A True Mystery. Random House, 2002.

> Beverly Monroe was a successful patents analyst at Philip Morris and a mother of three children. When she fell in love with the romantic Polish count, Roger de la Burde, a tobacco research chemist, she fell hard. Then

Burde committed suicide. However, the police began to think it was murder, and she confesses to the crime. The evidence began to reveal that Burde was more than Monroe knew, but then maybe Beverly was not what she seemed, either.

Affairs; Suicide; Virginia—Richmond

Tidyman, Ernest.

Dummy. Little, Brown, 1974.
Donald Lang, known as "The Dummy" in his Chicago neighborhood, was the last person seen with a prostitute who was found murdered. When he was put on trial, the task was how to properly defend a man who could not speak, write, or read lips and had never learned sign language.

Handicapped; Illinois—Chicago

Waller, George.

Kidnap: The Story of the Lindbergh Case. Dial, 1961.
This work tells the story of the famous Lindbergh kidnapping in four parts: the crime, the capture, the trial, and the appeal.

Kidnapping; New Jersey—Hopewell

Wambaugh, Joseph.

The Blooding. Morrow, 1989.
Two teenagers were raped and murdered near a psychiatric hospital. One victim was found on the Black Path between a construction site and the hospital. The other was found in Ten Pound Lane, again near the hospital. The police were desperate to solve the crime, until Alec Jeffreys discovered a way to conduct genetic fingerprinting and solved two terrible crimes by testing the entire village.

DNA; England—Leicestershire; Rape

Wright, William.

The Von Bülow Affair. Delacorte, 1983.
Martha "Sunny" Crawford Von Bülow suffered an overdose of insulin that put her into a coma. This was not the first such incident in her life, so suspicion fell on her husband. Claus Von Bülow had married the heiress and manipulated her life for his gain. Then he was on the world stage when he went on trial.

Rhode Island—Newport; Trials; Uxoricide

Chapter 5

Criminal Detectives

The criminal detectives discussed in this chapter are the companions to the mystery and detective heroes covered in the companion volume to this book, *Make Mine a Mystery*. The difference between the two is that in this book we are looking at protagonists whose moral compass does not always lead them down the right path. Instead, these fictional characters are often led down the dark path of criminal behavior, making them as dangerous as any criminal antagonist.

Cops Gone Bad

Society expects that those individuals who are appointed to enforce the law will not descend to the level of those who break it. The books listed in this section prove that that is not always the way law enforcement occurs in many societies.

Benchmark Cops Gone Bad Novels

Ambler, Eric.

The Mask of Dimitrios. UK: Hodder & Stoughton, 1939. (U.S.: *Coffin for Dimitrios*, Knopf, 1939).

> Charles Latimer, an author of mysteries, is traveling when he meets Turkish Colonel Haki, a fan of Latimer's espionage novels. Haki shares a tale about master criminal Dimitrios Makropolous, whose story so fascinates Latimer that he begins to search for the truth about this criminal. As the search progresses, Latimer begins to wonder if he is the victim of a masterful manipulation.

> Authors; Balkans; Turkey—Istanbul

Caspary, Vera.

Laura. Houghton Mifflin, 1943.

> When Mark McPherson, the investigating officer who tries to solve the murder of Laura Hunt, falls in love with her portrait, he discovers two other men who also loved the woman when she was alive.

> New York—New York; Romance

Thompson, Jim.

Pop. 1280. Fawcett, 1964.

In Potts County, Texas, Nick Corey has been sheriff for a long time. He lives with a wife who hates him and a brother-in-law who is a petty criminal. From Corey's easygoing manner and the way the people he knows push him around, it would seem he is mild mannered. In reality, he is plotting his revenge against those who have not shown him respect and to get himself reelected as sheriff.

Elections; Revenge; Texas—Pottsville

Vidocq, François Eugéne.

Mémoires de Vidocq, Chef de la Police de Sureté, jusqu'en 1827. France: Tenon, 1828–1829. (UK: *Memoirs of Vidocq, principal agent of the French police until 1827*, Hunt and Clarke, 1828–1829) (U.S.: *Vidocq: The Personal Memoirs of the First Great Detective*, Houghton Mifflin, 1935).

After being captured and jailed in the La Force Prison, the former soldier Vidocq offered his services as a police spy. He rose in the ranks of the Sûreté until he became the head of the detective branch. This work recounts his life from his birth until he resigned from the force in 1827. This may be the world's first work of faction; the debate continues about how honest and forthright Vidocq was in re-creating his life.

Detectives; France; Sûreté

Cops Gone Bad Novels

Claudel, Philippe.

Les Âmes Grises. France: Éditions Stock, 2003. (UK: *Grey Souls*, Weidenfeld & Nicolson, 2005). (U.S.: *By a Slow River*, Knopf, 2006).

This novel has an unreliable narrator who tells tales from a number of different time periods. For example, in 1917 a ten-year-old girl is found strangled in a small French village while the battles of World War I rage nearby. To lay before the reader who the most likely suspects are, the policeman narrator takes us back to the arrival of the new schoolteacher and how that affected the town's prosecutor, Pierre-Ange Destinat. "The Case" falls under the domain of the judge and the colonel, two men who rule the town, with ominous consequences. Only in the last pages of the work do we understand who is guilty of all the crimes in this novel.

France; Historical; World War I

Francisco, Ruth.

Good Morning, Darkness. Mysterious Press, 2004.

Laura Finnegan is a magnet for romance. Her boyfriend, real estate agent Scott Goodsell, obsesses about her after Laura breaks off their relationship. Reggie

Brooks, an African American LAPD detective who has been teaching her self-defense to protect herself from Scott, yearns to get closer. A Mexican fisherman, who regularly spies on her, finds an arm while fishing on Venice Beach. It is clear that Laura went missing after she was seen by Scott having a date with another man, but she also quit her job and told everyone she was moving to the East. Brooks, obsessed with Laura, is willing to put his life on the line to find out if the body on the beach was Laura.

California—Los Angeles; Fishermen; Missing persons; Obsession

Goodis, Davis.

Of Missing Persons. Morrow, 1950.

Captain Paul Ballard is the head of the Missing Persons Bureau. Burnt out by all that he sees in the big unnamed city where he works, it is difficult to get past his hardened exterior. Even his wife, Claire, struggles with his obsession with doing his job. When Myra Nichols refuses to admit her husband is dead, suspicion falls on the registered nurse who is assigned to help the woman. This time Ballard is willing to put his career on the line to prove that Jean Landis did not do what she is accused of.

Missing persons; Obsession

Night Squad. Fawcett, 1961.

When things go south for cop Corey Bradford, he is fired from the police force on a charge of corruption. Desperate when someone tries to kill him, he hires on with mobster Walter Grogan for protection. That brings him to the attention of the special police unit known as The Night Squad, who think a dirty ex-cop is a perfect candidate to turn into a mole in the mobster's gang.

Organized crime; Police corruption

Highsmith, Patricia.

A Dog's Ransom. Knopf, 1972.

Edward Reynolds lives with his wife, Greta, and their beloved poodle, Lisa. Their neighbor, Kenneth Rowajinski, takes out his frustrations with the world on them by killing Lisa. Kenneth then begins to send ransom notes to the couple, trying to extort their emotions as much as ransom. When the case is turned over to Clarence Duhamell, a rookie cop, he turns out to be as obsessive as the perpetrator, and the consequences are tragic.

Dogs; New York—New York; Obsession

Kernick, Simon.

The Business of Dying. UK: Transworld, 2002. (U.S.: St. Martin's Minotaur, 2002).

Dennis Milne has taken it upon himself as a police officer to moonlight as a hit man, taking out all the bad guys vigilante-style on the orders of Raymond Keen, a businessman who might be a mobster. When his latest hit turns out to be two customs agents and an accountant, he is conflicted because the men were guilty of corruption. Meanwhile, as a cop he is searching for the killer of a hooker named Miriam Fox, whom he wants to avenge. Then he finds out there may be a witness to his latest hit.

England—London; Hit men; Police corruption

The Crime Trade. UK: Bantam, 2004. (U.S.: St. Martin's Minotaur, 2004).
When an operation against Columbian drug lords goes awry, Stegs Jenner's partner is killed. DI John Gallen believes that perhaps the fatal shot was fired by Jenner. He and his partner need to know who killed their informer, Slim Robbie O'Brien, the man who set up the sting in the first place.

Drugs; England—London; Police corruption

A Good Day to Die. UK: Bantam, 2005. (U.S.: St. Martin's Minotaur, 2006).
Mick Kane is a former police officer named Dennis Milne, who has turned vigilante, killing hoods for hire. When a former friend, Detective Asif Malik, is murdered, Kane risks everything to hunt down his killers.

England—London; Hit men

Kertész, Imre.

Detektívtörténet. Hungary: Szepirodalmi, 1977. (U.S.: *Detective Story*, Knopf, 2008).
Fallout from a fallen dictatorial regime: What happens when a torturer is imprisoned for crimes committed under the previous government? Antonio Martens has asked for the opportunity to write out his confession in the deaths of prominent opposition leader, department store magnate Federigo Salinas and his worthless son, Enrique. Should the determination of what is right and wrong be left to those who hold power?

Central America; Political crimes; Torture

Landay, William.

Mission Flats. Delacorte, 2003.
Police chief Ben Truman is trying to solve a murder in his own small town, Versailles, Maine, by walking the mean streets of a Boston neighborhood called Mission Flats. After he finds the body of a Boston DA in a remote Maine cabin, he seeks the advice of a retired Boston cop named John Kelly and moves to the big city to take on the people who live there, including Kelly's daughter, with surprising results. The question is, Who is manipulating whom in this narrative?

Maine—Versailles; Massachusetts—Boston, Mission Flats; Mothers and sons

McDermid, Val.

A Place of Execution. UK: HarperCollins, 1999. (U.S.: St. Martin's Minotaur, 2000).
George Bennett is willing to bare his soul to journalist Catherine Heathcote. The subject is the disappearance of thirteen-year-old Alison Carter from the gated community of Scardale in Derbyshire in 1963. This was Detective Inspector Bennett's first case. What has always haunted Bennett is his inability to piece together the puzzle, which included no corpse and a closed community. Thirty

years later, just before publication of his story, Bennett withdraws from the interview, hiding new evidence that will reveal the truth. The dogged journalist is not about to give up that easy, and as Carter struggles to go over the ground Bennett covered years earlier, she finds the community is still a closed book to outsiders.

Children in jeopardy; England—Derbyshire, Burxon; England—Derbyshire, Scardale

McKinty, Adam.

Hidden River. Scribner, 2005.

Alexander Lawson loses his homicide detective job in Belfast when he steals drugs to support his heroin habit. All seems lost, and he heads to America with his friend, John. Lawson's troubles mean he is the perfect man for the job when a grieving father in Denver needs a private investigation into the death of Lawson's old girlfriend, Victoria Patawasti. When Lawson learns that Victoria might have uncovered some dirty deeds at the environmental agency where she works, he decides to go undercover and hunt down her killer.

Colorado—Denver; Drugs; Environment

O'Connell, Jack.

Box Nine. Mysterious Press, 1992.

When a new drug called Lingo hits the streets, it causes murderous rampages, and Lieutenant Lenore Thomas is assigned the job of tracking it down. Meanwhile, her twin brother Ike is working at the post office and finding odd things in box number nine. Each investigator has to deal with sexual tensions, odd partners, and a decaying city that is the setting for this unusual thriller.

Drugs; Massachusetts—Quinsigamond

Word Made Flesh. HarperFlamingo, 1999.

Gilrein is an ex-cop, now driving a cab on the weird streets of Quinsigamond. He has never recovered from the death of his wife, also a cop, who was killed on the job. Then some new evidence comes his way, and Gilrein decides to seek revenge on those who might have taken his wife away.

Massachusetts—Quinsigamond; Revenge

Parker, T. Jefferson.

Silent Joe. Hyperion, 2001.

Joe Trona was saved from the orphanage by Orange County Supervisor Will Trona despite Joe's badly scarred face. Will helps Joe grow into the man he needs to be, but Joe is unable to prevent Will from being assassinated one night. When Joe sets out to avenge his adoptive father's death, he discovers that Will was trying to find a missing eleven-year-old girl. Although Joe may discover who killed his father, he might also discover some things about Will that he may wish were left a secret.

Adoption; California—Orange County; Fathers and sons; Politics

Perry, Thomas.

Pursuit. Random House, 2002.

When profiler Daniel Millikan is called into a case in which thirteen people have been murdered in a Louisville restaurant, he is frustrated to find that the police are not making any progress with the usual methods. He decides he can do a better job working with a rogue named Roy Prescott, an expert at catching the bad guys the hard way.

Kentucky—Louisville; Profilers

Raymond, Derek.

How the Dead Live. UK: Alison, 1986.

Marianne Mardy has gone missing in Wiltshire, and a detective is dispatched to figure it all out. When he arrives on the scene he finds both the husband, Dr. William Mardy, and the locals all uninterested in her whereabouts. Suspicious of the good doctor, who lives in a gothic-like setting, the detective soon discovers the meaning of corruption.

England—Wiltshire, Thornhill; Husbands and wives

Simon, Michael.

Dirty Sally. Viking, 2004.

Dan Reles, an expatriated Easterner, is the only Jewish cop on the Austin, Texas, police force in 1988. Pulled into an investigation of the death of a prostitute named Nikki, Dan finds he needs to deal with residual feelings from the death of his partner, Joey Velez. Soon Reles finds himself on suspension, which leads to probation. But body parts are being sent to some influential businessmen, so he is pulled back in. When his investigation traces major dirty money, the detective heads to the capitol to find the truth.

Prostitutes; Texas—Austin

Spillane, Mickey.

Dead Street. Hard Case, 2007.

When NYPD detective Jack Stang hears his fiancée, missing twenty years and presumed dead, is alive in Florida, he thinks it is good news. Then he discovers that Bette, the victim of a car crash, is blind and has no memories of her previous life with him. However, the men who kidnapped her years ago are still looking for her and are still willing to silence her in case a stray memory should surface.

Amnesia; Florida; Kidnapping; Retirement communities

Thompson, Jim.

The Transgressors. New American Library, 1961.

In a rough and tumble Texas town, the local deputy sheriff, Tom Lord, is laying for a local tough while living with a prostitute named Joyce. Driven to a confrontation, Lord kills Aaron McBride in a fight. Then the victim's widow comes from Fort Worth with vengeance on her mind, bringing in tow the mob muscle needed to get the job done.

Revenge; Texas—Pardee County

Waites, Martyn.

Candleland. UK: Allison & Busby, 2000.

Detective Inspector Henry Moir is leaving his home turf to head to London to find his daughter, a heroin junkie with AIDs. To help in the search, he is bringing along his journalist friend Stephen Larkin, a man damaged by the loss of his own wife and child to a different crusade, and a photographer named Andy Brennan. What the trio find in London, especially at the runaway shelter Candleland, is complicated and chilling.

Drugs; England—London; Runaways

Winslow, Don.

The Power of the Dog. Knopf, 2005.

When Art Keller is assigned by the DEA to the Mexican–U.S. border, he is not prepared for what he will encounter. By becoming friends with the Barrera brothers, he will eventually have to decide between them and his beliefs when their uncle Miguel makes it an issue to maintain his drug empire.

Drug Enforcement Agency; Drugs; Mexico—Culiacan

The Dawn Patrol. Knopf, 2008.

Ex-cop Boone Daniels is haunted by a case he failed to close when working for the San Diego P.D. Now, working part time as a PI and surfing each day with his posse, called The Dawn Patrol, he is pulled back into the fire when a lawyer named Petra Hall hires him to do an investigation. Little does Boone realize that while he is chasing an arson case around Silver Dan's Strip Club, he will also be chasing ghosts from his past.

Arson; California—San Diego; Children in jeopardy

True Crime Cops Gone Bad

Blakeslee, Nate.

Tulia: Race, Cocaine and Corruption in a Small Texas Town. Public Affairs, 2005.

When Tulia narcotics officer Tom Coleman decided to improve his record by making thirty-nine drug arrests of innocent citizens, he opened a can of worms on the border that exposed a racist and corrupt small town judicial system. Thanks to the dedicated work of NAACP Legal Defense Fund attorney Vanita Grupta, his malfeasance was brought to light, but only after families were separated and people were sent to jail for long terms.

Drugs; Police corruption; Texas—Tulia

Cea, Robert.

No Lights No Siren: The Corruption and Redemption of an Inner City Cop. Morrow, 2005.

Robert Cea began his career in the police force as an upbeat patrolman. But years working the "Badlands" of Brooklyn turned him into a man willing to use the laws of the streets to bring order to his beat. After lying on the stand to convict criminals and planting evidence to make convictions more likely, he quit the police force.

New York—New York; Police corruption

Earley, Pete.

Circumstantial Evidence: Death, Life and Justice in a Southern Town. Bantam, 1995.

Monroeville, Alabama, was the hometown of Ronda Morrison, who was murdered in the back room of a dry cleaning store. A black man, Walter McMillan, was arrested three months later. His trial lasted three days, and he spent six years on death row. Bryan Stevenson, a Harvard-educated attorney with an interest in death row inmates, decided that McMillan was innocent and set about proving how bad police procedure had led to shortcuts in the courtroom.

Alabama—Monroeville; Capital punishment; Trials

Fuhrman, Mark.

Murder in Brentwood. Regnery, 1997.

When Mark Fuhrman got the call that took him to the murder scene and the bodies of Nicole Brown Simpson and Ron Goldman, little did he know that he would end up the focus of the trial and that he would watch O. J. Simpson walk free. Here he tells his side of the story.

California—Los Angeles; Simpson, O. J.; Trials

O'Donnell, Lawrence, Jr.

Deadly Force: The True Story of How a Badge Can Become a License to Kill. Morrow, 1983.

When African American James Bowden Jr. was shot to death in his car on the streets of Boston, it was dismissed by most, including the police department, as just another justified police shooting. But when lawyer Lawrence O'Donnell was brought in by Bowden's widow, Patricia, the policeversion of the events began to unravel.

Massachusetts—Boston; Police corruption; Trials

Shapiro, Fred.

Whitmore. Bobbs-Merrill, 1969.

Janice Whylie and Emily Hoffert were brutally murdered in 1963 in Manhattan in the apartment that they shared with another girl. Eight months later the murder of a black woman in Brooklyn led the police to George Whitmore Jr., who quickly confessed to that crime and the other two. The problem was that he was not guilty of the latter.

New York—New York; Race relations; Trials

Summerscale, Kate.

The Suspicions of Mr. Whicher: A Shocking Murder and the Undoing of a Great Victorian Detective. Walker, 2008.

In 1860 in England, a three-year-old boy named Saville Kent was found murdered in the outdoor bathroom on the estate where his family lived. The case was assigned to Scotland Yard Det.-Insp. Jonathan Jack Whicher. Although he did his best to find a suspect, it was not until five years had passed and a killer had confessed that the murderer was tried and Whicher's reputation was restored.

Children in jeopardy; England; Scotland Yard

Wambaugh, Joseph.

Fire Lover. Morrow, 2002.

John Orr was a cop wannabe but can never quite make the grade in a police department. However, his work as an arson investigator for the Glendale Fire Department was superb. Then he decided to write a fiction book about a fireman/arsonist, and some of the details were too close to the facts known in a real serial arson case in which four people had died.

Arson; California— Glendale

Lawyers Gone Bad

What are the temptations facing a person who defines what the law means? Many, apparently, as the books listed in the following section showcase how the temptations of twisting the law to serve a purpose prove irresistible to these individuals.

Benchmark Lawyers Gone Bad Novel

Traver, Robert.

Anatomy of a Murder. St. Martin's, 1958.

When his ten-year run as the DA ends with the election of a war hero, Paul "Polly" Biegler has to decide what to do. When he gets a call from Laura Mannion, whose husband, Lieutenant Frederic Mannion, has been arrested for shooting a Thunder Bay hotel owner named Barney Quill, he discovers he can turn from prosecution to defense and get back in the game.

Michigan—Upper Peninsula; Trials

Lawyers Gone Bad Novels

Abbott, Megan.

Die a Little. Simon & Schuster, 2005.

Orphaned early in life, brother and sister Bill and Lora King have a special bond. When femme fatale Alice Steele enters Bill's life, the young district attorney's office investigator finds himself ensnared in her web. Only his sister's loyalty and her persistent investigation save him from his fate.

Brothers and sisters; California—Hollywood; California—Pasadena; Historical

Clark, Martin.

The Legal Limit. Knopf, 2008.

When brothers Mason and Gates Hunt are parties to a crime, they vow to keep it a secret between the two of them. Mason is able to become a lawyer, but his brother goes to jail for a crime unrelated to the family secret. However, Gates decides his get-out-of-jail-free card is his brother, whom he is not shy about blackmailing.

Brothers; Virginia—Stuart

de Kretser, Michelle.

The Hamilton Case. Little Brown, 2004.

The Hamilton Case is told in three parts. The first section is the first-person narration of Sam Obeysekere, an elderly lawyer, who tells about his life in Ceylon and his education at Oxford. The second section of the book is an omniscient look at the Hamilton case, in which a rich white planter's murder, originally blamed on locals, leads to the prosecution of another white man for the death of the first. In the third section of the book, the omniscient point of view completes the story of Sam's life and fills in the details of how he came to be a prosecutor.

Ceylon—Colombo; Ceylon—Kijygana; Ceylon—Nuwara Eliya; Colonialism; Mothers and sons; Trials

Phillips, Scott.

The Ice Harvest. Ballantine, 2000.

It is Christmas Eve, 1979, and mob lawyer Charlie Arglist is thinking of ending his working relationship with his partner, Vic Cavanaugh, and the local mobster, Bill Gerard. He will leave Wichita with the money he has scammed from the strip bars he has been running with Vic, but first he has to deal with club owner Renata. She has a photograph that could be used for blackmail, and when he stops to deal with her, he may lose his opportunity to get out of town, especially when people start to end up dead.

Blackmail; Christmas; Embezzlement; Historical; Kansas—Wichita; Lawyers; Organized crime

The Walkaway. Ballantine, 2002.

It is 1989 when ex-cop Gunther Fahnstiel wanders away from his Alzheimer's ward in search of a suitcase filled with money he hid away ten years earlier, after the events in *The Ice Harvest.* His wife, Dot, does not care, because she knows the money has already been recovered and spent. But Gunther's stepson Sidney cares enough about the money to try to find him. Meanwhile, in a flashback from 1952, we hear the story of how Gunther was a cop who might have been as deep into the underworld of Wichita as the bad men he was supposed to be apprehending.

Amnesia; Historical; Kansas—Wichita; Missing money

Pyper, Andrew.

Lost Girls. Delacorte, 2000.

A pompous and drug-addicted Toronto attorney heads north to Murdoch, Ontario, Canada, where two missing teenagers are believed to have drowned in the murky waters of Lake St. Christopher. Their high school English teacher, Thomas Tripp, is accused of murder, and Bartholomew Crane is assigned to defend the man. But what passes for reality in this gothic setting, especially when Crane is not in control of his own senses, stretches the boundaries between reality and hallucination before the truth is revealed about what happened on that eerie lake.

Canada—Ontario—Murdoch, Lake St. Christopher; Children in jeopardy; Drugs; Trials

Private Investigators Gone Bad

When the legal system of the cops, lawyers, and courts fails an individual, people with the means can try to hire justice by working with a private investigator. The hope is that the money also buys loyalty, a wish that does not always come true, as shown by the books listed in this section.

Benchmark Private Investigators Gone Bad Novel

Hammett, Dashiell.

The Maltese Falcon. Knopf, 1930.

The beautiful and captivating Miss Wonderly wanders into the Spade and Archer Detective Agency, and Miles Archer agrees to follow her down a blind alley, only to end up murdered. Sam Spade, Archer's partner, decides to avenge his death, and he is given the opportunity when Miss Wonderly returns to the agency, this time confessing to be Brigid O'Shaughnessy. Brigid blames a man named Floyd Thursby for Archer's death, and as Spade begins to investigate, he discovers the real reason for the murder may be a jeweled bird known as The Maltese Falcon.

Antiquities; California—San Francisco

Private Investigators Gone Bad Novels

Abe, Kobo.

Moetsukita chizu. Japan: Shincho-sha, 1967. (U.S.: *The Ruined Map*, Knopf, 1969).

Ten paces from a streetlight, over a manhole, Haru Nemuro's husband disappeared. She has waited six months for his return before hiring a private detective. Convinced that her husband's return to the house for a paperclip on the morning of his disappearance is significant, she has been barely on the edge of control and dependent on the strange investigation of her brother. The PI hopes a missed rendezvous with a coworker, and the papers that were to have been exchanged, hold the clue to his disappearance. Ultimately, the plot is really not all that important, except to provide an avenue through which the PI begins to lose control of his own identity and to merge with the missing man's wife.

Japan—Tokyo; Missing persons; Obsession; Private investigators

Banks, Ray.

Saturday's Child. UK: Polygon, 2006. (U.S.: Harcourt, 2006).

Callum Innes has just been released from Strangeways Prison and is trying to go straight as a PI in Manchester. But his former criminal boss, "Uncle" Morris Tiernan, has one last job he wants Innes to do for the gang: find Tiernan's sixteen-year-old daughter Alison, who has run off with a blackjack dealer. Cal discovers that although he may be searching for the daughter, he may also have to protect Morris from his son, intent on overthrowing his father and taking over his criminal empire.

England—Manchester; England—Newcastle; Ex-convicts; Fathers and sons; Organized crime

Barnes, Jonathan.

The Somnambulist. UK: Gollancz, 2007. (U.S.: Morrow, 2007).

Set in Victorian London, this is the story of declining magician Edward Moon, no longer wanted by his audience for his prestidigitation nor by the police for his amazing detective skills. Left to perform on stage with a strange partner known as The Somnambulist, he is forgotten until he is approached one last time when the bizarre murder of an actor confounds the police. What they discover will shake the very foundations of London's society and reveal a vast conspiracy.

England—London; Historical; Magicians; Private investigators; Somnambulism; Victorian England

Bloch, Robert.

Shooting Star. Ace, 1958.

Mark Clayburn is a one-eyed PI who also is a literary agent. When he is offered the opportunity to look into the murder of actor Dick Ryan, he reluctantly accepts, because there are some Westerns that could see the light of day if he can clear up the actor's name. What surprises the PI so much is how reluctant everyone is to discuss the actor or his drug use.

California—Los Angeles; Drugs; Motion pictures; Westerns

Chabon, Michael.

The Final Solution: A Story of Detection. Fourth Estate, 2004.

One day a nine-year-old mute German-Jewish boy carrying an African gray parrot named Bruno crosses paths with an eighty-nine-year-old retired world famous detective in Sussex. The murder of Richard Woolsey Shane does not intrigue the old man to leave his bee-keeping behind. But when Bruno is bird-napped, evidently because of the string of German numbers the bird utters, the old man is roused to practice his skills one more time.

Children in jeopardy; England—Sussex, South Downs; Espionage; Historical; Holmes, Sherlock; Mutes; Parrots; World War II

Ellin, Stanley.

The Eighth Circle. Random House, 1958.

Murray has fallen in love with Ruth, the fiancée of a cop named Arnold, who is under indictment. Hired by Arnold's rather naïve lawyer to prove that Arnold is innocent, Murray may be more interested in making the cop look bad.

New York—New York; Private investigators; Triangles (Interpersonal relations)

Gores, Joe.

Interface. M. Evans, 1974.

Neil Fargo is a man who walks with his feet in both worlds. Although he has paying clients in the investigative business, he is also running heroin.

When his own partner rips him off, he is not disinclined to seek justice by the methods he learned in the Special Forces.

Drugs; California—San Francisco

Hammett. Putnam, 1975.

It is 1928, and Dashiell Hammett is trying to establish himself as a novelist in San Francisco, having retired from the PI business. When Victor Atkinson, an old PI acquaintance, is murdered while working for the committee to reform the city, Hammett is driven to investigate out of guilt for not helping the cause. What he discovers is that his nerves are shot, his skills are lacking, and he may be tossing aside his literary life.

California—San Francisco; Private investigators

Dead Man. Mysterious, 1993.

Eddie Dain is a PI who specializes in technology. His wife and son are murdered after he offends the wrong people, so Eddie transforms himself a number of times, moving about the country, carrying the Tibetan Book of the Dead, and administering the justice that will give him peace.

California—San Francisco; Louisiana; Nevada—Las Vegas; Revenge

Cases. Mysterious, 1999.

Pierce "Dunc" Duncan is wandering the United States after graduating from Notre Dame in 1953, retracing the journey the author took as a young man. As Dunc moves across the landscape, his adventures toughen him up, but nothing can prepare him for the deadly adventure awaiting him when he reaches the mean streets of the Bay Area.

California—San Francisco; Coming-of-age; Travel

Hiaasen, Carl.

Tourist Season. Putnam, 1986.

Brian Keyes is a former newspaper reporter who operates a private investigator agency in Miami. A Shriner goes missing, possibly eaten by an alligator. The president of the local Chamber of Commerce has been chopped up, stuffed in a suitcase with an alligator shoved down his throat, and set to float in the bay. A terrorist group called Las Noches de Diciembre begins to make claims, and then a Canadian goes missing. When an old journalist pal seems a little too obsessed with the development of his beloved Florida and the influx of tourists, Keyes begins to wonder about the real motive behind the murders.

Florida—Miami; Tourism

Hjortsberg, William.

Falling Angel. Harcourt Brace Jovanovich, 1978.

Harry Angel is a New York PI hired by Louis Cyphre to find Johnny Favorite, a nightclub singer who has gone missing. As the case progresses, Harry begins to realize that he may have a devil of a client.

Devil; Historical; New York—New York; Private investigators

Lethem, Jonathan.

Gun, with Occasional Music. Harcourt Brace, 1994.

In a bold near future, asking questions is forbidden, which makes it difficult for PI Conrad Metcalf. Although genetically engineered animals do most of the work, it is unexpected that one might be a murderer. But when urologist Dr. Maynard Stanhunt is killed, it is up to the memory detective Metcalf to figure out who done it.

California—Oakland; Private investigators; Science fiction

Motherless Brooklyn. Doubleday, 1999.

Lionel "Freakshow" Essrog is a Tourette's syndrome sufferer who is taken from the St. Vincent's Orphanage to become a part of Frank Minna's limo service and detective agency. Then one night Frank enters a Brooklyn Zen center wearing a wire, and his four detectives fail to keep him from being taken for a ride. Forced to overcome his problem to become a leader of men, Lionel sets out to discover who murdered his mentor.

Maine; New York—New York; Private investigators; Tourette's syndrome; Zen Buddhism

Levien, David.

City of the Sun. Doubleday, 2008.

Twelve-year-old Jamie Gabriel disappears from his paper route in suburban Indianapolis, and his parents, Paul and Carol, are frustrated when the police cannot discover what happened. Desperate, they turn to PI Frank Behr, a former cop with a bad reputation. With Paul as his partner, Frank heads to Mexico to find the boy and end the ordeal.

Indiana—Indianapolis; Kidnapping; Mexico

Millar, Margaret.

How Like an Angel. Random House, 1962.

Joe Quinn is a PI working security in Las Vegas, where he has saddled himself with a big gambling debt. Hitching a ride to Southern California to pick up $300, he finds himself dumped at a religious colony called The Tower. He is surprised to discover that Sister Blessing of the Salvation, despite a vow of poverty, has $120 to hire him to locate a man named Patrick O'Gorman. When people start dying in The Tower, he knows he has stirred up trouble.

California—Chicote; California—San Felice; Cults

Perry, Thomas.

Silence. Harcourt, 2007.

Private investigator Jack Till thought he was doing Wendy Harper a favor when he taught her how to disappear. When she went missing, the bad men who were after her thought she was dead. But years later, when her former business partner, Eric Fuller, is being framed for her murder,

Fuller wants Till to bring Harper back from the dead. Then maybe hired guns Paul and Sylvie Turner can really put her away forever.

Private investigators

Fidelity. Harcourt, 2008.

Los Angeles private investigator Phil Kramer is murdered one night. Feeling righteous, his wife, Emily, and his staff begin an investigation into his death. Emily does not like what she finds out about Phil, but she likes it even less when the man who killed him, Jerry Hobart, asks to add her name to his list. Hobart is mad at his client, mad at Emily, and about to do something about it.

California—Los Angeles; Husbands and wives; Private investigators

Rhoades, J. D.

Jack Keller series.

In this series by J. D. Rhoades, Desert Storm service has left bounty hunter Jack Keller with issues that sometimes make him as scary as the people he is hunting. The following seres titles are listed in order of publication.

The Devil's Right Hand. St. Martin's Minotaur, 2005.

Jack Keller works for Angela out of her bail bondsman shop. In this case they are after a man who jumped bail after being arrested for burglary. What the bail bondsmen do not know is that DeWayne Puryear has killed a member of the Lumbee Indian tribe whose son is a mobster. What Jack finds on his side of the law is an untrustworthy cop. On the other side is a Native American seeking revenge for his father's murder.

Bail bondsman; Native Americans; North Carolina—Fayetteville; Post-traumatic stress disorder/syndrome

Good Day in Hell. St. Martin's Minotaur, 2006.

Jack is working on a bail enforcement case that puts him on the trail of Laurel Marks, a young, rich, and dangerous woman. At the same time, his lover, Sheriff's Deputy Marie Jones, is investigating a death in a gas station robbery and a killing spree that began in a church. Soon it becomes evident that they are looking for the same people. When the local media become involved on the side of the crooks, it makes the good guys' jobs that much harder.

Bail bondsman; North Carolina

Safe and Sound. St. Martin's Minotaur, 2007.

Jack finds himself hunting the daughter of David Lundgren, an Army Delta Force veteran, and perhaps a man who shares the same trauma that Jack still battles each day. Then Lundgren disappears, and Jack has to deal with army bureaucracy to find out why the members of an elite unit may be finding life stateside a challenge. Could it be their choices overseas are coming home to roost?

Afghanistan conflict; Children in jeopardy; Kidnapping; North Carolina—Fayetteville; United States Army

Rifkin, Shepard.

The Murderer Vine. Fawcett Gold Medal, 1971.

In the historical South, where the movement to register black voters led to murder, three civil rights workers are murdered. One of the men's father is angry enough to hire New York PI Joe Dunne and his partner, Kirby, and send them to Mississippi to find out who murdered his son. And then kill the responsible parties.

Civil rights; Mississippi—Jackson; Race relations; Revenge

Swierczynski, Duane.

Secret Dead Men. Point Blank, 2004.

The Association took out investigative journalist Del Farmer years ago, but he lives on through a process that lets his essence survive in the body of others. He can control his "new" body, and he uses his hosts to investigate murders, hoping to exact revenge on The Association by using all the talents of the dead that he has collected over the years.

Fantasy; Ghosts; Historical; Revenge

Part III

Topics

Chapter 6

Bibliographies

Adey, Robert.

Locked Room Murders and Other Impossible Crimes: A Comprehensive Bibliography. Revised and expanded ed. Crossover Press, 1991. 0-9628870-0-5.
> An outstanding example of a dedicated fan publishing his own notes for the edification of other fans.

Barzun, Jacques, and Wendell Hertig Taylor.

A Catalogue of Crime: Being a Reader's Guide to the Literature of Mystery, Detection, and Related Genres. Harper & Row, 1989. 0060157968.
> Get an arrogant and delightfully opinionated look at mystery by reading the reviews of these experts.

Bleiler, Richard.

Reference Guide to Mystery and Detective Fiction. Libraries Unlimited, 1999.
> This work does a fine job of reviewing available sources for research in the genre.

Bourgeau, Art.

The Mystery Lover's Companion. Crown, 1986.
> Philadelphia bookstore owner Bourgeau lists his favorites.

Breen, Jon L.

What about Murder? A Guide to Books about Mystery and Detective Fiction. Scarecrow, 1981. 0-8108-1413-7.

What about Murder? (1981–1991): A Guide to Books about Mystery and Detective Fiction. Scarecrow, 1993. 0-8108-2609-7.
> If you want evaluations of books that talk about mysteries, Breen's annotated bibliography is the best place to look.

Burgess, Michael, and Jill H. Vassilakos.

Murder in Retrospect: A Selective Guide to Historical Mystery Fiction. Libraries Unlimited, 2005. 1-59158-087-0.

> Geared toward readers and librarians, this annotated guide provides a broad overview of the historical mystery genre, defining it as mystery set more than fifty years before the novel was written.

Contento, William G., and Martin H. Greenberg, eds.

Index to Crime and Mystery Anthologies. G. K. Hall, 1991. 0-8161-8629-4.

> A great place to check for hard-to-find mystery short stories.

Cook, Michael L.

Monthly Murders: A Checklist and Chronological Listing of Fiction in the Digest-size Mystery Magazines in the United States and England. Greenwood Press, 1982. 0313231265.

> This massive work attempts to organize the short stories in the field.

Mystery Fanfare: A Composite Index to Mystery and Related Fanzines, 1963–1981. Bowling Green State University Popular Press, 1983. 0879722290.

> Fans produce a lot of writings about the field, and dedicated bibliographer Cook indexed their work for this period.

Gannon, Michael B.

Blood, Bedlam, Bullets, and Badguys: A Reader's Guide to Adventure Suspense Fiction. Libraries Unlimited, 2004.

> A readers' advisory guide to the world of suspense and thrillers.

Green, Joseph, and Jim Finch.

Sleuths, Sidekicks, and Stooges. Scolar, 1997.

> This enormous work organizes the genre by characters. Its strength is that besides the lead characters, it gives equal attention to the sidekick assistants and the authorities that the detective defies.

Hagen, Ordean A.

Who Done It? A Guide to Detective, Mystery, and Suspense Fiction. R. R. Bowker, 1969. Out-of-print.

> The first book-length published bibliography in the field. Errors occurred, but it was the first major effort to list titles in the genre.

Hubin, Allen J., ed.

Crime Fiction IV: A Comprehensive Bibliography, 1749–2000. Locus Press, 2003.

> The CD-ROM version of this work is an updated version that can be used on any PC or Apple with a CD-ROM drive and a standard Web browser.

Machler, Tasha.

Murder by Category: A Subject Guide to Mystery Fiction. Scarecrow, 1991.
Machler, a bookstore owner, organized some mysteries into about a hundred subject categories.

Melvin, David Skene, and Ann Skene Melvin.

Crime, Detective, Espionage, Mystery, and Thriller Fiction and Film: A Comprehensive Bibliography of Critical Writing Through 1979. Greenwood, 1980.
Gathering secondary source references into one index, the compilers of this work included English- and non-English-language sources.

Menendez, Albert J.

The Subject Is Murder. Garland, 1986.

The Subject Is Murder: Volume 2. Garland, 1990.
The first volume has twenty-five subject areas; the second volume updates some old and adds some new categories while trying to organize the genre by subject.

Mundell, E. H., and G. Jay Rausch.

The Detective Short Story: A Bibliography and Index. Kansas State University Library, 1974.
An expansion of the Queen title listed below. Mundell and Rausch updated the old work and included items overlooked by Queen.

Niebuhr, Gary Warren.

Make Mine a Mystery: A Reader's Guide to Mystery and Detective Fiction. Libraries Unlimited, 2004.
A readers' advisory guide to mystery books in series.

Pronzini, Bill, and Marcia Muller.

1001 Midnights: The Aficionado's Guide to Mystery and Detective Fiction. Arbor House, 1986.
PI authors and married couple Pronzini and Muller put together this comprehensive list of best books in the field.

Queen, Ellery.

Queen's Quorum. Little, Brown, 1951.

Queen, Ellery, ed.

The Detective Short Story: A Bibliography. Little, Brown, 1942.
> The master mystery authors and publishers of *Ellery Queen Mystery Magazine* provide an early overview of the state of the art in the short story.

Stiwell, Steven A., and Charles Montney, eds.

What Mystery Do I Read Next?: A Reader's Guide to Recent Mystery Fiction. 2nd ed. Edited by Steven A. Stiwell and Charles Montney. Gale Research, 1999. 0787615927.
> Two editions of this source were published before it disappeared.

Chapter 7

Encyclopedias

Ashley, Mike.

The Mammoth Encyclopedia of Modern Crime Fiction. Carroll & Graf, 2003. 0786710063.
> This big paperback contains tons of information about contemporary writers in the genre.

The Mammoth Encyclopedia of Modern Crime Fiction: The Authors, Their Works, and Their Most Famous Creations. Carroll & Graf, 2002.
> A comprehensive, inexpensive reference guide to and overview of the genre of crime fiction.

Barnett, Colleen A.

Mystery Women: An Encyclopedia of Leading Women Characters in Mystery Fiction. Volume 1: 1860–1979. Ravenstone, 1997. *Volume 2: 1980–1989.* Poisoned Pen, 2002. 1890208698. *Volume III (1990–1999), Part 1: A–L.* Poisoned Pen Press, 2004. 1590580494.
> This work assembles the greats from the beginning of the genre to 1999 in three volumes.

Brunsdale, Mitzi.

Gumshoes: A Dictionary of Fictional Detectives. Greenwood, 2006. 0-313-33331-9.
> Series detectives' lives are explained in this one-volume resource.

DeAndrea, William L.

Encyclopedia Mysteriosa. Prentice Hall, 1994. 0-671-85025-3.
> The late mystery critic put this tome together to update or replace the *Encyclopedia of Mystery and Detection*, but it may be marred by some factual errors and limited coverage. Both volumes should be kept. It did win the 1994 Edgar award for best reference book.

Herbert, Rosemary, ed.

The Oxford Companion to Crime & Mystery Writing. Oxford University Press, 1999.
> This work provides a comprehensive overview of the entire genre.

Lachman, Marv, Otto Penzler, Charles Shibuk, and Chris Steinbrunner, eds.

Encyclopedia of Mystery & Detection. McGraw-Hill, 1976. Out of print.
> The first, and still the best, mainstream attempt to outline the genre for the average reader.

Murphy, Bruce F.

The Encyclopedia of Murder and Mystery. St. Martin's Minotaur, 1999.
> A personalized look at the genre.

Penzler, Otto, Chris Steinbrunner, and Marvin Lachman.

Detectionary: A Biographical Dictionary of Leading Characters in Mystery Fiction. Overlook, 1977.
> This dictionary-format work is divided into four sections: detectives, rogues and helpers, cases, and movies.

Rollyson, Carl, ed.

Critical Survey of Mystery and Detective Fiction. Salem Press, 2008.
> This five-volume set provides a detailed analysis of the lives and writings of major contributors to mystery and detective fiction.

St. James Guide to Crime and Mystery Writers. St. James Press, 1996. $160.00. 0-7867-1048-8.
> The best single-volume reference work for fans and researchers.

Winks, Robin, and Maureen Corrigan, eds.

Mystery and Suspense Writers. Charles Scribner's Sons, 1998. 0684805219.
> This two-volume work is a compilation of scholarly articles on the entire genre.

Chapter 8

Filmography

Cameron, Ian.

A Pictorial History of Crime Films. Hamlyn, 1975.
There is some text here, but the majority of this book is stills from all the great films.

Christopher, Nicholas.

Somewhere in the Night: Film Noir and the American City. Free, 1997.
A novelist and poet examines the nuances of this film style.

Crowther, Bruce.

Film Noir: Reflections in a Dark Mirror. Continuum, 1989.
A history of this film style.

Everson, William K.

The Detective in Film. Citadel, 1972.
This well-illustrated guide features the greatest detectives filmed from 1903 to 1972.

Hardy, Phil, ed.

The BFI Companion to Crime. University of California Press, 1997. 0520215389.
This British filmography offers a complete and detailed guide to crime on film.

Hirsch, Foster.

The Dark Side of the Screen: Film Noir. Barnes, 1981.
A serious study of this film style by a master reviewer.

Martin, Richard.

Mean Streets and Raging Bulls: The Legacy of Film Noir in Contemporary American Cinema. Scarecrow, 1997.

Muller, Eddie.

Dark City: The Lost World of Film Noir. St. Martin's Press, 1998. 0312180764.
> An overview of this style of film by a contemporary master of its complexities.

Silver, Alain, and Elizabeth Ward.

Film Noir: An Encyclopedic Reference to the American Style. 3rd ed. Overlook, 1992.
> A large, comprehensive look at this film style.

Stephens, Michael L.

Film Noir: A Comprehensive Illustrated Reference to Movies, Terms and Persons. McFarland, 1995.
> Stephens provides full film entries and lots of photographs.

Tuska, Jon.

The Detective in Hollywood. Doubleday, 1978.
> This is an overview with lots of pictures by film critic Tuska.

Chapter 9

Guides

Benvenuti, Stefano, and Gianni Rizzoni.

The Whodunit: An Informal History of Detective Fiction. Macmillan, 1979.
    This historical guide was compiled by two Italian critics of the field.

Breen, Jon L.

Novel Verdicts: A Guide to Courtroom Fiction. 2nd ed. Scarecrow Press, 1999.
0-8108-3674-2.
    Lifelong reader and review Breen has put together a comprehensive guide to this
    subgenre.

Gorman, Ed, Martin H. Greenberg, Larry Segriff, and Jon L. Breen, eds.

The Fine Art of Murder: The Mystery Readers Indispensable Companion. Carroll
and Graf, 1993. 0-88184-972-3.
    This Anthony Award–winning title is a cornucopia of mystery trivia for any fan,
    similar in style to the groundbreaking *Murder Ink*.

Grape, Jan, Dean James, and Ellen Nehr, eds.

Deadly Women: The Woman Mystery Reader's Indispensable Companion. Carroll
& Graf, 1998. 0-7867-0468-3.
    A compilation of articles by and about women in the field of mysteries. Absolutely
    a delightful by-the-nightstand book full of trivia.

Heising, Willetta L.

Detecting Men and *Detecting Men Pocket Guide.* Purple Moon Press, 1998.
0-9644593-3-7 & 0-9644593-4-5.

Detecting Women 3 and *Detecting Women Pocket Guide.* Purple Moon Press, 1999.
0-9644593-35-3 (set).
    These readers' guides and checklists feature more than 600 series by women and
    men. The pocket guides can be carried into a bookstore or library as a shopping
    guide.

Jakubowski, Maxim.

100 Great Detectives: Famous Mystery Writers Examine Their Favourite Fictional Investigators. Carroll & Graf, 1991.

> Famous mystery writers examine their favorite mystery characters in this guide edited by London bookstore owner Jakubowski.

King, Nina, and Robin Winks.

Crime of the Scene: A Mystery Novel Guide for the International Traveller. St. Martins, 1997. 0312151748.

> A perfect companion for the "mysterious" traveler.

Nichols, Victoria, and Susan Thompson.

Silk Stalkings: More Women Write of Murder. Scarecrow Press, 1998. 0-810-83393-X.

> A delightful spin through the accomplishments of women in the mystery genre, this book is the second edition of this guide.

Ousby, Ian.

Guilty Parties: A Mystery Lover's Companion. Thames & Hudson, 1997. 0500279780.

> As much fun as *Murder Ink*, this fannish review of mystery fiction is full of surprises and is wonderfully illustrated.

Penzler, Otto.

The Great Detectives: A Host of the World's Most Celebrated Sleuths Are Unmasked by Their Authors. Little, Brown, 1978.

> This work includes the words of the creators as they dissect their own creations.

The Private Lives of Private Eyes: Spies, Crime Fighters, and Other Good Guys. Grosset and Dunlap, 1977.

> Using the characters as the approach, famed bookstore owner and collector Penzler outlines the lives of these fictional people.

[Reader's Guide to . . .]

> Each of the volumes in this series offers annotated titles in its area, along with special indexes to guide a reader through the genre.

Jarvis, Mary Johson.

A Reader's Guide to the Suspense Novel. G. K. Hall, 1997. 0-8161-1804-3.

Lachman, Marvin.

A Reader's Guide to the American Novel of Detection. G. K. Hall, 1993. 0-8161-1803-5.

Niebuhr, Gary Warren.

A Reader's Guide to the Private Eye Novel. G. K. Hall, 1993. 0-8161-1802-7.

Oleksiw, Susan.

A Reader's Guide to the Classic British Mystery. G. K. Hall, 1988. 0-8161-8787-3 (hardcover). Mysterious Press, 1989. 0-89296-968-7 (softcover, out-of-print).

Stone, Nancy-Stephanie.

A Reader's Guide to the Spy and Thriller Novel. G. K. Hall, 1997. 0-8161-1800-0.

Vicarel, JoAnn.

A Reader's Guide to the Police Procedural Novel. G. K. Hall, 1995. 0-8161-1801-9.

Siegel, Jeff.

The American Detective: An Illustrated History. Taylor, 1993.
  This colorful approach to the detective story includes reproductions of book covers, as well as media stills and posters.

Stine, Kate, ed.

The Armchair Detective Book of Lists. Mysterious Press, 1995. 0-89296-423-5.
  A small book of lists full of the kind of trivia that mystery fans will just love to read. The second edition of this book won an Anthony Award as the best mystery nonfiction book of 1995.

Swanson, Jean, and Dean James.

By a Woman's Hand: A Guide to Mystery Fiction by Women. 2nd ed. Berkley, 1996. 0425154726.
  An informal, encyclopedic look at the women who have had an impact on the genre.

Swanson, Jean, Dean James, and Anne Perry.

Killer Books: A Reader's Guide to Exploring the Popular World of Mystery and Suspense. Berkley, 1998. 0425162184. $13.00.
  For the fan reader, this book is a marvelous overview of the field, including books, movies, and TV shows.

Trott, Barry.

Read On . . . Crime Fiction. Libraries Unlimited, 2007. 978-1591583738.
  This book provides reading lists for every taste.

Winn, Duilys.

Murder Ink: The Mystery Reader's Companion. Workman, 1977. (2nd ed., Workman, 1984).

This classic volume was one of the first fannish publications in the field. It is full of trivia about the field. The second edition was its equal in fun and facts.

Chapter **10**

History and Criticism

Bailey, Frankie Y.

Out of the Woodpile: Black Characters in Crime and Detective Fiction. Greenwood Press, 1991. 0313266719.

> From slaves to assimilation, Bailey tries to trace the path of African American characters in mysteries.

Ball, John.

The Mystery Story. University of California, San Diego, 1976.

> Examining every facet of the mystery story, including its origins, history, subgenres, authors, and characters, this work was produced as a companion to a reprint series the university was issuing in the 1970s.

Binyon, T. J.

Murder Will Out: The Detective in Fiction. Oxford, 1989.

> Tracing the history of mystery from Poe to the present, this work provides an overview of the development of the genre.

Bloom, Harold, ed.

Classic Crime and Suspense Writers. Chelsea House, 1995. 0791022315.

> This work studies Ambler, Buchan, Cain, Chandler, du Maurier, Fleming, Greene, Hammett, Hornung, John D. MacDonald, Ross Macdonald, Thompson, and Woolrich.

Classic Mystery Writers. Chelsea House, 1995. 0791022358.

> This work studies Berkeley/Iles, Chesterton, Christie, Collins, Crofts, Doyle, Freeman, Poe, Post, Rinehart, Sayers, Van Dine, and Wallace.

Modern Crime and Suspense Writers. Chelsea House, 1995. 0791022471.

> This work studies Bloch, Condon, Dahl, Deighton, Ellroy, Harris, Highsmith, le Carre, Leonard, Ludlum, Parker, Spillane, and Vachss.

Modern Mystery Writers. Chelsea House, 1995. 0791023761.

> This works studies Allingham, Blake, Brown, Carr, Crispin, Gardner, Himes, Innes, Marsh, Millar, Queen, Stout, and Tey.

Craig, Patricia, and Mary Cadogan.

The Lady Investigates: Women Detectives and Spies in Fiction. Oxford, 1981.
    The majority of this work is an analysis of women characters in the formative years of the mystery.

Davis, David Brion.

Homicide in American Fiction, 1798–1860. Cornell, 1968.
    This critical study looks at the formative fiction that led to the creation of the modern mystery.

Dove, George N.

The Reader and the Detective Story. Bowling Green State University Popular Press, 1997.
    This work of criticism takes the unique approach of tying the mystery to the process of reading and enjoying fiction.

Eames, Hugh.

Sleuths, Inc.: Studies of Problem Solvers. Lippincott, 1978.
    This work studies the contributions of Doyle, Simenon, Hammett, Ambler, and Chandler.

Haycraft, Howard.

The Art of the Mystery Story: A Collection of Critical Esays. Carroll & Graf, 1946.
    A collection of major essays written by practitioners in the field.

Murder for Pleasure: The Life and Times of the Detective Story. D. Appleton-Century, 1941.
    This classic work of criticism and history was the standard against which all other criticism was measured for many years.

Klein, Kathleen Gregory.

The Woman Detective: Gender and Genre. University of Illinois, 1988.
    A study of the role of women in the history of the genre.

Landrum, Larry.

American Mystery Novels and Detective Novels: A Reference Guide. Greenwood Press, 1999. 0313213879.
    This book does a very through job of explaining the forces that created the mystery as a modern genre, from its roots to the literary influences that shape it today.

Lehman, David.

The Perfect Murder: A Study in Detection. University of Michigan, 1999.
An examination of the reasons readers enjoy reading about murder. This is an enlarged and expanded update to the original 1989 edition.

1

Lindsay, Elizabeth Blakesley.

Great Women Mystery Writers. 2nd ed. Greenwood, 2007.
Essays and bibliographies of major female contributors to the genre are provided by an impressive list of mystery fans and scholars.

2

Moore, Lewis D.

Cracking the Hard-Boiled Detective: A Critical History from the 1920S to the Present. McFarland, 2006. 0-7864-25681-4.
A critical review that traces the hard-boiled form from its birth in the 1920s to the present.

3

4

Murch, A. E.

The Development of the Detective Novel. Greenwood, 1968.
From its earliest ancestors through the Golden Age, this work attempts to trace the origins of the contemporary mystery.

5

Niebuhr, Gary Warren.

Make Mine a Mystery. Libraries Unlimited, 2003. 1-56308-784-7.
An explanation of the mystery for librarians that tries to identify the best mystery fiction collection.

6

Read 'Em Their Writes: A Handbook for Mystery and Crime Fiction Book Discussions. Libraries Unlimited, 2006.
A guide for starting a mystery book club with tips, background information, and sample questions provided for 100 mysteries.

7

Panek, Leroy Lad.

An Introduction to the Detective Story. Bowling Green University Popular Press, 1987.
This overview of the history of the mystery looks at early contributors and then covers the various subgenres.

8

The Origins of the American Detective Story. McFarland, 2006. 0-7864-2776-0.
From turn-of-the-century publications, theories are drawn about the evolution of the mystery novel as we know it.

9

10

Probable Cause: Crime Fiction in America. Bowling Green University Popular Press, 1990.

> Panek provides an overview of the first 100 years of crime fiction in America by putting together basic facts and observations that explain how the literature developed.

Schwartz, Saul.

The Detective Story: An Introduction to the Whodunit. National Textbook, 1978.

> A textbook for teaching the mystery.

Symons, Julian.

Bloody Murder: From the Detective Story to the Crime Novel. 3rd ed. Mysterious Press, 1992. 0-89296-496-0.

> The most respected contemporary analytical look at the detective story by the late British critic and writer of mystery fiction.

Great Detectives: Seven Original Investigations. Abrams, 1981.

> A look at the lives of Sherlock Holmes, Miss Marple, Nero Wolfe, Ellery Queen, Maigret, Hercule Poirot, and Philip Marlowe.

Thomson, H. Douglas.

Masters of Mystery: A Study of the Detective Story. Collins, 1931.

> This work may be the first attempt to create an overview of the field.

Walton, Priscilla L., and Manina Jones.

Detective Agency: Women Rewriting the Hard-Boiled Tradition. University of California, 1999.

> A look at the effect of women in an area of the genre that traditionally was reserved for men.

Willett, Ralph.

The Naked City: Urban Crime Fiction in the USA. Manchester University, 1996.

> City by city, this guide provides an overview of crime-related fiction as it developed in urban America.

Winks, Robin W.

Detective Fiction: A Collection of Critical Essays. Prentice Hall, 1981.

> This collection contains most of the major essays on the field through 1981, including the famous Edmund Wilson essay, "Who Cares Who Killed Roger Ackroyd?"

Modus Operandi: An Excursion into Detective Fiction. Godine, 1982.

> A collection of contemporary criticism of the field by a historian and reviewer.

Chapter 11

Journals

Alfred Hitchcock Mystery Magazine
 Davis Publications
 380 Lexington
 New York, NY 10017
 $30 (13 issues)
 Fiction, some reviews

Cads
 9 Vicarage Hill
 South Benfleet, Essex, England SS7 1PA
 $9 per issue
 Commentary and reviews

Clues: A Journal of Detection
 c/o Heldref Publications
 1319 18th Street NW
 Washington, DC 20036-1802
 $57 per year individual, $117 per year institutional
 Academic-style publication, with each issue focusing on one subject

Crime Spree
 536 South 5th Street, Suite 1A
 Milwaukee, WI 53204
 $20 (6 issues)
 Interviews, features, reviews

Deadly Pleasures
 PO Box 839
 Farmington, UT 84025-0839
 $18 (4 issues)
 Interviews, features, reviews

Ellery Queen Mystery Magazine
 Davis Publications
 380 Lexington
 New York, NY 10017
 $30 for 13 issues
 Fiction, some reviews

Mystery News

262 Hawthorn Village Commons, No. 152
Vernon Hills, IL 60061
$25 (6 issues)
Interviews, features, reviews

Mystery Readers Journal

Part of membership in the organization Mystery Readers International

Mystery Scene

331 W 57th Street Suite 148
New York, NY 10019-3101
$32 (5 issues)
Interviews, features, reviews

Chapter **12**

Book Review Sources

Booklist

Regular columns of review. In addition, each spring this magazine does a mystery issue, which provides a great list of titles for selection purposes.

Library Journal

Regular columns of reviews.

Publishers Weekly

Regular columns of reviews. In addition, each fall this magazine does a "Mystery Category Closeup," which provides an overview of the mystery genre from the industry point of view.

Additional book review sources are listed in Chapter 11.

Chapter 13

Conventions

Boulchercon, the World Mystery Convention, is held once a year in the fall of the year. the convention is named for Anthony Boucher, a respected mystery reviewer and author. This fans' convention has grown in its thirty-plus years to include authors, agents, publishers, and booksellers' concerns as well. Each Boulchercon maintains its own Web site, but the main page can be found at www. boulchercon.info.

Left Coast Crime Conference is held each spring in a city in the Western United States. The convention is similar to a Boulchercon, but its emphasis is on celebrating the authors of this region. Each Left Coast Conference maintains its own Web site.

Malice Domestic was created to extend the work being done to elevate the status of women in the genre. Its goal is to celebrate the soft-boiled mystery, but traditional mystery readers will find that most of their authors are eligible for discussion at this convention. The convention is held each spring near the nation's capital. Its Web site is www.malicedomestic.org.

Magna Cum Murder originated as an alumni activity for Ball State University. The convention has grown into a regional mystery convention, which works very hard to bring two or three major international mystery stars each year. Web site: www.magnacummurder.com.

Chapter 14

Mystery Bookstores

Mystery bookstores were a rarity until the 1980s, when there was a boom in store openings. At the end of the 1990s, we witnessed the opposite when independent mystery booksellers found themselves competing with large national chain bookstores and the Internet.

Here is a sample of some of the best mystery bookstores.

Murder One (www.murderone.co.uk)

The Mysterious Bookshop (www.mysteriousbookshop.com)

The Poisoned Pen Mystery Bookstore (www.poisonedpen.com)

Sleuth of Baker Street (www.abebooks.com/home/sleuthbooks)

Chapter 15

Online Resources

General Sites

ClueLass Home Page (www.cluelass.com)

Mystery Listservs

dorothyl: www.dorothyl.com

fictionl: www.webrary.org/rs/flmenu.html

rara-avis: www.miskatonic.org/rara-avis/

Readers' Advisory Sites

The Mystery Reader (www.themysteryreader.com)

Stop, You're Killing Me (www.stopyourekillingme.com)

Chapter 16

Organizations

Mystery Readers International

PO Box 8116
Berkeley, CA 94707

$22.50 per year for a membership and subscription to *Mystery Readers Journal*, a thematic magazine that is worth the price of admission.

Mystery Writers of America

17 East 47th Street, 6th floor
New York, NY 10017

$65 a year for membership for professional writers and associates plus a subscription to *The Third Degree*, the group's official newsletter. Membership is also included in the regional MWA chapter (the Midwest Chapter publishes its own newsletter, *Clues*). Membership includes the official Edgar Award program.

Private Eye Writers of America

330 Surrey Road
Cherry Hill, NY 08002

$50 a year for membership for professional writers and associates plus a subscription to *Reflections in a Private Eye*, the official newsletter.

Sisters in Crime

PO Box 442124
Lawrence, KS 66044
Web site: www.books.com/sinc

Membership for those who support women writers in the mystery field.

Chapter 17

Publishers

Bookwire's index to publishers: www.bookwire.com/index.publishers.html

Major Publishers

Penguin: www.penguinputnam.com/clubppi/index.htm

Random House: www.randomhouse.com/BB/MOTI

St. Martin's Minotaur: www.minotaurbooks.com/

Simon & Schuster: www.simonsays.com/email_update.cfm

Small Presses

Poisoned Pen Press: www.poisonedpenpress.com/

Author Index and Biographical Notes

Authors listed here are found in Part II.

Abe, Kobo, 158

Kobo Abe was born in 1924 in Tokyo, Japan, the son of a doctor. He earned an M.D. from Tokyo University in 1948, but was a novelist and playwright his entire adult life. Abe married an artist named Machi Yamada, and they had one daughter. He died in 1993 from heart failure.

Abbott, Megan, 28, 122, 156

Megan Abbott was born in Detroit, Michigan, in 1971. Her mother was a writer. Megan earned a B.A. from the University of Michigan and a Ph.D. from New York University in 2000. She has taught at New York University and the State University of New York at Oswego. Web site: www. meganabbott.com

Alexander, Shana, 68, 86, 103

Born in 1925 in New York City, Shana Alexander received a B.A. from Vassar College in 1945. She spent the early part of her career as a journalist until she became a full-time writer in 1979. She died of cancer in 2005.

Ambler, Eric, 147

Born in 1909 in London, England, Eric Ambler was the son of music hall performers. He attended the Northampton Polytechnic branch of the University of London from 1924 to 1927, but left before graduating. Ambler worked in various careers—as an engineering apprentice, a vaudevillian, and an advertising man. From 1940 until 1946 he served in the British Army's artillery corps. His first novel, *The Dark Frontier*, appeared in 1936. Over the course of his career, he received an Academy Award nomination for the screenplay for *The Cruel Sea*, and a Golden Dagger award for *A Passage of Arms*, *The Light of Day* (also an Edgar Award), *Dirty Story*, and *The Levanter*. The Mystery Writers of America made Amber a Grand Master in 1975, and the Crime Writers Association gave him the Diamond Dagger for lifetime achievement in 1986. He was twice married. Ambler died in 1998.

Amiel, Barbara, 139

Barbara Amiel was born in 1940 in Hertfordshire, England, the daughter of a lawyer father and nurse mother. She emigrated to Canada in 1948 and earned a B.A. from the University of Toronto in 1963. She was married to co-author George Jonas, but they are divorced, and she has been married three other times.

Anastasia, George, 36

A reporter for the *Philadelphia Inquirer*, George Anastasia has been twice nominated for the Pulitzer Prize. He lives in New Jersey with his wife.

Anderson, Edward, 41

Edward Anderson was born in Texas in 1905. He rose from being a printer's apprentice to a reporter', then spent time traveling in Europe before returning to America during the Great Depression. He wrote one other novel besides the one featured in this book, titled *The Hungry Men*, about the world of hobos. Setting novels aside, he had a rather unsuccessful career in Hollywood as a screenwriter before returning to a reporting role for the *Sacramento Bee*. The last years of his life were spent dealing with family troubles and ill-health. He died in 1969 in Texas.

Aronson, Steven M. L., 142

Steven M. L. Aronson was educated at Yale University. He has worked as a book editor in the publishing field. He lives in New York City.

Atkinson, Jim, 69

Jim Atkinson is the founding editor of "*D*" magazine and a contributing editor to *Texas Monthly* magazine.

Atwood, Margaret, 74

Margaret Atwood was born on November 18, 1939, in Ottawa, Ontario, Canada. She has a B.A. from the University of Toronto and an M.A. from Radcliffe College in Cambridge, MA. From 1964 through 1989, Atwood taught in various university settings. She holds sixteen honorary degrees from various universities around the world. Living in Toronto, Ontario, Canada, she is a full-time writer. Web site: www.owtoad.com

Banks, Ray, 158

Ray Banks was born in Kirkcaldy, Scotland. He went to university for two years but dropped out to be a double-glazing salesman, croupier, and dole monkey. He now lives with his wife in Newcastle-upon-Tyne, England. Web site: www.thesaturdayboy.com

Bardin, John Franklin, 75

John Franklin Bardin was born in 1916 in Cincinnati, Ohio, the son of a merchant. He worked in advertising and as a managing editor for a number of firms and publications before becoming a freelance writer in 1971. Bardin died in New York City in 1981.

Barnes, Jonathan, 159 Jonathan Barnes graduated from Oxford with a first in English literature. He is a reviewer and lives in London.

Barnes, Margaret Anne, 69 Margaret Anne Barnes was a newspaper reporter in Georgia. She retired to Orlando, Florida.

Baron, Alexander, 75 Joseph Alexander Baron was born in 1917. He served in the British Army from 1939 to 1945. After the war he worked for three years as a journalist before becoming a full-time writer.

Bean, Fred, 28 Fred Bean has worked as a horse trainer, livestock auctioneer, and Western writer.

Behn, Noel, 136 Born in 1928 in Chicago, Noel Behm earned a B.A. from Stanford in 1950. He served in counterintelligence with the U.S. Army from 1952 to 1953. From 1954 on, he worked in various capacities in the theater. He died of a heart attack in 1998.

Benioff, David, 29 Born David Friedman, he is the son of the former head of Goldman Sachs. David earned a B.A. from Dartmouth College and an M.F.A. from the University of California Irvine. He worked as a bouncer and a high school English teacher before becoming a screenwriter and novelist.

Berkow, Ira, 51 Ira Berkow was born in 1940 in Chicago, Illinois. He earned a B.A. from Miami University in 1963. He has worked as a journalist and editor since 1965.

Biggers, Earl Derr, 15 Earl Derr Biggers was born in 1884 in Warren, Ohio. He earned a B.A. from Harvard University in 1907. He wrote for the *Traveler*, a Boston newspaper, from 1908 to 1912. The rest of his life he was a playwright and novelist, including his long-running mystery series about the Honolulu detective Charlie Chan. He died in 1933.

Bigsby, Christopher, 91 Christopher Bigsby was born in 1941 in Dundee, Scotland. He earned a B.A. from the University of Sheffield in 1962 and an M.A. in 1964. His Ph.D. from the University of Nottingham was earned in 1966. Bigsby is a professor of American literature at the University of East Anglia, Norwich. He is also the author of more than forty nonfiction books and is considered one of the premier experts on American playwright Arthur Miller. *Beautiful Dreamer* is his fourth novel after *Hester: A Novel*, about the heroine of *The Scarlet Letter* (1994), *Pearl* (1995), and *Still Lives* (1996).

Black, David, 69 David Black is a novelist and nonfiction writer who lives in New York City.

Blake, Nicholas, 41

Cecil Day-Lewis was born in 1904 in Ballintubber, Ireland, the son of a minister. He attended Wadham College at Oxford. During his career as a poet, translator of Virgil, critic, and editor, he taught at Oxford, Trinity College and Harvard, among others. As Nicholas Blake, he wrote a series of mystery novels starring the character Nigel Strangeways. He died in 1972.

Blakeslee, Nate, 153

Nate Blakeslee earned a B.A. from Southwestern University in 1992. He is a former editor of the *Texas Observer* and lives with his wife in Austin, Texas.

Blanchard, Alice, 105

Alice Blanchard grew up in Connecticut and studied creative writing and filmmaking at Emerson and Harvard. She is the author of a collection of short stories, *The Stuntman's Daughter* (University of North Texas, 1996), which won the Katharine Anne Porter Prize. Her novels include *Darkness Peering* (Bantam, 1999) and *Life Sentences* (Warner, 2005). She has also received a PEN Syndicated Fiction Award, a New Literary Award, and a Centrum Artists in Residence Fellowship. She and her husband live in Los Angeles.

Bledsoe, Jerry, 51, 116

Jerry Bledsoe was born in Danville, Virginia, in 1941. He served in the U.S. Army from 1960 to 1963 and then spent the rest of his life as a journalist.

Bloch, Robert, 15, 159

Robert Bloch was born in Chicago, Illinois, in 1917, the son of a bank cashier father and a mother who was a teacher. He lived his early life in Milwaukee before moving West. Bloch's long literary career spans many genres, with the novel *Psycho* as his greatest claim to fame. He died from cancer in Los Angeles in 1994.

Block, Lawrence, 16, 75, 76, 77

Lawrence Block was born in Buffalo, New York, in 1938. He attended Antioch College in the late 1950s and worked as an editor for an agent and a publishing company before becoming a full-time writer. Block has not been out of print since 1961 and writes a number of different series in crime fiction as well as stand-alone thrillers. A number of his works have been filmed. He lives in New York City with his wife, Lynne, a painter. Web site: www.lawrenceblock.com/index_flash.htm

Bloom, John, 69

John Bloom was born in 1959 in Frontage, Texas, the son of a miner. He has been an auto mechanic, television and radio personality, comedian, journalist, and author. He was the host of *Joe Bob's Drive-in Theater*, on The Movie Channel from 1986 to 1996.

Blum, Howard, 36

Howard Blum was born in 1948 in New York City. He attended Stanford University. Twice nominated for the Pulitzer Prize, Blum worked as a journalist for the *New York Times* and the *Village Voice* before becoming a full-time author.

Bock, Charles, 122

Charles Bock's grandfather, father, and now his brothers run a pawn shop in Las Vegas, Nevada. Charles has an M.F.A. from Bennington College and lives in New York City. Web site: www.beautifulchildren.net

Bojanowski, Marc, 122

Marc Bojanowski was born in 1977 in Healdsburg, California. He has an M.F.A. from the University of California at Berkeley. He lives in Northern California.

Bommersbach, Jana, 103

Jana Bommersbach works as an investigative journalist in the Phoenix area, where she also resides.

Bourdain, Anthony, 41

Anthony Bourdain was born in 1956 in Leonia, New Jersey, the son of a record executive father and a mother who was an editor at the *New York Times*. He attended Vassar College and the Culinary Institute of America. He was the chef at Brasserie Les Halles, the Supper Club, and Vince & Linda at One Fifth, all in New York City. He was the host of *A Cook's Tour* on the Food Network and is currently the host of the Travel Channel's program *No Reservations*. Web site: www.travelchannel.com/TV_Shows/Anthony_Bourdain

Bowker, David, 29

David Bowker was born in Manchester, England. He is a journalist and author.

Braddon, Mary Elizabeth, 123

Mary Elizabeth Braddon published more than eighty novels during the Victorian period. She capitalized on the success of Wilkie Collin's *The Woman in White* to launch a writing career in the crime field. During this period many writers appeared in the "yellowback" format in England, and Braddon was one of the leading female authors. Braddon also edited two literary magazines and wrote plays and poetry in addition to her fiction.

Bradley, James, 123

James Bradley was born in Adelaide, South Australia, in 1967. He studied at the University of Adelaide, where he received a law degree, and at the University of South Australia and the Australian Film, Television and Radio School. He has worked as a law clerk, judge's associate, solicitor, research assistant, and editor. Bradley's book of poetry, *Paper Nautilus*, was shortlisted for the National Book Council Award in Australia. He lives in Sydney.

Brand, Christianna, 86

Christianna Brand was born in 1907 in Malaya, the daughter of a rubber planter. She was a mystery novelist and freelance writer. She died in 1988.

Breslin, Jimmy, 29, 36

Jimmy Breslin was born in 1930 in Jamaica, New York. Breslin began his career as a copyboy at the Long island Press. He worked as a sportswriter for many years and then became a well respected columnist, novelist, and freelance journalist.

Brewer, Gil, 11, 55

Gil Brewer was born in 1922. He served in the U.S. Army during the Second World War in France and Belgium. He was severely wounded and received a VA disability pension. He worked as a warehouseman, gas station attendant, cannery worker, and bookseller before becoming a full-time writer of over thirty paperback originals. He died in 1983 in St. Petersburg, Florida, from acute alcoholism.

Brown, Fredric, 91, 106, 123

Fredric Brown was born in 1906 in Cincinnati, Ohio, the son of a journalist. He attended two different colleges before working as an office worker for twelve years. He was an employee of the *Milwaukee Journal* newspaper from 1936 to 1947, when he became a full-time writer. Brown wrote in many genres, including some classic science fiction. He won the Edgar Allan Poe Award for best first mystery novel from the Mystery Writers of America in 1948 for *The Fabulous Clipjoint*, a coming-of-age mystery that launched his *Ed and Am Hunter series*. He died in Tucson, Arizona, in 1972.

Bruen, Ken, 12, 56

Ken Bruen was born in 1951 in Galway, Ireland. He has a Ph.D. from Trinity College. He worked all over the world as an English teacher. On one of his journeys, he was jailed and tortured in a South American country. He now lives in Galway. Web site: www.kenbruen.com

Bryan, Patricia L., 137

Patricia L. Bryan is a professor of law at the University of North Carolina. She lives in Chapel Hill, North Carolina, with her husband and coauthor Thomas Wolf and their three sons.

Bugliosi, Vincent, 69, 116

Vincent Bugliosi was born in 1934 in Hibbing, Minnesota. He earned a B.B.A. in 1956 from the University of Miami. He served in the U.S. Army after college. His LL.B. was earned from the University of California, and he has worked in the Los Angeles County District Attorney's office as well as in private practice. His biggest claim to fame was bringing down the Manson family and his book, *Helter Skelter*, earned an Edgar Award from the Mystery Writers of America.

Bunker, Edward, 16, 24, 41, 56, 61, 77

Edward Bunker was born in Hollywood, California, in 1933, the son of a set designer. By age ten, he was in reform school. Although once on the FBI's Ten Most Wanted List, his greatest claim to fame is that at seventeen he became the youngest criminal sent to San Quentin. His first novel, *No Beast So Fierce*, was published in 1972. Bunker appeared as an actor in the films *Reservoir Dogs* and *Heat*. He died in Burbank, California, in 2005.

Burn, Gordon, 116

Gordon Burn was born in 1948 in Newcastle, England, the son of a factory worker. He earned a B.A. from the University of London in 1969. He has been a freelance writer his entire adult life. His novel, *Alma*, won the Whitbread Prize for best first novel in 1991.

Burnett, W. R., 11, 27

William Riley Burnett was born in Springfield, Ohio, in 1899. After attending the Miami Military Institute and Ohio State University, he worked as a shop steward in a factory and as an insurance salesman. After working six years as a statistician for the Ohio Department of Labor Relations, he became a full-time novelist and screenwriter and ultimately produced thirty-six novels, sixty screenplays, and numerous songs and plays. The Mystery Writers of America made him a Grand Master for his contributions to crime literature. He died of heart failure in Santa Monica, California, in 1982.

Cain, James M., 11, 28, 49, 55, 61

James M. Cain was born in Annapolis, Maryland, to an educator and an opera singer. After graduating from college at the young age of seventeen, Cain served in the army in World War I and then as a journalist before embarking on a career as a novelist. Cain's novels were a steady source for Hollywood studios, and Cain also spent some time in Hollywood unsuccessfully trying to be a screenwriter. While he wrote until he died in his eighties, Cain's early novels were far more successful than his later works.

Cain, Paul, 28

George Carrol Sims was born in 1902 in Des Moines, Iowa. Besides his Paul Cain pseudonym, he also wrote screenplays under the name Peter Ruric. Sims worked in the film industry as an art decorator and production assistant. He died from cancer in 1966 in Los Angeles, California.

Cain, Tom, 16

Tom Cain is the pseudonym of an award-winning British journalist.

Capote, Truman, 11, 103

Truman Streckfus Persons was born in 1924 in New Orleans, Louisiana. His father was a nonpracticing lawyer and his mother, a former Miss Alabama, eventually divorced his father. Sent to be cared for by relatives in Monroeville, Alabama, Truman met his childhood friend, Harper Lee, who eventually would make him a character in her book *To Kill a Mockingbird*. Bouncing between his never-do-well father and a mother who did not want him, Truman eventually was adopted by Joseph G. Capote, who had married Truman's mother. He began his career as a newspaper clipper and cartoon cataloger for the *New Yorker* magazine. Over time, through his writing of stories, novels, plays, and screenplays, Capote managed to create a world around himself that brought him both fame and notoriety. His short stories won the O. Henry Award in 1946, 1948, and 1951. *In Cold Blood* received the Mystery Writers of America Edgar Award in 1966. Capote died in Los Angeles, California, in 1984, from complications brought on by alcohol and drug abuse.

Carcaterra, Lorenzo, 86

Lorenzo Carcaterra was born in 1954 in Hell's Kitchen, New York City, the son of a butcher. After reform school, he earned a B.S. from St. John's University. He has worked as a reporter, editor, television screenwriter, and freelance writer.

Carnahan, Matthew, 42

Matthew Carnahan was born in 1961 in California. He attended New York University and the Neighborhood Playhouse School of Theatre. He claims to have held over seventy different jobs, including deckhand and circus worker. He has been a novelist, playwright, and television and film director and producer. He is the life partner of actress Helen Hunt and they have two children. Web site: www.matthewcarnahan.com

Carpenter, Don, 56

Don Carpenter was born in 1931 in Berkeley, California. His family moved to Portland, where he graduated from high school. After service in the Air Force during the Korean War, he earned a B.S. from Portland State College. After earning an M.A. from San Francisco State College, he taught English. After the publication of his first novel, he moved to Mill Valley, California, and became a full-time writer. In addition to writing nine novels and various short story collections, Carpenter was a Hollywood scriptwriter. Divorced, and ill but still writing, he committed suicide by gunshot in 1995.

Carr, A. H. Z., 16 — Albert H. Z(olotkoff) Carr was born in 1902 in Chicago, Illinois. He earned a B.S. from the University of Chicago in 1921. He was an editor, business assistant, and freelance writer before becoming an economic advisor to President Harry Truman. He held various positions in the business community before he died of a heart attack in New York City.

Carr, Howie, 37 — Howie Carr was born in Portland, Maine, in 1952. He is a graduate of the University of North Carolina and has been a broadcaster and a journalist.

Cartwright, Gary, 70 — Gary Cartwright was raised in the Dallas area, where he later worked as a reporter for area newspapers. He lives in Austin.

Caspary, Vera, 106, 147 — Vera Caspary was born in 1899 in Chicago, Illinois, the daughter of a department store buyer. She was married to film producer I. G. Goldsmith. Caspary served as editor of *Dance* magazine from 1925 to 1927, but the rest of her life she was a freelance author of books, plays, and screenplays.

Cea, Robert, 154 — Robert Cea resigned from the New York police department as a highly decorated officer. He now writes screenplays for film and television.

Century, Douglas, 37 — Douglas Century is a contributing writer to many journals and magazines.

Chabon, Michael, 159 — Michael Chabon was born in 1963 in Washington, D.C., the son of two lawyers. Chabon earned a B.A. from the University of Pittsburgh in 1984 and an M.F.A. from the University of California–Irvine in 1987. His publications include *The Mysteries of Pittsburgh* (1988), *A Model World, and Other Stories* (1991), *Wonder Boys* (1995—New York Times Notable), *Werewolves in Their Youth* (1999), *The Amazing Adventures of Kavalier and Clay* (2000 National Book Critics Circle Award nomination, PEN/Faulkner Award for Fiction shortlist, and Pulitzer Prize for Fiction), *Summerland* (2002) and *The Yiddish Policemen's Union* (2007). His first marriage was to poet Lollie Groth. His second wife is mystery writer Ayelet Waldman, and they have three children. They live in Berkeley, California. Web site: www.michaelchabon.com

Chavarría, Daniel, 17 — Daniel Chavarría was born in 1933 in Uruguay. He immigrated to Cuba, where he is a professor of classics at the University of Havana.

Chessman, Caryl, 70   Caryl Chessman was born in 1921 in St. Joseph, Michigan. He was convicted of being the notorious "Red Light Bandit" in California. His method was to pull over unsuspecting motorists with a red light and then rob them, also raping the women. He was sentenced to death and placed on death row in San Quentin Prison in 1948. He was executed on May 2, 1960, for his crimes.

Chester, Giraud, 70   Giraud Chester was born in 1922 in New York City. He has been an educator, a writer, an advertising executive, and a television producer, including a span as executive vice president of Goodson-Todman Productions.

Chester, Lewis, 25   Lewis Chester worked as a journalist for the *London Sunday Times*.

Choi, Susan, 91   Susan Choi was born in South Bend, Indiana, in 1969. She earned a B.A. at Yale in 1990 and an M.F.A. from Cornell in 1995. Her novel, *American Woman*, was a Pulitzer Prize finalist. She lives in Brooklyn with her husband and two sons. Web site: www.susanchoi.com

Chute, Verne, 92   Verne Chute was born in California in 1899. He was the author of crime, science fiction, and Western stories and two novels under the name Dustin C. Scott. He died in Sun City, Arizona, in 1986.

Clark, Martin, 156   Martin Clark graduated from Davidson College and the University of Virginia School of Law. He now serves as a judge. He is the author of two previous novels.

Clark, Robert, 78   Robert Clark was born in 1952 in St. Paul, Minneapolis. He is the author of the novel *In the Deep Midwinter* (1997), and the nonfiction books *River of the West* (1995) and *The Solace of Food: A Life of James Beard* (1993). He lives in Seattle with his wife and two children.

Claude, Philippe, 148   Philippe Claude was born in 1962. He is a college educated man who has worked as a teacher of handicapped children and at the prison in Nancy, France. He is a professor of literature at the University of Nancy. In 2005 he won the Prix Renaudot award and Sweden's Martin Beck Award for *Les Âmes grises*. Web site: www.philippeclaudel.com

Cohen, Rich, 37   Born in 1968 in Libertyville, Illinois, the son of a Jewish business strategist, Rich Cohen grew up hearing war stories about Jewish gangsters. Cohen earned a B.A. from Tulane University and has worked as a writer and an editor.

Colapinto, John, 92

John Colapinto is a journalist and author who lives in New York City with his wife and son.

Coleman, Jonathan, 24

Jonathan Coleman was born in 1951 in Hattiesburg, Missouri, the son of parents who were retailers. He earned a B.A. from the University of Virginia in 1973. He worked as an editorial assistant and editor for a number of publishing concerns and as a producer at CBS before becoming a full-time writer in 1986.

Collins, Max (Allan), 78, 79

Max Allan Collins is a publishing phenomenon whose production includes novels, novelizations, nonfiction, plays, screenplays, and filmmaking. His private eye series featuring Nate Heller is one of the most revered historical series in the mystery genre. His graphic novel *Road to Perdition* was the basis of the Sam Mendes film starring Tom Hanks and Paul Newman. His novelizations have covered such entertainment efforts as *Saving Private Ryan* and *NYPD Blues*. Collins lives in Muscatine, Iowa, with his wife and fiction collaborator, author Barbara Collins.

Collins, Wilkie, 10, 62, 91, 121

A friend of Charles Dickens, British author Collins produced two works that help laid the foundation for crime fiction, along with the works of Edgar Allan Poe and Charles Dickens. Although his output was minimal, the success of his works led to great popularity and financial reward. Web site: www.deadline.demon.co.uk/wilkie/wilkie.htm

Condon, Richard, 17

Richard Condon was born in 1915 in New York City. He had a high school education. He worked for Walt Disney Productions from 1936 to 1941 as a publicist in New York. He then moved to other film companies until becoming a full-time novelist in 1957. He died in 1996 in Dallas, Texas.

Connelly, Michael, 42, 106, 123

Michael Connelly was born in 1956. He attended the University of Florida and worked on Florida newspapers. He was a Pulitzer Prize finalist for feature writing with two other journalist for coverage of an airline crisis and the consequences to the survivors. He then moved to the crime beat on the *Los Angeles Times*, which is where he got his inspiration to write his first novel, about LAPD homicide investigator Harry Bosch. He is now a full-time novelist, having written series books about Harry Bosch, Mickey Haller, Rachel Walling, and Terry McCaleb. Web site: www.michaelconnelly.com

Conrad, Mark T., 17

Mark T. Conrad is an assistant professor of philosophy at Marymount Manhattan College in New York City. He is the author of *The Simpsons and Philosophy* and *Woody Allen and Philosophy*.

Cook, Thomas H., 62, 92, 103, 124

Thomas H. Cook was born in 1947 in Fort Payne, Alabama. He received degrees in English and philosophy from Georgia State College (1969) and graduate degrees in American history from Hunter College, City University of New York (1972), and Columbia University (1976). While attending school, he supported himself in a variety of jobs, from advertising executive for U.S. Industrial Chemicals, to clerk-typist for the Association for Help of Retarded Adults. He taught college English and history at DeKalb Community College in Clarkson, Georgia, for three years before deciding, upon publication of his first book, to become a full-time writer. Cook is the author of over twenty books, including two works of true crime. His novels have been nominated for the Edgar Allan Poe Award, the Macavity Award, and the Dashiell Hammett Prize.

Cooke, John Peyton, 107

John Peyton Cooke was born in Amarillo, Texas, in 1967, and grew up in Laramie, Wyoming. He attended the University of Wisconsin, where he also was a police stenographer for the Madison Police Department. He eventually moved to New York, where he worked in the publishing industry. Cooke now lives in Toronto, Ontario, Canada. Web site: johnpeytoncooke.com

Cooley, Robert, 37

Robert Cooley was a Chicago attorney who worked for the mob. After wearing a wire and testifying in nine trials, he was forced to move about the country to avoid a retribution hit.

Corbett, David, 29, 124

David Corbett was born in 1953 in Columbus, Ohio. He earned a B.S. from Ohio State University in 1976 and worked as a private detective in San Francisco from 1983 to 1996. He then worked as an office manager in his wife's law office, until her death from cancer in 2001. He lives in Northern California, where he continues to write. Web site: www.davidcorbett.com

Cornwell, John, 86

John Cornwell was born in England in 1940. He has worked as a journalist and an investigative reporter. He is a novelist as well as a nonfiction writer.

Cowan, Rick, 37

Rick Cowan is a New York police officer in the Organized Crime Investigation Division.

Cray, Ed, 116	Ed Cray was born in 1933 in Cleveland, Ohio, the son of a laundry owner father and a mother who was a schoolteacher. Cray served in the U.S. Army from 1952 to 1954. He earned a B.A. from the University of California in 1957. His first job was as a folklore and folk song instructor. He became a freelance writer in 1964 and eventually became a professor of journalism.
Cummings, John, 37	John Cummings is the co-author of *Goombata: The Improbable Rise and Fall of John Gotti and His Gang*.
de Ford, Miriam Allen, 137	Miriam Allen deFord was born in 1888 in Philadelphia, Pennsylvania. She earned a A.B. from Temple University. She worked as a journalist, an insurance claim adjuster and a freelance writer. The book in this volume won the Edgar Award in 1961. She was twice married and died in 1975.
de Kretser, Michelle, 156	Michelle de Kretser was born in Sri Lanka (formerly Ceylon) in 1958, the daughter of a judge. She immigrated to Australia at age fourteen in 1972. Michelle attended Melbourne University, where she studied French, and she also studied in Paris. Her first novel, *The Rose Grower*, was published in 1999. She has taught literature at Melbourne University. Michelle has also worked as an editor for *Lonely Planet* and as a reviewer for a newspaper. *The Hamilton Case* is her second novel.
DeMarinis, Rick, 124	Rick DeMarinis was born in 1937 in New York City. He served in the U.S. Air Force from 1954 to 1958 and was an engineer in the aerospace industry. He earned a B.A. from the University of Montana in 1961 and an M.A. in 1967. He taught at the University of Montana and San Diego State University and is now a professor emeritus at the University of Texas at El Paso.
Denton, Bradley, 107	Bradley Denton was born in 1958. He earned an M.A. from the University of Kansas in creative writing. He is a full-time writer.
Dershowitz, Alan M., 70	Alan M. Dershowitz was born in Brooklyn, New York, in 1938. He earned a B.A. from Brooklyn College in 1959 and an LL.B. from Yale in 1962. He has been a lawyer, educator, writer, editor, lecturer, and radio talk show host. He taught at Harvard Law School from 1964 to 1993.
Detroit, Michael, 38	Michael Detroit is the pseudonym of a writer who lives in California.

Dickens, Charles, 10, 105, 121

Born in Portsmouth, England, into a family that eventually would have eight children, Charles Dickens's spent a happy childhood on the south coast of England. After the family moved to London and his father served a jail term for debt, he was forced to work to support his family. Although educated at the Welling Academy, Dickens never attended college and was essentially self-educated while working at various jobs, including as a law clerk and journalist. By 1837 he had published his first book, and he was recognized in his own day as one of the greatest novelists of all time. Web site: www.dickensfellowship.org

Dobyns, Stephen, 107

Stephen Dobyns was born in 1941 in Orange, New Jersey, and is the son of an Episcopal minister. He attended Shimer College and Wayne State University before earning an M. F. A. from the University of Iowa. He has taught English, worked as a reporter, and been a writer since 1971. Besides being a novelist, Dobyns is an award-winning poet. All of the books in his long-running mystery series about private detective Charlie Bradshaw have "Saratoga" in the title.

Dodge, David, 17

David Dodge was born in 1910 in Berkeley, California. He was a high school graduate and worked as a bank clerk, ship's fireman, social worker, and public accountant from 1935 to 1942. Dodge served in the U.S. Naval Reserve from 1941 to 1945. He died in San Miguel de Allende, Mexico, in 1974.

Dolnick, Edward, 25

Edward Dolnick was born in 1952. He is the former chief science writer at the *Boston Globe*. He lives near Washington, D.C.

Doolittle, Sean, 93

Sean Doolittle was born in 1971. He lives with his wife and children in Omaha, Nebraska. Web site: seandoolittle.com

Dorsey, Tim, 18, 19, 20

Tim Dorsey was born in Indiana but raised in Florida. He has a B.S. in transportation from Auburn University. He has served as the police reporter for *The Alabama Journal*, and as a reporter for *The Tampa Tribune*. He was the night editor for the *Tribune* when he quit in 1999 to write full time. Web site: www.timdorsey.com

Dostoevsky, Fyodor, 10, 62

Fyodor Dostoevsky was born in Moscow in October 1821. His mother died when he was a teenager, and his father was murdered while Fyodor was away at school. Graduating from college as an engineer, Dostoevsky chose to follow his love of reading into a career as a writer. Achieving success early, his literary achievements did not keep him from being imprisoned in 1848 for political activity and put before a firing squad. Saved by a pardon, he was sentenced to hard labor in Siberia until 1859, when he returned to St. Petersburg to resume his writing. His life there was difficult and sad but allowed him to produce his greatest works.

Dreiser, Theodore, 10, 63

Born in 1871 in Terre Haute, Indiana, Dreiser's early life was spent as a reporter while working his way to New York City. He based his first novel, *Sister Carrie*, on his sister's, life but its failure led him to give up writing, and he spent some time in a sanitarium. Dreiser later went on to write one of the great novels of American literature, *An American Tragedy*. He died of a heart attack in December 1945.

Dumas, Timothy, 137

Timothy Dumas was born and raised in Greenwich, Connecticut. Now the managing editor of the *Greenwich News*, he lives in Stamford, Connecticut.

du Maurier, Daphne, 124

Daphne du Maurier was born in 1907 in London, England, the daughter of actors. In 1932 she married Frederick Arthur Montague Browning, a lieutenant general. They had three children. Ms. du Maurier was a full-time writer from 1931 until her death in Cornwall in 1989. She published fifteen novels during her career, as well as short stories, nonfiction, and plays. In 1969 she received the Dame Commander, Order of the British Empire. Web site: www.dumaurier.org

Duncombe, Stephen, 48

Stephen Duncombe earned a B.A. from the State University of New York in 1988 and a Ph.D. from the City University of New York in 1993. He has worked as an educator.

Earley, Pete, 154

Pete Earley was born in 1951 in Douglas, Arizona. He earned a B.S. from Phillips University in 1973. He worked as a journalist in Kansas, Oklahoma, and Washington, D.C. He has been a freelance writer since 1986. He lives in Chantilly, Virginia. Web site: www.peteearley.com/bio/index.html.

Earling, Debra Magpie, 93

Debra Magpie Earling was born in 1957 in Spokane, Washington. She is a member of the Confederated Salish and Kootenai Tribes of the Flathead Reservation. She was married in 1974 but is now divorced. She left high school before graduation. After earning a GED, she was a public defender on the reservation from 1985 to 1986. Debra earned a B.A. from the University of Washington in 1986. From 1991 to 1998, she was an instructor in Native American studies and creative writing at Montana State University. From Cornell University, she earned an M.A. in 1991 and an M.F.A. in 1992. She is currently an associate professor of English at the University of Montana.

Edgerton, Clyde, 20

Clyde Edgerton was born in 1944 in Durham, North Carolina, the son of an insurance salesman. He earned a B.A., M.A.T., and Ph.D. from the University of North Carolina. He served five years as a fighter pilot in the U.S. Air Force. He is the author of numerous novels that are set in the South. Web site: clydeedgerton.com

Eichenwald, Kurt, 52

Kurt Eichenwald was born in 1961 in Dallas, Texas. He is a graduate of Swarthmore College. He has been an investigative journalist in New York City since 1987 and has twice received the Pulitzer Prize.

Elkind, Peter, 117

Peter Elkind is an editor at *Texas Monthly* who broke the Genene Jones case. He lives in Dallas, Texas, with his wife and son.

Ellin, Stanley, 159

Stanley Ellin was born in Brooklyn in 1916. He attended Brooklyn College and earned a B.A. in 1936. He worked for a newspaper distributor until serving in the armed forces during World War II. In 1946, Ellin became a full-time writer and eventually became a master of the short story form. He was made a Grand Master by the Mystery Writers of America.

Ellis, David, 94

David Ellis graduated from Northwestern Law School and is an attorney in private practice in Chicago, where he lives with his wife, Susan. He published *Line of Vision* in 2001 and since then has written *Life Sentence* (2003), *Jury of One* (2004), *In the Company of Liars* (2005), and *Eye of the Beholder* (2007). Web site: www.davidellis.com

Enger, Lin, 125

Englade, Ken, 60

English, T. J., 38

Evans, Wanda Webb, 104

Fanning, Diane, 117

Farber, Myron, 117

Farrell, Harry, 25

Faust, Christa, 94

Fay, Stephen, 25

Fearing, Kenneth, 94

Lin Enger grew up in Minnesota. He earned an MFA from the Iowa Writers' Workshop and is the director of the MFA program for Minnesota State University. He collaborated with his brother Leif on a series of mystery novels under the pseudonym L. L. Enger. Enger lives in Moorhead, Minnesota, with his wife and children. Web site: www.lin-enger.com

Bon in Memphis, Tennessee, in 1938, Ken Englade earned a B.A. from Louisiana State University in 1960. He has worked as a reporter and a freelance writer for his entire adult life.

T. J. English is a New York City writer specializing in writing about organized crime.

Wanda Webb Evans is a former columnist for the Lubbock *Avalanche-Journal*.

Dianne Fanning is a freelance writer who lives in New Braunfels, Texas.

Myron Farber was a *New York Times* reporter nominated for the Pulitzer Prize for his reporting on the Dr. X case and also eventually was pardoned by the governor of New Jersey for a contempt conviction associated with the same case.

Harry Farrell was born in 1924 in San Jose, California. He worked from 1946 to 1986 as a journalist and earned a B.A. from San Jose State College in 1948. He He lives in San Jose.

Christa Faust was born in 1969 in New York City. She is a former Times Square peep booth girl and a professional dominatrix. Web site: www.christafaust.com

Stephen Fay was born in Littleborough, England, in 1938, the son of a journalist. He earned a B.A. from the University of New Brunswick in 1958 and an M.A. in 1959 from the London School of Economics and Political Science. He worked as an economist before becoming a journalist at the *London Sunday Times*.

Kenneth Fearing was born in 1902 in Oak Park, Illinois, the son of an attorney. He earned a B.A. from the University of Wisconsin in 1924. He was a freelance writer and editor from 1927 to 1961. He died in 1961.

Fergus, Jim, 94

Jim Fergus lives in Arizona, where he works as a freelance journalist. He is the author of two nonfiction books, *A Hunter's Road* (1992) and *The Sporting Road* (1999). His first novel, *One Thousand White Women: The Journals of May Dodd*, was published in 1998 and was the winner of the Mountains and Plains Booksellers Award.

Feuerlight, Roberta Strauss, 87

Roberta Strauss Feuerlight was born in New York City. She is the author of numerous books, including *Reign of Terror: World War I* and *Joe McCarthy and McCarthyism*.

Finkel, Michael, 87

Born in 1969, Michael Finkel grew up in Bozeman, Montana. His career as a journalist brought him to the *New York Times Magazine*. He was fired for writing an article about a composite character trapped in slave labor in Mali. At the same time, he found out a murderer was living in Mexico, impersonating him. Finkel now lives in Bozeman.

Fisher, Jim, 137

Jim Fisher served as a special agent for the FBI from 1966 to 1972. He is currently a professor in the Department of Political Science and Criminal Justice at Edinboro University of Pennsylvania.

Fisher, Steve, 29

Steve Fisher was born in 1913 in Marine City, Michigan. He was raised in Los Angeles by his actress mother. He joined the U.S. Navy at age sixteen and served for four years in submarines. Fisher began his writing career working for the pulps. With limited success as a novelist and short story writing, Fisher turned to screen writing in Hollywood with some success both in the film and television industry. He died in California in 1980.

Fitzgerald, F. Scott, 49

F. Scott Fitzgerald was born in 1896 in St. Paul, Minnesota. Fitzgerald was named for an ancestor on his father's side, who wrote the national anthem. He left the Midwest to attend Princeton University from 1913 to 1917. Fitzgerald served in the U.S. Army in Europe during World War I rising to the rank of second lieutenant. After the war, his first published novel, *This Side of Paradise*, received public acclaim. He married Zelda Sayre in 1920, and their stormy and strange relationship became legendary. The couple had one son. Fitzgerald also published *The Beautiful and the Damned* (1922), *Tender Is the Night* (1934), and *The Last Tycoon* (unfinished when published in 1941). He worked occasionally as a screenwriter in Hollywood for the studios, including working on *Gone With the Wind*. Fitzgerald died of a heart attack in 1940.

Floyd, Bill, 107 Bill Floyd graduated from Appalachian State University. He lives in Morrisville, North Carolina, with his wife.

Flynn, Kevin, 70 Kevin Flynn was born in 1957. He earned a law degree from Notre Dame University and works as an Assistant U.S. District Attorney for the District of Columbia.

Fosburgh, Lacey, 137 Lacey Fosburgh was born in 1942 in New York City, the daughter of a writer father and a public relations executive mother. She earned a B.A. from Sarah Lawrence College in 1964. She worked as a journalist, freelance writer, and educator. She died of breast cancer in 1993.

Fowles, John, 108 John Fowles was born in 1926 in Leigh-on-Sea, Essex, England. He served in the Royal Marines, rising to the rank of lieutenant. Fowles attended the University of Edinburgh while a Marine and New College, Oxford, where he earned a B.A. in 1950. Fowles taught from 1951 until 1963, when he published this book. Additional novels include the much acclaimed *The Magus* (1966) and *The French Lieutenant's Woman* (1969). Fowles married twice and died on November 5, 2005.

France, Johnny, 104 Johnny France is the sheriff of Madison County, Montana.

Francisco, Ruth, 148 Ruth Francisco studied voice and drama in New York before working in the film industry in Hollywood. She is the author of *Confessions of a Deathmaiden* and *The Secret Memoirs of Jacqueline Kennedy Onassis*.

Frank, Gerold, 117 Gerold Frank was born in Cleveland in 1907. He earned a B.A. from Ohio State University in 1929 and an M.A. from Western Reserve University in 1933. He was a journalist his entire adult life. He died in 1998.

Frasca, John, 138 John Frasca was born in 1916 in Lynn, Massachusetts, the son of a contractor. He earned a B.A. from Mississippi College in 1940. Frasca served in the U.S. Marine Corps from 1942 to 1945, rising to the rank of first lieutenant. He worked as a rewriter, a reporter, an editor, and a freelance writer. He died in Tampa, Florida, in 1979.

Fuhrman, Mark, 117, 154 Mark Fuhrman was born in 1952 in Eatonville, Washington. He was a U.S. Marine and served two tours of duty in Vietnam. Fuhrman served with the Los Angeles Police Department for twenty years, including time as a detective on the O. J. Simpson case. Since retiring from the LAPD, he has worked as an electrician's apprentice and a sawmill worker, bused tables in a restaurant, and been a radio talk show host. He lives in Idaho.

Gentry, Curt, 116, 138	Born in 1931 in Lamar, Colorado, Curt Gentry was the son of a city clerk. He earned a B.A. from San Francisco State College. He served in the U.S. Air Force from 1950 to 1954, including one year in Korea as editor of the Air Force newspaper. He has been a full-time writer since 1961.
Giancana, Antoinette, 38	Antoinette Giancana is the daughter of Sam Giancana, the man who replaced Al Capone as the head of the Chicago mob.
Girard, James Preston, 108	James Preston Girard was born in 1944 in Tillamook, Oregon, the son of a teacher father and a bookkeeper mother. He earned a B.A. in 1966 from the University of Kansas and an M.A. from Johns Hopkins University in 1967. He has worked as an educator, a reporter, a political scriptwriter, and a public relations officer. Web site: thelateman.com
Gischler, Victor, 20, 30, 95	Victor Gischler was born in 1969 in Sanford, Florida, the son of a real estate father and a massage therapist mother. He has a Ph.D. in English from the University of Southern Mississippi and teaches creative writing at Rogers State University in Claremore, Oklahoma. Web site: victorgischler. blogspot.com
Glynn, Jonny, 108	Jonny Glynn is a writer and actor who has performed with the Royal Shakespeare Company.
Godfrey, Ellen, 71	Ellen Godfrey was born in 1942 in Chicago, Illinois. She earned a B.A. from Stanford University in 1963. She has been a teacher and worked in the software industry before becoming a full-time writer in 1996.
Goines, Donald, 79	Donald Goines was born in 1937 in Detroit, Michigan. He attended Catholic schools in Detroit but left early to join the U.S. Air Force from 1951 to 1954. Goines returned from the military a heroin addict. He took up the criminal life to feed his habit and ended up being arrested fifteen times and serving seven prison terms. In prison he read *Iceberg Slim* and took up writing. In 1974, Goines was murdered in Highland Park, Michigan, during a robbery that may have been related to his drug use.
Golden, Harry, 138	Born Harry Goldhurst in 1902 in New York City, Golden was the son of a newspaper editor. He legally changed his name in the 1930s. His entire career was spent working for various newspapers in New York City and Charlotte. He died in Charlotte in 1981.

The Goldman Family, 104

Since Ron Goldman was murdered along with Nicole Brown Simpson in 1994, the family has been on a mission to see that O. J. Simpson is proven guilty of this crime.

Goodis, David, 11, 63, 79, 95, 96, 125, 149

David Goodis was born in Philadelphia, Pennsylvania, in 1917. Goodis graduated from Temple University with a B.Sc. in journalism. While working for an advertising agency, he wrote his first book, *Retreat from Oblivion*, in 1939. He moved to New York, where he wrote for the pulps, spent his time in Hollywood writing for the film industry and for hardcover publishers, then finished his career back in his hometown writing paperback originals.

Goodman, Carol, 63

Carol Goodman earned a B.A. from Vassar College and an M.F.A for New School University. She taught Latin in Austin, Texas, before moving to New York City to teach, write, and live.

Gores, Joe, 80, 108, 159

Joe Gores was born in 1931 in Rochester, Minnesota, the son of an accountant. He earned an A.B. from the University of Notre Dame in 1953 and an M.A. from Stanford in 1961. He served in the U.S. Army from 1958 to 1959. After holding down a variety of jobs and going in and out of school, Gores became a private investigator from 1955 to 1962. He then taught in Africa for a year before becoming the manager and auctioneer at the San Francisco office of Automobile Auction. He has been a full-time writer since 1976.

Gottlieb, Eli, 96

Eli Gottlieb lives in Boulder, Colorado. His previous novel, *The Boy Who Went Away*, won the Rome Prize and the 1998 McKitterick Prize from the British Society of Authors and was a *New York Times* Notable book. Web site: www.eligottlieb.com

Gourevitch, Philip, 104

Philip Gourevitch was born in 1961. He earned a B.A. from Cornell and an M.F.A. in fiction writing from Columbia University. He has worked as a journalist, including time at the *New Yorker* magazine. He won the National Book Critics Circle Award for general nonfiction in 1999 (and many other awards) for his first book, *We Wish to Inform You That Tomorrow We Will Be Killed with Our Families: Stories from Rwanda*.

Gray, John MacLachlan, 108

John MacLachlan Gray was born in 1946 in Ottawa, Ontario, Canada, the son of a Royal Canadian Air Force officer and a mother who was a biologist. He earned a B.A. from Mount Allison University and an M.A. from the University of British Columbia. He spent many years in the theater world as an actor, composer, and director.

Graysmith, Robert, 118

Robert Gray Smith was born in 1942 in Pensacola, Florida, the son of an Air Force lieutenant colonel. He earned a B.F.A. from California College of Arts and Crafts in 1965 and was a political cartoonist. In 1976 he legally changed his name to Graysmith, and since 1983 he has been a full-time writer. His book *Zodiac* was a best seller and was the basis for a major motion picture.

Green, George Dawes, 125

George Dawes Green was born in 1954 in Idaho, the son of a newspaperman. He attended high school in Georgia. In the late 1970s and early 1980s, he wrote for *Suburbia Today* magazine in New York City. From 1984 to 1991, he owned a clothing manufacturing and exporting business in Guatemala. He has been a full-time writer since 1991. In addition to this title, he has written the screenplays for this novel and the novel *The Juror* (1995). He lives in Key West, Florida.

Green, Norman, 30, 96

Norman Green was born in 1954 in Massachusetts. He now lives in New Jersey with his wife.

Greene, Graham, 50

Graham Greene was born in 1904 in Berkhamsted, Hertfordshire, England. He earned a B.A. from Balliol College, Oxford. Greene was a film critic in his early years. Besides the title included in this book, he wrote many novels, plays, and screenplays, earning a literary reputation. Greene and his wife, Vivien, had two children. He died in 1991 in Vevey, Switzerland.

Greene, Robert W., 52

Robert Greene was born in Jamaica, New York, the son of an attorney father and a teacher mother. He attended Fordham University from 1947 to 1950 and then began a career in journalism.

Gresham, William Lindsay, 57

William Lindsay Gresham was born in Baltimore in 1909. He was always interested in sideshows and carnivals and wrote nonfiction about that subject as well as the book featured in this book. Living an unhappy life caused partially by his alcoholism, Gresham took his own life in a hotel in New York in 1962.

Grisham, John, 138

John Grisham was born in 1955 in Jonesboro, Arkansas, the son of a construction worker. He earned a B.S. from Mississippi State University and a J.D. from the University of Mississippi. He worked as a lawyer from 1981 to 1990 and served in the Mississippi House of Representatives from 1984 to 1990. He is now an internationally famous and best-selling novelist. Web site: www.randomhouse.com/features/grisham

Grubb, Davis, 125

Davis Grubb was born in 1919 in Moundsville, West Virginia. He attended Carnegie Institute of Technology and briefly worked in the radio industry. Grubb was a full-time writer from 1944 until his death in 1980.

Guterson, David, 126

David Guterson was born in 1956 in Seattle, Washington, the third of five children. His father was a criminal defense attorney. Guterson earned a B.A. in English from the University of Washington in 1978. In 1982 he earned an M.A. in creative writing from the same university. He was a high school English teacher on Bainbridge Island, Washington, from 1984 until 1994. While teaching, he wrote magazine articles, including some published in *Sports Illustrated* and *Harpers' Magazine*. He is now a contributing editor at *Harpers'*. His first book, a collection of short stories called *The Country Ahead of Us, the Country Behind* (1989), was published in 1989. He has also written *East of the Mountains* (1999). In 1992 a nonfiction title, *Why Homeschooling Makes Sense*, was published. He is married, and he and his wife Robin have four children.

Guthrie, Allan, 20, 42

Allan Guthrie was born in Orkney, England. He has lived in Edinburgh for most of his life, and his wife's name is Donna. Web site: www.allanguthrie.co.uk/Guthrie/allan.htm

Haddon, Mark, 126

Mark Haddon was born in 1962 in Northampton, England. Haddon earned a B.A. in education from Merton College at Oxford in 1981 and an M.A. from Edinburgh University in 1984. He has worked with autism and multiple sclerosis patients. He was also an illustrator and cartoonist, including the cartoon strip, *Men—A User's Guide*. He is the creator of *Microsoap*, an award-winning television series for children. He has authored (and in some cases illustrated) eighteen books for children. His newest work is *The Talking Horse and the Sad Girl and the Village Under the Sea* (2005), a collection of poetry. He is married to Sos Eltis, an educator, and they have one daughter. They live in Oxford. Web site: www.markhaddon.com

Hall, B. C., 118

B(axter) C(larence) Hall was born in 1936 in Buckhorn, Arkansas. He earned a B.A. from Henderson State University in 1959 and an M.F.A. in 1961 from the University of Iowa. He has worked as a reporter and an editor as well as a professor of journalism.

Hamilton, Donald, 80

Donald Hamilton was born in 1916 in Uppsala, Sweden. His family immigrated to the United States when he was eight. Hamilton earned a B.S. from the University of Chicago in 1938. He served four years in the U.S. Naval Reserve, rising to the rank of lieutenant. He worked as a photographer before becoming a full-time writer.

Hammer, Richard, 38

Richard Hammer was born in 1928 in Hartford, Connecticut. He earned an A.B. from Syracuse University in 1950 and an M.A. from Trinity College in 1951. He worked as a news assistant and editor for a number of publications. His book, *The Vatican Connection*, won the Edgar Award from the Mystery Writers of America.

Hammett, Dashiell, 11, 28, 158

Samuel Dashiell Hammett was born in 1894 in St. Mary, Maryland. He attended Baltimore Polytechnic Institute but left high school at age fourteen. Hammett held a variety of jobs but worked for the Pinkerton National Detective Agency from 1915 until 1918 and again from 1919 until 1921. Hammett served in the U.S. Army Ambulance Corps from 1918 through 1919. For the rest of his life he suffered from the tuberculosis he contracted while serving, and from alcoholism. His first detective fiction appeared in *Black Mask* magazine in 1923. His later years were spent in the company of playwright Lillian Hellman and in dodging the Internal Revenue Service, which eventually garnisheed his royalties. He died in 1961 of lung cancer.

Harris, Thomas, 12, 109

Thomas Harris was born in 1940 in Jackson, Mississippi, the son of an electrical engineer father and a mother who taught high school. He earned a B.A. in 1964 from Baylor University. He worked as a police report in Waco and for the Associated Press in New York City. Since 1974, he has been a full-time writer.

Harrison, Colin, 126

Colin Harrison was born in 1960 in New York City, the son of a headmaster father and the actress Jean Spencer. He earned a B.A. from Haverford College and an M.F.A. from the University of Iowa in 1986. He has worked as an editor at a variety of publications while also teaching at Columbia University.

Harrison, Kathryn, 87

Kathryn Harrison was born in Los Angeles, California, in 1961. She attended Stanford University and the University of Iowa Writers' Workshop. She is a former editor for Viking and now lives in Los Angeles.

Harwell, Fred, 138

Fred Harwell has a law degree from the University of North Carolina at Chapel Hill. He has been a reporter and the executive director of the North Carolina Center for Public Policy.

Hassler, Jon, 80

Jon Francis Hassler was born in 1933 in Minneapolis, Minnesota, the son of a grocer and a teacher. He earned a B.A. from St. John's University in 1955 and an M.A. from the University of North Dakota in 1960. He has taught English on the high school, college, and university levels. He lives in Sauk Rapids, Minnesota, with his wife, Marie.

Hendricks, Vicki, 20, 80

Vicki Hendricks was born in 1951 in Covington, Kentucky, the daughter of a salesman. She earned a B.S. from the Ohio State University in 1973, an M.A. from Florida Atlantic in 1979, and an M.F.A. from Florida International University in 1992. She was a professor at Broward Community College from 1981 until 1996. She is now a full-time writer. Web site: www.vickihendricks.com

Hiaasen, Carl, 160

Carl Hiaasen was born in 1953 in Fort Lauderdale, Florida, the son of a lawyer and a homemaker. He earned a B.S. from the University of Florida in 1974. Since then, Hiaasen has worked as a reporter or columnist. He has been married twice and has two children. Web site: www.carlhiaasen.com

Higgins, George V., 12, 21, 57

George V. Higgins was born in Brockton, Massachusetts, in 1939. He earned a B.A. from Boston College in 1961, an M.A. from Stanford University in 1965, and a J.D. from Boston College in 1967. He worked as a reporter from 1962 to 1967, when he was admitted to the Massachusetts Bar. He worked for many years in the various attorney general's offices prosecuting organized crime until he opened his own law firm in 1973. He has also taught law. Twice married, Higgins has two children.

Highsmith, Patricia, 11, 63, 81, 96, 110, 111, 126, 149

Mary Patricia Highsmith was born in 1921 in Fort Worth, Texas, to a graphic artist father and a fashion illustrator mother. Her parents divorced early in her life and she was raised by her maternal grandmother. When her mother, Mary, remarried, she moved her daughter to New York City, but Highsmith lived her entire life resenting the fact that her mother did not love her. After attending Barnard College, she wrote text for comic books, including *Superman* and *Batman*. Her first novel, *Strangers on a Train*, was published in 1950 and became a successful film directed by Alfred Hitchcock. Despite some early popularity, her novels never gained her wealth or fame in America, and she lived out her life in Europe. Highsmith died of lung cancer in Locarno, Switzerland, in 1995.

Hill, Russell, 57

Russell Hill was born in 1935 in Spring Valley, Illinois, the son of two teachers. He earned a B.A. from the University of California at Berkeley in 1958 and an M.A. from San Francisco State University in 1976. Hill taught English in the Tamalpais High School District, Marin County, California, for twenty-five years.

Hjortsberg, William, 160

William Hjortsberg was born in New York City in 1941, the son of a restaurateur. He has a B.A. from Dartmouth Collge and has studied at both Yale and Stanford. He has been a writer and teacher his entire adult life.

Hodel, Steve, 139

Steve Hodel was born in 1941 in Los Angeles, California, the son of a surgeon. He served in the U.S. Navy as a medic before spending twenty-four years with the LAPD, including time as a homicide investigator. He retired from the force and now works as a private investigator.

Hodgson, Ken, 21

Ken Hodgson was born in 1945 in Canon City, Colorado, the son of a miner. Besides working in a mental hospital and owning an air compressing business, Hodgson owned The Payroll, a historic gold mine. He is the author of numerous Westerns and mysteries. He lives in Tucumcari, New Mexico, or San Angelo, Texas, with his wife, Rita.

Hoffman, William, 96

William Hoffman was born in 1925 in Charleston, West Virginia, the son of a coal miner. His parents divorced shortly after his birth. He was raised by his grandmother and schooled at the Kentucky Military Institute. From 1943 until 1946, Hoffman served in the U.S. Army, where he saw action in Normandy and the Battle of the Bulge. He earned a B.A. from Hampden-Sydney College in 1949 and then did graduate studies at Washington and Lee University in law and at the University of Iowa Writers' Workshop. From 1952 until 1959 he was an assistant professor at Hampden-Sydney. At that point in his life he became a full-time writer. From 1966 until 1970, he was a writer-in-residence at the college. His first novel was published in 1957, and since then he has written over fifteen novels or collections of short stories. Hoffman married Alice Sue Richardson in 1957, and they have two daughters. He lives on a farm in Charlotte County, Virginia.

Holmes, Paul, 87	Paul Holmes was born in 1901 in Milton, Wisconsin, the son of a tobacco dealer. He earned an A.B. in 1921 from the University of Wisconsin. He studied law at the University of Wisconsin and was admitted to the bar in 1927. He worked as a journalist and editor his entire adult life. Holmes died in 1985, in Pompano Beach, Florida.
Hopley, George, 11, 97, 127	*See* Woolrich, Cornell.
Horne, Jed, 88	Jed Horne was born in 1948. He is a 1966 graduate of the Deerfield Academy. He is the city editor for the New Orleans *Times-Picayune*.
Howard, Clark, 25, 139	Clark Howard was born in Tennessee in 1934. He was educated in Chicago and served his country as a marine. Besides his many nonfiction books, Howard is also the author of fourteen novels.
Hume, Fergus, 10, 122	Fergus Hume was born in England, but his family emigrated to New Zealand. Hume became an attorney and moved to Australia. He self-published his first novel, *The Mystery of a Hansom Cab*, in 1886. He sold the rights to his novel, and despite its being one of the best selling novels of this period, he did not receive any royalties. However, his success did allow him to return to England, where he lived out the rest of his life as a novelist and short story writer.
Humes, Edward, 39, 52	Edward Humes was born in Philadelphia, Pennsylvania. He earned a B.A. from Hampshire College in 1979. He worked for a number of magazines and journals. Humes won a Pulitzer Prize in 1989.
Hunter, Stephen, 97	Stephen Hunter was born in 1946 in Kansas City, Missouri, the son of an educator father and a business executive mother. He earned a B.S.J. from Northwestern University in 1968. He served in the U.S. Army from 1968 to 1970. He has worked as a copy reader, a book review editor, and a film critic at the *Baltimore Sun*. Web site: www.stephenhunter.net
Hurwitz, Ken, 69	Ken Hurwitz was born in Milwaukee, Wisconsin, in 1948, the son of a lawyer. He earned an A.B. from Harvard in 1970.
Huston, Charlie, 30, 31	Charlie Huston was born in Oakland, California. He has worked as an actor, bartender, waiter, novelist, and comic-book writer. He is married to the actress Virginia Louise Smith.

Hyde, Christopher, 111	Christopher Hyde was born in 1949 in Ottawa, Ontario, Canada, the son of an author father and child psychologist-mother. He has been a full-time writer since 1977.
Indiana, Gary, 118	Born in 1950 in Derry, New Hampshire, Gary Indiana is the son of a lumber company owner. He attended the University of California at Berkeley before launching a career as a writer.
Inness-Brown, Elizabeth, 127	Elizabeth Inness-Brown was born in 1954 in Rochester, New York, the daughter of a surgeon. In 1976 she earned a B.A. in English from St. Lawrence University. Her M.F.A. in creative writing, earned in 1978, is from Columbia University. Inness-Brown has held a number of positions in various academic settings, and is now on the faculty of Vermont College. She published two collections of short stories before publishing the novel discussed in this book. She lives in Colchester, Vermont.
Irish, William, 11, 74, 97, 127	*See* Woolrich, Cornell.
Jackson, Joe, 104	Joe Jackson is a four-time Pulitzer Prize nominee. He lives in Virginia Beach, Virginia.
Japrisot, Sebastian, 81	Jean Baptiste Rossi was born in 1931 in Marseille, France. He studied at a Jesuit university until he was asked to leave and then studied philosophy at the Sorbonne. His first novel, published under his own name, was a scandalous account of a love affair between a nun and a teenaged boy. During his lifetime he was a novelist, film director, screenwriter, and translator. Under the pseudonym Sebastien Japrisot he wrote eleven novels, including the one discussed in this book. Rossi died in Vichy, France, in 2003.
Jentz, Terri, 139	Terri Jentz is a screenwriter who also writes about being a victim of crime.
Jonas, George, 139	George Jonas was born in 1935 in Budapest, Hungary, the son of a lawyer. He emigrated to Canada in 1956. He has been an editor and a television producer. He was married to coauthor Barbara Amiel, but they are divorced.
Jones, Elwyn, 71	Elwyn Jones was born in 1923 in Aberdare, Wales, the son of a coal miner. He worked as a reporter before working in radio and television as an editor and producer. He died in 1982 in Wales.

Junger, Sebastian, 88

Sebastian Junger was born in Boston, Massachusetts, in 1962, the son of a physician father and a mother who was an artist. He earned a B.A. from Wesleyan Univeristy in 1984. He has been a freelance writer his entire career.

Kates, Brian, 139

Brian Kates was born in Flushing, New York, in 1946. He earned a B.A. from Pennsylvania Military College in 1968. He was in the U.S. Army Military Police Corps from 1968 to 1972. He has worked as a reporter, an editor, and an educator.

Katzenbach, John, 111

John Katzenbach was born in 1950 in Princeton, New Jersey, to an attorney and a psychoanalyst. He earned an A.B. from Bard College in 1972 and has worked as a criminal court reporter for *The Miami Herald* and *Miami News* and as a feature writer for the *Herald's Tropic* magazine. He is married to Madeleine H. Blais, a journalist and writer, and they have two children.

Kennedy, Ludovic, 140

Born in 1919 in Edinburgh, Scotland, Ludovic Kenney was the son of a naval officer. He earned an M.A. in politics from Christ Church, Oxford. He has been a secretary, librarian, lecturer, media personality, and an editor.

Kernick, Simon, 97, 149

Simon Kernick was born in 1966 in Slough, England. He graduated from the Brighton Polytechnic in 1991 and has worked various jobs, including as a laborer on a road-building gang, a stockroom assistant for a major IT company, a Christmas tree uprooter, and a fruit picker. Web site: www.simonkernick.com

Kersh, Gerald, 31, 64

Gerald Kersh was born in 1911 in Teddington-on-Thames, Middlesex, England. He was a cinema manager, cook, bouncer, baker, and wrestler in the 1930s. Kersh served in the Coldstream Guards during World War II and ended up in the Films Division of the Ministry of Information. He immigrated to the United States in the 1940s and became a U.S. citizen in 1959. He died in 1968.

Kertész, Imre, 150

Imre Kertész was born in Budapest, Hungary, in 1929. He was imprisoned in two concentration camps during World War II. He served in the Hungarian Army from 1951 to 1953. He has worked as a journalist and a translator. He received the Nobel Prize for Literature in 2002.

Keyes, Daniel, 88, 118, 140	Daniel Keyes was born in 1927 in Brooklyn, New York. He earned an A.B. in psychology from Brooklyn College in 1950 and an A.M. in 1961. He became a fiction editor before becoming an educator. He finished his career as a professor of English and creative writing at Ohio University. His most famous work, *Flowers for Algernon*, won the Hugo in 1959 as a short story and won the Nebula Award in 1966 for the novel version.
Keyes, Edward, 118	Edward Keyes was born in New York City in 1927, the son of a banker. Keyes served in the U.S. Army Air Corps from 1945 to 1946. He earned a B.A. from Fordham University in 1949. He has worked in public relations and as a journalist and a freelance writer.
Khadra, Yamina, 81	Mohammed Moulessehoul was born in 1956 in Algeria. He entered the Algerian Army at the age of nine and served as an officer before immigrating to France. He is married to Yasmina Khadra. When his novels angered his superior officers in the army, he used his wife's name as a pseudonym. He is the author of many novels, including *Les hirondelles de Kaboul* (2002) (*The Swallows of Kabul*, US, 2004), and the *Inspector Brahim Llob series*. In 2000 he and his wife went into exile in France. They now live in Mexico. The novel discussed in this book was first published in France under the title *L'attentat*. Web site: www.yasmina-khadra.com
King, Laurie R., 128	Laurie Richardson was born in Northern California in 1952, the daughter of a furniture restorer father and a librarian mother. She earned a B.A. in comparative religion and an M.A. in Old Testament theology from the University of California at Santa Cruz. She married Noel Q. King in 1977. She is the author of the *Kate Martinelli series* and the *Mary Russell series*. Web site: www.laurierking.com
Kirino, Natsuo, 57, 128	Mariko Hasioka was born in 1951 in Kanazawa, Ishikawa, Japan. Under the pseudonym Natsuo Kirino, she has risen to be one of the leading female Japanese crime writers. Kirino is a much-decorated writer, having won the 1993 Edogawa Rampo Prize for mystery fiction for her debut novel, *Kao ni furikakeru ame* (*Rain Falling on My Face*), the 1997 Grand Prix for Crime Fiction (and an Edgar nomination in 2003) for *Out*, and the 1999 Naoki Prize for her novel *Yawarakana hoho* (*Soft Cheeks*).
Kleiman, Dena, 140	Dena Kleiman is a reporter for the *New York Times*.

Kurins, Andris, 39

Andris Kurins is an FBI agent and author. He lives in Connecticut.

Lancaster, Bob, 118

Bob Lancaster was born in 1943 in Sheridan, Arkansas, the son of a carpenter. He attended Harvard University before starting a career as a newspaperman.

Landay, William, 111, 150

William Landay was born in 1964 in Boston, Massachusetts. Landay graduated from Yale University before earning a J.D. from the Boston College Law School in 1990. Landay worked for many years in the Middlesex, Massachusetts, district attorney's office. Web site: www.williamlanday.com

Lankford, Terrill Lee, 97

Terrill Lee Lankford is a screenwriter, director, and producer in Hollywood. He owns Mysteries, Movies & Mayhem bookstore in Los Angeles, California. Web site: www.terrillleelankford.com

Lansdale, Joe R., 65

Joe R. Lansdale was born in 1951 in Gladewater, Texas, the son of a mechanic father and a saleswoman. He attended Tyler Junior College, the University of Texas, and Stephen F. Austin State University. He has worked at various jobs, including as a bouncer and goat farmer. Lansdale has practiced karate for over thirty years. He has written novels in many genres and brought home awards in all of them. He lives in Nacogdoches, Texas, with his wife, Karen.

Larson, Erik, 118

Erik Larson was born in Brooklyn, New York, in 1954. He earned a B.A. from the University of Pennsylvania in 1976 and an M.S. from Columbia University in 1978. He has worked as a teacher and a journalist. Larson lives in Seattle, Washington, with his wife and three daughters.

Lee, Harper, 81

Nelle Harper Lee was born in 1926 in Monroeville, Alabama, the daughter of a lawyer and a homemaker. She attended grade school with Truman Capote, who became the model for Dill in the novel discussed in this book. After graduating from Huntingdon College, she studied law at the University of Alabama and spent one year at Oxford University. In the 1950s she worked as an airline reservation clerk in New York City, until she wrote this novel. It is her only published novel. She also contributed some articles to *Vogue* and *McCall's* magazines. She divides her time between New York City and Monroeville.

Lefkowitz, Bernard, 88	Bernard Lefkowitz was born in 1937 in New York City. He earned a B.A. from City College in 1959. He worked for the Peace Corp, as a journalist, and as an educator. He worked as a freelance writer until his death from cancer in 2004.
Lehane, Dennis, 82	Dennis Lehane was born in 1965 in Dorchester, Massachusetts, the son of a factory foreman and a school cafeteria worker. He earned a B.A.S. from Eckerd College in 1988 and an M.F.A. from the Florida International University in 1993. Lehane has taught mentally handicapped children, taught English, and worked as a chauffeur. He created the series about private eye characters Patrick Kenzie and Angela Gennaro in 1994 with *A Drink Before the War*, winner of the Shamus Award for best first private eye novel of the year. These novels were followed by *Darkness, Take My Hand* (1996), *Sacred* (1998), *Gone, Baby, Gone* (1999), and *Prayers for Rain* (2000). After *Mystic River*, he wrote a second stand-alone novel, *Shutter Island* (2003), and *The Given Day* (2008). Web site: www.dennislehanebooks.com
Lehr, Dick, 39, 71	Dick Lehr was born in 1944. He earned a B.A. from Harvard College and a J.D. from the University of Connecticut School of Law. He has used his legal knowledge in his writing while serving as a journalist in Connecticut and in Boston, Massachusetts.
Lethem, Jonathan, 161	Jonathan Lethem was born in 1964 in Brooklyn, New York, the son of an artist father and activist mother. He was educated at Bennington College but dropped out to hitchhike across the country. He settled in California, where he clerked in a bookstore and published short stories. His first novel, *Gun with Occasional Music*, was published in 1994, to great acclaim. He has since moved back to Brooklyn and published ten additional works. Web site: www.jonathanlethem.com
Levien, David, 161	David Levien cowrote the screenplays for *Ocean's 13*, *Runaway Jury*, *Rounders*, and several other major films. He lives in Connecticut.
Levin, Hillel, 37	Hillel Levin was born in Bridgeport, Connecticut, in 1954. He earned a B.A. from Johns Hopkins in 1976 and an M.A. in 1977. He has worked as an author, journalist, and business owner.

Levin, Ira, 112

Ira Levin was born in New York City in 1929, the son of a toy importer. He earned an A.B. from New York University in 1950. He served in the U.S. Army Signal Corps from 1953 to 1955. He was a novelist and playwright his entire adult life. He died in New York City in 2007.

Levison, Iain, 112

Iain Levison was born in 1963 in Scotland but was raised in the United States. He served with the Royal Highland Fusiliers. After holding forty-two jobs in ten years, he wrote the nonfiction book *A Working Stiff's Manifesto: A Memoir of Thirty Jobs I Quit, Nine That Fired Me, and Three I Can't Remember*. He lives in Philadelphia, Pennsylvania.

Levitt, Leonard, 140

Leonard Levitt was born in New York City in 1941. He earned an A.B. from Dartmouth College in 1963 and an M.S. from Columbia University in 1967. He has worked in the Peace Corps, been an AP reporter, has taught at Columbia, and has worked as a freelance writer.

Lincoln, Victoria, 140

Victoria Lincoln was born in 1940 in Fall River, Massachusetts. She earned an A.B. in 1926 from Radcliffe College. She was a full-time writer her entire adult life. She died from cancer in 1981 in Baltimore, Maryland.

Lindsay, Jeff, 12, 112, 113

Jeffry P. Lindsay was born in 1952. He graduated from Middlebury College in 1975 with a double major in playwriting and directing. He is married to Hilary Hemingway, Ernest Hemingway's niece, and they have three daughters. They live in Cape Coral, Florida. Jeff is a karate world champion.

Lindsey, Robert, 25

Born in 1935 in Glendale, California, Robert Lindsey was the son of an engineer. He earned a B.A. from San Jose State University in 1956 and had a long career as a reporter before becoming a full-time writer in 1986. His book, *The Falcon and the Snowman: A True Story of Friendship and Espionage* (Simon & Schuster, 19790 was a huge best seller and was made into a movie.

Linklater, Magnus, 25

Magnus Linklater was born in 1942 in Orkney, Scotland, the son of a writer father and a mother who was a politician. He earned a B.A. from Trinity Hall, Cambridge, in 1964. He served in the Seaforth Highlanders from 1960 to 1964. He has worked as a journalist and editor for various publications.

Lippman, Laura, 58

Laura Lippman was born in Georgia but has adopted Baltimore, Maryland, as her permanent hometown. She is a former journalist, including a stint with the *Baltimore Sun*, and made her character, Tess Monaghan, a downsized reporter, who learns during the series how to become a private investigator. After seven books in the *Monaghan series*, Lippman began to write stand-alone novels as well. Many of her novels have received awards or nominations in the crime writing field. Lippman lives with another former *Baltimore Sun* reporter, David Simon, who wrote *Homicide: A Year on the Killing Streets* and then produced and wrote the accompanying television shows, *Homicide: Life on the Street* and *The Wire*.

Maas, Peter, 39, 72

Peter Maas was born in New York City in 1929. He earned a B.A. from Duke University in 1949. After service in the navy, Maas worked as a reporter based in New York City. He died there in 2001.

MacDonald, John D., 113

John D. MacDonald was born in 1916 in Sharon, Pennsylvania. He earned a B.S. from Syracuse University in 1938 and an M.B.A. from Harvard University in 1939. He served in the U.S. Army from 1940 to 1946, rising to the rank of lieutenant colonel in the Office of Strategic Services. After a brief time in the investment and insurance industry, he was a full-time author for the rest of his life. He died after having heart surgery in Milwaukee, Wisconsin, in 1986.

Macintyre, Ben, 48

Ben Macintyre was born in 1963 and educated at Cambridge. He has been a journalist, including stints as foreign affairs reporter for the *Sunday Correspondent* and the *Times* bureau chief in Paris.

MacLean, Harry N., 119

Harry N. MacLean earned a B.A. in psychology from Lawrence University and then attended the University of Denver, where he earned both an M.A. and a law degree. He has worked as a lawyer in the Denver area.

Mailer, Norman, 71

Norman Mailer was born in Long Branch, New Jersey, in 1923, the son of an accountant father and a mother who ran a small business. He graduated from Harvard in 1943 and served in the U.S. Army during World War II. He became one of America's preeminent writers and worked as a producer and director in the film industry. He was decorated with numerous literary awards, including the Pulitzer Prize. Mailer died in November 2007.

Manchette, Jean-Patrick, 82, 98

Jean-Patrick Manchette was born in France in 1942. He was an amateur jazz saxophonist and political activist who wrote screenplays and novels. His work in the field of noir is considered defining within the French neo-polar genre. He wrote ten novels and then abandoned the field. He died from lung cancer in 1995.

Marlowe, Dan J., 65, 98

Dan J. Marlowe was born in 1914 in Lowell, Massachusetts, the son of a printing press mechanic. Marlowe attended the Bently School of Accounting and Finance and worked in accounting, insurance, and public relations, and as a newspaper columnist. He was also a member of the City Council of Harbor Beach, Michigan. He became a novelist only after the sudden death of his wife at the age of forty-three. After a trip to Florida in 1977, he had severe memory loss. He moved to Los Angeles and lived with Al Nussbaum, a bank robber with whom he had an on-again, off-again friendship during most of his writing career. He died in 1987.

Martin, J(ulia) Wallis, 65, 98

Julia Wallis Martin was born in 1957. Her mother left her father, and through a series of affairs and bad marriages, tried to raise Julia. Depressed and addicted to pills, Julia's mother attempted suicide. She eventually died of cancer when her daughter was seventeen. Julia moved to Oxford, where she worked as a waitress and had one short story published. At the age of twenty she was tragically widowed when her first husband, Terry Flahery, was killed in an automobile accident. She has a son named James from that marriage. At age twenty-seven, she married a man who took her to South Africa for seven years, where Julia worked as an editor in a publishing house. Her marriage ended when violence in the country drove her and her son back to England without her husband. Her novel, *A Likeness in Stone*, was published in 1998 by J. Wallis Martin. *The Bird Yard* (1999) followed, written by Julia Wallis Martin, as were *The Long Close Call* (2000) and *Dancing with the Uninvited Guest* (2002). She is now married to screenwriter Russell Murray and they live in a cottage in Somerset, England. Web site: www.gregoryandcompany.co.uk/pages/authors/index.asp?AuthorID=37

Matheson, Richard, 113, 128

Richard Matheson was born in 1926 in Allendale, New Jersey, the son of a floor installer. He served in the U.S. Army during World War II. He earned a B.A. from the University of Missouri in 1949. He spent his entire life as a writer in the publishing, theater, television, and film industries. He is equally famous in science fiction, fantasy, and crime fiction.

Mattson, Andrew, 48

Andrew Mattson is an instructor at the State University of New York.

Mayer, Robert, 141

Born in New York City in 1939, Robert Mayer earned a B.A. from City College of New York and an M.A. from Columbia University. He has worked on various newspapers in various capacities since 1960. He lives in New Mexico.

McCarthy, Cormac, 58

Charles McCarthy, named for his father, was born in 1933 in Providence, Rhode Island. His first name was legally changed to Cormac, which is Gaelic for "son of Charles." At age four, his family moved to Knoxville, Tennessee. From 1951 to 1952 he attended the University of Tennessee. Subsequently, McCarthy served in the Air Force (1953–1956). Although he returned to the university after his military service, he left before completing a degree. He moved to Chicago, worked as an auto mechanic, and had a son, Cullen, from his marriage to Lee Holleman. They divorced prior to the beginning of his writing career. McCarthy received the National Book Award for fiction and National Book Critics Award for fiction for *All the Pretty Horses*. He married Anne DeLisle in 1965 and was divorced in 1978. McCarthy moved to El Paso, Texas. He was married a third time in 1998 to his Jennifer, and they have one child. They live in Santa Fe, New Mexico. Web site: www.cormacmccarthy.com

McClintick, David, 52

David McClintick was born in 1940 in Hays, Kansas. He earned a B.A. from Harvard University in 1962. He served in the U.S. Army's Intelligence Branch from 1964 to 1968. After serving nine years as an investigative reporter for the *Wall Street Journal*, he became a full-time freelance writer.

McConnell, Malcolm, 104

Malcolm McConnell was born in Elmhurst, Illinois, in 1939, the son of an engineer. He earned a B.A. from the University of Wisconsin in 1962. He served in the U.S. Foreign Service from 1963 to 1969. He is a full-time freelance writer and novelist.

McCoy, Horace, 11, 31, 58

Horace McCoy was born in Tennessee in 1897, the son of a railroad conductor. Early in his life he wandered the South, working as a mechanic, traveling salesperson, and cab driver. After a few years as a journalist, he tried his hand as a freelance writer in Hollywood and then eventually had a twenty-year run with the studios. He wrote only six novels in and died of a heart attack in 1955.

McDermid, Val, 150

Val McDermid was born in 1955 in Kirkcaldy, Scotland. She received a B.A. in English from St. Hilda's College, Oxford, in 1975. From 1975 to 1991 she worked as a journalist in Devon and Manchester, England, as well as Glasgow, Scotland, before becoming a full-time writer. Her first novel, *Report for Murder*, was published in 1987 and featured reporter Lindsay Gordon. Her series about P. I. Kate Brannigan includes *Dead Beat* (1992), *Kick Back* (1993), *Crackdown* (1994), *Clean Break* (1995), *Blue Genes* (1996), and *Star Struck* (1998). Her series about clinical psychologist Dr Tony Hill and Detective Chief Inspector Carol Jordan includes *The Mermaids Singing* (1995; received the Gold Dagger Award from the Crime Writers Association and the French Grand Prix des Romans d'Aventure for Mauvais Signes), *The Wire in the Blood* (1997), *The Last Temptation* (2002), *The Torment of Others* (2004), and *Beneath the Bleeding* (2007). In addition to *A Place of Execution*, she has written two other stand-alone novels, *Killing the Shadows* (2000) and *The Distant Echo* (2003; Barry Award for the Best British Crime Novel and the Sherlock Award), two collections of short stories, *The Writing on the Wall* (1997), *Stranded* (2005), *The Grave Tattoo* (2006), and a nonfiction work on the fictional female PI, called *A Suitable Job for a Woman* (1994). Web site: www.valmcdermid.com

McDougal, Dennis, 88

Dennis McDougal was a reporter for the *Los Angeles Times*. He lives in California.

McGinniss, Joe, 61

Joe McGinniss was born in 1942 in New York City, the son of a travel agent. He earned a B.S. from Holy Cross College in 1964. After four years of working as a reporter, he began a distinguished career as a freelance writer.

McKinty, Adrian, 151

Adrian McKinty was born in Carrickfergus, Northern Ireland. He attended Oxford University and immigrated to the United States in 1992. He has been an attorney, an educator, and a writer.

McNamara, Eileen, 89

Eileen McNamara is a staff writer for the *Boston Globe Magazine*.

Meyer, Deon, 82

Deon Meyer was born in 1958 in Paarl, Western Cape, South Africa. He attended Potchefstroom University and served in the military. He lives in Melkbosstrand and is married and has two children. He worked as a journalist and an Internet consultant before becoming a full-time writer. Web site: www.deonmeyer.com/index.html

Meyer, Gerald, 119
Gerald Meyer (also know as G. J. Meyer and Gerald Justin Meyer) was born in 1940. He was a writer and journalist as well as the vice president for communications at McDonnell Douglas.

Millar, Margaret, 98, 129, 161
Margaret William was born in 1915 in Kitchener, Ontario, Canada, the daughter of a businessman. She attended schools in Canada before moving to California and marrying Kenneth Millar (aka Ross Macdonald) in 1938. Margaret Millar was a screenwriter in Hollywood as well as a novelist. She died of a heart attack in 1994 in Santa Barbara, California.

Miller, Gene, 141
Gene Miller was born in 1928 in Evansville, Indiana. He earned a B.A. from Indiana University in 1950. Miller served in the U.S. Army from 1951 to 1953. He was a reporter his entire adult life, including time on the *Wall Street Journal* and the *Miami Herald*.

Miller, Wade, 42
Wade Miller is the pseudonym of two men who first met when they were twelve years old. The two friends attended San Diego State University, served in the U.S. Air Force, and then returned to San Diego. Forming a writing team, the two produced thirty-three books before Bill Miller (b. 1920) passed away in 1961 of a heart attack. Bob Wade (b. 1920) continued to write on his own for a few years and then gave up his novel-writing career to become a television and movie screenwriter. The pair are most famous for writing the book *Badge of Evil*, which Orson Welles made into the film *Touch of Evil*, and for the long-running *Max Thursday* private investigator series.

Mills, Mark, 82
Mark Mills was born in 1967. He lives in London with his family. He is a screenwriter and has written works including *The Reckoning* (2003), *Global Heresy* (2002), *The Lost Son* (1999), and *One Night Stand* (1993). He is also the author of *The Savage Garden* (Putnam, 2007).

Mitchell, Corey, 119
Corey Mitchell lives in San Antonio, Texas. He is a law school graduate and the author of numerous nonfiction works.

Moore, Susanna, 129
Susanna Moore was born in Bryn Mawr, Pennsylvania, in 1948, the daughter of a physician. She attended private schools in Honolulu, Hawaii. From 1967 to 1980 she was a script reader for the motion picture industry and then a motion picture art director from 1980 to 1982. She is now a full-time novelist. Web site: www.randomhouse.com/author/results.pperl?authorid=21133

Muller, Eddie, 59

Eddie Muller was born in 1959 in San Francisco, California, the son of a sportswriter who would become the model for his series character Billy Nichols. Muller attended San Francisco Art Institute and has developed an interest in film noir that has led him to create film festivals and write nonfiction criticism. Web site: www. eddiemuller.com

Murray, Sabina, 113

Sabina Murray was born in 1968. She grew up in Australia and the Philippines. She has a B.A. from Mount Holyoke College and an M.A. from the University of Texas. She is married to poet John Hennessey, and they have two children. Her work has received numerous awards, including the PEN/Faulkner Award in 2003 for the work *The Caprices*. She is on the faculty of the University of Massachusetts.

Naifeh, Steven, 72

Steven Naifeh was born in 1952 in Tehran, Iran. A U.S. citizen, Naifeh received an A.B. from Princeton University and a J.D. from Harvard. His art has been exhibited throughout the world. With his writing partner he received a National Book Award nomination and a Pulitzer Prize for *Jackson Pollock: An American Saga*.

Neff, James, 141

James Neff attended Norte Dame and the University of Texas. After a career in journalism at the *Cleveland Plain Dealer*, he became a professor of journalism at Ohio State University. He lives in Seattle, Washington, where he is senior editor at the *Seattle Times*.

Norris, Frank, 99

Frank Norris was born in 1870 in Chicago, Illinois, the son of a wholesale jeweler and real estate investor father and an actress mother. Norris studied painting at the Atelier Julien, then attended the University of California at Berkeley and Harvard University. He worked as the foreign correspondent for the *San Francisco Chronicle* in South Africa and as a McClure Syndicate war correspondent in Cuba in 1898. After a short life as a novelist, essayist, and poet, he died of appendicitis in 1902, in San Francisco, California.

Nunn, Kem, 65, 83

Kem Nunn was born in 1948 in Pomona, California. He has an M.F.A. from the University of California.

O'Brien, Darcy, 89

Darcy O'Brien was born in Los Angeles, California, in 1939, the son of two film actors. He earned an A.B. from Princeton in 1961, an M.A. from the University of California, Berkeley in 1963, and a Ph.D. in 1965. O'Brien worked as a college instructor from 1970 to 1996. He died of a heart attack in 1998 in Tulsa, Oklahoma.

O'Brien, Joseph F., 39   Joseph F. O'Brien is an FBI agent and author. He lives in upstate New York.

O'Connell, Jack, 83, 114, 151   Jack O'Connell was born in 1959 in Worcester, Massachusetts, the son of a businessman father and a nurse mother. He earned a B.A. from the College of Holy Cross in 1981.

O'Connor, Joseph, 99   Joseph O'Connor was born in 1963 in Glenageary, Ireland. His mother died in an automobile accident in 1985. O'Connor's famous siblings are Sinead O'Connor, the singer, and Eimear, the painter. He also has two brothers. O'Connor earned a B.A. in English and modern American literature in 1984 and an M.A. in Anglo-Irish literature in 1986, all from University College in Dublin. While working as a full-time writer, critic, and playwright, he also earned an M.A. in screenwriting from the Northern School of Film and Television at the University of Leeds.

O'Donnell, Lawrence, Jr., 154   Born in 1951 in Boston, Massachusetts, Lawrence O'Donnell Jr. earned a B.A. from Harvard in 1976.

Olsen, Jack, 26, 119, 141   Jack Olsen was born in 1925 in Indianapolis, Indiana. After serving in the army during World War II, Olsen attended the University of Pennsylvania. From 1947 on he worked as a journalist, until becoming a full-time writer in 1960. He was nominated five times for a Pulitzer Prize. He died of a heart attack in 2002.

O'Malley, Suzanne, 142   Born in 1951 in Cedar Rapids, Iowa, Suzanne O'Malley earned a B.A. from the University of Texas in 1973. She has worked as a writer and editor for such diverse entities as *Esquire* magazine and *Dining Out*. She has also worked in the television industry as a freelance producer. She lives in New York City and Houston.

O'Neill, Gerard, 39   Gerard O'Neill was born in Boston, Massachusetts, in 1942, the son of a post office official and a nurse. He earned a B.A. from Stonehill College and an M.S. from Boston University. He has worked his entire career at the *Boston Globe* in various capacities.

Oney, Steve, 142   Steve Oney attended the University of Georgia and Harvard University. He worked for many years on the *Atlanta Journal-Constitution* magazine. He lives in Los Angeles, California.

Pamuk, Orhan, 129

Ferit Orhan Pamuk was born in Istanbul, Turkey, in 1952. His father was a civil engineer and a university teacher who maintained an affluent, secular home for Pamuk until he was thirty. Pamuk attended Robert College in Istanbul and received a B.A. in journalism. He attended Istanbul Technical University, studying architecture, before dropping out to be a full-time novelist. Pamuk has refused to allow his first novel to be translated into English; his second novel has only been translated into French; his novel *The White Castle* was the first translated into English. Pamuk married Aylin Turegen, a historian, and they had one daughter, named Ruya (b. 1991), before divorcing in 2001. Pamuk has received a number of international awards, culminating with the Nobel Prize for literature in 2006. In Turkey, because of his opposition to fundamentalist religion, his comments on the Armenian genocide, and his outspoken criticism of Turkey's war on the Kurds, he has been criticized by the government, and criminal charges were pressed against him. Pamuk now lives in the United States and is a professor of comparative literature at Columbia University. Web site: www.orhanpamuk.net; Reader's Guide: faculty.gvsu.edu/websterm/Pamuk.html

Parker, T. Jefferson, 151

T(homas) Jefferson Parker was born in Los Angeles, California. He attended the University of California, Irvine, where he earned a B.A. in 1976. He worked for a variety of newspapers, including the *Newport Ensign and Daily Pilot*. He is the author of the *Merci Rayborn series*. Parker won the Southern California Booksellers Association Book Award in 2003 for *Cold Pursuit* and the Edgar Allan Poe Award in 2005 for *California Girl*. Web site: www.tjeffersonparker.com

Peace, David, 114

David Peace was born in 1967 in Ossett, West Yorkshire, England. After studying at Manchester Polytechnic, he taught English in Istanbul, Turkey, for three years. In 1994 he moved to Tokyo, Japan, and has lived there since.

Pearl, Matthew, 66

Matthew Pearl was born in 1975 in New York. He has a B.A. in English and American literature from Harvard University and graduated in 2000 from the Yale Law School. Pearl has been a teaching fellow in literature at Harvard University and currently is an adjunct professor at Emerson College. He is an editor and provided the introduction to a translation of *The Inferno* by Dante Alighieri published in 2003. Pearl received the Dante Prize from the Dante Society of America in 1998 for his senior thesis on the Dante Club. He lives in Cambridge, Massachusetts. Web site: www.thedanteclub.com

Pears, Iain, 130

Iain Pears was born in 1955 in Coventry, England, the son of an industrialist father and a mother who was a magistrate. He attended Wadham College at Oxford and earned a B.A. in 1977 and an M.A. in 1979. His doctorate in philosophy was earned at Wolfson College, Oxford, in 1982. From 1983 to 1984, Pears was a Reuters News Agency correspondent in Rome. He worked in the banking industry from 1984 until 1987, when he began postdoctoral work at Yale University as a Getty Fellow. Pears married Ruth Harris in 1985; they have one son, and live in Oxford.

Pearson, John, 40

John Pearson was born in 1930. He has worked as a journalist for the *London Sunday Times* and *The Economist*.

Pelecanos, George, 130

George Pelecanos was born in Washington, D.C., in 1957. He worked as a bartender and a shoe salesman before becoming a full-time writer. He served as a producer, writer, and story editor for the HBO series *The Wire*. He lives in Silver Spring, Maryland, with his wife and three children. Web site: www.hachettebookgroupusa.com/features/georgepelecanos

Perry, Thomas, 21, 32, 50, 99, 152, 161

Thomas Perry was born in 1947 in Tonawanda, New York, the son of two teachers. He earned a B.A. in 1969 from Cornell University and a Ph.D. in 1974 from the University of Rochester. He worked for one year as a commercial fisherman before working in the field of education for nine years. He then became a writer on the *Simon & Simon* television show for five years. He is now a full-time writer.

Phillips, Scott, 114, 157

Scott Phillips was born in Wichita, Kansas. He worked as a bookseller, and he lived in Paris for many years working as a translator and an English teacher. Scott also lived in California when he worked as a screenwriter. He lives in St. Louis with his wife and daughter. Web site: scottphillipsauthor.com

Picoult, Jodi, 83

Jodi Picoult ("pee- koe") was born in 1966, in New York, the daughter of Myron Michel (a securities analyst) and Jane Ellen (a nursery school director) Picoult. She earned a B.A. from Princeton University in 1987, where she studied creative writing and had two short stories published in *Seventeen Magazine*. Picoult worked as a technical writer for a Wall Street brokerage firm, as a copywriter at an ad agency, as an editor at a textbook publisher, and as an eighth-grade English teacher. She then attended Harvard to pursue a master's in education, which she earned in 1990. In 2003 she was awarded the New England Bookseller Award for Fiction. She has also been the recipient of the Margaret Alexander Edwards Award for Young Adult Fiction, the Book Browse Diamond Award for novel of the year, a lifetime achievement award for mainstream fiction from the Romance Writers of America, and Waterstone's Author of the Year in the UK. She has provided five stories for the DC Comics *Wonder Woman* series. She is married to Timothy Warren van Leer, a technical sales representative, and they have three children. The family lives on a farm in Hanover, New Hampshire. Web site: www.jodipicoult.com

Pierre, D. B. C., 130

D. B. C. Pierre was born in 1961 in Reynella, South Australia, Australia, the son of a geneticist. He has lived in Mexico, England, and Ireland. He has worked as a writer, cartoonist, graphic designer, photographer, and filmmaker. His first novel, *Vernon God Little*, received the Bollinger Everyman Wodehouse Prize for Comic Writing, the Booker Prize, and the Whitbread Award.

Pietrusza, David, 26

Born in 1949 in Amsterdam, New York, David Pietrusza earned a B.A. and M.A. from the State University of New York. He is the public information officer for the New York State Governor's Office of Regulatory Reform. He has written or edited more than three dozen books.

Pileggi, Nicholas, 40

Nicholas Pileggi was born in 1933 in New York City, the son of a shoe store owner. He attended Long Island University. He has been a reporter and editor in New York City his entire adult life.

Pistone, Joseph D., 40

Joseph D. Pistone was born in Paterson, New Jersey, the son of a bar manager. After working as a teacher and in naval intelligence, he was recruited by the FBI. He served undercover in the New York mob for six years. After that, he worked as a security consultant.

Pomeroy, Sarah B., 142
Sarah B. Pomeroy was born in 1938 in New York City, the daughter of a real estate investor father and a mother who taught elementary school. She earned an A.B. from Barnard College in 1957 and an M.A. from Columbia University in 1960, followed by a Ph.D. in 1961. She has taught at the University of Texas, and has been on the staff of Hunter College since 1964.

Prendergast, Alan, 72
Alan Prendergast was born in 1956 in Denver, Colorado, the son of a dentist father and a mother who was a teacher. He earned a B.A. from Colorado College in 1978 and has worked as an editor and writer.

Preston, Douglas, 120
Douglas Preston was born in 1956 in Cambridge, Massachusetts, the son of a lawyer father and a mother who was a professor. He attended Pomona College and earned a B.A. in 1978. He worked as an editor at the American Museum of Natural History. He is now a freelance writer and lives in New Mexico. Web site: www.prestonchild.com

Price, Richard, 42
Richard Price was born in New York City in 1949. He earned a B.S. from Cornell University in 1971 and an M.F.A. from Columbia University in 1976. From 1973 to 1980 he was an educator, and he has been a full-time writer since then.

Protess, David, 89
David Protess was born in 1946 in Brooklyn, New York. He earned a B.A. in 1968, a M.A. in 1970, and a Ph.D., all from the University of Chicago. He has worked his entire adult life as an educator and is an independent investigative journalist.

Puzo, Mario, 12, 32, 33, 59
Mario Puzo was born in 1920 in New York, the son of a railroad trackman. He was educated at Columbia University, served in World War II in Germany, and held various jobs before becoming a full-time writer. His *Godfather* novels revolutionized readers' conceptions of the mob and led him to a successful and recognized career as a screenwriter in Hollywood. He died of heart failure in New York in 1999.

Pyper, Andrew, 157
Andrew Pyper was born in Stratford, Ontario, Canada, in 1968. He received a B.A. from McGill University and then a law degree from the University of Toronto. His collection of short stories, *Kiss Me*, was published in 1996. His other novels are *The Trade Mission* (2003; also, *Dark Descent*) and *The Wildfire Season* (2005). He lives in Toronto. Web site: andrewpyper.com

Rabe, Peter, 11, 33, 130

Peter Rabinowitsch was born in Germany in 1921. He immigrated to the United States in 1938. He earned a Ph.D. from Western Reserve University and worked as a psychology instructor at California Polytechnic State University. He died of lung cancer in 1990 in Atascadero, California.

Raymond, Derek, 152

Born in 1931 in London, Robert William Arthur Cook was the son of a businessman. He attended Eton College and served in the British Army. He wrote as Robin Cook and Derek Raymond. He died from cancer in 1991.

Rayner, Richard, 26

Richard Rayner was born in Bradford, England, in 1955. He is a graduate of Cambridge University and now lives in Los Angeles with his wife and children.

Reasoner, James, 99

James Reasoner has written many books under many names, including Dana Fuller Ross. He lives in Texas with his wife Livia, also an author. Web site: home.flash.net/~livia/index.html

Reit, Seymour, 26

Seymour Reit was born in 1918 in New York City. He earned an A.B. from New York University in 1938. Reit served in the U.S. Army Air Force during World War II and earned a Bronze Star while serving as a camouflage and photo intelligence officer. As an animator, Reit created Casper the Friendly Ghost. He died in New York City in 2001.

Revoyr, Nina, 66

Born in Japan in 1969, Nina Revoyr is the daughter of a Japanese woman and a white American father. She was educated at Yale University and earned an M.F.A. in creative writing from Cornell. She has worked in Japan teaching English and with Head Start in Los Angeles. Her first novel, *The Necessary Hunger*, was published in 1997.

Rhoades, J. D., 162

J. D. Rhoades was born in North Carolina. He has worked as a radio news reporter, club DJ, television cameraman, ad salesman, waiter, practicing attorney, and newspaper columnist. He lives in Carthage, North Carolina. Web site: www.jdrhoades.com

Rifkin, Shepard, 163

Shepard Rifkin was born in 1918 in New York City. He attended City College and spent some time in the Merchant Marines during the Second World War. After holding many part-time jobs, he became a full-time writer.

Robins, Natalie, 142   Natalie Robins was born in 1938 in Bound Brook, New Jersey. She earned a B.A. from Mary Washington College in 1960 and has worked her entire adult life as a writer, including four volumes of poetry.

Robotham, Michael, 100   Michael Robotham was born in 1960. For years, he worked as an investigative journalist in Australia, England, and Africa. In 1993 he quit journalism to become a ghostwriter for twelve biographies of famous people. After writing the novel discussed in this book, Robotham wrote *Lost* (2005) and *Pitter Patter* (2006). He lives in Sydney, Australia, with his wife and three daughters. Web site: www.michaelrobotham.com

Rossner, Judith, 130   Judith Rossner was born in New York City in 1935. She attended City College. She was a writer her entire adult life. She died in 2005.

Rozan, S. J., 33   S. J. Rozan was born in the Bronx, New York. She has a B.A. from Oberlin College and an M.Arch. from the State University of New York. S. J. worked as an architect until 2004, when she became a full-time novelist. She lives in New York City.

Rubinstein, Julian, 89   Julian Rubinstein writes for a variety of magazines. He lives in New York.

Ruddick, James, 143   James Ruddick was born in Elmira, New York, in 1923. He is an ordained Roman Catholic priest. He has worked as a journalist, as educator, and a writer.

Ruiz Zafón, Carlos, 100   Carlos Ruiz Zafón was born in 1964 and grew up in Barcelona. Prior to writing the novel discussed in this book, he was the author of four young adult titles: *Las Luces de Septiembre* (*The Lights of September*), *Marina* (*Navy*), *El Palacio de la Medianoche* (*The Palace of the Medianochel*), *El Príncipe de la Niebla* (*The Principle of the Frog*). He lives in Los Angeles.

Rule, Ann, 52, 72, 120, 143, 144   Ann Rule was born in 1935 in Lowell, Michigan, the daughter of two teachers. She earned a B.A. from the University of Washington in 1954 and a graduate degree in police science from the same institute. She worked as a police officer in Seattle before becoming a best-selling author of more than a dozen true crime books.

Russell, Francis, 90   Francis Russell was born in 1910 in Boston, Massachusetts. He earned an A.B. from Bowdoin College in 1933 and an A.M. from Harvard in 1937. He served in the Canadian Army Intelligence Corps from 1941 to 1946.

St. James, James, 53

Once a "celebutante" in the New York club scene, James St. James now lives in Los Angeles, California.

Sakey, Marcus, 59

Marcus Sakey was born in Flint, Michigan. He graduated from the University of Michigan. He spent ten years in the advertising business. He now lives in Chicago, Illinois, with his wife, g.g. Web site: www.marcussakey.com

Sanders, Lawrence, 34

Lawrence Sanders was born in 1920 in Brooklyn, New York. After three years on the Macy's Department store staff in New York, he joined the U.S. Marine Corps, serving until 1946 and rising to the rank of sergeant. He joined the editorial staffs of *Mechanix Illustrated*, *Science*, and *Mechanics* and wrote for men's magazines until the publication of his first novel in 1970 at age fifty. He went on to be a best-selling author of many works of fiction. He died in 1998 in Pompano Beach, Florida.

Saul, Jamie M., 131

Jamie M. Saul was born in New York City. He earned a B.A. from Indiana State University. He has been a scholarship student at Bread Loaf Writers' Conference, and his short fiction has been published in various magazines. He has served as a guest professor at Yale University. Web site: www.authortracker.ca/author.asp?a=authorid&b=28341

Savage, Mildred, 72

Mildred Savage was born in New London, Connecticut. She earned a B.A. from Wellesley College. She has been a freelance writer and novelist her entire life.

Schickler, David, 100

David Schickler has a B.A. from Georgetown and is a graduate of the Columbia University M.F.A. creative writing program. He taught English and drama at a Vermont boarding school and a private school in Rochester, NY He lives in New York with his wife and baby boy. Web site: www.davidschickler.com.

Schiller, Lawrence, 90

Lawrence Schiller was born in 1936 in New York City, the son of a merchant father and a mother who was a department store buyer. He earned a B.A. from Pepperdine College in 1958. He has been a writer, a director, producer, photographer, cinematographer, film editor, and actor.

Schone, Mark, 27

Mark Schone was born in 1960. He is a freelance journalist.

Schulberg, Budd, 34

Budd Schulberg was born in New York in 1914. His father B. P. Schulberg was chief of production for Paramount Studios. Educated at Dartmouth College, Schulberg was a writer his entire life, creating novels, plays and screenplays. His screenplay for *On the Waterfront* received the Academy Award in 1954. Married four times, he now lives on Long Island, New York.

Schutz, Benjamin M., 131

Benjamin M. Schutz was born in 1949 in Washington, D.C. He earned a B.A. from Lafayette College and a Ph.D. from Catholic University of America in 1977. He was a clinical psychologist for three years before spending the rest of his career as a forensic psychologist. He was married to his wife JoAnne and they had two boys and lived in the northern Virginia suburbs near Washington, D.C. He was the author of the Leo Haggerty private eye series. Schutz died in 2008 from a heart attack.

Schutze, Jim, 73, 144

Jim Schutze was born in Alexandria, Virginia, in 1946, the son of an Episcopalian priest. He earned a B.A. from the University of Michigan in 1971. He has worked as a journalist.

Schwartz-Nobel, Loretta, 53

Loretta Schwartz-Nobel is an investigative journalist working for the *Philadelphia Inquirer* who lives in Philadelphia.

Serrano, Richard A., 144

Richard A. Serrano was born in Kansas City, Missouri, in 1953. He has spent his life as a journalist and has twice been awarded a Pulitzer Prize.

Setterfield, Diane, 83

Diane Setterfield was born in 1964 in Reading, England. She attended Bristol University and has taught English to the French and French to the English. She is married to Peter Whittall, an accountant, and they live in Harrowgate, Yorkshire. Web site: www.thethirteenthtale.com

Shapiro, Fred, 155

Fred Shapiro was born in 1931 in Washington, D.C. He earned an A.B. in 1952 from the University of Missouri and served in the U.S. Army from 1953 to 1954. He has worked as a journalist for his entire adult life, including a thirty-year stint as staff writer on the *New Yorker*.

Sherman, Dayne, 131

Dayne Sherman was born in 1970 in Hammond, Louisiana. He earned a B.A. from Southeastern Louisiana University and an M.A. from Louisiana State University. He has worked as a librarian. Sherman is married and has one son. Web site: www.daynesherman.com

Shreve, Anita, 131	Anita Shreve was born in 1946 to an airline pilot and a homemaker. She attended Tufts University and earned an M.A. from Amherst College. Anita has worked as a high school English teacher and an instructor in creative writing. She has worked as a freelance journalist, including three years in Nairobi, Kenya. She has served as the deputy editor of *Viva* magazine, editor of *US Magazine,* and special issues writer for *Newsweek* magazine. Her short story, "Past the Island, Drifting," won the O. Henry Award in 1976. She has written five nonfiction works and eleven novels. Anita has been married three times, most recently to an insurance agent. She lives in Longmeadow, Massachusetts.
Shubin, Seymour, 100	Seymour Shubin was born in 1921 in Philadelphia, Pennsylvania. He earned a B.S. from Temple University in 1943. He worked as an editor in the publishing industry from 1943 to 1969.
Sidor, Steven, 101	Steven Sidor was born in Chicago. He attended Grinnell College and the University of North Carolina at Chapel Hill. His short stories have appeared in a variety of print and online publications. His second novel, *Bone Factory,* was published in 2005. He lives with his wife and children near the Fox River in the greater Chicago area. Web site: www.stevensidor.com
Siegel, Barry, 144	Barry Siegel attended the Columbia University Graduate School of Journalism. He has worked as a *Los Angeles Times* reporter and received a Pulitzer Prize for journalism in 2002.
Simmons, Kelly, 132	Kelly Simmons works as a journalist before starting a career in advertising. She is the president of Bubble advertising. Web site: bykellysimmons.com
Simon, Michael, 152	Michael Simon was born in Levittown, New York. He has worked as an actor and as a Texas probation officer. He is a playwright and has taught at Brooklyn College and New York University. Web site: www.michaelsimon.info
Singular, Stephen, 40	Stephen Singular was born in 1950 in Emporia, Kansas. He earned a B.A. from the University of Kansas in 1972. After working eight years as a freelance writer, Singular became a reporter for the *Denver Post* in 1982.

Skármeta, Antonio, 43	Antonio Skármeta was born in Antofagast, Chile, in 1940. He earned an M.A. from Columbia University. He was a professor of contemporary Latin American literature at the University of Chile in the 1970s and then taught screenwriting at the German Academy of Film and Television from 1978 to 1981. He then worked as a freelance writer, filmmaker, journalist, television host, and book translator. His novel *Il Postino* (*The Postman*) was made into an acclaimed film.
Smith, Gregory White, 72	Born in 1951 in Ithaca, New York, Gregory White Smith earned a B.A. from Colby College and a J.D. at Harvard. He has been a writer, lawyer, and art collector. With his writing partner he received a National Book Award nomination and a Pulitzer Prize for *Jackson Pollock: An American Saga*.
Smith, Mitchell, 84	Mitchell Smith was born in 1935 in Oneonta, New York, the son of a doctor father and a nurse mother. He attended Columbia College from 1954 to 1958 and then served in the U.S. Army in intelligence from 1958 to 1960.
Smith, Peter Moore, 132	Peter Moore Smith was born in 1965 in Panama. He earned a B.A. from Columbia University, an M.Ed. from Northern Arizona University, and an M.F.A. from the University of Iowa's Writer's Workshop.
Spezi, Mario, 120	Mario Spezi is an Italian journalist whose career has revolved around the serial killer known as The Monster of Florence.
Spillane, Mickey, 152	Frank Morrison "Mickey" Spillane was born in 1918 in Brooklyn, New York. He attended Kansas State College and served in the U.S. Army Air Force during World War II as a fighter pilot. Upon returning from the war, Spillane turned an idea for a comic book character into private investigator Mike Hammer. He became one of America's all-time best-selling fiction authors and even had a chance to act in a Hollywood movie as his fictional creation. Mickey Spillane was a Jehovah's Witness. He died in 2006 in Murrells Inlet, South Carolina.
Stannard, David E., 73	David E. Stannard was born in 1941 in Teaneck, New Jersey, to a businessman father and a mother who was a translator. He earned an A.B. from San Francisco State College in 1971, an M.A. from Yale in 1972, an M.Phil. in 1973, and a Ph.D. in 1975. He is the American studies professor at the University of Hawai'i.

Stansberry, Domenic, 50, 101, 114

Domenic Stansberry was born in 1952 in Washington, D.C., the son of an aerospace engineer. He earned a B.A. from Portland State University in 1977, an M.A. from Colorado State University in 1980, and an M.F.A. from the University of Massachusetts in 1984. Stansberry was a newspaper writer in Northampton, Massachusetts, from 1981 to 1983. He worked as an instructor from 1984 to 1986 and again from 1990 to 1992. He has worked in public relations, marketing, and media relations and is the cofounder of Black River Publishing. He lives in Corte Madera, California, with his wife, poet Gillian Conoley, and their daughter, Gillis. Web site: www.domenicstansberry.com

Stark, Richard, 43, 44, 45, 46, 47

See Westlake, Donald

Starr, Jason, 12, 47, 50, 56, 60, 66, 101

Jason Starr was born in 1966 in New York City. He earned a B.A. from Binghamton University in 1988 and an M.F.A. from Brooklyn College in 1990. He has worked as a telemarketer and a writer. Web site: www.jasonstarr.com

Stashower, Daniel, 145

Daniel Stashower was born in 1960 in Cleveland, Ohio, the son of an advertising executive father and an interior designer mother. Stashower was a professional magician from 1974 to 1979. He earned a B.A. from Northwestern University in 1982 and an M.F.A. from Columbia University in 1984. He worked as a copywriter while in school and then was a staff writer at Time-Life Books for two years. He now is a full-time freelance writer and has written crime novels and a biography of Sherlock Holmes's creator, Arthur Conan Doyle. Web site: www.stashower.com

Stella, Charlie, 34, 35, 132

Carmello "Charlie" Stella was born in 1956 in New York City. He earned a B.A. from Brooklyn College in 1982. Charlie has worked as a football coach, a window cleaner, and a word processor. He is also an off-off-off Broadway playwright. Web site: www.charliestella.com

Stewart, James B., 53, 120

James B. Stewart was born in 1957 in Quincy, Illinois. He has degrees from DePauw University and the Harvard Law School. He has worked as a writer, a journalist, an educator, and an attorney. He won the Pulitzer Prize in 1988.

Stout, Rex, 132	Rex Stout is one of the most revered American Golden Age mystery writers, having created the <u>Nero Wolfe/Archie Goodwin series</u>. Stout was born in 1886 in Noblesville, Indiana. He was public-school educated in Topeka, Kansas. In his youth, he worked all over the United States as a cook, a salesperson, a bookkeeper, a Pueblo guide, a bellhop, a hotel manager, an architect, a cabinetmaker, and a magazine writer. Stout served in the U.S. Navy from 1906 to 1908. He invented a school banking system that employed him from 1916 to 1927. He then moved to Paris to write for two years. Eventually the success of his mystery novels let him live out his life as a mystery writer. He died in 1975 in Danbury, Connecticut.
Stowers, Carlton, 27, 145	Born in 1942 in Brownwood, Texas, Carlton Stowers studied religion at the University of Texas. Since 1966 he has worked as a journalist with various Texas newspapers.
Sullivan, Robert, 145	Justice Robert Sullivan graduated from Harvard in 1938 and the Boston College Law School in 1941. He was appointed to the highest trial court in Massachusetts in 1958 when he was forty-one. He lives in Boston.
Summerscale, Kate, 155	Kate Summerscale was born in 1965. She has attended Oxford University and Stanford University. She has worked as a journalist.
Swan, Mary, 51	Mary Swan lives with her husband and daughter near Toronto, Ontario, Canada. She is the winner of the 2001 O. Henry Award for short fiction.
Swierczynski, Duane, 47, 133, 163	Duane Swierczynski was born in 1972. He lives in Philadelphia, Pennsylvania, where he is editor-in-chief of the *Philadelphia City Paper*. Web site: www.duaneswierczynski.com
Swindle, Howard, 145	Howard Swindle is an editor at the *Dallas Morning News*.
Tartt, Donna, 133	Donna Tartt was born in Greenwood, Mississippi, on December 23, 1963, to Don and Taylor Tartt. She has one sister. Donna wrote her first poem at age five and had a sonnet published at age thirteen. She attended the University of Mississippi for one semester and then Bennington College. At Bennington, she wrote *The Secret History* (1992), which eventually was published with a big advance and much ballyhoo. She lives in New York City.

Taylor, John, 145

John Taylor was born in 1995 in Yokosuka, Japan, the son of a diplomat. He has a B.A. from the University of Chicago, earned in 1977. He worked at *Newsweek* and *Business Week* before becoming a senior writer for *Esquire*. He lives in East Moriches, New York.

Thiong'o, Ngúgí wa, 133

Ngúgí wa Thiong'o (known as Ngúgí) was born in 1938 in Kamiriithu, near Limuru, Kiambu District, while Kenya was a British-ruled colony. He was the fifth child of the third of his father's four wives. Raised as a Christian, he was educated at Makerere University in Kampala, Uganda, and the University of Leeds. His writing often reflects the conflict between his Gikuyu heritage and his Christian/Western upbringing. Ngúgí worked as a reporter and lectured at various colleges. In 1977 he was arrested for his writing, which was viewed by the now-independent Kenyan government as a threat. Held for one year without a trial, Ngúgí was released but not reinstated at the university, so he went into exile in 1982. From this point forward, he began to use Gikuyu, his native tongue, as his primary language in his writings. Ngúgí taught at Yale University before he became the professor of comparative literature and performance studies at New York University in 1992, where he held the Erich Maria Remarque Chair.

Thompson, Jim, 11, 35, 48, 51, 60, 67, 84, 115, 133, 148, 153

Born the son of a sheriff, Thompson failed to finish high school due to an illness. While working the oil fields of Texas, he began to contribute articles about his experiences to various journals. After being admitted as a special student to the University of Nebraska, Thompson dropped out after dabbling in the English and journalism departments. While drifting from job to job, he never lost interest in writing and had his first novel published in 1942. Although he eventually found a home in the paperback original publishing industry and produced over thirty novels, his writing attracted little attention until he was rediscovered during a renaissance in noir literature during the 1980s.

Thompson, Thomas, 105

Thomas Thompson was born in 1933 in Fort Worth, Texas, the son of two educators. He earned a B.A. in 1955 from the University of Texas and then worked as a reporter and editor. Thompson died from cancer in 1982.

Thomson, David, 67   David Thomson was born in 1941 in London, England. He attended Dulwich College and the London School of Film Technique. He immigrated to the United States in 1975. Thomson is a film critic, biographer, historian, and novelist. He has taught film studies at Dartmouth College. He lives in San Francisco, California.

Thornburg, Newton, 101   Newton Thornburg was born in 1930 in Harvey, Illinois. He earned a B.A. from the University of Iowa in 1951 and studied at the Writers Workshop in New York City. He worked as an advertising copywriter from 1960 to 1970 before becoming a full-time writer.

Tidyman, Ernest, 49, 146   Ernest Tidyman was born in 1928 in Cleveland, Ohio, the son of a journalist. He worked as a journalist for many years and eventually became a full-time writer of novels (including Shaft), nonfiction, and screenplays. He won an Academy Award for the screenplay for the film *The French Connection*. Tidyman died in London in 1984 of a perforated ulcer.

Traver, Robert, 156   Robert Traver is the pseudonym of John D(onaldson) Voelker. Voelker was born in 1903 in Ishpeming, Michigan, the son of a saloon keeper. He earned an L.L.B. in 1928 from the University of Michigan. He was the prosecuting attorney for Marquette County, Michigan, from 1934 to 1952 and then became a Michigan Supreme Court justice from 1957 to 1960. He was the author of four novels and numerous works of nonfiction. He died of a heart attack in 1991 in Marquette, Michigan.

Tucker, John C., 73   John C. Tucker was born in 1934. He attended Princeton University and then practiced law in Chicago, Illinois, until 1985. He lives in Tidewater, Virginia.

Vidocq, François Eugéne, 9, 148   François Eugéne Vidocq was a soldier, privateer, smuggler, and spy before the Paris police began using him for security services in 1812. Most famous for coining the phrase "set a thief to catch a thief," Vidocq founded the Police de Sûreté and went on to immortalize himself in a series of books that most likely were ghostwritten by another writer. It was Vidocq's adventures that inspired America's Edgar Allan Poe when he turned to writing crime fiction. After his resignation from the Sûreté, Vidocq founded a series of private detective agencies. Web site: www.vidocq.org/vidocq.html

Volkman, Ernest, 37   Ernest Volkman is the co-author of *Goombata: The Improbable Rise and Fall of John Gotti and His Gang*.

Waites, Martyn, 153

Born 1963, in Newcastle upon Tyne, England, Martyn Waites attended drama school and worked as a comic and an actor. He has been a published author since 1997.

Waiwaiole, Lono, 84, 85

Lono Waiwaiole was born in San Francisco, California. He has worked as a newspaper and magazine editor, sports information officer, and professional poker player. He taught secondary school in Portland, Oregon, before moving to Hilo, Hawaii to teach. Lono now resides in Portland.

Walker, Kent, 27

Kent Walker lives in California. He is the son of Sante Kimes, a con artist and murderer.

Waller, George, 146

Walter, Jess, 85

Jess Walter is a career journalist. Besides his professional writing, he has authored short stories, essays, and screenplays. He has also written the nonfiction book *Every Knee Shall Bow* (1995) and the novels *Over Tumbled Graves* (2001), *Land of the Blind* (2003), and *The Zero* (2006). His wife's name is Anne, and they have two children. He lives in Spokane, Washington. Web site: www.jesswalter.com

Walters, Minette, 68, 102, 134, 135

Minette Walters was born in 1949 in Bishop's Stortford, England, the daughter of an army captain and an artist. Minette graduated from Durham University. In 1978 she married Alec Walters, and they have two sons. She worked as an editor in London for *IPC Magazine*, a romantic fiction publication, writing articles, short stories, and novelettes for the publication. She then became a freelance writer for numerous women's magazines. After her second son began full-time school, Walters began to write her first novel. She has been a full-time writer ever since. Her first five books were adapted for television by the BBC. She lives in an eighteenth-century manor house in Dorchester in Dorset. Web site: www.minettewalters.co.uk

Wambaugh, Joseph, 146, 155

Joseph Wambaugh was born in 1937 in East Pittsburgh, Pennsylvania, the son of a police officer. Wambaugh served in the U.S. Marine Corps from 1954 to 1957. He earned an A.A. from Chaffey College in 1958, and a B.A. in 1960 and an M.A. in 1968 from California State College. Wambaugh served with the Los Angeles Police Department from 1960 until 1974. He is now a full-time writer and lives in Rancho Mirage, California.

Warden, Rob, 89
Rob Warden is a legal affairs writer and political consultant in Chicago.

Watson, Larry, 135
Larry Watson was born in 1947 in Rugby, North Dakota, the son of a sheriff. He has a B.A. and an M.A. from the University of North Dakota. Watson earned a Ph.D. in the creative writing program at the University of Utah. Watson taught writing and literature at the University of Wisconsin—Stevens Point from 1979 until 2004. He is currently a visiting professor at Marquette University. Watson also wrote *In a Dark Time* (1980), *Justice* (1995), *White Crosses* (1997), *Laura* (2000), and *Orchard* (2003). He lives with his wife, Susan, in rural Wisconsin and they have two daughters. Web site: larry-watson.com

Weiss, Mike, 73
Mike Weiss was born in 1942 in Washington, D.C., the son of an accountant father and bursar mother. He earned a B.A. from Knox College in 1964 and an M.F.A. from John Hopkins in 1965. He has worked his entire life as a journalist and writer. He is the author of the Ben Henry mystery novels.

Welch, Louise, 135
Louise Welch is a Scottish writer whose first book won The Crime Writers Association's John Creasey Dagger for the best first crime novel.

Westlake, Donald, 22, 23, 24, 68
Donald Westlake was born in Brooklyn, New York, in 1933. He attended Champlain College and the State University of New York at Binghamton as well as serving in the Air Force from 1954 to 1856. He became a professional writer in 1959 as has written under his own name and at least a dozen pseudonyms including Richard Stark. In 1992, the Mystery Writers of America made him a Grand Master.

Wignall, Kevin, 85
Kevin Wignall was born in Herentals, Belgium, the son of a British soldier. He lived in various countries around the world before settling in Western England. He is a former English teacher and now full-time novelist. Web site: www.kevinwignall.com

Willeford, Charles, 135
Charles Ray Willeford III was born in 1919 in Arkansas but lived most of his youth in Los Angeles before running away from home. He served in the military in various capacities from 1935 to 1956. His first novel was published in 1953, and he was one of the more successful paperback writers of the period. His series character, Hoke Moseley, was a financial and critical success for the author at the end of his career. He died of a heart attack in 1988.

Williams, Charles, 115, 136

Charles Williams was born in San Angelo, Texas. He served in the U.S. Merchant Marines. He worked in the electronics and radio industry before becoming a full-time novelist. Three years after the death of his wife, Williams committed suicide in Los Angeles in 1975.

Williams, Darren, 136

Darren Williams was born in Australia in 1967. His first novel, *Swimming in Silk*, was published in 1995 and won the Australian/Vogel Literary Award. Living in London with his social worker wife, Williams was set to give up the writing life when his second novel, *Angel Rock*, was accepted for publication.

Wilson, Robert, 68

Robert Wilson was born in 1957. After graduating from Oxford University in 1979 with a degree in English, he worked in Crete leading archeological tours and as an advertising man in a business agency, and lived and worked in Africa. He is the author of the *Bruce Medway series*.

Winslow, Don, 35, 85, 153

Don Winslow was born in 1953 in New York City, the son of a naval officer father and a librarian mother. He earned a B.A. and an M.A. and has worked as an actor, director, movie theater manager, safari guide, and private investigator. He lives in San Diego, California, with his wife and child. Web site: www.donwinslow.com

Wolf, Thomas, 137

Thomas Wolf earned an M.F.A. from the Iowa Writers' Workshop. He is a writing consultant for the Association of American Medical Colleges. He lives in Chapel Hill, North Carolina, with his wife and coauthor Patricia L. Bryan, and their three sons.

Wolfe, Linda, 90

Born to an accountant and a singer in 1935 in New York, Linda Wolfe earned a B.A. from Brooklyn College in 1958 and an M.A. from New York University in 1960. She worked as an assistant editor, a researcher, and a writer.

Woodley, Richard, 40

Richard Woodley is a novelist and screenwriter.

Woodrell, Daniel, 85

Daniel Woodrell was born in 1953 in Springfield, Missouri, the son of a salesman father and a nurse mother. Woodrell served in the U.S. Marine Corp as a sharpshooter. He earned a B.G.S. from the University of Kansas, and a B.G.S. in 1980 and an M.F.A from the University of Iowa in 1983. He lives in Eureka Springs, Arkansas.

Woolrich, Cornell, 11, 36, 74, 102, 116, 136

Cornell George Hopley-Woolrich was born in New York City in 1903, the son of a civil engineer. He traveled throughout Mexico and Central America with his father after his parents divorced but then lived from age twelve with his mother. He dropped out of college in 1926 when his first jazz age novel was published. After a series of those, he turned to crime writing. He also wrote as George Hopley and William Irish. After his mother's death in 1957, he essentially had a mental breakdown and wrote very little. He died from a stroke in New York City in 1968.

Wright, William, 146

William Wright was born in Philadelphia, Pennsylvania, in 1930. He earned a B.A. at Yale University in 1952 and then served as a translator in the U.S. Army for three years. He worked as an editor for most of his professional life before becoming a full-time writer.

Zierold, Norman, 53

Norman Zierold was born in 1927 in South Amana, Iowa, the son of a professional singer. He earned a B.A. from Harvard in 1949 and an M.A. from the University of Iowa in 1951. He has worked as an advertising salesman, a promotion writer, an editor, and a teacher. He has been a freelance writer since 1964.

Zuckoff, Mitchell, 71

Mitchell Zuckoff was born in Brookly, New York, in 1962, the son of a history teacher and a bookkeeper. He earned a B.A. from the University of Rhode Island and an M.A. from the University of Missouri. He has spent his entire adult life as a journalist and writer. He lives in Boston.

Title Index

About the Author, Colapinto, John, 92
Absent Friends, Rozan, S. J., 33
Accident Man, The, Cain, Tom, 16
Acid Row, Walters, Minette, 68
Adios Muchachos, Chavarría, Daniel, 17
Adventures of Caleb Williams, Godwin, William, 9
After Dark, My Sweet, Thompson, Jim, 60
Airman and the Carpenter, The: The Lindbergh Kidnapping and the Framing of Richard Hauptmann, Kennedy, Ludovic, 140
Amagansett, Mills, Mark, 82
American Detective, The, Siegel, Jeff, 177
American Mystery Novels and Detective Novels, Landrum, Larry, 180
American Tragedy, An, Dreiser, Theodore, 10, 62
Âmes Grises, Les, Claudel, Philippe, 148
Anatomy of a Killer, Rabe, Peter, 33,
Anatomy of a Murder, Traver, Robert, 156
And Never Let Her Go: Thomas Capano: The Deadly Seducer, Rule, Ann, 144
And the Dead Shall Rise: The Murder of Mary Phagan and the Lynching of Leo Frank, Oney, Steve, 142
Anderson Tapes, The, Sanders, Lawrence, 34
Angel of Montague Street, The, Green, Norman, 30
Angel Rock, Williams, Darren, 136
Animal Factory, Bunker, Edward, 61
Anyone's Daughter, Alexander, Shana, 103
"Are You There Alone?": The Unspeakable Crimes of Andrea Yates, O'Malley, Suzanne, 142
Armadale, Collins, Wilkie, 91
Armchair Detective Book of Lists, The, Stine, Kate, 177
Art of the Mystery Story, The, Haycraft, Howard, 180
Ask the Parrot, Stark, Richard, 47
At Mother's Request: A True Story of Money, Murder and Betrayal, Coleman, Jonathan, 24

Atomic Lobster, Dorsey, Tim, 20
Attack, The, Khadra, Yamina, 81

Backflash, Stark, Richard, 46
Bad News, Westlake, Donald E., 23
Baiale de la Victoria, El, Skármeta, Antonio, 43
Ballad of the Whiskey Robber: A True Story of Bank Heists, Ice Hockey, Transylvanian Pelt Smuggling, Moonlighting Detectives and Broken Hearts, Rubinstein, Julian, 89
Bank Shot, Westlake, Donald E., 22
Beast in View, Millar, Margaret, 98
Beautiful Children, Bock, Charles, 122
Beautiful Cigar Girl, The: Mary Rogers, Edgar Allan Poe, and the Invention of Murder, Stashower, Daniel, 145
Beautiful Dreamer, Bigsby, Christopher, 91
Bedelia, Caspary, Vera, 106
Before He Wakes: A True Story of Money, Marriage, Sex and Murder, Bledsoe, Jerry, 51
Benim Adim Kirmizi, Pamuk, Orhan, 129
Benny Muscles In, Rabe, Peter, 33
Beyond Reason: The True Story of a Shocking Double Murder, a Brilliant and Beautiful Virginia Socialite, and a Deadly Psychotic Obsession, Englade, Ken, 60
BFI Companion to Crime, The, Hardy, Phil, 173
Bible Salesman, The, Edgerton, Clyde, 20
Big Bamboo, The, Dorsey, Tim, 19
Big Bounce, Leonard, Elmore, 12
Big Bucks: The True, Outrageous Story of the Plymouth Mail Robbery and How They Got Away with It, Tidyman, Ernest, 49
Big Clock, The, Fearing, Kenneth, 94
Bird Yard, The, Martin, J, Wallis, 65
Bitter Harvest: A Woman's Fury, a Mother's Sacrifice, Rule, Ann, 143
Black Alibi, Woolrich, Cornell, 116
Black Angel, The, Woolrich, Cornell, 136

Black Curtain, The, Woolrich, Cornell, 102

Black Dahlia Avenger: The True Story, Hodel, Steve, 139

Black Friday, Goodis, David, 79

Black Gold, Bean, Fred, 28

Black Ice Score, The, Stark, Richard, 45

Black Mass: The Irish Mob, the FBI and a Devil's Deal, Lehr, Dick, and Gerard O'Neill, 39

Black Path of Fear, The, Woolrich, Cornell, 36

Blackburn, Denton, Bradley, 107

Bleak House, Dickens, Charles, 10

Blind Assassin, The, Atwood, Margaret, 74

Blind Eye: How the Medical Establishment Let a Doctor Get Away with Murder, Stewart, James B., 120

Blonde, The, Swierczynski, Duane, 133

Blood and Money, Thompson, Thomas, 105

Blood, Bedlam, Bullets, and Badguys, Gannon, Michael B., 168

Blood Echoes: The True Story of an Infamous Mass Murder and Its Aftermath, Cook, Thomas H., 103

Blood Will Tell: The Murder Trials of T, Cullen Davis, Cartwright, Gary, 70

Blooding, The, Wambaugh, Joseph, 146

Bloody Murder, Symons, Julian, 182

Blunderer, The, Highsmith, Patricia, 126

Bobbed Haired Bandit, The: A True Story of Crime and Celebrity in 1920s New York, Duncombe, Stephen, and Andrew Mattson, 48

Bobby Gold Stories, The, Bourdain, Anthony, 41

Bodies Electric, Harrison, Colin, 126

Born to Kill: America's Most Notorious Vietnamese Gang and the Changing Face of Organized Crime, English, T., J., 38

Boss of Bosses: The Fall of the Godfather: The FBI and Paul Catellano, O'Brien, Joseph F., and Andrus Kurins, 39

Boston Strangler, The, Frank, Gerold, 117

Box Nine, O'Connell, Jack, 151

Boy Who Followed Ripley, The, Highsmith, Patricia, 110

Boys in the Trees, The, Swan, Mary, 51

Branded Woman, Miller, Wade, 42

Breakdown: Sex, Suicide, and the Harvard Psychiatrist, McNamara, Eileen, 89

Breaker, The, Walters, Minette, 134

Breakheart Hill, Cook, Thomas H., 124

Breakout, Stark, Richard, 46

Breathtaker, The, Blanchard, Alice, 105

Bride Wore Black, The, Woolrich, Cornell, 136

Broker, The, Collins, Max (Allan), 78

Broker's Wife, The, Collins, Max (Allan), 78

Brothers Bulger, The: How They Terrorized and Corrupted Boston For a Quarter Century, Carr, Howie, 37

Burden of Proof: The Case of Juan Corona, Cray, Ed, 116

Burglar, The, Goodis, David, 79

Burglar in the Closet, The, Block, Lawrence, 76

Burglar in the Library, The, Block, Lawrence, 77

Burglar in the Rye, The, Block, Lawrence, 77

Burglar on the Prowl, The, Block, Lawrence, 77

Burglar Who Liked to Quote Kipling, The, Block, Lawrence, 76

Burglar Who Painted Like Mondrian, The, Block, Lawrence, 76

Burglar Who Studied Spinoza, The, Block, Lawrence, 76

Burglar Who Thought He Was Bogart, The, Block, Lawrence, 77

Burglar Who Traded Ted Williams, The, Block, Lawrence, 76

Burglars Can't Be Choosers, Block, Lawrence, 75

Burn, Doolittle, Sean, 93

Burning Marguerite, Inness-Brown, Elizabeth, 127

Business of Dying, The, Kernick, Simon, 149

Bust, Bruen, Ken and Jason Starr, 56

Butcher's Boy, The, Perry, Thomas, 32

Butcher's Moon, Stark, Richard, 46

By a Slow River, Claudel, Philippe, 148

By a Woman's Hand, Swanson, Jean, and Dean James, 177

By Persons Unknown: The Strange Death of Christine Demeter, Jonas, George, and Barbara Amiel, 139

By Reason of Doubt: The Belshaw Case, Godfrey, Ellen, 71

By Two and Two: The Scandalous Story of Twin Sisters Accused of a Shocking Crime of Passion, Schutze, Jim, 144

Cadillac Beach, Dorsey, Tim, 19
California Fire and Life, Winslow, Don, 35
Candleland, Waites, Martyn, 153
Cape May Court House, Schiller, Lawrence, 90
Careless Whispers, Stowers, Carlton, 27
Carnivore's Inquiry, A, Murray, Sabina, 113
Cases, Gores, Joe, 160
Catalogue of Crime, A, Barzun, Jaques, and Wendell Hertig Taylor, 167
Caught Stealing, Huston, Charlie, 31
Caveman's Valentine, The, Green, George Dawes, 125
Cell 2455 Death Row, Chessman, Caryl, 70
Chain of Evidence: A True Story of Law Enforcement and One Woman's Bravery, Detroit, Michael, 38
Charlie Opera, Stella, Charlie, 35
Chasing the Dime, Connelly, Michael, 123
Chatham School Affair, The, Cook, Thomas H., 92
Cheapskates, Stella, Charlie, 132
Child of Rage, Thompson, Jim, 134
Church of Dead Girls, The, Dobyns, Stephen, 107
Circumstantial Evidence: Death, Life and Justice in a Southern Town, Earley, Pete, 154
Citizen Vince, Walter, Jess, 85
City of the Sun, Levien, David, 161
Classic Crime and Suspense Writers, Bloom, Harold, 179
Classic Mystery Writers, Bloom, Harold, 179
Clean Up, The, Doolittle, Sean, 93
Clod of Wayward Marl, A, DeMarinis, Rick, 124
Closing Time: The True Story of the "Goodbar" Murder, Fosburgh, Lacey, 137
Cloud of Unknowing, The, Cook, Thomas H., 62
Coffin for Dimitrios, Ambler, Eric, 147
Cogan's Trade, Higgins, George V., 21
Cold Caller, Starr, Jason, 50
Cold Case, A, Gourevitch, Philip, 104
Collector, The, Fowles, John, 108
Comeback, Stark, Richard, 46
Confession, The, Stansberry, Domenic, 114
Conviction: Solving the Moxley Murder, Levitt, Leonard, 140
Cottonwood, Phillips, Scott, 114

Count and the Confession, The: A True Mystery, Taylor, John, 145
Cracking the Hard-Boiled Detective, Moore, Lewis D., 181
Crime and Punishment, Dostoevsky, Fyodor, 10, 62
Crime, Detective, Espionage, Mystery, and Thriller Fiction and Film, Melvin, David Skene, and Ann Skene Melvin, 169
Crime Fiction IV, Hubin, Allen J., 168
Crime of the Scene, King, Nina, and Robin Winks, 176
Crime of the Century: The Lindbergh Kidnapping and the Framing of Richard Hauptmann, Kennedy, Ludovic, 140
Crime Trade, The, Kernick, Simon, 150
Criminal, The, Thompson, Jim, 134
Critical Survey of Mystery and Detective Fiction, Rollyson, Carl, 172
Cropper's Cabin, Thompson, Jim, 133
Cruel Doubt, McGinniss, Joe, 61
Cry of the Owl, The, Highsmith, Patricia, 64
Curious Incident of the Dog in the Night Time, The, Haddon, Mark, 126
Cutter and Bone, Thornburg, Newton, 101
Cutting Room, The, Welch, Louise, 135

Daddy Cool, Goines, Donald, 79
Dancer and the Thief, The, Antonio Skármeta, 43
Dangerous Man, A, Huston, Charlie, 31
Dante Club, The, Pearl, Matthew, 66
Dark Arena, The, Puzo, Mario, 59
Dark as Night, Conrad, Mark T., 17
Dark City, Muller, Eddie, 174
Dark Passage, Goodis, David, 11, 95
Dark Room, The, Walters, Minette, 102
Dark Side of the Screen, The, Hirsch, Foster, 173
Darker Place, A, King, Laurie R, 128
Darkly Dreaming Dexter, Lindsay, Jeff, 112
Dawn Patrol, The, Winslow, Don, 153
Day They Stole the Mona Lisa, The, Reit, Seymour, 26
Dead Aim, Perry, Thomas, 99
Dead by Sunset: Perfect Husband, Perfect Killer? Rule, Ann, 72
Dead Calm, Williams, Charles, 115
Dead Cat Bounce, Green, Norman, 30

Dead Man, Gores, Joe, 160
Dead Street, Spillane, Mickey, 152
Deadline at Dawn, Irish, William, 97
Deadly Edge, Stark, Richard, 45
*Deadly Force: The True Story of How a Badge
    Can Become a License to Kill,*
    O'Donnell, Lawrence, Jr., 154
Deadly Percheron, The, Bardin, John
    Franklin, 75
*Deadly Silence, A: The Ordeal of Cheryl
    Pierson; a Case of Incest and Murder,*
    Kleiman, Dena, 140
Deadly Women, Grape, Jan, Dean James,
    and Ellen Nehr, 175
Dealer, The, Collins, Max (Allan), 78
Dearly Devoted Dexter, Lindsay, Jeff, 112
Death and Life of Bobby Z, The, Winslow,
    Don, 85
*Death at the Priory: Sex, Love, and Murder in
    Victorian England,* Ruddick, James,
    143
Death Benefits, Perry, Thomas, 50
Death in Belmont, A, Junger, Sebastian, 88
*Death in White Bear Lake, A: The True
    Chronicle of an All-American Town,*
    Siegel, Barry, 144
*Death Sentence: The True Story of Velma
    Barfield's Life, Crimes and Execution,*
    Bledsoe, Jerry, 116
*Death Shift, The: The True Story of Nurse
    Genene Jones and the Texas Baby
    Murders,* Elkind, Peter, 117
Death You Deserve, The, Bowker, David, 29
Deep Water, Highsmith, Patricia, 64
Den of Thieves, Stewart, James B., 53
*Desire Street: A True Story of Death and
    Deliverance in New Orleans,* Horne,
    Jed, 88
Detecting Men/Detecting Men Pocket Guide,
    Heising, Willetta L., 175
*Detecting Women 3/Detecting Women Pocket
    Guide,* Heising, Willetta L., 175
Detectionary, Penzler, Otto, Chris
    Steinbrunner, and Marvin
    Lachman, 172
Detective Agency, Walton, Priscilla L., and
    Manina Jones, 182
Detective Fiction, Winks, Robin W., 182
Detective in Film, The, Everson, William K.,
    173
Detective in Hollywood, The, Tuska, Jon, 174
Detective Short Story, The, Queen, Ellery,
    170
Detective Story, Kertész, Imre, 150
Detective Story, The, Schwartz, Saul, 182
Detektívtörténet, Kertész, Imre, 150
*Devil in the White City, The: Murder, Magic,
    and Madness at the Fair That Changed
    America,* Larson, Eric, 118
Devil's Peak, Meyer, Deon, 82
Devil's Redhead, The, Corbett, David, 29
Devil's Right Hand, The, Rhoades, J. D.,
    162
Development of the Detective Novel, The,
    Murch, A. E., 181
Dexter in the Dark, Lindsay, Jeff, 113
Die a Little, Abbott, Megan, 156
Digger's Game, The, Higgins, George V.,
    57
Dirt, Doolittle, Sean, 93
Dirty Money, Stark, Richard, 47
Dirty Sally, Simon, Michael, 152
Dirty White Boys, Hunter, Stephen, 97
Disappearance of Dr, Parkman, The,
    Sullivan, Robert, 145
*Disco Bloodbath: A Fabulous But True Tale of
    Murder in Clubland,* St. James,
    James, 53
Distance, The, Muller, Eddie, 59
"Doc": The Rape of the Town of Lovell,
    Olsen, Jack, 141
Dog Eat Dog, Bunker, Edward, 77
Dog Fighter, The, Bojanowski, Marc, 122
Dog's Ransom, ,A, Highsmith, Patricia, 149
Done for a Dime, Corbett, David, 124
*Donnie Brasco: My Undercover Life in the
    Mafia; a True Story by FBI Agent
    Joseph D. Pistone,* Pistone, Joseph D.,
    with Richard Woodley, 40
Don't Ask, Westlake, Donald E., 23
Double Indemnity, Cain James J., 11, 49,
*Double Play: The San Francisco City Hall
    Killings,* Weiss, Mike, 73
Down There, Goodis, David, 80
*Drake's Fortune: The Fabulous True Story of
    the World's Greatest Confidence
    Artist,* Rayner, Richard, 26
Dreams of Ada, The, Mayer, Robert, 141
Drowned Hopes, Westlake, Donald E., 23
Dummy, Tidyman, Ernest, 146
Dust Devils, The, Reasoner, James, 99

Earth to Earth, Cornwell, John, 86
Earthquake Weather, Lankford, Terrill Lee, 97
Echo, The, Walters, Minette, 102
Eddie's World, Stella, Charlie, 34
Education of a Felon: A Memoir, Bunker, Edward, 24
Eighth Circle, The, Ellin, Stanley, 159
Encyclopedia Mysteriosa, DeAndrea, William L., 171
Encyclopedia of Murder and Mystery, Murphy, Bruce F., 172
Encyclopedia of Mystery & Detection, Lachman, Marv, Otto Penzler, Charles Shibuk, and Chris Steinbrunner, 172
End of the Night, The, MacDonald, John D., 113
Engaged to Murder: The Inside Story of the Main Line Murders, Schwartz-Nobel, Loretta, 53
Every Breath You Take: A True Story of Obsession, Revenge and Murder, Rule, Ann, 144
Every Secret Thing, Lippman, Laura, 58
Everything She Ever Wanted: A True Story of Obsessive Love, Murder & Betrayal, Rule, Ann, 143
Evidence of Love, Bloom, John, and Jim Atkinson, 69
Executioner's Song, The, Mailer, Norman, 71

Fake I.D., Starr, Jason, 47
Falling Angel, Hjortsberg, William, 160
Far Cry, The, Brown, Fredric, 123
Fast One, Cain, Paul, 28
Fidelity, Perry, Thomas, 162
Fiend in Human, The, Gray, John MacLachlan, 108
Film Noir, Crowther, Bruce, 173
Film Noir, Silver, Alain, and Elizabeth Ward, 174
Film Noir, Stephens, Michael L., 174
Final Justice: The True Story of the Richest Man Ever Tried for Murder, Naifeh, Steven, and Gregory White Smith, 72
Final Solution, The: A Story of Detection, Chabon, Michael, 159
Finding Maubee, Carr, A H. Z., 16

Fine Art of Murder, The, Gorman, Ed, Martin H. Greenberg, Larry Segriff, and Jon L. Breen, 175
Fire in the Flesh, Goodis, David, 63
Fire Lover, Wambaugh, Joseph, 155
Firebreak, Stark, Richard, 46
First Quarry, The, Collins, Max (Allan), 79
Flashfire, Stark, Richard, 46
Flight of an Angel, Chute, Vern, 92
Florida Roadkill, Dorsey, Tim, 18
For the Dogs, Wignall, Kevin, 85
Fortunate Pilgrim, The, Puzo, Mario, 32
Fox Evil, Walters, Minette, 68
Frame-up: The Incredible Case of Tom Mooney and Warren Billings, Gentry, Curt, 138
Friends of Eddie Coyle, The, Higgins, George V., 12, 21
Fright, Hopley, George, 97
Fury on Sunday, Matheson, Richard, 113

Game for the Living, A, Highsmith, Patricia, 64
Gang That Couldn't Shoot Straight, The, Breslin, Jimmy, 29
Gangland: How the FBI Broke the Mob, Blum, Howard, 36
Gathering of Saints, A: A True Story of Money, Murder and Deceit, Lindsey, Robert, 25
Getaway, The, Thompson, Jim, 48
Ghosts of Hopewell, The: Setting the Record Straight in the Lindbergh Case, Fisher, Jim, 137
Girl with the Long Green Hair, The, Block,, Lawrence, 16
Give Us a Kiss, Woodrell, Daniel, 85
Glass Cell, The, Highsmith, Patricia, 127
Glass Key, The, Hammett, Dashiell, 11, 28
Godfather, The, Puzo, Mario, 12, 32
Golden Gizmo, The, Thompson, Jim, 67
Gone in the Night: The Dowaliby Family's Encounter with Murder and the Law, Protess, David, and Rob Warden, 89
Good Behavior, Westlake, Donald E., 23
Good Day in Hell, Rhoades, J., D., 162
Good Day to Die, A, Kernick, Simon, 150
Good Morning, Darkness, Francisco, Ruth, 148
Good People, Sakey, Marcus, 59

Good Rat, The: A True Story, Breslin, Jimmy, 36

Goombata: The Improbable Rise and Fall of John Gotti and His Gang, Cummings, John, and Ernest Volkman, 37

Great Detectives, Symons, Julian, 182

Great Detectives, The, Penzler, Otto, 176

Great Fall, A, Savage, Mildred, 72

Great Gatsby, The, Fitzgerald, F. Scott, 49

Great Short Stories of Detection, Mystery & Horror, Sayers, Dorothy L., 9

Great Women Mystery Writers, Lindsay, Elizabeth Blakesley, 181

Green Eagle Score, The, Stark, Richard, 45

Green River, Running Red: The Real Story of the Green River Killer—America's Deadliest Serial Murderer, Rule, Ann, 120

Greentown: Murder and Mystery in Greenwich, America's Wealthiest Community, Dumas, Timothy, 137

Grey Souls, Claudel, Philippe, 148

Grifters, The, Thompson, Jim, 48

Grifter's Game, Block, Lawrence, 16

Guilty Parties, Ousby, Ian, 176

Gumshoes, Brunsdale, Mitzi, 171

Gun Monkeys, Gischler, Victor, 30

Gun, with Occasional Music, Lethem, Jonathan, 161

Hamilton Case, The, de Kretser, Michelle, 156

Hammerhead Ranch Motel, Dorsey, Tim, 18

Hammett, Gores, Joe, 160

Handle, The, Stark, Richard, 44

Hannibal, Harris, Thomas, 109

Hannibal Rising, Harris, Thomas, 109

Hard Feelings, Starr, Jason, 66

Hard Rain Falling, Carpenter, Don, 56

Harder They Fall, The, Schulberg, Budd, 34

Hastened to the Grave: The Gypsy Murder Investigation, Olsen, Jack, 26

Heart Full of Lies: A True Story of Death and Desire, Rule, Ann, 52

Heaven Knows Who, Brand, Christianna, 86

Hell of a Woman, A, Thompson, Jim, 51

Helter Skelter: The True Story of the Manson Murders, Bugliosi, Vincent, and Curt Gentry, 116

Hidden River, McKinty, Adrian, 151

Hoax: The Inside Story of the Howard Hughes–Clifford Irving Affair, Fay, Stephen, Lewis Chester, and Magnus Linklater, 25

Homicide in American Fiction, 1798–1860, Davis, David Brion, 180

Honor Killing: How the Infamous "Massie Affair" Transformed Hawai'i, Stannard, David E., 73

Hot Rock, The, Westlake, Donald E., 22

How Like a God, Stout, Rex, 132

How Like an Angel, Millar, Margaret, 161

How the Dead Live, Raymond, Derek, 152

Hunter, The, Stark, Richard, 43

Hurricane Punch, Dorsey, Tim, 19

I: The Creation of a Serial Killer, Olsen, Jack, 120

I Married a Dead Man, Irish, William, 74

Ice Harvest, The, Phillips, Scott, 157

Ice House, The, Walters, Minette, 102

If I Did It: Confessions of the Killer, The Goldman Family, 104

If You Really Loved Me: A True Story of Desire and Murder, Rule, Ann, 143

Iguana Love, Hendricks, Vicki, 20

In a Child's Name: The Legacy of a Mother's Murder, Maas, Peter, 72

In Broad Daylight, MacLean, Harry N., 119

In Cold Blood: A True Account of a Multiple Murder and Its Consequences, Capote, Truman, 11, 103

In the Best of Families: The Anatomy of a True Tragedy, McDougal, Dennis, 88

In the Cut, Moore, Susanna, 129

Incident at Big Sky: The True Story of Sheriff Johnny France and the Capture of the Mountain Men, France, Johnny, and Malcolm McConnell, 104

Indecent Exposure: A True Story of Hollywood and Wall Street, McClintick, David, 52

Index to Crime and Mystery Anthologies, Contento, William G., and Martin H. Greenberg, 168

Infanta, Meyer, Deon, 82

Informant, The: A True Story, Eichenwald, Kurt, 52

Innocent Man, The: Murder and Injustice in a Small Town, Grisham, John, 138

Instance of the Fingerpost, An, Pears, Iain, 130

Interface, Gores, Joe, 159
Introduction to the Detective Story, A, Panek, Leroy Lad, 181
Invitation to a Lynching, Miller, Gene, 141
Island, Perry, Thomas, 21

Jimmy Bench Press, Stella, Charlie, 35
Jimmy the Kid, Westlake, Donald E., 22
Judgment Day, Lancaster, Bob, and B. C. Hall, 118
Judgment Ridge: The True Story Behind the Dartmouth Murders, Lehr, Dick, and Mitchell Zuckoff, 71
Jugger, The, Stark, Richard, 44
Justice Crucified: The Story of Sacco and Vanzetti, Feuerlight, Roberta Strauss, 87

Kidnap: The Story of the Lindbergh Case, Waller, George, 146
Kill-off, The, Thompson, Jim, 67
Killer Books, Swanson, Jean, Dean James, and Anne Perry, 177
Killer Inside Me, The, Thompson, Jim, 115
Killer's Wife, The, Floyd, Bill, 107
Killtown, Stark, Richard, 44
Kiss Before Dying, A, Levin, Ira, 112
Kiss Tomorrow Goodbye, McCoy, Horace, 31

Lady Audley's Secret, Braddon, Mary Elizabeth, 123
Lady Investigates, The, Craig, Patricia, and Mary Cadogan, 180
Lament for a Lover, Highsmith, Patricia, 126
Last Days of Il Duce, The, Stansberry, Domenic, 101
Last Don, The, Puzo, Mario, 33
Last Gangster, The: From Cop to Wiseguy to FBI Informant: Big Ron Previte and the Fall of the American Mob, Anastasia, George, 36
Last Match, The, Dodge, David, 17
Last Quarry, The, Collins, Max (Allan), 79
Last Two to Hang, A, Jones, Elwyn, 71
Late Man, A, Girard, James Preston, 108
L'attentat, Khadra, Yamina, 81
Laura, Caspary, Vera, 147
Leather Maiden, Lansdale, Joe R., 65
Leavenworth Train: A Fugitive's Search for Justice in the Vanishing West, Jackson, Joe, 104

Legal Limit, The, Clark, Martin, 156
Lenient Beast, The, Brown, Fredric, 106
Light of Day, Saul, Jamie M., 131
Lights Out, Starr, Jason, 67
Likeness in Stone, A, Martin, J. Wallis, 98
Lindbergh: The Crime, Behn, Noel, 136
Line of Vision, Ellis, David, 94
Listening Walls, The, Millar, Margaret, 129
Little Boy Blue, Bunker, Edward, 56
Little Caesar, Burnett, W. R., 11, 27
Little Friend, The, Tartt, Donna, 133
Little Girl Is Dead, A, Golden, Harry, 138
Locked Room Murders and Other Impossible Crimes, Adey, Robert, 167
Long Dimanche de Fiançailles, Un, Japrisot, Sébastien, 81
Looking for Mr. Goodbar, Rossner, Judith, 130
Los Angeles, Smith, Peter Moore, 132
Lost Girls, Pyper, Andrew, 157
Love Hunter, The, Hassler, Jon, 80
Lowlife, The, Baron, Alexander, 75
Lush Life, Price, Richard, 42

Madman's Tale, The, Katzenbach, John, 111
Mafia Princess: Growing Up in Sam Giancana's Family, Giancana, Antoinette, 38
Mafiya, Stella, Charlie, 35
Make Mine a Mystery, Niebuhr, Gary Warren, 169, 181
Maltese Falcon, The, Hammett, Dashiell, 158
Mammoth Encyclopedia of Modern Crime Fiction, Ashley, Mike, 171
Man on a Leash, Williams, Charles, 136
Man Who Killed Shakespeare, The, Hodgson, Ken, 21
Man Who Robbed the Pierre, The: The Story of Bobby Comfort, Berkow, Ira, 51
Man with the Getaway Face, The, Stark, Richard, 43
Manchurian Candidate, The, Condon, Richard, 17
Manifesto for the Dead, Stansberry, Domenic, 50
Mask of Dimitrios, The, Ambler, Eric, 147
Master of the Delta, Cook, Thomas H., 92
Masters of Mystery, Thomson, H. Douglas, 182

Max, The, Bruen, Ken, and Jason Starr, 56

May God Have Mercy: A True Story of Crime and Punishment, Tucker, John C., 73

McTeague: A Story of San Francisco, Norris, Frank, 99

Mean Justice: A Town's Terror, a Prosecutor's Power, a Betrayal of Innocence, Humes, Edward, 52

Mean Streets and Raging Bulls, Martin, Richard, 173

Mémoires de Vidocq, Chef de la Police de Sureté, jusqu'en 1827, Vidocq, François Eugéne, 148

Memoirs of Vidocq, Principal Agent of the French Police until 1827, Vidocq, François Eugéne, 148

Memphis Murders, The, Meyer, Gerald, 119

Menaced Assassin, Gores, Joe, 108

Metzger's Dog, Perry, Thomas, 21

Miami Purity, Hendricks, Vicki, 80

Michigan Murders, The, Keyes, Edward, 118

Midnight Assassin: A Murder in America's Heartland, Bryan, Patricia L., and Thomas Wolf, 137

Minds of Billy Milligan, The, Keyes, Daniel, 140

Misbegotten Son, The: A Serial Killer and His Victims: The True Story of Arthur J, Shawcross, Olsen, Jack, 119

Mission Flats, Landay, William, 150

Mississippi Mud: A True Story from a Corner of the Deep South, Humes, Edward, 39

Modern Crime and Suspense Writers, Bloom, Harold, 179

Modern Mystery Writers, Bloom, Harold, 179

Modus Operandi, Winks, Robin W., 182

Moetsukita chizu, Abe, Kobo, 158

Mona, Block, Lawrence, 16

Money Shot, Faust, Christa, 94

Mongol Reply, The, Schutz, Benjamin M., 131

Monster of Florence, The, Preston, Douglas, and Mario Spezi, 120

Montana 1948, Watson, Larry, 135

Monthly Murders, Cook, Michael L., 168

Moon in the Gutter, The, Goodis, David, 125

Moonstone, The, Collins, Wilkie, 10, 62

Motherless Brooklyn, Lethem, Jonathan, 161

Mourner, The, Stark, Richard, 44

Mr. White's Confession, Clark, Robert, 78

Mulberry Tree, The, Frasca, John, 138

Murder at the Met: Based on the Exclusive Account of Detectives Mike Struk and Jerry Giorgio of How They Solved the Phantom of the Opera Case, Black, David, 69

Murder by Category, Machler, Tasha, 169

Murder Exchange, The, Kernick, Simon, 97

Murder for Pleasure, Haycraft, Howard, 180

Murder in Brentwood, Fuhrman, Mark, 154

Murder in Coweta County, Barnes, Margaret Anne, 69

Murder in Little Egypt, O'Brien, Darcy, 89

Murder in Retrospect, Burgess, Michael, and Jill H. Vassilakos, 168

Murder in Spokane: Catching a Serial Killer, Fuhrman, Mark, 117

Murder Ink, Winn, Dilys, 178

Murder Me for Nickels, Rabe, Peter, 33

Murder of a Shopping Bag Lady, The, Kates, Brian, 139

Murder of Regilla, The: A Case of Domestic Violence in Antiquity, Pomeroy, Sarah B., 142

Murder Will Out, Binyon, T. J., 179

Murderer Vine, The, Rifkin, Shepard, 163

"My Husband's Trying to Kill Me!": A True Story of Money, Marriage, and Murderous Intent, Schutze, Jim, 73

My Name Is Red, Pamuk, Orhan, 129

Mystery and Suspense Writers, Winks, Robin, and Maureen Corrigan, 172

Mystery Fanfare, Cook, Michael L., 168

Mystery of Edwin Drood, The, Dickens, Charles, 10, 105

Mystery Lover's Companion, The, Bourgeau, Art, 167

Mystery of a Hansom Cab, The, Hume, Fergus, 10, 122

Mystery Story, The, Ball, John, 179

Mystery Women, Barnett, Colleen A., 171

Mystic River, Lehane, Dennis, 82

Naked City, The, Willett, Ralph, 182

Name of the Game Is Death, The, Marlowe, Dan J., 98

Napoleon of Crime, The: The Life and Times of Adam Worth, Master Thief, Macintyre, Ben, 48

Night and the City, Kersh, Gerald, 31
Night Has a Thousand Eyes, Hopley,
    George, 127
Night of the Hunter, The, Grubb, Davis, 125
Night of the Jabberwock, The, Brown,
    Fredric, 91
Night Squad, Goodis, David, 149
Night Walker, Hamilton, Donald, 80
Nightfall, Goodis, David, 95
Nightlife, Perry, Thomas, 114
Nightmare Alley, Gresham, William
    Lindsay, 56
Ninth Juror, The, Chester, Giraud, 70
No Beast So Fierce, Edward Bunker, 41
No Country for Old Men, McCarthy,
    Cormac, 58
No House Limit, Fisher, Steve, 29
*No Lights No Siren: The Corruption and
    Redemption of an Inner City Cop*, Cea,
    Robert, 154
No Pockets in a Shroud, McCoy, Horace, 58
No Way Out, Fearing, Kenneth, 94
Nobody Runs Forever, Stark, Richard, 47
Nobody's Perfect, Westlake, Donald E., 22
Nothing Man, The, Thompson, Jim, 115
Nothing More Than Murder, Thompson,
    Jim, 67
Nothing Personal, Starr, Jason, 66
Novel Verdicts, Breen, Jon L., 175
Now You See Him, Gottlieb, Eli, 96
*Nutcracker: Money, Madness, Murder: A
    Family Album*, Alexander, Shana, 68

Of Missing Persons, Goodis, David, 149
Oliver Twist; or, the Parish Boy's Progress,
    Dickens, Charles, 10, 121
Omnibus of Crime, The, Sayers, Dorothy L.,
    9
100 Great Detectives, Jakubowski, Maxim,
    176
*One of Ours: Timothy McVeigh and the
    Oklahoma City Bombing*, Serrano,
    Richard A., 144
1001 Midnights, Pronzini, Bill, and Marcia
    Muller, 169
Operation Overkill, Marlowe, Dan J., 98
Orange Crush, Dorsey, Tim, 18
Origins of the American Detective Story, The,
    Panek, Leroy Lad, 181
*Our Guys: The Glen Ridge Rape and the
    Secret Life of the Perfect Suburb*,
    Lefkowitz, Bernard, 88

Out, Kirino, Natsuo, 57
Out of the Woodpile, Bailey, Frankie Y., 179
Outfit, The, Stark, Richard, 43
*Overbury Affair, The: The Murder Trail That
    Rocked the Court of King James I*, de
    Ford, Miriam Allen, 137
*Oxford Companion to Crime & Mystery
    Writing, The*, Herbert, Rosemary,
    172

Perfect Murder, The, Lehman, David, 181
Perma Red, Earling, Debra Magpie, 93
Person of Interest, A, Choi, Susan, 91
*Personal Memoirs of the First Great
    Detective, The*, Vidocq, François
    Eugéne, 148
Petals of Blood, Thiong'o, Ngúgí wa, 133
Petit Bleu de la Côte ouest, Manchette,
    Jean-Patrick, 98
Phantom Lady, Irish, William, 74
Pick-up, Willeford, Charles, 135
Pictorial History of Crime Films, A,
    Cameron, Ian, 173
Pistol Poets, The, Gischler, Victor, 95
Place of Execution, A, McDermid, Val, 150
Plain Truth, Picoult, Jodi, 83
Playback, Stark, Richard, 43
Plunder Squad, Stark, Richard, 45
Poet, The, Michael Connelly, 106
Point Blank, Stark, Richard, 43
*Poison Tree, The: A True Story of Family
    Violence and Revenge*, Prendergast,
    Alan, 72
Pomona Queen, Nunn, Kem, 66
Pop. 1280, Thompson, Jim, 148
Position du Tireur Couché, La , Manchette,
    Jean-Patrick, 82
Postman Always Rings Twice, The, Cain,
    James M., 11, 55
Power of the Dog, The, Winslow, Don, 153
Prelude to a Certain Midnight, Kersch,
    Gerald, 64
Primary Target, Collins, Max (Allan), 79
*Private Disgrace, A: Lizzie Borden by
    Daylight*, Lincoln, Victoria, 140
Private Lives of Private Eyes, Penzler, Otto,
    176
Probable Cause, Panek, Leroy Lad, 182
Profession of Violence, The, Pearson, John,
    40
Prone Gunman, The, Manchette,
    Jean-Patrick, 82

Pursuit, Perry, Thomas, 152

Quarry, Collins, Max (Allan), 78
Quarry's Cut, Collins, Max (Allan), 78
Quarry's Deal, Collins, Max (Allan), 78
Quarry's Greatest Hits, Collins, Max
    (Allan), 79
Quarry's List, Collins, Max (Allan), 78
Queenpin, Abbott, Megan, 28
Queen's Quorum, Queen, Ellery, 169

Rain Dogs, Doolittle, Sean, 93
Rare Coin Score, The, Stark, Richard, 44
Raveling, Smith, Peter Moore, 132
Rawhead, Bowker, David, 29
Read 'Em Their Writes, Niebuhr, Gary
    Warren, 181
Read On . . . Crime Fiction, Trott, Barry, 177
Reader and the Detective Story, The, Dove,
    George N., 180
*Reader's Guide to the American Novel of
    Detection, A*, Lachman, Marvin, 176
Reader's Guide to Classic British Mystery, A,
    Oleksiw, Susan, 177
*Reader's Guide to the Police Precedural
    Novel, A*, Vicarel, JoAnn, 177
Reader's Guide to the Private Eye Novel, A,
    Niebuhr, Gary Warren, 177
*Reader's Guide to the Spy and Thriller Novel,
    A*, Stone, Nancy-Stephanie, 177
Reader's Guide to the Suspense Novel, A,
    Jarvis, Mary Johnson, 176
Real World, Kirino, Natsuo, 128
Rebecca, du Maurier, Daphne, 124
Recoil, Thompson, Jim, 84
Recollections of a Detective-Police Officer, 10
Red Dragon, Harris, Thomas, 12, 109
Red Leaves, Cook, Thomas H., 124
*Reference Guide to Mystery and Detective
    Fiction*, Bleiler, Richard, 167
*Relentless Pursuit: A True Story of Family,
    Murder and the Prosecutor Who
    Wouldn't Quit*, Flynn, Kevin, 70
Rendezvous in Black, Woolrich, Cornell, 74
*Rescue Artist, The: A True Story of Art,
    Thieves, and the Hunt for a Missing
    Masterpiece*, Dolnick, Edward, 25
*Reversal of Fortune: Inside the von Bülow
    Case*, Dershowitz, Alan M., 70
Riaru Warudo, Kirino, Natsuo, 128
Ride the Nightmare, Matheson, Richard,
    128

Ripley Under Ground, Highsmith, Patricia,
    110
Ripley Under Water, Highsmith, Patricia,
    111
Ripley's Game, Highsmith, Patricia, 110
Road to Ruin, The, Westlake, Donald E., 24
Robbie's Wife, Hill, Russell, 57
*Rothstein: The Life, Times and Murder of the
    Criminal Genius Who Fixed the 1919
    World Series*, Pietrusza, David, 26
Ruined Map, The, Abe, Kobo, 158
Run Lethal, Stark, Richard, 44

Safe and Sound, Rhoades, J. D., 162
Saturday's Child, Banks, Ray, 158
*Savage Grace: The True Story of Fatal
    Relations in a Rich and Famous
    American Family*, Robins, Natalie
    and Steven M. Aronson, 142
Savage Night, Guthrie, Allan, 20
Savage Night, Thompson, Jim, 35
Scold's Bridle, The, Walters, Minette, 102
Score, The, Stark, Richard, 44
Screaming Mimi, The, Brown, Fredric, 106
Sculptress, The, Walters, Minette, 134
Secret Dead Men, Swierczynski, Duane,
    163
Seduction of Water, The, Goodman, Carol,
    63
Serenade, Cain, James M., 61
Serpent Girl, Carnahan, Matthew, 42
Seven Days of Peter Crumb, The, Glynn,
    Jonny, 108
Seven Keys to Baldpate, Biggers, Earl Derr,
    15
Seventh, The, Stark, Richard, 44
Shadow Boxer, Muller, Eddie, 59
Shadow of the Wind, The, Ruiz Zafón,
    Carlos, 100
Shakedown, Stella, Charlie, 35
Shape of Snakes, The, Walters, Minette,
    135
Sheppard Murder Case, The, Holmes, Paul,
    87
Shooting Dr. Jack, Green, Norman, 30
Shooting Star, Bloch, Robert, 159
Shotgun Opera, Gischler, Victor, 95
Shroud for Jesso, A, Rabe, Peter, 130
Sicilian, The, Puzo, Mario, 33
Silence, Perry, Thomas, 161
Silence of the Lambs, The, Harris, Thomas,
    12, 109

Silent Joe, Parker, T, Jefferson, 151

Silk Stalkings, Nichols, Victoria, and Susan Thompson, 176

Since the Layoffs, Levison, Iain, 112

Sister Carrie, Dreiser, Theodore, 10

Six Against the Rock, Howard, Clark, 25

Six Bad Things, Huston, Charlie, 31

Skin Palace, The, O'Connell, Jack, 83

Skin River, Sidor, Steven, 101

Slasher, The, Collins, Max (Allan), 78

Slayground, Stark, Richard, 45

Sleepers, Carcaterra, Lorenzo, 86

Sleeping Dogs, Perry, Thomas, 32

Sleuths, Inc., Eames, Hugh, 180

Sleuths, Sidekicks, and Stooges, Green, Joseph, and Jim Finch, 168

Slide, Bruen, Ken, and Jason Starr, 56

Small Death in Lisbon, A, Wilson, Robert, 68

Small Sacrifices: A True Story of Passion and Murder, Rule, Ann, 143

Snow Falling on Cedars, Guterson, David, 126

Sombra del Viento, La, Ruiz Zafón, Carlos, 100

"Somebody Is Lying": The Story of Dr. X, Farber, Myron, 117

Somebody's Husband, Somebody's Son: The Story of the Yorkshire Ripper, Burn, Gordon, 116

Someone Is Bleeding, Matheson, Richard, 113

Somewhere in the Night, Christopher, Nicholas, 173

Somnambulist, The, Barnes, Jonathan, 159

"Son": A Psychopath and His Victims, Olsen, Jack, 119

Son of a Grifter: The Twisted Tale of Sante and Kenny Kimes, the Most Notorious Con Artists in America, Walker, Kent, and Mark Schone, 27

Song Is You, The, Abbott, Megan, 122

Sour Lemon Score, The, Stark, Richard, 45

South of Heaven, Thompson, Jim, 134

Southland, Revoyr, Nina, 66

Spiderweb, Bloch, Robert, 15

Split, The, Stark, Richard, 44

St. James Guide to Crime and Mystery Writers, Rollyson, Carl, 172

Standing Still, Simmons, Kelly, 132

Star of the Sea, O'Connor, Joseph, 99

Stark, Bunker, Edward, 16

Steel Hit, The, Stark, Richard, 43

Sting Man, The: Inside ABSCAM, Greene, Robert W., 52

Stingray Shuffle, Dorsey, Tim, 19

Stone City, Smith, Mitchell, 84

Story-Teller, The, Highsmith, Partricia, 127

Strange Piece of Paradise, Jentz, Terri, 139

Stranger Beside Me, The, Rule, Ann, 120

Stranger in My Grave, A, Millar, Margaret, 129

Strangers on a Train, Highsmith, Patricia, 11, 63

Strangler, The, Landay, William, 111

Strangler, Mitchell, Corey, 119

Stark, Bunker, Edward, 16

Street of No Return, Goodis, David, 95

Subject Is Murder, The, Menendez, Albert J., 169

Suicide Squeeze, Gischler, Victor, 20

Suspect, Robotham, Michael, 100

Suspects, Thomson, David, 67

Suspension of Mercy, A, Highsmith, Patricia, 127

Suspicions of Mr. Whicher, The: A Shocking Murder and the Undoing of a Great Victorian Detective, Summerscale, Kate, 155

Sweet and Vicious, Schickler, David, 100

Sweet Slow Death, Block, Lawrence, 16

Swell Looking Babe, A, Thompson, Jim, 60

Swift Justice: Murder and Vengeance in a California Town, Farrell, Harry, 25

Takedown: The Fall of the Last Mafia Empire, Cowan, Rick, and Douglas Century, 37

Talked to Death: The Life and Murder of Alan Berg, Singular, Stephen, 40

Talented Mr. Ripley, The, Highsmith, Patricia, 110

Tangled Web, A, Blake, Nicholas, 41

Tapping the Source, Nunn, Kem, 65

Texas by the Tail, Thompson, Jim, 60

They Shoot Horses, Don't They? McCoy, Horace, 58

Thieves Like Us, Anderson, Edward, 41

Third Man, The, Graham, Greene, 50

Thirteenth Tale, The, Setterfield, Diane, 83

This Sweet Sickness, Highsmith, Patricia, 64

Those Who Walk Away, Highsmith, Patricia, 81

Three Month Fever: The Andrew Cunanan Story, Indiana, Gary, 118

Three Musketeers, The, Dumas, Alexander, 9

Three Sisters in Black, Zierold, Norman, 53

361, Westlake, Donald E, 68

Three to Kill, Manchette, Jean-Patrick, 98

Tidewater Blood, Hoffman, William, 96

Tijuana Straits, Nunn, Kem, 83

Till Death Us Do Part: A True Murder Mystery, Bugliosi, Vincent, and Ken Hurwitz, 69

Time of Predators, A, Gores, Joe, 80

To Kill a Mockingbird, Lee, Harper, 81

To the Last Breath: Three Women Fight for the Truth Behind a Child's Tragic Murder, Stowers, Carlton, 145

Tokyo Year One, Peace, David, 114

Too Late to Say Goodbye: A True Story of Murder and Betrayal, Rule, Ann, 120

Torpedo Juice, Dorsey, Tim, 19

Torsos, Cooke, John Peyton, 107

Tough Jews, Cohen, Rich, 37

Tough Luck, Starr, Jason, 60

Tourist Season, Hiaasen, Carl, 160

Tragedy in Dedham: The Story of the Sacco-Vanzetti Case, Russell, Francis, 90

Trail of Blood: A Father, a Son and a Tell-tale Crime Scene Investigation, Evans, Wanda Webb, 104

The Transgressors, Thompson, Jim, 153

Trespasses: Portrait of a Serial Rapist, Swindle, Howard, 145

Trial by Ordeal, Chessman, Caryl, 70

Triggerfish Twist, Dorsey, Tim, 18

True Deliverance, A: The Joan Little Case, Harwell, Fred, 138

True Story: Murder, Memoir, Mea Culpa, Finkel, Michael, 87

Trunk Murderess, The: Winnie Ruth Judd: The Truth About an American Crime Legend Revealed at Last, Bommersbach, Jana, 103

Tulia: Race, Cocaine and Corruption in a Small Texas Town, Blakeslee, Nate, 153

Turnaround, The, Pelecanos, George, 130

25th Hour, The, Benioff, David, 29

Twisted City, Starr, Jason, 101

Two Faces of January, The, Highsmith, Patricia, 96

Two-Way Split, Guthrie, Allan, 42

Unabomber: A Desire to Kill, Graysmith, Robert, 118

Undiscovered Country, Enger, Lin, 125

Unfinished Murder: The Capture of a Serial Rapist, Neff, James, 141

Unveiling Claudia: A True Story of Serial Murder, Keyes, Daniel, 88

Valachi Papers, The, Maas, Peter, 39

Vatican Connection, The, Hammer, Richard, 38

Vengeance Man, The, Marlowe, Dan J., 65

Vengeful Virgin, The, Brewer, Gil, 55

Vernon God Little, Pierre, D. B. C., 130

Very Long Engagement, A, Japrisot, Sébastien, 81

Very Much a Lady: The Untold Story of Jean Harris and Dr, Herman Tarnower, Alexandra, Shana, 86

Vidocq: The Personal Memoirs of the First Great Detective, Vidocq, François Eugéne,

Void Moon, Connelly, Michael, 42

Von Bülow Affair, The, Wright, William, 146

Walkaway, The, Phillips, Scott, 157

Waltz into Darkness, Irish, William, 127

Wasted: The Preppie Murder, Wolfe, Linda, 90

Watch Your Back! Westlake, Donald E., 24

Waterfront, Schulberg, Budd, 34

Way Past Legal, Green, Norman, 96

Weight of Water, The, Shreve, Anita, 131

Welcome to the Fallen Paradise, Sherman, Dayne, 131

Westies, The: Inside the Hell's Kitchen Irish Mob, English, T. J., 38

Whaleboat House, The, Mills, Mark, 82

What about Murder?, Breen, Jon L., 167

What about Murder? (1981–1991), Breen, Jon L., 167

What Mystery Do I Read Next?, Stilwell, Steven A., and Charles Montney, 170

What's So Funny?, Westlake, Donald E., 24

What's the Worst That Could Happen?, Westlake, Donald E., 23

Wheelman, The, Swierczynski, Duane, 47

When Corruption Was King: How I Helped the Mob Rule Chicago, Then Brought the Outfit Down, Cooley, Robert, with Hillel Levin, 37

While They Slept: An Inquiry into the Murder of a Family, Harrison, Kathryn, 87

Whitmore, Shapiro, Fred, 155

Who Don't It?, Hagen, Ordean A., 168

Whodunit, The, Benvenuti, Stefano, and Gianni Rizzoni, 175

Why Me?, Westlake, Donald E., 22

Wild Girl, The: The Notebooks of Ned Giles, 1932, Fergus, Jim, 94

Wild Town, Thompson, Jim, 115

Wiley's Lament, Waiwaiole, Lono, 84

Wiley's Refrain, Waiwaiole, Lono, 85

Wiley's Shuffle, Waiwaiole, Lono, 84

Winter of Frankie Machine, The, Winslow, Don, 36

Wireless, O'Connell, Jack, 114

Wisdom of the Bones, Hyde, Christopher, 111

Wiseguy: Life in a Mafia Family, Pileggi, Nicholas, 40

Witness to Myself, Shubin, Seymour, 100

Woman Detective, The, Klein, Kathleen Gregory, 180

Woman in White, The, Collins, Wilkie, 10, 121

Word Made Flesh, O'Connell, Jack, 151

Wounded and the Slain, The, Goodis, David, 96

Wrack, Bradley, James, 123

Written in Blood: A True Story of Murder and a Deadly 16-Year-Old Secret That Tore a Family Apart, Fanning, Diane, 117

Wrong Man, The: The Final Verdict on the Dr, Sam Sheppard Murder Case, Neff, James, 141

Zebra: The True Account of the 179 Days of Terror in San Francisco, Howard, Clark, 139

Subject Index

ABSCAM bribery scandal
  Greene, Robert W., *The Sting Man*, 52
Academia
  Cook, Thomas H., *The Chatham School Affair*, 92
  DeMarinis, Rick, *A Clod of Wayward Marl*, 124
  Gischler, Victor, *The Pistol Poets*, 95
  Moore, Susanna, *In the Cut*, 129
  Saul, Jamie M., *Light of Day*, 131
Acquittals
  Neff, James, *The Wrong Man*, 141
Actors and actresses
  Abbott, Megan, *The Song Is You*, 122
  Bardin, John Franklin, *The Deadly Percheron*, 75
  Dorsey, Tim, *The Big Bamboo*, 19
Adoption
  Parker, T. Jefferson, *Silent Joe*, 152
  Siegel, Barry, *A Death in White Bear Lake*, 144
Adultery
  Cain, James M., *The Postman Always Rings Twice*, 55
  Highsmith, Patricia, *Deep Water*, 64
  Rule, Ann, *And Never Let Her Go*, 144
Affairs
  Alexandra, Shana, *Very Much a Lady*, 86
  Bloom, John, and Jim Atkinson, *Evidence of Love*, 69
  Bruen, Ken, and Jason Starr
    Bust, 56
    Slide, 56
  Cook, Thomas H., *The Chatham School Affair*, 92
  Irish, William, *Phantom Lady*, 74
  Taylor, John, *The Count and the Confession*, 146
Afghanistan conflict
  Rhoades, J. D., *Safe and Sound*, 162
African Americans
  Cook, Thomas H., *Breakheart Hill*, 124
  Lee, Harper, *To Kill a Mockingbird*, 82

Albinos
  Smith, Peter Moore, *Los Angeles*, 132
Alcatraz prison
  Howard, Clark, *Six Against the Rock*, 25
Alcohol
  Sidor, Steven, *Skin River*, 101
Alcoholism
  Brown, Fredric, *The Screaming Mimi*, 106
  Goodis, David, *Street of No Return*, 95
  Willeford, Charles, *Pick-up*, 135
Alighieri, Dante
  Pearl, Matthew, *The Dante Club*, 66
Amish
  Picoult, Jodi, *Plain Truth*, 83
Amnesia
  Chute, Vern, *Flight of an Angel*, 92
  Clark, Robert, *Mr. White's Confession*, 78
  Phillips, Scott, *The Walkaway*, 157
  Spillane, Mickey, *Dead Street*, 152
  Walters, Minette, *The Dark Room*, 102
Amusement parks
  Stark, Richard, *Slayground*, 45
Anti-Semitism
  Golden, Harry, *A Little Girl Is Dead*, 138
  Singular, Stephen, *Talked to Death*, 40
Antiquities
  Hammett, Dashiell, *The Maltese Falcon*, 158
Apaches
  Fergus, Jim, *The Wild Girl*, 94
Archaeologists
  Bradley, James, *Wrack*, 123
Armed robbery
  Guthrie, Allan, *Two-Way Split*, 42
Arson
  Goodis, David, *Fire in the Flesh*, 63
  Rule, Ann, *Bitter Harvest*, 143
  Wambaugh, Joseph, *Fire Lover*, 155
  Winslow, Don
    California Fire and Life, 36
    The Dawn Patrol, 153

Art
    Dolnick, Edward, *The Rescue Artist*, 24
    Highsmith, Patricia, *Ripley Under
        Ground*, 110
    Pamuk, Orhan, *Benim Adim Kirmizi*,
        129
    Reit, Seymour, *The Day They Stole the
        Mona Lisa*, 26
    Stark, Richard, *Plunder Squad*, 45
    Westlake, Donald E.
        Nobody's Perfect, 22
        Watch Your Back! 24
Asian Americans
    Choi, Susan, *A Person of Interest*, 92
Asperger's syndrome
    Haddon, Mark, *The Curious Incident of
        the Dog in the Night Time*, 126
Assassination
    Collins, Max (Allan), *Primary Target*, 79
    Condon, Richard, *The Manchurian
        Candidate*, 17
    Dorsey, Tim, *Orange Crush*, 18
    Gischler, Victor
        Gun Monkeys, 30
        Shotgun Opera, 95
    Perry, Thomas, *The Butcher's Boy*, 32
    Weiss, Mike, *Double Play*, 73
Attorneys
    Humes, Edward, *Mean Justice*, 52
Auctions
    Welch, Louise, *The Cutting Room*, 135
Authors
    Ambler, Eric, *The Mask of Dimitrios*, 147
    Biggers, Earl Derr, *Seven Keys to
        Baldpate*, 15
    Block, Lawrence, *The Burglar in the Rye*,
        77
    Bowker, David, *Rawhead*, 29
    Colapinto, John, *About the Author*, 92
    DeMarinis, Rick, *A Clod of Wayward
        Marl*, 124
    Dorsey, Tim, *Stingray Shuffle*, 19
    Goodman, Carol, *The Seduction of
        Water*, 63
    Ruiz Zafón, Carlos, *La Sombra del
        Viento*, 100
    Setterfield, Diane, *The Thirteenth Tale*,
        84
Autism
    Haddon, Mark, *The Curious Incident of
        the Dog in the Night Time*, 126
Auto accidents
    Schiller, Lawrence, *Cape May Court
        House*, 90

Automobile theft
    Edgerton, Clyde, *The Bible Salesman*, 20
Automobiles
    Westlake, Donald E., *The Road to Ruin*, 24

Bail bondsmen
    Rhoades, J. D.
        The Devil's Right Hand, 162
        Good Day in Hell, 162
Ballet
    Antonio Skármeta, *The Dancer and the
        Thief*, 43
Bank robbery
    Anderson, Edward, *Thieves Like Us*, 41
    Goodis, David, *Nightfall*, 95
    Higgins, George V., *The Friends of Eddie
        Coyle*, 21
    Marlowe, Dan J., *The Name of the Game
        Is Death*, 98
    Stark, Richard
        Flashfire, 46
        Nobody Runs Forever, 47
    Swierczynski, Duane, *The Wheelman*, 47
    Thompson, Jim, *The Getaway*, 48
    Westlake, Donald E., *Bank Shot*, 22
Bars
    Fosburgh, Lacey, *Closing Time*, 137
    Westlake, Donald E., *Watch Your Back!*
        24
Baseball
    Huston, Charlie, *A Dangerous Man*, 31
    Pietrusza, David, *Rothstein*, 26
    Starr, Jason, *Lights Out*, 67
Baseball cards
    Block, Lawrence, *The Burglar Who
        Traded Ted Williams*, 76
    Gischler, Victor, *Suicide Squeeze*, 20
Basque Americans
    Mills, Mark, *Amagansett*, 83
Battlefield executions
    Japrisot, Sébastien, *Un Long Dimanche
        de Fiançailles*, 81
Bed and breakfasts
    Block, Lawrence, *The Burglar in the
        Library*, 77
Bibliomystery
    Ruiz Zafón, Carlos, *La Sombra del
        Viento*, 100
Bicycles
    Breslin, Jimmy, *The Gang That Couldn't
        Shoot Straight*, 29
Bigamy
    Braddon, Mary Elizabeth, *Lady
        Audley's Secret*, 123

Bikers
  Detroit, Michael, *Chain of Evidence*, 38
Biographers
  Setterfield, Diane, *The Thirteenth Tale*, 84
Black Dahlia murder
  Hodel, Steve, *Black Dahlia Avenger*, 139
Black Muslims
  Howard, Clark, *Zebra*, 139
Blackmail
  Phillips, Scott, *The Ice Harvest*, 157
  Starr, Jason, *Nothing Personal*, 66
Bodyguards
  Huston, Charlie, A *Dangerous Man*, 31
  Kernick, Simon, *The Murder Exchange*, 97
  Wignall, Kevin, *For the Dogs*, 85
Bogart, Humphrey
  Block, Lawrence, *The Burglar Who Thought He Was Bogart*, 77
Bombs
  Choi, Susan, *A Person of Interest*, 92
  Graysmith, Robert, *Unabomber*, 118
  Serrano, Richard A., *One of Ours*, 144
Bookies
  Pietrusza, David, *Rothstein*, 26
  Thompson, Jim, *A Swell-Looking Babe*, 60
Bookstores
  Block, Lawrence, *The Burglar Who Liked to Quote Kipling*, 76
Boston Strangler
  Junger, Sebastian, *A Death in Belmont*, 88
  Landay, William, *The Strangler*, 112
Bounty hunters
  Stark, Richard, *Nobody Runs Forever*, 47
Boxing
  Muller, Eddie, *The Distance*, 59
  Schulberg, Budd, *The Harder They Fall*, 34
Brainwashing
  Condon, Richard, *The Manchurian Candidate*, 17
Brothers
  Clark, Martin, *The Legal Limit*, 156
  Goodis, David, *Down There*, 80
  Kersh, Gerald, *Night and the City*, 31
  Landay, William, *The Strangler*, 112
  Meyer, Gerald, *The Memphis Murders*, 119
  Schulberg, Budd, *Waterfront*, 34
Brothers and sisters
  Abbott, Megan, *Die a Little*, 156
  Cook, Thomas H., *The Cloud of Unknowing*, 62

Burglars
  Block, Lawrence, *Burglars Can't Be Choosers*, 75
Cannibalism
  Murray, Sabina, *A Carnivore's Inquiry*, 113
Capers
  Rubinstein, Julian, *Ballad of the Whiskey Robber*, 90
Capital punishment
  Bledsoe, Jerry, *Death Sentenc*, 116
  Earley, Pete, *Circumstantial Evidence*, 154
  Jones, Elwyn, *The Last Two to Hang*, 71
  Tucker, John C., *May God Have Mercy*, 73
Captivity
  Fowles, John, *The Collector*, 108
Carnivals
  Gresham, William Lindsay, *Nightmare Alley*, 57
Carroll, Lewis
  Brown, Fredric, *The Night of the Jabberwock*, 91
Casinos
  Connelly, Michael, *Void Moon*, 42
  Stark, Richard, *Backflash*, 46
  Westlake, Donald E., *Bad News*, 23
Central Intelligence Agency
  Perry, Thomas, *Metzger's Dog*, 21
Child abuse
  Prendergast, Alan, *The Poison Tree*, 72
Child murderers
  Lippman, Laura, *Every Secret Thing*, 58
Children in jeopardy
  Bock, Charles, *Beautiful Children*, 122
  Bunker, Edward, *Little Boy Blue*, 56
  Chabon, Michael, *The Final Solution*, 159
  Cook, Thomas H., *Red Leaves*, 124
  Dobyns, Stephen, *The Church of Dead Girls*, 107
  Elkind, Peter, *The Death Shift*, 117
  Golden, Harry, *A Little Girl Is Dead*, 138
  Grubb, Davis, *The Night of the Hunter*, 125
  Hyde, Christopher, *Wisdom of the Bones*, 111
  Kersch, Gerald, *Prelude to a Certain Midnight*, 64
  Lehane, Dennis, *Mystic River*, 82
  Lippman, Laura, *Every Secret Thing*, 58
  Martin, J. Wallis, *The Bird Yard*, 65

Children in jeopardy (*cont.*)
    McDermid, Val, *A Place of Execution*, 151
    Olsen, Jack, *The Misbegotten Son*, 119
    O'Malley, Suzanne, "*Are You There Alone?*", 142
    Oney, Steve, *And the Dead Shall Rise*, 142
    Prendergast, Alan, *The Poison Tree*, 72
    Protess, David, and Rob Warden, *Gone in the Night*, 89
    Pyper, Andrew, *Lost Girls*, 157
    Rhoades, J. D., *Safe and Sound*, 162
    Rule, Ann, *Small Sacrifices*, 143
    Saul, Jamie M., *Light of Day*, 131
    Siegel, Barry, *A Death in White Bear Lake*, 144
    Smith, Peter Moore, *Raveling*, 132
    Stowers, Carlton, *To the Last Breath*, 145
    Summerscale, Kate, *The Suspicions of Mr. Whicher*, 155
    Thompson, Jim, *Child of Rage*, 134
    Walters, Minette
        The Breaker, 134
        The Scold's Bridle, 102
    Williams, Darren, *Angel Rock*, 136
    Winslow, Don, *The Dawn Patrol*, 153
Christmas
    Phillips, Scott, *The Ice Harvest*, 157
Civil rights
    Rifkin, Shepard, *The Murderer Vine*, 163
Club scene
    St. James, James, *Disco Bloodbath*, 53
Cocaine
    Dorsey, Tim, *Florida Roadkill*, 18
Coins
    Block, Lawrence, *The Burglar Who Studied Spinoza*, 76
    Stark, Richard, *The Rare Coin Score*, 44
Cold cases
    Gourevitch, Philip, *A Cold Case*, 104
Colonialism
    de Kretser, Michelle, *The Hamilton Case*, 156
    Thiong'o, Ngũgĩ wa, *Petals of Blood*, 133
Comic books
    Bock, Charles, *Beautiful Children*, 122
Coming-of-age
    Carnahan, Matthew, *Serpent Girl*, 42
    Dickens, Charles, *Oliver Twist; or, the Parish Boy's Progress*, 121
    Earling, Debra Magpie, *Perma Red*, 93
    Enger, Lin, *Undiscovered Country*, 125
    Fergus, Jim, *The Wild Girl* 94

Gores, Joe, *Cases*, 160
    Haddon, Mark, *The Curious Incident of the Dog in the Night Time*, 126
    Inness-Brown, Elizabeth, *Burning Marguerite*, 127
    Lee, Harper, *To Kill a Mockingbird*, 82
    Lehane, Dennis, *Mystic River*, 82
    Ruiz Zafón, Carlos, *La Sombra del Viento*, 100
    Tartt, Donna, *The Little Friend*, 133
    Watson, Larry, *Montana 1948*, 135
Commercial crimes
    Eichenwald, Kurt, *The Informant*, 52
Con artist
    Bunker, Edward, *Stark*, 16
    Dodge, David, *The Last Match*, 17
    Hodgson, Ken, *The Man Who Killed Shakespeare*, 21
    Rayner, Richard, *Drake's Fortune*, 26
Confessions
    The Goldman Family, *If I Did It*, 104
Construction
    Bojanowski, Marc, *The Dog Fighter*, 122
Convicts. *See also* Ex-convicts
    Walters, Minette, *The Sculptress*, 134
Corporations
    Harrison, Colin, *Bodies Electric*, 126
Corruption
    Dumas, Timothy, *Greentown*, 137
    Humes, Edward, *Mississippi Mud*, 39
    Levitt, Leonard, *Conviction*, 140
    McCoy, Horace
        No Pockets in a Shroud, 58
        Kiss Tomorrow Goodbye, 32
    Schulberg, Budd, *Waterfront*, 34
Cruise ships
    Dorsey, Tim, *Atomic Lobster*, 20
    Stark, Richard, *Backflash*, 46
Cults
    King, Laurie R., *A Darker Place*, 128
    Millar, Margaret, *How Like an Angel*, 161
Custody of children
    Schutz, Benjamin M., *The Mongol Reply*, 131

Dams
    Westlake, Donald E., *Drowned Hopes*, 23
Dance marathons
    McCoy, Horace, *They Shoot Horses, Don't They?*, 58
Dante. *See* Alighieri, Dante

Dartmouth College
  Lehr, Dick, and Mitchell Zuckoff,
      Judgment Ridge, 71
Death row
  Chessman, Caryl
      Cell 2455 Death Row, 70
      Trial by Ordeal, 70
Dentists
  Block, Lawrence, *The Burglar in the
      Closet*, 76
Depression
  Walters, Minette, *Fox Evil*, 68
Detectives
  Vidocq, François Eugéne, *Mémoires de
      Vidocq, Chef de la Police de Sureté,
      jusqu'en 1827*, 148
Developers
  Dorsey, Tim, *Torpedo Juice*, 19
Devil
  Hjortsberg, William, *Falling Angel*, 160
Diamonds
  Stark, Richard, *The Black Ice Score*, 45
  Collins, Wilkie, *The Moonstone*, 62
Diana, Princess of Wales (1961–1997)
  Cain, Tom, *The Accident Man*, 16
Diplomats
  Stark, Richard, *The Mourner*, 44
Dismemberment
  Kirino, Natsuo, *Out*, 57
Divorce
  Highsmith, Patricia, *Deep Water*, 64
  Rule, Ann, *Every Breath You Take*, 144
  Schutz, Benjamin M., *The Mongol Reply*,
      131
  Schutze, Jim, "*My Husband's Trying to
      Kill Me!*", 73
  Stowers, Carlton, *To the Last Breath*, 145
DNA
  Wambaugh, Joseph, *The Blooding*, 146
  Westlake, Donald E., *Bad News*, 23
Docks
  Goodis, David, *The Moon in the Gutter*,
      125
Doctors
  Alexandra, Shana, *Very Much a Lady*,
      86
  Farber, Myron, "*Somebody Is Lying*",
      117
  Olsen, Jack, "*Doc*", 141
Dogs
  Bojanowski, Marc, *The Dog Fighter*, 122
  Haddon, Mark, *The Curious Incident of
      the Dog in the Night Time*, 126

Highsmith, Patricia, *A Dog's Ransom*,
      149
Drowning
  Cook, Thomas H., *The Cloud of
      Unknowing*, 62
Drug Enforcement Agency
  Waiwaiole, Lono, *Wiley's Lament*, 84
  Winslow, Don
      The Death and Life of Bobby Z., 85
      The Power of the Dog, 153
Drugs
  Benioff, David, *The 25th Hour*, 29
  Blakeslee, Nate, *Tulia*, 154
  Bloch, Robert, *Shooting Star*, 159
  Block, Lawrence, *Mona*, 16
  Bruen, Ken, and Jason Starr, *Slide*, 56
  Bunker, Edward, *Stark*, 16
  Collins, Max (Allan), *The Broker*, 78
  Corbett, David
      The Devil's Redhead, 29
      Done for a Dime, 124
  Detroit, Michael, *Chain of Evidence*, 38
  Dickens, Charles, *The Mystery of Edwin
      Drood*, 105
  Doolittle, Sean
      The Cleanup, 93
      Rain Dogs, 93
  Dorsey, Tim, *Atomic Lobster*, 20
  Gischler, Victor, *The Pistol Poets*, 95
  Gores, Joe, *Interface*, 160
  Hendricks, Vicki, *Iguana Love*, 20
  Kernick, Simon, *The Crime Trade*, 150
  McCarthy, Cormac, *No Country for Old
      Men*, 58
  McKinty, Adrian, *Hidden River*, 151
  O'Connell, Jack, *Box Nine*, 151
  Perry, Thomas, *Metzger's Dog*, 21
  Pyper, Andrew, *Lost Girls*, 157
  Sakey, Marcus, *Good People*, 59
  Starr, Jason, *Twisted City*, 101
  Waites, Martyn, *Candleland*, 153
  Waiwaiole, Lono, *Wiley's Lament*, 84
  Williams, Charles, *Man on a Leash*, 136
  Winslow, Don
      The Death and Life of Bobby Z., 85
      The Power of the Dog, 153
  Woodrell, Daniel, *Give Us a Kiss*, 86
Dry cleaners
  Hendricks, Vicki, *Miami Purity*, 81

Earthquakes
  Lankford, Terrill Lee, *Earthquake
      Weather*, 98

Elections
  Dorsey, Tim, *Orange Crush*, 18
  Thompson, Jim, *Pop. 1280*, 148
Emasculation
  Thompson, Jim, *The Nothing Man*, 115
Embezzlement
  McClintick, David, *Indecent Exposure*,
    52
  Phillips, Scott, *The Ice Harvest*, 157
  Swan, Mary, *The Boys in the Trees*, 51
  Thompson, Jim, *A Hell of a Woman*, 51
Enforcers
  Higgins, George V., *The Digger's Game*,
    57
England, Victorian. *See* Victorian England
Environment
  McKinty, Adrian, *Hidden River*, 151
  Nunn, Kem, *Tijuana Straits*, 83
Escapes
  Bommersbach, Jana, *The Trunk
    Murderess*, 103
Espionage
  Chabon, Michael, *The Final Solution*,
    159
Estates
  du Maurier, Daphne, *Rebecca*, 125
  Westlake, Donald E., *The Road to Ruin*,
    24
Evangelists
  Stark, Richard, *Comeback*, 46
Excavations
  Bradley, James, *Wrack*, 123
Ex-convicts. *See also* Convicts
  Banks, Ray, *Saturday's Child*, 158
  Bourdain, Anthony, *The Bobby Gold
    Stories*, 41
  Bunker, Edward, *Dog Eat Dog*, 77
  Green, Norman, *Way Past Legal*, 96
  Lippman, Laura, *Every Secret Thing*, 58
  Nunn, Kem, *Ponoma Queen*, 66
  Stella, Charlie
    Cheapskates, 132
    Jimmy Bench Press, 35
  Thompson, Jim, *Recoil*, 84
Executions
  Mailer, Norman, *The Executioner's
    Song*, 71

Factory workers
  Kirino, Natsuo, *Out*, 57
False accusations
  Irish, William, *Phantom Lady*, 74
  Woolrich, Cornell, *The Black Path of
    Fear*, 36

False arrest
  Price, Richard, *Lush Life*, 43
False confessions
  Keyes, Daniel, *Unveiling Claudia*, 88
  Miller, Gene, *Invitation to a Lynching*,
    141
  Stansberry, Domenic, *The Confession*,
    115
False identity
  Braddon, Mary Elizabeth, *Lady
    Audley's Secret*, 123
  Collins, Wilkie, *Armadale*, 91
  Finkel, Michael, *True Story*, 87
  Goodis, David, *Dark Passage*, 95
  Hamilton, Donald, *Night Walker*, 80
  Highsmith, Patricia, *This Sweet
    Sickness*, 64
  Irish, William, *I Married a Dead Man*, 74
False imprisonment
  Highsmith, Patricia, *The Glass Cell*, 127
  Woolrich, Cornell, *The Black Angel*, 136
Families
  Cook, Thomas H.
    The Cloud of Unknowing, 62
    Red Leaves, 124
  Collins, Wilkie, *Armadale*, 91
  Cornwell, John, *Earth to Earth*, 86
  Flynn, Kevin, *Relentless Pursuit*, 71
  Guthrie, Allan, *Savage Night*, 20
  Williams, Darren, *Angel Rock*, 136
  Woodrell, Daniel, *Give Us a Kiss*, 86
Family feuds
  Hoffman, William, *Tidewater Blood*, 96
Fantasy
  Swierczynski, Duane, *Secret Dead Men*,
    163
Farms
  Cornwell, John, *Earth to Earth*, 86
  Hill, Russell, *Robbie's Wife*, 57
Fascism
  Singular, Stephen, *Talked to Death*, 40
Fathers and daughters
  Blanchard, Alice, *The Breathtaker*, 106
  Highsmith, Patricia, *Those Who Walk
    Away*, 81
  Hopley, George, *Night Has a Thousand
    Eyes*, 127
  Waiwaiole, Lono, *Wiley's Lament*, 84
Father and sons
  Banks, Ray, *Saturday's Child*, 158
  Cook, Thomas H.
    Master of the Delta, 92
    Red Leaves, 124
  Enger, Lin, *Undiscovered Country*, 125

Flynn, Kevin, *Relentless Pursuit*, 71
Gottlieb, Eli, *Now You See Him*, 96
Hodel, Steve, *Black Dahlia Avenger*, 139
O'Brien, Darcy, *Murder in Little Egypt*, 90
Parker, T. Jefferson, *Silent Joe*, 152
Thompson, Jim
 The Criminal, 134
 Cropper's Cabin, 133
 Texas by the Tail, 60
Williams, Charles, *Man on a Leash*, 136
Federal Bureau of Investigation
 Blum, Howard, *Gangland*, 36
 Eichenwald, Kurt, *The Informant*, 52
 Graysmith, Robert, *Unabomber*, 118
 Harris, Thomas
  Hannibal, 109
  Red Dragon, 109
  The Silence of the Lambs, 109
 King, Laurie R., *A Darker Place*, 128
 O'Brien, Joseph F., and Andrus Kurins,
  Boss of Bosses, 39
Female bonding
 Kirino, Natsuo, *Out*, 57
Firefighters
 Rozan, S. J., *Absent Friends*, 34
Fishermen
 Francisco, Ruth, *Good Morning,
  Darkness*, 149
 Mills, Mark, *Amagansett*, 83
Flathead Indians
 Earling, Debra Magpie, *Perma Red*, 93
Football
 Stark, Richard, *The Seventh*, 44
Forensics
 Evans, Wanda Webb, *Trail of Blood*, 104
Forgery
 Colapinto, John, *About the Author*, 92
Fortune telling
 Gresham, William Lindsay, *Nightmare
  Alley*, 56
Fox hunting
 Walters, Minette, *Fox Evil*, 68
Frames
 Block, Lawrence, *Burglars Can't Be
  Choosers*, 75
Friendship
 Gottlieb, Eli, *Now You See Him*, 96
 Lehane, Dennis, *Mystic River*, 82
Funerals
 Doolittle, Sean, *Dirt*, 93

Gambling
 Baron, Alexander, *The Lowlife*, 75
 Fisher, Steve, *No House Limit*, 30

Highsmith, Patricia, *Ripley's Game*, 110
Rabe, Peter, *Murder Me for Nickels*, 33
Stark, Richard
 Ask the Parrot, 47
 The Handle, 44
Starr, Jason, *Tough Luck*, 60
Thompson, Jim
 A Swell-Looking Babe, 60
 Texas by the Tail, 60
Gangs
 Bunker, Edward, *Dog Eat Dog*, 77
 Cook, Thomas H., *Blood Echoes*, 103
 Goodis, David
  Black Friday, 80
  The Burglar, 79
  Nightfall, 95
 MacDonald, John D., *The End of the
  Night*, 113
 McCoy, Horace, *Kiss Tomorrow
  Goodbye*, 32
 Westlake, Donald E., *The Hot Rock*, 22
Germany
 history (1945–1955)
  Puzo, Mario, *The Dark Arena*, 59
Ghosts
 Collins, Wilkie, *The Woman in White*,
  121
 Setterfield, Diane, *The Thirteenth Tale*, 84
 Swierczynski, Duane, *Secret Dead Men*,
  163
Gold
 Thompson, Jim, *The Golden Gizmo*, 67
Governors
 Dorsey, Tim, *Orange Crush*, 18
Grandfathers
 Dorsey, Tim, *Cadillac Beach*, 19
Grave robbery
 Westlake, Donald E., *Bad News*, 23
Great Britain. *See also* Victorian England
 history (Restoration, 1660–1688)
  Pears, Iain, *An Instance of the
   Fingerpost*, 130
Great Depression (1929–1939)
 Atwood, Margaret, *The Blind Assassin*,
  75
Greed
 Norris, Frank, *McTeague*, 99
Grief
 Walters, Minette, *Fox Evil*, 68
Guilt
 Goodis, David, *Fire in the Flesh*, 63
Guns
 Higgins, George V., *The Friends of Eddie
  Coyle*, 20

Gurus
  Bloch, Robert, *Spiderweb*, 16
Gypsies
  Olsen, Jack, *Hastened to the Grave*, 26

Handicapped
  Japrisot, Sébastien, *Un Long Dimanche de Fiançailles*, 81
  Tidyman, Ernest, *Dummy*, 146
Hansom cabs
  Hume, Fergus, *The Mystery of a Hansom Cab*, 122
Harbors
  Schulberg, Budd, *Waterfront*, 34
Hate crimes
  Bigsby, Christopher, *Beautiful Dreamer*, 91
Haunted houses
  Setterfield, Diane, *The Thirteenth Tale*, 84
Hearst, Patty
  Alexander, Shana, *Anyone's Daughter*, 103
Hell's Angels
  Detroit, Michael, *Chain of Evidence*, 38
High school athletics
  Lefkowitz, Bernard, *Our Guys*, 88
Historical
  Abbott, Megan, *Die a Little*, 156
  Barnes, Jonathan, *The Somnambulist*, 159
  Bean, Fred, *Black Gold*, 28
  Bojanowski, Marc, *The Dog Fighter*, 122
  Bradley, James, *Wrack*, 123
  Caspary, Vera, *Bedelia*, 106
  Chabon, Michael, *The Final Solution*, 159
  Claudel, Philippe, *Les Âmes Grises*, 148
  Cook, Thomas H., *The Chatham School Affair*, 92
  Cook, Thomas H., *Master of the Delta*, 92
  Cooke, John Peyton, *Torsos*, 106
  Earling, Debra Magpie, *Perma Red*, 93
  Edgerton, Clyde, *The Bible Salesman*, 20
  Gray, John MacLachlan, *The Fiend in Human*, 108
  Green, Norman, *The Angel of Montague Street*, 30
  Grubb, Davis, *The Night of the Hunter*, 125
  Guterson, David, *Snow Falling on Cedars*, 126

Haddon, Mark, *The Curious Incident of the Dog in the Night Time*, 126
Hjortsberg, William, *Falling Angel*, 160
Hodgson, Ken, *The Man Who Killed Shakespeare*, 21
Hyde, Christopher, *Wisdom of the Bones*, 111
Irish, William, *Waltz Into Darkness*, 128
Japrisot, Sébastien, *Un Long Dimanche de Fiançailles*, 81
Landay, William, *The Strangler*, 112
Mills, Mark, *Amagansett*, 83
Muller, Eddie, *The Distance*, 59
Muller, Eddie, *Shadow Boxer*, 59
Pamuk, Orhan, *Benim Adim Kirmizi*, 129
Peace, David, *Tokyo Year One*, 114
Phillips, Scott
  Cottonwood, 114
  The Ice Harvest, 157
  The Walkaway, 157
Shreve, Anita, *The Weight of Water*, 131
Swan, Mary, *The Boys in the Trees*, 51
Swierczynski, Duane, *Secret Dead Men*, 163
Thompson, Jim, *The Criminal*, 134
Walter, Jess, *Citizen Vince*, 85
Hit men
  Bowker, David, *Rawhead*, 29
  Bruen, Ken, and Jason Starr, *Bust*, 56
  Cain, Tom, *The Accident Man*, 16
  Collins, Max (Allan)
    The Broker, 78
    The Broker's Wife, 78
    The Dealer, 78
    The First Quarry, 79
    The Last Quarry, 79
    The Slasher, 78
  Gischler, Victor
    Gun Monkeys, 30
    Shotgun Opera, 95
  Goines, Donald, *Daddy Cool*, 79
  Gores, Joe, *Menaced Assassin*, 108
  Huston, Charlie, *A Dangerous Man*, 31
  Kernick, Simon
    The Business of Dying, 150
    A Good Day to Die, 150
  Levison, Iain, *Since the Layoffs*, 112
  Manchette, Jean-Patrick
    Petit Bleu de la Côte ouest, 98
    La Position du Tireur Couché, 82
  Perry, Thomas
    The Butcher's Boy, 32
    Sleeping Dogs, 32

Rabe, Peter, *Anatomy of a Killer*, 33
Schutze, Jim, *"My Husband's Trying to Kill Me!"*, 73
Skármeta, Antonio, *The Dancer and the Thief*, 43
Stark, Richard, *Firebreak*, 46
Stowers, Carlton, *Careless Whispers*, 27
Swierczynski, Duane, *The Blonde*, 133
Thompson, Jim, *Savage Night*, 35
Walter, Jess, *Citizen Vince*, 85
Wignall, Kevin, *For the Dogs*, 85
Winslow, Don, *The Winter of Frankie Machine*, 36
Hoboes
Thompson, Jim, *South of Heaven*, 134
Hockey
Rubinstein, Julian, *Ballad of the Whiskey Robber*, 90
Holmes, Oliver Wendell, Sr.
Pearl, Matthew, *The Dante Club*, 66
Holmes, Sherlock
Chabon, Michael, *The Final Solution*, 159
Homeless
Green, George Dawes, *The Caveman's Valentine*, 125
Kates, Brian, *The Murder of a Shopping Bag Lady*, 139
Walters, Minette, *The Echo*, 102
Homosexuality
Cain, James M., *Serenade*, 61
Carpenter, Don, *Hard Rain Falling*, 56
Cooke, John Peyton, *Torsos*, 106
Indiana, Gary, *Three Month Fever*, 118
Walters, Minette, *The Ice House*, 102
Welch, Louise, *The Cutting Room*, 135
Honeymoons
Highsmith, Patricia, *Those Who Walk Away*, 81
Williams, Charles, *Dead Calm*, 115
Hospitals
Farber, Myron, *"Somebody Is Lying"*, 117
Hotels
Berkow, Ira, *The Man Who Robbed the Pierre*, 51
Biggers, Earl Derr, *Seven Keys to Baldpate*, 15
Dorsey, Tim, *Hammerhead Ranch Motel*, 18
Goodman, Carol, *The Seduction of Water*, 63
Millar, Margaret, *Beast in View*, 98
Thompson, Jim

A Swell-Looking Babe, 60
Texas by the Tail, 60
Wild Town, 115
House detectives
Thompson, Jim, *Wild Town*, 115
Housing projects
Walters, Minette, *Acid Row*, 68
Hughes, Howard
Fay, Stephen, Lewis Chester, and Magnus Linklater, *Hoax*, 25
Hunting
Hassler, Jon, *The Love Hunter*, 80
Hurricanes
Dorsey, Tim
Hammerhead Ranch Motel, 18
Hurricane Punch, 19
Husbands and wives
Bledsoe, Jerry, *Before He Wakes*, 51
Bryan, Patricia L., and Thomas Wolf, *Midnight Assassin*, 137
Caspary, Vera, *Bedelia*, 106
Fanning, Diane, *Written in Blood*, 117
Goodis, David, *The Wounded and the Slain*, 96
Irish, William, *Phantom Lady*, 74
Millar, Margaret, *The Listening Walls*, 129
Norris, Frank, *McTeague*, 99
Perry, Thomas, *Fidelity*, 162
Pomeroy, Sarah B., *The Murder of Regilla*, 142
Protess, David, and Rob Warden, *Gone in the Night*, 89
Raymond, Derek, *How the Dead Live*, 152
Ruddick, James, *Death at the Priory*, 143
Rule, Ann, *Heart Full of Lies*, 52
Thompson, Jim, *The Getaway*, 48

Identity theft
Highsmith, Patricia
Ripley Under Ground, 110
The Talented Mr. Ripley, 110
Illumination
Pamuk, Orhan, *Benim Adim Kirmizi*, 129
Immigration
O'Connor, Joseph, *Star of the Sea*, 99
Incest
Kleiman, Dena, *A Deadly Silence*, 140
Robins, Natalie, and Steven M. Aronson, *Savage Grace*, 142
Infanticide
Elkind, Peter, *The Death Shift*, 117
Picoult, Jodi, *Plain Truth*, 83

Infidelity
  Hopley, George, *Fright*, 97
  Stansberry, Domenic, *The Confession*,
    115
Informants
  Anastasia, George, *The Last Gangster*,
    36
  Blum, Howard, *Gangland*, 36
  Cooley, Robert, with Hillel Levin,
    When Corruption Was King, 37
  Eichenwald, Kurt, *The Informant*, 52
  English, T. J., *Born to Kill*, 38
  Stark, Richard, *Nobody Runs Forever*, 47
Inheritance
  Coleman, Jonathan, *At Mother's
    Request*, 24
  Sherman, Dayne, *Welcome to the Fallen
    Paradise*, 131
  Walters, Minette, *The Scold's Bridle*, 102
Insider trading
  Stewart, James B., *Den of Thieves*, 53
Insurance fraud
  Cain, James M., *Double Indemnity*, 49
  Perry, Thomas, *Death Benefits*, 50
  Rule, Ann, *Heart Full of Lies*, 52
  Thompson, Jim, *Nothing More Than
    Murder*, 67
  Westlake, Donald E., *Nobody's Perfect*,
    22
  Zierold, Norman, *Three Sisters in Black*,
    53
Islamic culture
  Pamuk, Orhan, *Benim Adim Kirmizi*,
    129
Islands
  Inness-Brown, Elizabeth, *Burning
    Marguerite*, 127
  Shreve, Anita, *The Weight of Water*, 131
  Stark, Richard, *The Handle*, 44

James I, King of England (1566–1625)
  de Ford, Miriam Allen, *The Overbury
    Affair*, 137
Japanese Americans
  Guterson, David, *Snow Falling on
    Cedars*, 126
  Revoyr, Nina, *Southland*, 66
Jewels
  Block, Lawrence, *The Burglar in the
    Closet*, 76
  Bunker, Edward, *No Beast So Fierce*, 41
  Dorsey, Tim, *Cadillac Beach*, 19
  Goodis, David, *The Burglar*, 79
  Miller, Wade, *Branded Woman*, 42

Schickler, David, *Sweet and Vicious*, 100
Stark, Richard
  Breakout, 46
  Richard, *Flashfire*, 46
Stella, Charlie, *Eddie's World*, 34
Westlake, Donald E.
  The Hot Rock, 22
  *What's the Worst That Could
    Happen?*, 23
  Why Me?, 22
Jews
  Cohen, Rich, *Tough Jews*, 37
Journalists
  Brown, Fredric
    The Night of the Jabberwock, 91
    The Screaming Mimi, 106
  Doolittle, Sean, *Dirt*, 93
  Gray, John MacLachlan, *The Fiend in
    Human*, 108
  Guterson, David, *Snow Falling on
    Cedars*, 126
  Lansdale, Joe R., *Leather Maiden*, 65
  Starr, Jason, *Twisted City*, 101
  Walters, Minette
    The Echo, 102
    The Sculptress, 134
Junkyards
  Green, Norman, *Shooting Dr. Jack*, 30
Juries
  Chester, Giraud, *The Ninth Juror*, 70

Kenya
  Thiong'o, Ngũgĩ wa, *Petals of Blood*, 133
Kidnapping
  Behn, Noel, *Lindbergh*, 136
  Cook, Thomas H., *Red Leaves*, 124
  Dorsey, Tim, *The Big Bamboo*, 19
  Farrell, Harry, *Swift Justice*, 25
  Fisher, Jim, *The Ghosts of Hopewell*, 137
  Fowles, John, *The Collector*, 108
  France, Johnny, and Malcolm
    McConnell, *Incident at Big Sky*,
    104
  Highsmith, Patricia, *The Boy Who
    Followed Ripley*, 110
  Kennedy, Ludovic, *The Airman and the
    Carpenter*, 140
  Levien, David, *City of the Sun*, 161
  Miller, Wade, *Branded Woman*, 42
  Rabe, Peter, *Benny Muscles In*, 33
  Rhoades, J. D., *Safe and Sound*, 162
  Simmons, Kelly, *Standing Still*, 132
  Spillane, Mickey, *Dead Street*, 152
  Starr, Jason, *Nothing Personal*, 66

Thompson, Jim, *After Dark, My Sweet*, 60

Waller, George, *Kidnap*, 146

Westlake, Donald E.
Good Behavior, 23
Jimmy the Kid, 22
The Road to Ruin, 24

Kipling, Rudyard
Block, Lawrence, *The Burglar Who Liked to Quote Kipling*, 76

Lawyers
Phillips, Scott, *The Ice Harvest*, 157

Lesbians
Revoyr, Nina, *Southland*, 66

Libraries
Block, Lawrence, *The Burglar in the Library*, 77

Lions
Hopley, George, *Night Has a Thousand Eyes*, 127

Longfellow, Henry Wadsworth
Pearl, Matthew, *The Dante Club*, 66

Lottery
Norris, Frank, *McTeague*, 99

Louvre
Reit, Seymour, *The Day They Stole the Mona Lisa*, 26

Lowell, James Russell
Pearl, Matthew, *The Dante Club*, 66

Lynching
Bigsby, Christopher, *Beautiful Dreamer*, 91
Farrell, Harry, *Swift Justice*, 25
Oney, Steve, *And the Dead Shall Rise*, 142

Magicians
Barnes, Jonathan, *The Somnambulist*, 159

Mail robbery
Tidyman, Ernest, *Big Bucks*, 49

Manson, Charles
Bugliosi, Vincent, and Curt Gentry, *Helter Skelter*, 116

Marathons
McCoy, Horace, *They Shoot Horses, Don't They?*, 58

Marriage
Dorsey, Tim, *Torpedo Juice*, 19
du Maurier, Daphne, *Rebecca*, 125
Khadra, Yamina, *L'attentat*, 81
Thompson, Jim, *A Hell of a Woman*, 51

Mathematics
Haddon, Mark, *The Curious Incident of the Dog in the Night Time*, 126

Matricide
Robins, Natalie, and Steven M. Aronson, *Savage Grace*, 142
Rule, Ann, *If You Really Loved Me*, 143

Memory
Clark, Robert, *Mr. White's Confession*, 78
Katzenbach, John, *The Madman's Tale*, 111
Millar, Margaret, *A Stranger in My Grave*, 129
Shubin, Seymour, *Witness to Myself*, 100
Woolrich, Cornell, *The Black Curtain*, 102

Mental health
McDougal, Dennis, *In the Best of Families*, 89
Thompson, Jim, *After Dark, My Sweet*, 60

Mercy killings
Hassler, Jon, *The Love Hunter*, 80

Mesmerism
Dickens, Charles, *The Mystery of Edwin Drood*, 105

Metropolitan Opera House
Black, David, *Murder at the Met*, 69

Mexican–American border
Nunn, Kem, *Tijuana Straits*, 83

Migrant workers
Cray, Ed, *Burden of Proof*, 116

Mines
Hodgson, Ken, *The Man Who Killed Shakespeare*, 21

Miniaturists
Pamuk, Orhan, *Benim Adim Kirmizi*, 129

Missing money
Phillips, Scott, *The Walkaway*, 157

Missing persons
Abbott, Megan, *The Song Is You*, 122
Abe, Kobo, *The Ruined Map*, 158
Dobyns, Stephen, *The Church of Dead Girls*, 107
Francisco, Ruth, *Good Morning, Darkness*, 149
Goodis, David, *Of Missing Persons*, 149
Nunn, Kem, *Tapping the Source*, 65
Smith, Peter Moore, *Los Angeles*, 132

Models
    Jonas, George, and Barbara Amiel, *By Persons Unknown*, 139
Molestation
    Starr, Jason, *Hard Feelings*, 66
Mona Lisa
    Reit, Seymour, *The Day They Stole the Mona Lisa*, 26
Mondrian, Piet
    Block, Lawrence, *The Burglar Who Painted Like Mondrian*, 76
Money laundering
    Dorsey, Tim, *Florida Roadkill*, 18
Mormons
    Alexander, Shana, *Nutcracker*, 69
    Lindsey, Robert, *A Gathering of Saints*, 26
    Olsen, Jack, *"Doc"*, 141
Mothers and daughters
    Goodman, Carol, *The Seduction of Water*, 63
    King, Laurie R., *A Darker Place*, 128
    Murray, Sabina, *A Carnivore's Inquiry*, 113
    Tartt, Donna, *The Little Friend*, 133
Mothers and sons
    Condon, Richard, *The Manchurian Candidate*, 17
    de Kretser, Michelle, *The Hamilton Case*, 156
    Landay, William, *Mission Flats*, 150
    McDougal, Dennis, *In the Best of Families*, 89
    Olsen, Jack, *"Son"*, 119
    Thompson, Jim, *The Grifters*, 48
    Walker, Kent, and Mark Schone, *Son of a Griftera*, 27
Motion pictures
    Bloch, Robert, *Shooting Star*, 159
    Dorsey, Tim, *The Big Bamboo*, 19
    Lankford, Terrill Lee, *Earthquake Weather*, 98
    McClintick, David, *Indecent Exposure*, 52
    Puzo, Mario, *The Last Don*, 33
    Smith, Peter Moore, *Los Angeles*, 132
    Stansberry, Domenic, *Manifesto for the Dead*, 50
    Thomson, David, *Suspects*, 67
Mountain men
    France, Johnny, and Malcolm McConnell, *Incident at Big Sky*, 104

Movie theaters
    O'Connell, Jack, *The Skin Palace*, 83
    Thompson, Jim, *Nothing More Than Murder*, 67
Mugging
    Price, Richard, *Lush Life*, 42
Multiple personalities
    Keyes, Daniel, *The Minds of Billy Milligan*, 140
Munch, Edvard
    Dolnick, Edward, *The Rescue Artist*, 24
Murder for profit
    Brewer, Gil, *The Vengeful Virgin*, 55
Musicians
    Corbett, David, *Done for a Dime*, 124
    Goodis, David, *Down There*, 80
    Mitchell, Corey, *Strangler*, 119
    Nunn, Kem, *Ponoma Queen*, 66
    Waiwaiole, Lono, *Wiley's Refrain*, 85
Mutes
    Chabon, Michael, *The Final Solution*, 159

Nanotechnology
    Swierczynski, Duane, *The Blonde*, 133
Native Americans
    Earling, Debra Magpie, *Perma Red*, 93
    Rhoades, J. D., *The Devil's Right Hand*, 162
    Watson, Larry, *Montana 1948*, 135
    Westlake, Donald E., *Bad News*, 23
Nazi Germany
    Wilson, Robert, *A Small Death in Lisbon*, 68
Neighborhoods
    Dorsey, Tim, *Triggerfish Twist*, 18
Newspapers
    Brown, Fredric, *The Night of the Jabberwock*, 91
    McCoy, Horace, *No Pockets in a Shroud*, 58
    Rozan, S. J., *Absent Friends*, 34
    Thompson, Jim
        The Criminal, 134
        The Nothing Man, 115
Nightclubs
    Kernick, Simon, *The Murder Exchange*, 97
Norwegian immigrants
    Shreve, Anita, *The Weight of Water*, 131
Nuns
    Westlake, Donald E., *Why Me?*, 22
Nurses
    Thompson, Jim, *The Grifters*, 48

Obsession
    Abe, Kobo, *The Ruined Map*, 158
    Brown, Fredric, *The Far Cry*, 123
    Fowles, John, *The Collector*, 108
    Francisco, Ruth, *Good Morning,*
        Darkness, 149
    Goodis, David, *Of Missing Persons*, 149
    Highsmith, Patricia, *A Dog's Ransom*,
        149
    Rule, Ann
        Every Breath You Take, 144
        Everything She Ever Wanted, 143
    Stansberry, Domenic, *The Last Days of*
        Il Duce, 101
    Stout, Rex, *How Like a God*, 132
Ocean travel
    O'Connor, Joseph, *Star of the Sea*, 99
Oedipal complex
    Thompson, Jim, *A Swell-Looking Babe*,
        60
Oil
    Bean, Fred, *Black Gold*, 28
Opera
    Cain, James M., *Serenade*, 61
Organized crime
    Abbott, Megan, *Queenpin*, 28
    Anastasia, George, *The Last Gangster*,
        36
    Banks, Ray, *Saturday's Child*, 158
    Bean, Fred, *Black Gold*, 28
    Blum, Howard, *Gangland*, 36
    Breslin, Jimmy
        The Gang That Couldn't Shoot
            Straight, 29
        The Good Rat, 36
    Burnett, W. R., *Little Caesar*, 27
    Cain, Paul, *Fast One*, 28
    Carr, Howie, *The Brothers Bulger*, 37
    Cohen, Rich, *Tough Jews*, 37
    Cooley, Robert, with Hillel Levin,
        When Corruption Was King, 37
    Cowan, Rick, and Douglas Century,
        Takedown, 37
    Cummings, John, and Ernest Volkman,
        Goombata, 37
    English, T. J.
        Born to Kill, 38
        The Westiesb, 38
    Fitzgerald, F. Scott, *The Great Gatsby*, 49
    Giancana, Antoinette, *Mafia Princess*,
        38
    Gischler, Victor
        Gun Monkeys, 30
        Shotgun Opera, 95

Goodis, David, *Night Squad*, 149
Gores, Joe, *Menaced Assassin*, 108
Green, Norman
    The Angel of Montague Street, 30
    Dead Cat Bounce, 30
    Shooting Dr. Jack, 30
Hammer, Richard, *The Vatican*
    Connection, 38
Hammett, Dashiell, *The Glass Key*, 28
Higgins, George V.
    Cogan's Trade, 21
    The Digger's Game, 57
Huston, Charlie, *Caught Stealing*, 31
Lehr, Dick, and Gerard O'Neill, *Black*
    Mass, 39
Maas, Peter, *The Valachi Papers*, 39
O'Brien, Joseph F., and Andrus Kurins,
    Boss of Bosses, 39
Pearson, John, *The Profession of*
    Violence, 40
Perry, Thomas
    The Butcher's Boy, 32
    Nightlife, 114
    Sleeping Dogs, 32
Phillips, Scott, *The Ice Harvest*, 157
Pileggi, Nicholas, *Wiseguy*, 40
Pistone, Joseph D., with Richard
    Woodley, *Donnie Brasco*, 40
Puzo, Mario
    The Fortunate Pilgrim, 32
    The Godfather, 32
    The Last Don, 33
    The Sicilian, 32
Rabe, Peter
    Benny Muscles In, 33
    Murder Me for Nickels, 33
Schulberg, Budd
    The Harder They Fall, 34
    Waterfront, 34
Stark, Richard
    Butcher's Moon, 46
    The Hunter, 43
    The Outfit, 43
    Plunder Squad, 45
Stella, Charlie
    Charlie Opera, 35
    Eddie's World, 34
    Jimmy Bench Press, 35
    Mafiya, 35
    Shakedown, 35
Thompson, Jim, *Savage Night*, 35
Walter, Jess, *Citizen Vince*, 85
Westlake, Donald E., *Watch Your Back!*
    24

Organized crime (*cont.*)
  Winslow, Don
    California Fire and Life, 36
    The Winter of Frankie Machine, 36
  Woolrich, Cornell, *The Black Path of
    Fear,* 36
Orphans
  Dickens, Charles, *Oliver Twist; or, the
    Parish Boy's Progress,* 121
Oxford University
  Martin, J. Wallis, *A Likeness in Stone,* 98
  Pears, Ian, *An Instance of the Fingerpost,*
    130

Palestinian–Israeli relations
  Khadra, Yamina, *L'attentat,* 81
Paranoia
  Gottlieb, Eli, *Now You See Him,* 96
  Green, George Dawes, *The Caveman's
    Valentine,* 125
Parents and children
  Englade, Ken, *Beyond Reason,* 61
Parkinson's disease
  Robotham, Michael, *Suspect,* 100
Parricide
  Harrison, Kathryn, *While They Slept,* 87
Parrots
  Chabon, Michael, *The Final Solution,*
    159
Patricide
  Alexander, Shana, *Nutcracker,* 69
  McGinniss, Joe, *Cruel Doubt,* 61
Pedophilia
  Martin, J. Wallis, *The Bird Yard,* 65
  Meyer, Deon, *Infanta,* 82
  Walters, Minette, *Acid Row,* 68
Peeping Toms
  Highsmith, Patricia, *The Cry of the Owl,*
    64
Penicillin
  Puzo, Mario, *The Dark Arena,* 59
Photography
  Fergus, Jim, *The Wild Girl,* 94
  O'Connell, Jack, *The Skin Palace,* 83
  Walters, Minette, *The Dark Room,* 102
Physicians
  O'Brien, Darcy, *Murder in Little Egypt,*
    89
  Rule, Ann, *Bitter Harvest,* 143
  Stewart, James B., *Blind Eye,* 121
  Thompson, Thomas, *Blood and Money,*
    105
Pimps
  Waiwaiole, Lono, *Wiley's Shuffle,* 84

Pipeline
  Thompson, Jim, *South of Heaven,* 134
Poe, Edgar Allan
  Connelly, Michael, *The Poet,* 106
  Stashower, Daniel, *The Beautiful Cigar
    Girl,* 145
Poisons
  Ruddick, James, *Death at the Priory,*
    143
Poker
  Waiwaiole, Lono, *Wiley's Refrain,* 85
Police
  Collins, Wilkie, *The Moonstone,* 62
Police corruption
  Blakeslee, Nate, *Tulia,* 154
  Cea, Robert, *No Lights No Siren,* 154
  Doolittle, Sean, *Rain Dogs,* 93
  Goodis, David, *Night Squad,* 149
  Kernick, Simon
    The Business of Dying, 150
    The Crime Trade, 150
  O'Donnell, Lawrence, Jr., *Deadly Force,*
    154
  Preston, Douglas, and Mario Spezi, *The
    Monster of Florence,* 120
Police pursuit
  Thompson, Jim, *The Getaway,* 48
Political crimes
  Kertész, Imre, *Detective Story,* 150
Politics
  Parker, T. Jefferson, *Silent Joe,* 152
  Rule, Ann, *And Never Let Her Go,* 144
Pollution
  Nunn, Kem, *Tijuana Straits,* 83
Pool
  Carpenter, Don, *Hard Rain Falling,* 56
Pornography
  Collins, Max (Allan), *The Slasher,* 78
  Faust, Christa, *Money Shot,* 94
  Millar, Margaret, *Beast in View,* 98
  Stella, Charlie, *Mafiya,* 35
  Welch, Louise, *The Cutting Room,* 135
Post partum depression
  O'Malley, Suzanne, *"Are You There
    Alone?",* 142
Post-traumatic stress disorder/syndrome
  Rhoades, J. D., *The Devil's Right Hand,*
    162
Poverty
  Earling, Debra Magpie, *Perma Red,* 93
Pregnancy
  Dreiser, Theodore, *An American
    Tragedy,* 63
  Levin, Ira, *A Kiss Before Dying,* 112

Priests
Schulberg, Budd, *Waterfront*, 34
Prison breaks
Goodis, David, *Dark Passage*, 95
Howard, Clark, *Six Against the Rock*, 25
Hunter, Stephen, *Dirty White Boys*, 97
Jackson, Joe, *Leavenworth Train*, 105
Stark, Richard, *Breakout*, 46
Prisons
Benioff, David, *The 25th Hour*, 29
Bruen, Ken, and Jason Starr, *The Max*, 56
Bunker, Edward
Animal Factory, 61
Education of a Felon, 24
Little Boy Blue, 56
Carpenter, Don, *Hard Rain Falling*, 56
Chessman, Caryl
Cell 2455 Death Row, 70
Trial by Ordeal, 70
Harris, Thomas, *The Silence of the Lambs*, 109
Harwell, Fred, *A True Deliverance*, 136
Highsmith, Patricia, *The Glass Cell*, 127
Muller, Eddie, *Shadow Boxer*, 59
Smith, Mitchell, *Stone City*, 84
Walters, Minette, *The Sculptress*, 134
Private investigators
Abe, Kobo, *The Ruined Map*, 158
Barnes, Jonathan, *The Somnambulist*, 159
Ellin, Stanley, *The Eighth Circle*, 159
Gores, Joe, *Hammett*, 160
Hjortsberg, William, *Falling Angel*, 160
Lethem, Jonathan
Gun, with Occasional Music, 161
Motherless Brooklyn, 161
Olsen, Jack, *Hastened to the Grave*, 26
Perry, Thomas
Fidelity, 162
Silence, 162
Private schools
Cook, Thomas H., *The Chatham School Affair*, 92
Profilers
Perry, Thomas, *Pursuit*, 152
Prosecutors
Katzenbach, John, *The Madman's Tale*, 111
Prostitutes
Connelly, Michael, *Chasing the Dime*, 123
Fuhrman, Mark, *Murder in Spokane*, 117
Goines, Donald, *Daddy Cool*, 79

Gray, John MacLachlan, *The Fiend in Human*, 108
Olsen, Jack, *The Misbegotten Son*, 119
Rule, Ann, *Green River, Running Red*, 120
Simon, Michael, *Dirty Simon*, 152
Stella, Charlie, *Mafiya*, 35
Thompson, Jim, *Child of Rage*, 134
Waiwaiole, Lono, *Wiley's Shuffle*, 84
Psychiatric hospitals
Katzenbach, John, *The Madman's Tale*, 111
Psychiatrists
Bardin, John Franklin, *The Deadly Percheron*, 75
Gresham, William Lindsay, *Nightmare Alley*, 56
Psychics
Hopley, George, *Night Has a Thousand Eyes*, 127
Psychologists
Robotham, Michael, *Suspect*, 100
Thompson, Jim, *Recoil*, 84
Psychotherapy
McNamara, Eileen, *Breakdown*, 89
Psychotics
Thompson, Jim, *The Killer Inside Me*, 115
Publishing
Fearing, Kenneth, *The Big Clock*, 94

Race relations
Barnes, Margaret Anne, *Murder in Coweta County*, 69
Bigsby, Christopher, *Beautiful Dreamer*, 91
Carpenter, Don, *Hard Rain Falling*, 56
Carr, A. H. Z., *Finding Maubee*, 16
Cook, Thomas H., *Breakheart Hill*, 124
Junger, Sebastian, *A Death in Belmont*, 88
Lee, Harper, *To Kill a Mockingbird*, 82
Miller, Gene, *Invitation to a Lynching*, 141
Pelecanos, George, *The Turnaround*, 130
Revoyr, Nina, *Southland*, 66
Rifkin, Shepard, *The Murderer Vine*, 163
Shapiro, Fred, *Whitmore*, 155
Walters, Minette, *The Shape of Snakes*, 135
Racism
Harwell, Fred, *A True Deliverance*, 138
Howard, Clark, *Zebra*, 139

Radicals
    Feuerlight, Roberta Strauss, *Justice
        Crucified*, 87
    Russell, Francis, *Tragedy in Dedham*, 90
Radio
    O'Connell, Jack, *Wireless*, 114
    Singular, Stephen, *Talked to Death*, 40
Railroads
    Dorsey, Tim, *The Stingray Shuffle*, 19
    Highsmith, Patricia, *Strangers on a
        Train*, 63
    Irish, William, *I Married a Dead Man*, 74
Rape
    Block, Lawrence, *The Burglar on the
        Prowl*, 77
    Goodis, David, *The Moon in the Gutter*,
        125
    Harwell, Fred, *A True Deliverance*, 138
    Keyes, Daniel, *The Minds of Billy
        Milligan*, 140
    Lee, Harper, *To Kill a Mockingbird*, 82
    Lefkowitz, Bernard, *Our Guys*, 88
    Neff, James, *Unfinished Murder*, 141
    Olsen, Jack
        "Doc", 141
        "Son", 119
    Stannard, David E., *Honor Killing*, 73
    Swindle, Howard, *Trespasses*, 145
    Thompson, Jim, *The Criminal*, 134
    Wambaugh, Joseph, *The Blooding*, 146
Rare books
    Ruiz Zafón, Carlos, *La Sombra del
        Viento*, 100
Rare documents
    Lindsey, Robert, *A Gathering of Saints*,
        26
Real estate
    Block, Lawrence, *The Girl with the Long
        Green Hair*, 16
Reconstructive surgery
    Stark, Richard, *The Man with the
        Getaway Face*, 43
Reform school
    Carcaterra, Lorenzo, *Sleepers*, 86
Refugees
    Graham, Greene, *The Third Man*, 50
Relics
    Westlake, Donald E.
        Don't Ask, 23
        What's So Funny?, 24
Religion
    Schickler, David, *Sweet and Vicious*, 100
    Westlake, Donald E., *Don't Ask*, 23

Repo men
    Gischler, Victor, *Suicide Squeeze*, 20
Reservations
    Earling, Debra Magpie, *Perma Red*, 93
Reservoirs
    Martin, J. Wallis, *A Likeness in Stone*, 98
Restaurants
    Bourdain, Anthony, *The Bobby Gold
        Stories*, 41
Retirement communities
    Spillane, Mickey, *Dead Street*, 152
Revenge
    Bloom, John, and Jim Atkinson,
        Evidence of Love, 69
    Collins, Max (Allan), *The Broker's Wife*,
        78
    Faust, Christa, *Money Shot*, 94
    Fitzgerald, F. Scott, *The Great Gatsby*, 49
    Goodis, David, *Street of No Return*, 95
    Gores, Joe
        Dead Man, 160
        A Time of Predators, 80
    Guthrie, Allan, *Two-Way Split*, 42
    Harris, Thomas, *Hannibal*, 109
    Highsmith, Patricia
        The Glass Cell, 127
        Ripley Under Water, 111
    Jentz, Terri, *Strange Piece of Paradise*,
        139
    Marlowe, Dan J., *The Name of the Game
        Is Death*, 98
    Matheson, Richard, *Ride the Nightmare*,
        128
    Meyer, Deon, *Infanta*, 82
    Millar, Margaret, *Beast in View*, 98
    Miller, Wade, *Branded Woman*, 42
    Muller, Eddie, *Shadow Boxer*, 59
    Nunn, Kem, *Ponoma Queen*, 66
    O'Connell, Jack, *Word Made Flesh*, 151
    Pelecanos, George, *The Turnaround*, 130
    Puzo, Mario, *The Dark Arena*, 59
    Rifkin, Shepard, *The Murderer Vine*, 163
    Sidor, Steven, *Skin River*, 101
    Stansberry, Domenic, *The Last Days of
        Il Duce*, 101
    Stark, Richard
        Deadly Edge, 45
        Dirty Money, 47
        The Hunter, 43
        The Jugger, 43
        The Outfit, 43
        Plunder Squad, 45
        The Sour Lemon Score, 43
    Starr, Jason, *Hard Feelings*, 66

Stella, Charlie
  Charlie Opera, 35
  Cheapskates, 132
  Mafiya, 35
Swierczynski, Duane, *Secret Dead Men*,
  163
Thompson, Jim
  Pop. 1280, 148
  The Transgressors, 153
Thompson, Thomas, *Blood and Money*,
  105
Walters, Minette, *The Shape of Snakes*, 135
Westlake, Donald E.
  361, 68
  *What's the Worst That Could
    Happen?*, 23
Wignall, Kevin, *For the Dogs*, 85
Woolrich, Cornell
  The Bride Wore Black, 136
  Rendezvous in Black, 74
Riots
  Goodis, David, *Street of No Return*, 95
  Walters, Minette, *Acid Row*, 68
Robbery
  Capote, Truman, *In Cold Blood*, 103
  Duncombe, Stephen, and Andrew
    Mattson, *The Bobbed Haired
    Bandit*, 48
  Starr, Jason, *Fake I.D.*, 47
Romance
  Anderson, Edward, *Thieves Like Us*, 41
  Block, Lawrence, *The Burglar Who
    Thought He Was Bogart*, 77
  Cain, James M., *The Postman Always
    Rings Twice*, 55
  Caspary, Vera, *Laura*, 147
  Doolittle, Sean, *The Cleanup*, 93
  Fitzgerald, F. Scott, *The Great Gatsby*, 49
  Guterson, David, *Snow Falling on
    Cedars*, 126
  Hammett, Dashiell, *The Glass Key*, 28
  Inness-Brown, Elizabeth, *Burning
    Marguerite*, 127
  Irish, William, *Waltz into Darkness*, 127
  Rabe, Peter, *Anatomy of a Killer*, 33
  Schickler, David, *Sweet and Vicious*, 100
Runaways
  Earling, Debra Magpie, *Perma Red*, 93
  Waites, Martyn, *Candleland*, 153

Sacco and Vanzetti
  Feuerlight, Roberta Strauss, *Justice
    Crucified*, 87
  Russell, Francis, *Tragedy in Dedham*, 90

Sailing
  Walters, Minette, *The Breaker*, 134
Salish
  Earling, Debra Magpie, *Perma Red*, 93
Scams
  Block, Lawrence, *The Girl with the Long
    Green Hair*, 16
  Chavarría, Daniel, *Adios Muchachos*, 17
  Thompson, Jim, *Texas by the Tail*, 60
Schizophrenia
  Cook, Thomas H., *The Cloud of
    Unknowing*, 62
  Smith, Peter Moore, *Raveling*, 132
School massacres
  Pierre, D. B. C., *Vernon God Little*, 130
Science fiction
  Lethem, Jonathan, *Gun, with Occasional
    Music*, 161
Scotland Yard
  Summerscale, Kate, *The Suspicions of
    Mr. Whicher*, 155
Self-help
  Bloch, Robert, *Spiderweb*, 16
September 11, 2001, terrorist attacks
  Rozan, S. J., *Absent Friends*, 34
Serial killer
  Blanchard, Alice, *The Breathtaker*, 106
  Bledsoe, Jerry, *Death Sentence*, 116
  Brown, Fredric
    The Lenient Beast, 106
    The Screaming Mimi, 106
  Bugliosi, Vincent, and Curt Gentry,
    Helter Skelter, 116
  Burn, Gordon, *Somebody's Husband,
    Somebody's Son*, 116
  Caspary, Vera, *Bedelia*, 106
  Connelly, Michael, *The Poet*, 106
  Cooke, John Peyton, *Torsos*, 106
  Cray, Ed, *Burden of Proof*, 116
  Denton, Bradley, *Blackburn*, 107
  Dobyns, Stephen, *The Church of Dead
    Girls*, 107
  Dorsey, Tim, *Hurricane Punch*, 19
  Elkind, Peter, *The Death Shift*, 117
  Farber, Myron, *"Somebody Is Lying"*,
    117
  Floyd, Bill, *The Killer's Wife*, 107
  Frank, Gerold, *The Boston Strangler*, 117
  Fuhrman, Mark, *Murder in Spokane*, 117
  Girard, James Preston, *The Late Man*,
    108
  Glynn, Jonny, *The Seven Days of Peter
    Crumb*, 108
  Gores, Joe, *Menaced Assassin*, 108

Serial killer (*cont.*)
  Gray, John MacLachlan, *The Fiend in
    Human,* 108
  Harris, Thomas
    Hannibal, 109
    Hannibal Rising, 109
    Red Dragon, 109
    The Silence of the Lambs, 109
  Hyde, Christopher, *Wisdom of the
    Bones,* 111
  Indiana, Gary, *Three Month Fever,* 118
  Katzenbach, John, *The Madman's Tale,*
    111
  Keyes, Edward, *The Michigan Murders,*
    118
  Landay, William, *The Strangler,* 112
  Larson, Eric, *The Devil in the White City,*
    118
  Lindsay, Jeff
    Darkly Dreaming Dexter, 112
    Dearly Devoted Dexter, 112
    Dexter in the Dark, 113
  Matheson, Richard
    Fury on Sunday, 113
    Someone Is Bleeding, 113
  Meyer, Gerald, *The Memphis Murders,*
    119
  Mitchell, Corey, *Strangler,* 119
  Murray, Sabina, *A Carnivore's Inquiry,*
    113
  O'Connell, Jack, *Wireless,* 114
  Olsen, Jack
    I: The Creation of a Serial Killer, 120
    The Misbegotten Son, 119
  Peace, David, *Tokyo Year One,* 114
  Perry, Thomas, *Nightlife,* 114
  Phillips, Scott, *Cottonwood,* 114
  Preston, Douglas, and Mario Spezi, *The
    Monster of Florence,* 120
  Rule, Ann
    Green River, Running Red, 120
    The Stranger Beside Me, 120
    Too Late to Say Goodbye, 120
  Stewart, James B., *Blind Eye,* 121
  Thompson, Jim, *The Nothing Man,* 115
  Woolrich, Cornell
    Black Alibi, 116
    The Bride Wore Black, 136
Sex
  Moore, Susanna, *In the Cut,* 129
  Rossner, Judith, *Looking for Mr.
    Goodbar,* 130
  Stout, Rex, *How Like a God,* 132
  Wolfe, Linda, *Wasted,* 90

Sex industry
  Waiwaiole, Lono, *Wiley's Lament,* 84
Sexual abuse
  Thompson, Jim, *Child of Rage,* 134
Sheriffs
  Thompson, Jim, *The Killer Inside Me,*
    115
Shipboard
  Shreve, Anita, *The Weight of Water,* 131
  Williams, Charles, *Dead Calm,* 115
Shipwrecks
  Bradley, James, *Wrack,* 123
Simpson, O. J.
  Fuhrman, Mark, *Murder in Brentwood,* 154
  The Goldman Family, *If I Did It,* 104
Sisters
  Atwood, Margaret, *The Blind Assassin,*
    75
  Tartt, Donna, *The Little Friend,* 133
  Zierold, Norman, *Three Sisters in Black,*
    53
Small town life
  Thompson, Jim, *The Kill-off,* 67
Sociopaths
  Glynn, Jonny, *The Seven Days of Peter
    Crumb,* 108
  Highsmith, Patricia
    Ripley Under Ground, 110
    The Talented Mr. Ripley, 110
  Walker, Kent, and Mark Schone, *Son of
    a Grifter,* 27
Somnambulism
  Barnes, Jonathan, *The Somnambulist,*
    159
South, The
  Cook, Thomas H., *Breakheart Hill,* 124
  Lee, Harper, *To Kill a Mockingbird,* 82
Spousal abuse
  Harrison, Colin, *Bodies Electric,* 126
Stadiums
  Stark, Richard, *The Seventh,* 44
Stalkers
  Floyd, Bill, *The Killer's Wife,* 107
Stamps
  Block, Lawrence, *The Burglar Who
    Painted Like Mondrian,* 76
Statutes
  Stark, Richard, *The Mourner,* 44
Suicide
  Cornwell, John, *Earth to Earth,* 86
  Goodis, David, *The Moon in the Gutter,*
    125
  Highsmith, Patricia
    A Suspension of Mercy, 127

Those Who Walk Away, 81
McCoy, Horace, *They Shoot Horses, Don't They?*, 58
McNamara, Eileen, *Breakdown*, 89
Perry, Thomas, *Dead Aim*, 99
Rule, Ann, *Too Late to Say Goodbye*, 91
Saul, Jamie M., *Light of Day*, 131
Tartt, Donna, *The Little Friend*, 133
Taylor, John, *The Count and the Confession*, 146

Sûreté
Vidocq, François Eugéne, *Mémoires de Vidocq, Chef de la Police de Sureté, jusqu'en 1827*, 148

Surfing
Nunn, Kem, *Tapping the Source*, 65

Surveillance
Sanders, Lawrence, *The Anderson Tapes*, 34

Symbionese Liberation Army
Alexander, Shana, *Anyone's Daughter*, 103

Tate, Sharon
Bugliosi, Vincent and Curt Gentry, *Helter Skelter*, 116

Taverns
Dorsey, Tim, *Torpedo Juice*, 19

Teachers
Schwartz-Nobel, Loretta, *Engaged to Murder*, 53

Teenaged mothers
Picoult, Jodi, *Plain Truth*, 83

Teenagers
Cook, Thomas H., *Red Leaves*, 124
Kirino, Natsuo, *Riaru Warudo*, 128

Telemarketing
Starr, Jason, *Cold Caller*, 50

Television shows
Highsmith, Patricia, *A Suspension of Mercy*, 127

Terminally ill
Hyde, Christopher, *Wisdom of the Bones*, 111

Terrorism
Dorsey, Tim, *Atomic Lobster*, 20
Khadra, Yamina, *L'attentat*, 81
Serrano, Richard A., *One of Ours*, 144

Terrorists
Choi, Susan, *A Person of Interest*, 92
Westlake, Donald E., *Why Me?*, 22

Texas Rangers
Bean, Fred, *Black Gold*, 28

Theology
Pears, Ian, *An Instance of the Fingerpost*, 130

Thieves
Macintyre, Ben, *The Napoleon of Crime*, 48

Thompson, Jim
Stansberry, Domenic, *Manifesto for the Dead*, 50

Tornadoes
Blanchard, Alice, *The Breathtaker*, 106

Torture
Kertész, Imre, *Detective Story*, 150

Tourette's syndrome
Lethem, Jonathan, *Motherless Brooklyn*, 161
Walters, Minette, *The Shape of Snakes*, 135

Tourism
Hiaasen, Carl, *Tourist Season*, 160

Tourist agency
Dorsey, Tim, *Cadillac Beach*, 19

Travel
Gores, Joe, *Cases*, 160

Travelers
Walters, Minette, *Fox Evil*, 68

Trench warfare
Japrisot, Sébastien, *Un Long Dimanche de Fiançailles*, 81

Trials
Black, David, *Murder at the Met*, 69
Bloom, John, and Jim Atkinson, *Evidence of Love*, 69
Brand, Christianna, *Heaven Knows Who*, 86
Bryan, Patricia L., and Thomas Wolf, *Midnight Assassin*, 137
Bugliosi, Vincent, and Ken Hurwitz, *Till Death Us Do Part*, 69
Capote, Truman, *In Cold Blood*, 103
Carcaterra, Lorenzo, *Sleepers*, 86
Cartwright, Gary, *Blood Will Tell*, 70
Chester, Giraud, *The Ninth Juror*, 70
Cook, Thomas H., *Blood Echoes*, 103
de Kretser, Michelle, *The Hamilton Case*, 156
Dershowitz, Alan M., *Reversal of Fortune*, 70
Earley, Pete, *Circumstantial Evidence*, 154
Ellis, David, *Line of Vision*, 94
Farber, Myron, *"Somebody Is Lying"*, 117

Trials (*cont.*)
    Feuerlight, Roberta Strauss, *Justice Crucified*, 87
    Flynn, Kevin, *Relentless Pursuit*, 71
    Frasca, John, *The Mulberry Tree*, 138
    Fuhrman, Mark, *Murder in Brentwood*, 154
    Gentry, Curt, *Frame-up*, 138
    Godfrey, Ellen, *By Reason of Doubt*, 71
    Grisham, John, *The Innocent Man, Murder and Injustice in a Small Town*, 138
    Guterson, David, *Snow Falling on Cedars*, 126
    Holmes, Paul, *The Sheppard Murder Case*, 87
    Horne, Jed, *Desire Street*, 88
    Humes, Edward, *Mean Justice*, 52
    Lancaster, Bob, and B. C. Hall, *Judgment Day*, 118
    Lee, Harper, *To Kill a Mockingbird*, 82
    MacLean, Harry N., *In Broad Daylight*, 119
    Mayer, Robert, *The Dreams of Ada*, 141
    Naifeh, Steven, and Gregory White Smith, *Final Justice*, 72
    Neff, James, *The Wrong Man*, 141
    O'Donnell, Lawrence, Jr., *Deadly Force*, 154
    O'Malley, Suzanne, *"Are You There Alone?"*, 142
    Oney, Steve, *And the Dead Shall Rise*, 142
    Prendergast, Alan, *The Poison Tree*, 72
    Protess, David, and Rob Warden, *Gone in the Night*, 89
    Pyper, Andrew, *Lost Girls*, 157
    Russell, Francis, *Tragedy in Dedham*, 90
    Savage, Mildred, *A Great Fall*, 72
    Schiller, Lawrence, *Cape May Court House*, 90
    Schutz, Benjamin M., *The Mongol Reply*, 131
    Schutze, Jim, *By Two and Two*, 144
    Shapiro, Fred, *Whitmore*, 155
    Stannard, David E., *Honor Killing*, 73
    Sullivan, Robert, *The Disappearance of Dr. Parkman*, 145
    Traver, Robert, *Anatomy of a Murder*, 156
    Tucker, John C., *May God Have Mercy*, 73
    Weiss, Mike, *Double Play*, 73
    Wolfe, Linda, *Wasted*, 90

    Wright, William, *The Von Bülow Affair*, 146
Triangles (Interpersonal relations)
    Abbott, Megan, *Queenpin*, 28
    Cain, James M.
        Double Indemnity, 49
        The Postman Always Rings Twice, 55
    Corbett, David, *The Devil's Redhead*, 29
    Dreiser, Theodore, *An American Tragedy*, 63
    Ellin, Stanley, *The Eighth Circle*, 159
    Ellis, David, *Line of Vision*, 94
    Guthrie, Allan, *Two-Way Split*, 42
    Highsmith, Patricia
        The Cry of the Owl, 64
        A Game for the Living, 64
        This Sweet Sickness, 64
        The Two Faces of January, 96
    Hill, Russell, *Robbie's Wife*, 57
    Rabe, Peter, *A Shroud for Jesso*, 130
    Thompson, Jim
        A Hell of a Woman, 51
        Nothing More Than Murder, 67
Truth
    Pears, Ian, *An Instance of the Fingerpost*, 130
Twins
    Schutze, Jim, *By Two and Two*, 144

Unabomber
    Graysmith, Robert, *Unabomber*, 118
Undertakers
    Doolittle, Sean, *Dirt*, 93
Unemployment
    Levison, Iain, *Since the Layoffs*, 112
United States Air Force
    Stark, Richard, *The Green Eagle Score*, 45
United States Army
    Rhoades, J. D., *Safe and Sound*, 162
Uxoricide
    Fanning, Diane, *Written in Blood*, 117
    Highsmith, Patricia
        The Blunderer, 126
        A Suspension of Mercy, 127
    Maas, Peter, *In a Child's Name*, 72
    Rule, Ann,
        Dead by Sunset, 72
        Too Late to Say Goodbye, 120
    Wright, William, *The Von Bülow Affair*, 146

Vatican
    Hammer, Richard, *The Vatican Connection*, 38

Victorian England. *See also* Great Britain
  Barnes, Jonathan, *The Somnambulist*, 159
  Dickens, Charles, *Oliver Twist; or, the Parish Boy's Progress*, 121
  Macintyre, Ben, *The Napoleon of Crime*, 48
  Ruddick, James, *Death at the Priory*, 143
Vietnamese conflict
  English, T. J., *Born to Kill*, 38
  Green, Norman, *The Angel of Montague Street*, 30
  Thornburg, Newton, *Cutter and Bone*, 101

Wall Street
  Stewart, James B., *Den of Thieves*, 53
War
  Japrisot, Sébastien, *Un Long Dimanche de Fiançailles*, 81
Waste removal
  Cowan, Rick, and Douglas Century, *Takedown*, 37
Watts Riot (1965)
  Revoyr, Nina, *Southland*, 66
Weddings
  Block, Lawrence, *The Burglar in the Library*, 77
Westerns
  Bloch, Robert, *Shooting Star*, 159
  Fergus, Jim, *The Wild Girl*, 94
  Phillips, Scott, *Cottonwood*, 114
Widows
  Atwood, Margaret, *The Blind Assassin*, 75
Wildfires
  Doolittle, Sean, *Burn*, 93

Wills
  Revoyr, Nina, *Southland*, 66
  Walters, Minette, *The Scold's Bridle*, 102
Winter weather
  Guterson, David, *Snow Falling on Cedars*, 126
Witness Protection Program
  Stella, Charlie, *Eddie's World*, 35
  Walter, Jess, *Citizen Vince*, 85
World Series
  Pietrusza, David, *Rothstein*, 26
World War I
  Claudel, Philippe, *Les Âmes Grises*, 148
  Japrisot, Sébastien, *Un Long Dimanche de Fiançailles*, 81
World War II
  Chabon, Michael, *The Final Solution*, 159
  Graham, Greene, *The Third Man*, 50
  Harris, Thomas, *Hannibal Rising*, 109
  Mills, Mark, *Amagansett*, 83
  Peace, David, *Tokyo Year One*, 114
  Puzo, Mario, *The Dark Arena*, 69
World Wide Web
  Connelly, Michael, *Chasing the Dime*, 123
World's Columbian Exposition of 1893
  Larson, Eric, *The Devil in the White City*, 118
Wrestling
  Dorsey, Tim, *Orange Crush*, 18

Yorkshire Ripper
  Burn, Gordon, *Somebody's Husband, Somebody's Son*, 116

Zen Buddhism
  Lethem, Jonathan, *Motherless Brooklyn*, 161

Locations Index

Countries Other Than the United States

Africa
  Dhaba
    Stark, Richard, *The Black Ice Score*,
      45
Australia
  Melbourne
    Hume, Fergus, *The Mystery of a*
      Hansom Cab, 122
  New South Wales
    Angel Rock
      Williams, Darren, *Angel Rock*,
        136
    Bradley, James, *Wrack*, 123
Austria
  Vienna
    Graham, Greene, *The Third Man*, 50

Balkans
  Ambler, Eric, *The Mask of Dimitrios*, 147
Bimini
  Hendricks, Vicki, *Iguana Love*, 20

Canada
  Emden
    Swan, Mary, *The Boys in the Trees*,
      51
  Ontario
    Jonas, George, and Barbara Amiel,
      By Persons Unknown, 139
    Murdock, Lake St. Christopher
      Pyper, Andrew, *Lost Girls*, 157
  Port Ticonderoga
    Atwood, Margaret, *The Blind*
      Assassin, 75
Caribbean
  Perry, Thomas, *Island*, 21
  St. Caro, Gracedieu
    Carr, A. H. Z., *Finding Maubee*, 16
Central America
  Kertész, Imre, *Detective Story*, 150
Ceylon
  Colombo
    de Kretser, Michelle, *The Hamilton*
      Case, 156

Kijygana
  de Kretser, Michelle, *The Hamilton*
    Case, 156
Nuwara Eliya
  de Kretser, Michelle, *The Hamilton*
    Case, 156
Chile
  Santiago
    Antonio Skármeta, *The Dancer and*
      the Thief, 43
Crete
  Highsmith, Patricia, *The Two Faces of*
    January, 96
Cuba
  Havana
    Chavarría, Daniel, *Adios*
      Muchachos, 17
    Woolrich, Cornell, *The Black Path of*
      Fear, 36

England
  General
    Braddon, Mary Elizabeth, *Lady*
      Audley's Secret, 123
    Summerscale, Kate, *The Suspicions*
      of Mr. Whicher, 155
    Walters, Minette, *The Sculptress*,
      134
  Bassingdale Estates
    Walters, Minette, *Acid Row*, 68
  Bath
    Perry, Thomas, *Sleeping Dogs*, 32
  Brighton
    Blake, Nicholas, *A Tangled Web*, 41
  Cambridge
    Setterfield, Diane, *The Thirteenth*
      Tale, 84
  Cloisterham
    Dickens, Charles, *The Mystery of*
      Edwin Drood, 105
  Cornwall
    du Maurier, Daphne, *Rebecca*, 125
  Cumberland
    Collins, Wilkie, *The Woman in*
      White, 121

England (*cont.*)
  Derbyshire
    Burxon
      McDermid, Val, *A Place of
        Execution,* 151
    Scardale
      McDermid, Val, *A Place of
        Execution,* 151
  Dorset
    General
      Hill, Russell, *Robbie's Wife,* 57
      Walters, Minette, *The Breaker,*
        134
    Dorchester
      Walters, Minette, *The Shape of
        Snakes,* 135
    Fontwell
      Walters, Minette, *The Scold's
        Bridle,* 102
    Shenstead
      Walters, Minette, *Fox Evil,* 68
  Hampshire
    Walters, Minette, *The Ice House,* 102
  Leicestershire
    Wambaugh, Joseph, *The Blooding,* 146
  Liverpool
    Robotham, Michael, *Suspect,* 100
  London
    Barnes, Jonathan, *The
      Somnambulist,* 159
    Baron, Alexander, *The Lowlife,* 75
    de Ford, Miriam Allen, *The
      Overbury Affair,* 137
    Dickens, Charles, *Oliver Twist; or,
      the Parish Boy's Progress,* 121
    Fowles, John, *The Collector,* 108
    Glynn, Jonny, *The Seven Days of
      Peter Crumb,* 108
    Gray, John MacLachlan, *The Fiend
      in Human,* 108
    Haddon, Mark, *The Curious
      Incident of the Dog in the
      Night Time,* 126
    Kernick, Simon
      The Business of Dying, 150
      The Crime Trade, 150
      A Good Day to Die, 150
      The Murder Exchange, 97
    Kersh, Gerald
      Night and the City, 31
      Prelude to a Certain Midnight,
        64
    Pears, Iain, *An Instance of the
      Fingerpost,* 130

    Pearson, John, *The Profession of
      Violence,* 40
    Robotham, Michael, *Suspect,* 100
    Ruddick, James, *Death at the Priory,*
      143
    Waites, Martyn, *Candleland,* 153
    Walters, Minette
      The Dark Room, 102
      The Echo, 102
      The Shape of Snakes, 135
    Westlake, Donald E., *Nobody's
      Perfect,* 22
  Manchester
    Banks, Ray, *Saturday's Child,* 158
    Bowker, David, *Rawhead,* 29
    Martin, J. Wallis, *The Bird Yard,* 65
  Marshfield
    Martin, J. Wallis, *A Likeness in
      Stone,* 98
  Mid-Devon
    Winkleigh
      Cornwell, John, *Earth to Earth,*
        86
  Newcastle
    Banks, Ray, *Saturday's Child,* 158
  Norfolk
    Thorpe Ambrose
      Collins, Wilkie, *Armadale,* 91
  Oxford
    Martin, J. Wallis, *A Likeness in
      Stone,* 98
    Pears, Iain, *An Instance of the
      Fingerpost,* 130
  Suffolk
    Highsmith, Patricia, *A Suspension
      of Mercy,* 127
  Sussex
    Lewes
      Fowles, John, *The Collector,* 108
    South Downs
      Chabon, Michael, *The Final
        Solution,* 159
  Swindon
    Haddon, Mark, *The Curious
      Incident of the Dog in the
      Night Time,* 126
  Wiltshire
    Thornhill
      Raymond, Derek, *How the
        Dead Live,* 152
  Workington
    Jones, Elwyn, *The Last Two to Hang,*
      71

Yorkshire
  Burn, Gordon, *Somebody's Husband,*
    Somebody's Son, 116
  Collins, Wilkie, *The Moonstone,* 62
  Setterfield, Diane, *The Thirteenth*
    Tale, 84

France
  General
    Claudel, Philippe, *Les Âmes Grises,*
      148
    Harris, Thomas, *Hannibal Rising,*
      109
    Manchette, Jean-Patrick, *La Position*
      du Tireur Couché, 82
    Vidocq, François Eugéne, *Mémoires*
      de Vidocq, Chef de la Police de
      Sureté, jusqu'en 1827, 148
  Landes
    Capbreton
      Japrisot, Sébastien, *Un Long*
        Dimanche de Fiançailles,
        81
  Paris
    Manchette, Jean-Patrick, *Petit Bleu*
      de la Côte oust, 98
    Reit, Seymour, *The Day They Stole*
      the Mona Lisa, 26
  Somme
    Bingo Crépuscule
      Japrisot, Sébastien, *Un Long*
        Dimanche de Fiançailles, 81
  Villeperce-sur-Seine
    Highsmith, Patricia
      The Boy Who Followed Ripley,
        110
      Ripley Under Ground, 110
      Ripley Under Water, 111
      Ripley's Game, 110

Germany
  Berlin
    Highsmith, Patricia, *The Boy Who*
      Followed Ripley, 110
  Bremen
    Puzo, Mario, *The Dark Arena,* 59
  Hamburg
    Highsmith, Patricia, *Ripley's Game,*
      110
  Hanover
    Rabe, Peter, *A Shroud for Jesso,* 130

Greece
  Athens
    Highsmith, Patricia, *The Two Faces*
      of January, 96

Hungary
  Rubinstein, Julian, *Ballad of the*
    Whiskey Robber, 90

India
  Collins, Wilkie, *The Moonstone,* 62
Israel
  Tel Aviv
    Khadra, Yamina, *L'attentat,* 81
Italy
  Florence
    Preston, Douglas and Mario Spezi,
      The Monster of Florence, 120
  Mongibello
    Highsmith, Patricia, *The Talented*
      Mr. Ripley, 110
  Rome
    Highsmith, Patricia, *Those Who*
      Walk Away, 81
    Pomeroy, Sarah B., *The Murder of*
      Regilla, 142
  Tuscany
    Wignall, Kevin, *For the Dogs,* 85
  Venice
    Highsmith, Patricia, *Those Who*
      Walk Away, 81

Jamaica
  Kingston
    Goodis, David, *The Wounded and*
      the Slain, 96
Japan
  Tokyo
    Abe, Kobo, *The Ruined Map,* 158
    Kirino, Natsuo
      Out, 57
      Riaru Warudo, 128
    Peace, David, *Tokyo Year One,* 114

Kenya
  Ilmorog
    Thiong'o, Ngúgí wa, *Petals of*
      Blood, 133

Mexico
  General
    Cain, James M., *Serenade,* 61
    Highsmith, Patricia, *A Game for the*
      Living, 64
    Levien, David, *City of the Sun,* 161
    McCarthy, Cormac, *No Country for*
      Old Men, 58
    Murray, Sabina, *A Carnivore's*
      Inquiry, 113

Mexico (*cont.*)
Canción
Bojanowski, Marc, *The Dog Fighter*,
122
Culiacan
Winslow, Don, *The Power of the
Dog*, 153
Mazatlán
Miller, Wade, *Branded Woman*, 42
Mexico City
Millar, Margaret, *The Listening
Walls*, 129
Sonora
Bauispe
Fergus, Jim, *The Wild Girl*, 94
Yucatán Peninsula
Huston, Charlie, *Six Bad Things*, 31
Morocco
Highsmith, Patricia, *Ripley Under
Water*, 111

Norway
Laurvig
Shreve, Anita, *The Weight of Water*,
131
Oslo
Dolnick, Edward, *The Rescue Artist*,
25

Pacific Ocean
Williams, Charles, *Dead Calm*, 115
Portugal
Lisbon
Wilson, Robert, *A Small Death in
Lisbon*, 68

Russia
St. Petersburg
Dostoevsky, Fyodor, *Crime and
Punishment*, 62

Scotland
Edinburgh
Guthrie, Allan
Savage Night, 20
Two-Way Split, 42
Glasgow
Brand, Christianna, *Heaven Knows
Who*, 86
Welch, Louise, *The Cutting Room*, 135
South Africa
Capetown
Meyer, Deon, *Infanta*, 82
South America
Ciudad Real
Woolrich, Cornell, *Black Alibi*, 116
Spain
Barcelona
Ruiz Zafón, Carlos, *La Sombra del
Viento*, 100
Switzerland
Aigle
Godfrey, Ellen, *By Reason of Doubt*, 71

Turkey
Istanbul
Ambler, Eric, *The Mask of Dimitrios*,
147
Pamuk, Orhan, *Benim Adim
Kirmizi*, 129

United States

Alabama
Choctaw
Cook, Thomas H., *Breakheart Hill*,
124
Huntsville
Schutze, Jim, *By Two and Two*, 144
Maycomb
Lee, Harper, *To Kill a Mockingbird*,
82
Monroeville
Earley, Pete, *Circumstantial
Evidence*, 154
Arizona
General
King, Laurie R., *A Darker Place*, 128

Phoenix
Bommersbach, Jana, *The Trunk
Murderess*, 103
Marlowe, Dan J., *The Name of the
Game Is Death*, 98
Tucson
Brown, Fredric, *The Lenient Beast*,
106

California
General
Alexander, Shana, *Anyone's
Daughter*, 103
Bunker, Edward, *Little Boy Blue*,
56

Cain, James M., *The Postman
    Always Rings Twice*, 55
Huston, Charlie, *Six Bad Things*, 31
Matheson, Richard, *Ride the
    Nightmare*, 128
Winslow, Don, *The Death and Life of
    Bobby Z*, 85
Alcatraz Island
    Howard, Clark, *Six Against the
        Rock*, 25
Bakersfield
    Humes, Edward, *Mean Justice*, 52
Brentwood
    The Goldman Family, *If I Did It*,
        104
Chicote
    Millar, Margaret, *How Like an
        Angel*, 161
Glendale
    Cain, James M., *Double Indemnity*,
        49
    Wambaugh, Joseph, *Fire Lover*, 155
Hollywood
    Abbott, Megan
        Die a Little, 156
        The Song Is You, 122
    Bugliosi, Vincent, and Curt
        Gentry, *Helter Skelter*, 116
    Lankford, Terrill Lee, *Earthquake
        Weather*, 98
    McClintick, David, *Indecent
        Exposure*, 52
    Stansberry, Domenic, *Manifesto for
        the Dead*, 50
Huntington Beach
    Nunn, Kem, *Tapping the Source*, 65
Los Angeles
    Bloch, Robert
        Shooting Star, 159
        Spiderweb, 16
    Bugliosi, Vincent, and Ken
        Hurwitz, *Till Death Us Do
        Part*, 69
    Bunker, Edward, *Dog Eat Dog*, 77
    Cain, Paul, *Fast One*, 28
    Chute, Vern, *Flight of an Angel*, 92
    Doolittle, Sean
        Burn, 93
        Dirt, 93
    Dorsey, Tim, *The Big Bamboo*, 19
    Francisco, Ruth, *Good Morning,
        Darkness*, 149
    Fuhrman, Mark, *Murder in
        Brentwood*, 154

Gores, Joe, *Menaced Assassin*, 108
Hodel, Steve, *Black Dahlia Avenger*,
    139
Millar, Margaret, *Beast in View*, 98
Perry, Thomas
    Fidelity, 162
    Metzger's Dog, 21
Puzo, Mario, *The Last Don*, 33
Revoyr, Nina, *Southland*, 66
Smith, Peter Moore, *Los Angeles*,
    132
Thompson, Jim
    The Golden Gizmo, 67
    The Grifters, 48
Waiwaiole, Lono, *Wiley's Shuffle*,
    84
Los Feliz
    Gores, Joe, *A Time of Predators*, 80
Oakland
    Lethem, Jonathan, *Gun, with
        Occasional Music*, 161
Oceanview
    Bunker, Edward, *Stark*, 16
Orange County
    Detroit, Michael, *Chain of Evidence*,
        38
    Parker, T. Jefferson, *Silent Joe*, 152
    Rule, Ann, *If You Really Loved Me*,
        143
    Winslow, Don, *California Fire and
        Life*, 36
Pacific City
    Thompson, Jim, *The Nothing Man*,
        115
Palos Verdes Estates
    McDougal, Dennis, *In the Best of
        Families*, 89
Pasadena
    Abbott, Megan, *Die a Little*, 156
Pomona
    Nunn, Kem, *Ponoma Queen*, 66
Rio Mirada
    Corbett, David, *Done for a Dime*,
        124
San Diego
    Winslow, Don
        The Dawn Patrol, 153
        The Winter of Frankie Machine,
        36
San Felice
    Millar, Margaret
        How Like an Angel, 161
        A Stranger in My Grave, 129

California (*cont.*)
    San Francisco
        Carpenter, Don, *Hard Rain Falling*,
            56
        Corbett, David, *The Devil's
            Redhead*, 29
        Gentry, Curt, *Frame-up*, 138
        Goodis, David, *Dark Passage*, 95
        Gores, Joe
            Cases, 160
            Dead Man, 160
            Hammett, 160
            Interface, 160
            Menaced Assassin, 108
        Hammett, Dashiell, *The Maltese
            Falcon*, 158
        Howard, Clark, *Zebra*, 139
        Muller, Eddie
            The Distance, 59
            Shadow Boxer, 59
        Norris, Frank, *McTeague*, 99
        Olsen, Jack, *Hastened to the Grave*,
            26
        Perry, Thomas, *Death Benefits*, 50
        Stansberry, Domenic, *The Last Days
            of Il Duce*, 101
        Weiss, Mike, *Double Play*, 73
        Willeford, Charles, *Pick-up*, 135
    San Jose
        Farrell, Harry, *Swift Justice*, 25
    San Quentin Prison
        Bunker, Edward, *Animal Factory*, 61
        Chessman, Caryl
            Cell 2455 Death Row, 70
            Trial by Ordeal, 70
    Santa Barbara
        Perry, Thomas, *Dead Aim*, 99
    Santa Monica
        Connelly, Michael, *Chasing the
            Dime*, 123
        Matheson, Richard, *Someone Is
            Bleeding*, 113
        McCoy, Horace, *They Shoot Horses,
            Don't They?*, 58
    Sausalito
        Stansberry, Domenic, *The
            Confession*, 115
    Tijuana River Valley
        Nunn, Kem, *Tijuana Straits*, 83
    Van Nuys
        Faust, Christa, *Money Shot*, 94
    Venice
        Carnahan, Matthew, *Serpent Girl*,
            42
    Yuba City
        Cray, Ed, *Burden of Proof*, 116
Catskills. *See under* New York
Colorado
    Denver
        McKinty, Adrian, *Hidden River*, 151
        Singular, Stephen, *Talked to Death*,
            40
Connecticut
    General
        Caspary, Vera, *Bedelia*, 106
    Greenwich
        Dumas, Timothy, *Greentown*, 137
        Levitt, Leonard, *Conviction*, 140
    Litchfield County
        Savage, Mildred, *A Great Fall*, 72

Delaware
    Wilmington
        Rule, Ann, *And Never Let Her Go*,
            144
District of Columbia. *See* Washington,
    D.C.

Florida
    General
        Dorsey, Tim
            Atomic Lobster, 20
            Florida Roadkill, 18
            Hurricane Punch, 19
            Orange Crush, 18
            Stingray Shuffle, 19
        Spillane, Mickey, *Dead Street*, 152
    Florida Keys
        Brewer, Gil, *The Vengeful Virgin*, 55
    Highland View
        Miller, Gene, *Invitation to a
            Lynching*, 141
    Hudson
        Marlowe, Dan J., *The Name of the
            Game Is Death*, 98
    Key West
        Dorsey, Tim, *Torpedo Juice*, 19
    Miami
        Dorsey, Tim, *Cadillac Beach*, 19
        Hendricks, Vicki
            Iguana Love, 20
            Miami Purity, 81
        Hiaasen, Carl, *Tourist Season*, 160
        Lindsay, Jeff
            Darkly Dreaming Dexter, 112
            Dearly Devoted Dexter, 112
            Dexter in the Dark, 113

Mulberry
    Frasca, John, *The Mulberry Tree*, 138
Orlando
    Gischler, Victor, *Gun Monkeys*, 30
Palm Beach
    Stark, Richard, *Flashfire*, 46
Pensacola
    Gischler, Victor, *Suicide Squeeze*, 20
Sarasota
    Rule, Ann, *Every Breath You Take*,
        144
Tampa Bay
    Dorsey, Tim
        Hammerhead Ranch Motel, 18
        Triggerfish Twist, 18

Georgia
  Atlanta
    Golden, Harry, *A Little Girl Is
        Dead*, 138
    Oney, Steve, *And the Dead Shall
        Rise*, 142
    Rule, Ann
        Everything She Ever Wanted,
         143
        Too Late to Say Goodbye, 120
  Coweta County
    Barnes, Margaret Anne, *Murder in
        Coweta County*, 69
  Marietta
    Oney, Steve, *And the Dead Shall
        Rise*, 142
  Seminole County
    Cook, Thomas H., *Blood Echoes*, 103

Hawai'i
  Big Island
    Waiwaiole, Lono, *Wiley's Refrain*,
        85
  Honolulu
    Stannard, David E., *Honor Killing*,
        73

Idaho
  Boise
    Carnahan, Matthew, *Serpent Girl*,
        42
Illinois
  General
    Eichenwald, Kurt, *The Informant*,
        52
  Carmel City
    Brown, Fredric, *The Night of the
        Jabberwock*, 91

  Chicago
    Brown, Fredric, *The Screaming
        Mimi*, 106
    Burnett, W, R., *Little Caesar*, 27
    Cooley, Robert, with Hillel Levin,
        When Corruption Was King,
        37
    Giancana, Antoinette, *Mafia
        Princess*, 38
    Larson, Eric, *The Devil in the White
        City*, 118
    Sakey, Marcus, *Good People*, 59
    Tidyman, Ernest, *Dummy*, 146
  Highland Woods
    Ellis, David, *Line of Vision*, 94
  Midlothian
    Protess, David, and Rob Warden,
        Gone in the Night, 89
  Saline County
    O'Brien, Darcy, *Murder in Little
        Egypt*, 89
Indiana
  Gilbert
    Saul, Jamie M., *Light of Day*, 131
  Indianapolis
    Levien, David, *City of the Sun*, 161
  Marion
    Maas, Peter, *In a Child's Name*, 72
Iowa
  General
    Rayner, Richard, *Drake's Fortune*,
        26
  Indianola
    Bryan, Patricia L., and Thomas
        Wolf, *Midnight Assassin*, 137
  Iowa City
    Collins, Max (Allan), *The First
        Quarry*, 79

Kansas
  General
    Denton, Bradley, *Blackburn*, 107
  Cottonwood
    Phillips, Scott, *Cottonwood*, 114
  Holcomb
    Capote, Truman, *In Cold Blood*, 103
  Kansas City
    Dreiser, Theodore, *An American
        Tragedy*, 63
  Prairie Village
    Rule, Ann, *Bitter Harvest*, 143
  Wichita
    Girard, James Preston, *The Late
        Man*, 108

Kansas (*cont.*)
  Phillips, Scott
    The Ice Harvest, 157
    The Walkaway, 157
Kentucky
  Louisville
    Perry, Thomas, *Pursuit*, 152

Louisiana
  General
    Gores, Joe, *Dead Man*, 160
  Baxter Parrish
    Mount Olive
      Sherman, Dayne, *Welcome to
        the Fallen Paradise*, 131
  New Orleans
    Horne, Jed, *Desire Street*, 88
    Inness-Brown, Elizabeth, *Burning
      Marguerite*, 127
    Irish, William, *Waltz into Darkness* ,
      127

Maine
  General
    Lethem, Jonathan, *Motherless
      Brooklyn*, 161
  Isle of Shoals, Smuttynose Island
    Shreve, Anita, *The Weight of Water*,
      131
  Machias, Green, Norman, *Way Past
    Legal*, 96
  Portland
    Murray, Sabina, *A Carnivore's
      Inquiry*, 113
  Versailles
    Landay, William, *Mission Flats*, 150
Maryland
  Baltimore
    Lippman, Laura, *Every Secret
      Thing*, 58
Massachusetts
  General
    Stark, Richard
      Ask the Parrot, 47
      Dirty Money, 47
      Nobody Runs Forever, 47
  Boston
    Carr, Howie, *The Brothers Bulger*, 37
    Frank, Gerold, *The Boston Strangler*,
      117
    Higgins, George V.
      Cogan's Trade, 21
      The Digger's Game, 57
      The Friends of Eddie Coyle, 21

Junger, Sebastian, *A Death in
    Belmont*, 88
Landay, William, *The Strangler*, 112
Lehr, Dick and Gerard O'Neill,
    Black Mass, 39
O'Donnell, Lawrence, Jr., *Deadly
    Force*, 154
Pearl, Matthew, *The Dante Club*,
    66
Sullivan, Robert, *The Disappearance
    of Dr. Parkman*, 145
East Buckingham
  Lehane, Dennis, *Mystic River*,
    82
Mission Flats
  Landay, William, *Mission
    Flats*, 150
Braintree
  Feuerlight, Roberta Strauss, *Justice
    Crucified*, 87
  Russell, Francis, *Tragedy in
    Dedham*, 90
Cambridge
  McNamara, Eileen, *Breakdown*, 89
Cape Cod
  Shubin, Seymour, *Witness to
    Myself*, 100
  Chatham
    Cook, Thomas H., *The
      Chatham School Affair*, 92
Denham
  Feuerlight, Roberta Strauss, *Justice
    Crucified*, 87
  Russell, Francis, *Tragedy in
    Dedham*, 90
Fall River
  Lincoln, Victoria, *A Private
    Disgrace*, 140
Little Wesley
  Highsmith, Patricia, *Deep Water*, 64
Plymouth
  Tidyman, Ernest, *Big Bucks*, 49
Quinsigamond
  O'Connell, Jack
    Box Nine, 151
    The Skin Palace, 83
    Wireless, 114
    Word Made Flesh, 151
Suffolk County
  Katzenbach, John, *The Madman's
    Tale*, 111
Michigan
  Detroit
    Goines, Donald, *Daddy Cool*, 79

Upper Peninsula
    Traver, Robert, *Anatomy of a
        Murder*, 156
Washtenaw County
    Keyes, Edward, *The Michigan
        Murders*, 118
Minnesota
  Battlepoint
    Enger, Lin, *Undiscovered Country*, 125
  Rookery,
    Hassler, Jon, *The Love Hunter*, 80
  St. Paul
    Clark, Robert, *Mr. White's
        Confession*, 78
  White Bear Lake
    Siegel, Barry, *A Death in White Bear
        Lake*, 144
Mississippi
  Alexandria
    Tartt, Donna, *The Little Friend*, 133
  Biloxi
    Humes, Edward, *Mississippi Mud*, 39
  Jackson
    Rifkin, Shepard, *The Murderer Vine*,
        163
  Lakeland
    Cook, Thomas H., *Master of the
        Delta*, 92
Missouri
  Kansas City
    Rule, Ann, *Bitter Harvest*, 143
  Ozarks
    Woodrell, Daniel, *Give Us a Kiss*, 86
  Skidmore
    Lancaster, Bob, and B. C. Hall,
        Judgment Day, 118
    MacLean, Harry N., *In Broad
        Daylight*, 119
  St. Louis
    Harris, Thomas, *Red Dragon*, 109
Montana
  General
    Graysmith, Robert, *Unabomber*, 118
    Hoffman, William, *Tidewater Blood*, 96
    Stark, Richard, *Firebreak*, 46
  Bentrock
    Watson, Larry, *Montana 1948*, 135
  Flathead Indian Reservation
    Earling, Debra Magpie, *Perma Red*,
        93
  Madison County
    France, Johnny, and Malcolm
        McConnell, *Incident at Big
        Sky*, 104

Perma
    Earling, Debra Magpie, *Perma Red*,
        93
Nebraska
  General
    Stark, Richard, *Flashfire*, 46
  Omaha
    Doolittle, Sean, *The Cleanup*, 93
  Sagamore
    Stark, Richard, *The Jugger*, 44
  Valentine
    Doolittle, Sean, *Rain Dogs*, 93
Nevada
  Coleville
    Williams, Charles, *Man on a Leash*,
        136
  Las Vegas
    Abbott, Megan, *Queenpin*, 28
    Bock, Charles, *Beautiful Children*,
        122
    Connelly, Michael, *Void Moon*, 42
    Fisher, Steve, *No House Limit*, 30
    Gores, Joe, *Dead Man*, 160
    Huston, Charlie, *A Dangerous Man*,
        31
    Puzo, Mario
        The Godfather, 32
        The Last Don, 33
    Stella, Charlie, *Charlie Opera*, 35
    Waiwaiole, Lono, *Wiley's Shuffle*,
        84
    Westlake, Donald E.
        Bad News, 23
        *What's the Worst That Could
          Happen?*, 23
New England
  Grain Island
    Inness-Brown, Elizabeth, *Burning
        Marguerite*, 127
New Hampshire
  General
    Perry, Thomas, *Death Benefits*, 50
  Hanover
    Lehr, Dick, and Mitchell Zuckoff,
        Judgment Ridge, 71
  Portsmouth
    Shreve, Anita, *The Weight of Water*,
        131
New Jersey
  General
    Stark, Richard, *The Man with the
        Getaway Face*, 43
  Atlantic City
    Block, Lawrence, *Mona*, 16

New Jersey (*cont.*)
   Bergen County
      Farber, Myron, "*Somebody Is
         Lying*", 117)
   Cape May Court House
      Schiller, Lawrence, *Cape May Court
         House*, 90
   East Orange
      Zierold, Norman, *Three Sisters in
         Black*, 53
   Glen Ridge
      Lefkowitz, Bernard, *Our Guys*, 88
   Hopewell
      Behn, Noel, *Lindbergh*, 136
      Fisher, Jim, *The Ghosts of Hopewell*,
         137
      Kennedy, Ludovic, *The Airman and
         the Carpenter*, 140
      Waller, George, *Kidnap*, 146
   Newark, Highsmith, Patricia, *The
      Blunderer*, 126
New Mexico
   Shakespeare
      Hodgson, Ken, *The Man Who Killed
         Shakespeare*, 21
   Taos
      Brown, Fredric, *The Far Cry*, 123
New York
   Arcadia
      Goodman, Carol, *The Seduction of
         Water*, 63
   Canarsie
      Starr, Jason, *Lights Out*, 67
   Catskills
      Goodman, Carol, *The Seduction of
         Water*, 63
   Great Neck
      Highsmith, Patricia, *Strangers on a
         Train*, 63
   Hudson River Valley
      Stark, Richard, *Backflash*, 46
   Long Island
      General
         Fitzgerald, F. Scott, *The Great
            Gatsby*, 49
      Amagansett
         Mills, Mark, *Amagansett*, 83
      Pearldale
         Thompson, Jim, *Savage Night*, 35
   Lycurgus
      Dreiser, Theodore, *An American
         Tragedy*, 63
   Monarch
      Gottlieb, Eli, *Now You See Him*, 96

   Monequois
      Stark, Richard, *The Green Eagle
         Score*, 45
New York
   Bardin, John Franklin, *The Deadly
      Percheron*, 75
   Benioff, David, *The 25th Hour*, 29
   Berkow, Ira, *The Man Who Robbed
      the Pierre*, 51
   Black, David, *Murder at the Met*, 69
   Block, Lawrence
      The Burglar in the Closet, 76
      The Burglar in the Rye, 77
      The Burglar on the Prowl, 77
      *The Burglar Who Liked to Quote
         Kipling*, 76
      *The Burglar Who Painted Like
         Mondrian*, 76
      *The Burglar Who Studied
         Spinoza*, 76
      *The Burglar Who Thought He
         Was Bogart*, 77
      *The Burglar Who Traded Ted
         Williams*, 76
      Burglars Can't Be Choosers, 75
   Blum, Howard, *Gangland*, 36
   Bourdain, Anthony, *The Bobby Gold
      Stories*, 41
   Breslin, Jimmy
      *The Gang That Couldn't Shoot
         Straight*, 29
      The Good Rat, 36
   Bruen, Ken, and Jason Starr
      Bust, 56
      Slide, 56
   Carcaterra, Lorenzo, *Sleepers*, 86
   Caspary, Vera, *Laura*, 147
   Cea, Robert, *No Lights No Siren*, 154
   Chester, Giraud, *The Ninth Juror*,
      70
   Colapinto, John, *About the Author*,
      92
   Cowan, Rick, and Douglas
      Century, *Takedown*, 37
   Cummings, John, and Ernest
      Volkman, *Goombata*, 37
   Dorsey, Tim, *Stingray Shuffle*, 19
   Duncombe, Stephen, and Andrew
      Mattson, *The Bobbed Haired
      Bandit*, 48
   Ellin, Stanley, *The Eighth Circle*, 159
   English, T. J.
      Born to Kill, 38
      The Westies, 38

Fearing, Kenneth, *The Big Clock,* 94
Fitzgerald, F. Scott, *The Great Gatsby,* 49
Fosburgh, Lacey, *Closing Time,* 137
Goodis, David, *Nightfall,* 95
Goodman, Carol, *The Seduction of Water,* 63
Gourevitch, Philip, *A Cold Case,* 104
Green, Norman
 The Angel of Montague Street, 30
 Dead Cat Bounce, 30
 Shooting Dr. Jack, 30
Harrison, Colin, *Bodies Electric,* 126
Highsmith, Patricia
 The Blunderer, 126
 A Dog's Ransom, 149
 The Glass Cell, 127
Hjortsberg, William, *Falling Angel,* 160
Huston, Charlie
 Caught Stealing, 31
 A Dangerous Man, 31
Irish, William, *Deadline at Dawn,* 97
Kates, Brian, *The Murder of a Shopping Bag Lady,* 139
Lethem, Jonathan, *Motherless Brooklyn,* 161
Maas, Peter, *The Valachi Papers,* 39
Matheson, Richard, *Fury on Sunday,* 113
Moore, Susanna, *In the Cut,* 129
Murray, Sabina, *A Carnivore's Inquiry,* 113
O'Brien, Joseph F., and Andrus Kurins, *Boss of Bosses,* 39
Pietrusza, David, *Rothstein,* 26
Pistone, Joseph D., with Richard Woodley, *Donnie Brasco,* 40
Price, Richard, *Lush Life,* 42
Puzo, Mario
 The Fortunate Pilgrim, 32
 The Godfather, 32
 The Sicilian, 33
Rossner, Judith, *Looking for Mr. Goodbar,* 130
Rozan, S. J., *Absent Friends,* 34
Sanders, Lawrence, *The Anderson Tapes,* 34
Schulberg, Budd
 The Harder They Fall, 34
 Waterfront, 34
Shapiro, Fred, *Whitmore,* 155

St. James, James, *Disco Bloodbath,* 53
Stark, Richard
 The Black Ice Score, 45
 The Hunter, 43
Starr, Jason
 Cold Caller, 50
 Fake ID, 47
 Hard Feelings, 66
 Nothing Personal, 66
 Tough Luck, 60
 Twisted City, 101
Stashower, Daniel, *The Beautiful Cigar Girl,* 145
Stella, Charlie
 Cheapskates, 132
 Eddie's World, 34
 Jimmy Bench Press, 34
 Mafiya, 35
 Shakedown, 35
Thompson, Jim, *Child of Rage,* 134
Westlake, Donald E.
 Bad News, 23
 Bank Shot, 22
 Don't Ask, 23
 Good Behavior, 23
 The Hot Rock, 22
 Jimmy the Kid, 22
 Nobody's Perfect, 22
 361, 68
 Watch Your Back! 23
 What's So Funny?, 23
 What's the Worst That Could Happen?, 23
 Why Me?, 22
Wolfe, Linda, *Wasted,* 90
Inwood Park
 Green, George Dawes, *The Caveman's Valentine,* 125
Olean
 Block, Lawrence, *The Girl with the Long Green Hair,* 16
Pattaskinnick
 Block, Lawrence, *The Burglar in the Library,* 77
Purchase
 Alexandra, Shana, *Very Much a Lady,* 86
Putkin's Corners
 Westlake, Donald E., *Drowned Hopes,* 23
Rochester
 Olsen, Jack, *The Misbegotten Son,* 119

New York (*cont.*)
  Selden
    Kleiman, Dena, *A Deadly Silence*, 140
  Upper Asquewan Falls
    Biggers, Earl Derr, *Seven Keys to Baldpate*, 15
  Watertown
    Olsen, Jack, *The Misbegotten Son*, 119

North Carolina
  General
    Clyde Edgerton, *The Bible Salesman*, 20
    Rhoades, J. D., *Good Day in Hell*, 162
  Cary
    Floyd, Bill, *The Killer's Wife*, 107
  Durham
    Bledsoe, Jerry, *Before He Wakes*, 51
    Fanning, Diane, *Written in Blood*, 117
  Fayetteville
    Rhoades, J. D.
      The Devil's Right Hand, 162
      Safe and Sound, 162
  Robeson County
    Bledsoe, Jerry, *Death Sentence*, 116
  Washington
    Harwell, Fred, *A True Deliverance*, 138
    McGinniss, Joe, *Cruel Doubt*, 61

North Dakota
  Copper Canyon
    Stark, Richard, *The Score*, 44

Ohio
  Bay Village
    Holmes, Paul, *The Sheppard Murder Case*, 87
    Neff, James, *The Wrong Man*, 141
  Cincinnati
    Stark, Richard, *Nobody Runs Forever*, 47
  Cleveland
    Cooke, John Peyton, *Torsos*, 107
    Neff, James, *Unfinished Murder*, 141
  Columbus
    Keyes, Daniel
      The Minds of Billy Milligan, 140
      Unveiling Claudia, 88
  Tyler
    Stark, Richard
      Butcher's Moon, 46
      Slayground, 45

Oklahoma
  General
    Anderson, Edward, *Thieves Like Us*, 41
    Gischler, Victor, *Shotgun Opera*, 95
    Hunter, Stephen, *Dirty White Boys*, 97
    Thompson, Jim, *Cropper's Cabin*, 133
  Ada
    Grisham, John, *The Innocent Man Murder and Injustice in a Small Town*, 138
    Mayer, Robert, *The Dreams of Ada*, 141
  Fumbee
    Gischler, Victor, *The Pistol Poets*, 95
  Oklahoma City
    Serrano, Richard A., *One of Ours*, 144
  Promise
    Blanchard, Alice, *The Breathtaker*, 106
Oregon
  General
    Olsen, Jack, *I: The Creation of a Serial Killer*, 120
  Cline Falls State Park
    Jentz, Terri, *Strange Piece of Paradise*, 139
  Lincoln County
    Finkel, Michael, *True Story*, 87
  Medford
    Harrison, Kathryn, *While They Slept*, 87
  Portland
    Carpenter, Don, *Hard Rain Falling*, 56
    Perry, Thomas, *Nightlife*, 114
    Rule, Ann, *Dead by Sunset*, 72
    Waiwaiole, Lono
      Wiley's Lament, 84
      Wiley's Refrain, 85
      Wiley's Shuffle, 84
  Springfield
    Rule, Ann, *Small Sacrifices*, 143
  Wallowa County
    Rule, Ann, *Heart Full of Lies*, 52
Ozarks
    Thornburg, Newton, *Cutter and Bone*, 101

Pennsylvania
  General
    Westlake, Donald E., *The Road to Ruin*, 24

Harrisburg
    Schwartz-Nobel, Loretta, *Engaged to Murder*, 53
Lancaster
    Picoult, Jodi, *Plain Truth*, 83
Langley
    Highsmith, Patricia, *The Cry of the Owl*, 64
Philadelphia
    Anastasia, George, *The Last Gangster*, 36
    Conrad, Mark T., *Dark as Night*, 17
    Goodis, David
        Black Friday, 80
        The Burglar, 79
        Down There, 80
        The Moon in the Gutter, 125
    Swierczynski, Duane
        The Blonde, 133
        The Wheelman, 47

Rhode Island
    Newport
        Dershowitz, Alan M., *Reversal of Fortune*, 70
        Wright, William, *The Von Bülow Affair*, 146

South Carolina
    Moline
        Marlowe, Dan J., *The Vengeance Man*, 65

Tennessee
    General
        Bigsby, Christopher, *Beautiful Dreamer*, 91
    Memphis
        Meyer, Gerald, *The Memphis Murders*, 119
Texas
    General
        Anderson, Edward, *Thieves Like Us*, 41
        Denton, Bradley, *Blackburn*, 107
        Hunter, Stephen, *Dirty White Boys*, 97
        McCarthy, Cormac, *No Country for Old Men*, 58
        Reasoner, James, *The Dust Devils*, 99
        Stark, Richard, *The Handle*, 44
        Thompson, Jim, *Wild Town*, 115

Alvin
    Stowers, Carlton, *To the Last Breath*, 145
Austin
    Simon, Michael, *Dirty Simon*, 152
Camp Rapture
    Lansdale, Joe R., *Leather Maiden*, 65
Central City
    Thompson, Jim, *The Killer Inside Me*, 115
Dallas
    Hyde, Christopher, *Wisdom of the Bones*, 111
    Schutze, Jim, *"My Husband's Trying to Kill Me!"*, 73
    Swindle, Howard, *Trespasses*, 145
Fort Worth
    Cartwright, Gary, *Blood Will Tell*, 70
    Naifeh, Steven, and Gregory White Smith, *Final Justice*, 72
    Thompson, Jim
        A Swell-Looking Babe, 60
        Texas by the Tail, 60
Houston
    Mitchell, Corey, *Strangler*, 119
    O'Malley, Suzanne, *"Are You There Alone?"*, 142
    Thompson, Thomas, *Blood and Money*, 105
Longview
    Bean, Fred, *Black Gold*, 28
Lubbock
    Evans, Wanda Webb, *Trail of Blood*, 104
Martirio
    Pierre, D. B. C., *Vernon God Little*, 130
Metcalf
    Highsmith, Patricia, *Strangers on a Train*, 63
Odessa
    Thompson, Jim, *South of Heaven*, 134
Pardee County
    Thompson, Jim, *The Transgressors*, 153
Pottsville
    Thompson, Jim, *Pop. 1280*, 148
San Antonio
    Elkind, Peter, *The Death Shift*, 117
    Rule, Ann, *Every Breath You Take*, 144

Texas (*cont.*)
  Tulia
    Blakeslee, Nate, *Tulia*, 154
  Waco
    Stowers, Carlton, *Careless Whispers*, 27
  Wylie
    Bloom, John, and Jim Atkinson, *Evidence of Love*, 69

Unknown state
  capital city
    Thompson, Jim, *Recoil*, 84
  Coltron
    McCoy, Horace, *No Pockets in a Shroud*, 58
  Homewood
    Collins, Max (Allan), *The Last Quarry*, 79
  Manduwoc
    Thompson, Jim, *The Kill-off*, 67
  Port City
    Collins, Max (Allan), *The Broker*, 78
  Stoneville
    Thompson, Jim, *Nothing More Than Murder*, 67
  Wesley
    Cook, Thomas H., *Red Leaves*, 124
Utah
  General
    Mailer, Norman, *The Executioner's Song*, 71
  Salt Lake City
    Alexander, Shana, *Nutcracker*, 69
    Coleman, Jonathan, *At Mother's Request*, 24
    Lindsey, Robert, *A Gathering of Saints*, 26

Vermont
  General
    Westlake, Donald E., *Don't Ask*, 23
  Chelsea
    Lehr, Dick, and Mitchell Zuckoff, *Judgment Ridge*, 71
  New Halcyon
    Colapinto, John, *About the Author*, 92
Virginia
  General
    Schutz, Benjamin M., *The Mongol Reply*, 131

Boonsboro
    Englade, Ken, *Beyond Reason*, 61
  Grundy
    Tucker, John C., *May God Have Mercy*, 73
  McLean
    Alexandra, Shana, *Very Much a Lady*, 86
  Richmond
    Taylor, John, *The Count and the Confession*, 146
  Stuart
    Clark, Martin, *The Legal Limit*, 156
  Tidewater,
    Hoffman, William, *Tidewater Blood*, 96

Washington
  Puget Sound
    San Piedro Island
      Guterson, David, *Snow Falling on Cedars*, 126
  Seattle
    Rule, Ann, *Green River, Running Red*, 120
  Spokane
    Fuhrman, Mark, *Murder in Spokane*, 117
    Olsen, Jack, "Son", 119
    Walter, Jess, *Citizen Vince*, 85
Washington, D.C.
    Flynn, Kevin, *Relentless Pursuit*, 71
    Greene, Robert W., *The Sting Man*, 52
    Pelecanos, George, *The Turnaround*, 130
West Virginia
  General
    Hoffman, William, *Tidewater Blood*, 96
  Moundsville
    Grubb, Davis, *The Night of the Hunter*, 125
Wisconsin
  Gunnar
    Sidor, Steven, *Skin River*, 101
  Janesville
    Schickler, David, *Sweet and Vicious*, 100
Wyoming
  Cheyenne
    Prendergast, Alan, *The Poison Tree*, 72
  Lovell
    Olsen, Jack, "Doc", 141

About the Author

GARY WARREN NIEBUHR is Library Director for the Village of Greendale in Wisconsin and the author of *Read 'Em Their Writes: A Handbook for Mystery and Crime Book Discussions* (Libraries Unlimited, 2006), which was nominated for an Anthony Award. His *Make Mine a Mystery* (Libraries Unlimited, 2003) won the Macavity Award, the Anthony Award, and The Kenneth Kingery Scholarly Book Award from the Council for Wisconsin Writers. He also wrote *A Reader's Guide to the Private Eye Novel* (1993), which was nominated for an Anthony Award.

In 2002, Gary received the Don Sandstrom Memorial Award for Lifetime Achievement in Mystery Fandom, and in 2004 he was the Fan Guest of Honor at Bouchercon: The World Mystery Convention and at the 1995 Magna Cum Murder. He also received the 2005 Margaret E. Monroe Award from the American Library Association in recognition of his contribution to the development of adult services in libraries. Gary is a contributing writer to Book Group Buzz, a *Booklist Magazine* blog, at http://book groupbuzz.booklistonline.com. Visit Gary at www.garywarrenniebuhr.com.